ADULT BULLYING—
A NASTY PIECE OF WORK

Translating a Decade of Research on Non-Sexual Harassment, Psychological Terror, Mobbing, and Emotional Abuse on the Job

Pamela Lutgen-Sandvik, Ph.D.

All proceeds from book sales support research to reduce workplace bullying, improve workplace communication, and build more respectful workplace climates and cultures.

Adult Bullying—A Nasty Piece of Work: Translating a Decade of Research on Non-Sexual Harassment, Psychological Terror, Mobbing, and Emotional Abuse on the Job

Printed in the United States of America
First Printing, 2013
ISBN-13: 978-1482613971
ISBN-10: 1482613972

ORCM Academic Press
1200 Pennsylvania Ave
St Louis MO 63130-1922

orgcommpress@gmail.com

Ordering Information: Amazon.com

DEDICATION

I dedicate this book to the hundreds of targeted employees who have shared their stories of workplace bullying and emotional abuse on the job. Your willingness to recount the extremely painful and professionally stigmatizing experiences of adult bullying helps everyone better understand workplace aggression and its toxic effects. Your willingness to speak contributes to raising the American consciousness about this pernicious toxin in modern workplaces and to building solutions for reducing and ending emotional and psychological abuse at work.

All proceeds from book sales support toward organizational research that seeks to reduce workplace bullying, improve workplace communication, and build workplaces that are more respectful.

ACKNOWLEDGEMENTS

In addition to the targeted workers who gave of their time and energy to assist in the research studies reported in this anthology, I would like to thank my collaborators for their energy, ideas, and insights as well as their permission to include revised versions of our originally co-authored pieces in this volume. (See First Publication Citations). I also wish to express my deepest appreciation to my husband who remains a steadfast champion of my work.

All names in this book are pseudonyms—organizations and people.

ADULT BULLYING—
A NASTY PIECE OF WORK

Translating a Decade of Research on Non-Sexual
Harassment, Psychological Terror, Mobbing, and
Emotional Abuse on the Job

Pamela Lutgen-Sandvik, Ph.D.
Associate Professor Organizational Communication
(http://www.ndsu.edu/pubweb/~lutgensa/)
Director, NDSU Communication
Research & Training Center
(http://www.commresearchtraining.com/)
Department of Communication
North Dakota State University

Other publications by Pamela Lutgen-Sandvik:

Lutgen-Sandvik, Pamela & Sypher, Beverly D. (2009). *Destructive Organizational Communication: Processes, Consequences, and Constructive Ways of Organizing.* New York: Routledge/Taylor & Francis.

See also Reference pages.

CONTENTS

Chapter   **page**

Chapter 1   Introduction
Pamela Lutgen-Sandvik .... (1)

Chapter 2   Prevalence, Perception, Degree, &
Impact of Adult Bullying in the American
Workplace
Pamela Lutgen-Sandvik, Sarah J. Tracy, &
Jess K. Alberts ....(12)

Chapter 3   Serial Bullying: How Employee Abuse
Starts, Ends, and Restarts with New Targets
Pamela Lutgen-Sandvik .... (34)

Chapter 4   "Take This Job and Shove It": How
Targets and Witnesses Fight Back When Faced
with Bullying
Pamela Lutgen-Sandvik .... (57)

Chapter 5   Explaining the Unexplainable: The
Painful Experiences of Workplace Bullying
Sarah J. Tracy, Pamela Lutgen-Sandvik, &
Jess K. Alberts .... (86)

Chapter 6   Does Age Matter? Older and Younger
Employees' Experiences of Workplace Bullying
Pamela Lutgen-Sandvik ....(111)

Chapter 7   Trauma and Stigma of Being Bullied:
Reconciling Crushed Beliefs and Salvaging
Self-Image
Pamela Lutgen-Sandvik & Lisa Farwell .... (124)

Chapter	page

Chapter 8 Toxic Organizing: How and Why
Workplaces Become Toxic
Pamela Lutgen-Sandvik &
Virginia McDermott .... (147)

Chapter 9 Communicative Nature of Bullying and
Responses to Bullying
Pamela Lutgen-Sandvik, Sarah J. Tracy, &
Jess K. Alberts .... (175)

Chapter 10 Attacking Our Own: A Deeper Look
at Why Women Bully Other Women
Pamela Lutgen-Sandvik, Elizabeth Dickinson, &
Karen A. Foss .... (194)

Chapter 11   Active and Passive Accomplices to
Workplace Bullying
Gary Namie & Pamela Lutgen-Sandvik .... (212)

Chapter 12   Making Sense of Supervisory Bullying
Pamela Lutgen-Sandvik &
Virginia McDermott .... (240)

Chapter 13   Profiles, Goals, and Tactics in Escalated
Bullying Conflicts: Targets, Witnesses, and Aggressors
Pamela Lutgen-Sandvik &
Courtney Vail Fletcher .... (269)

Chapter 14   How Positive Experiences at Work Can
Reduce Some of the Effects of Workplace Bullying
Pamela Lutgen-Sandvik &
Jacqueline Hood .... (294)

Chapter 15   Reversing the Effects of Bullying on
Workers, Workgroups, Workforces, and Workplaces
Pamela Lutgen-Sandvik .... (304)

Chapter	page

Chapter 16   What We Know about Workplace
Bullying: A Review
Pamela Lutgen-Sandvik & Sarah J. Tracy ...(324)

Permissions
.... (358)

Glossary
.... (361)

References
....(373)

About the Author
....(419)

First Publication Citations
.... (421)

LIST OF TABLES

Table Number, Title

Table 2.1: Hierarchy of Terms

Table 2.2.: Key Variables and Their Relationships to Each Other

Table 2.3: Prevalence Comparisons: Workplace Bullying and Aggression

Table 2.4: Negative Acts Compared: Targets and Non-Targets

Table 2.5: Averages – Bullying Degree & Work Quality Outcomes for Three Groups

Table 4.1: Types of Resistance and Descriptions

Table 5.1: Bullying Feels Like ...

Table 5.2: The Bully Seems to Be Like ...

Table 5.3: Being a Target of Bullying Feels Like

Table 6.1.A: Sample Comparisons Abuse Clusters

Table 6.1.B: Sample Comparisons Verbal Abuse

Table 6.2.A: Comparisons of Responses to Abuse

Table 6.2.B: Comparisons of Responses to Abuse in Clusters that Differ Significantly Between Groups

Table 7.1: Pre-Bullying Phase: Threats, Identity Work Types, and Remedial Goals

Table 7.2: Bullying Phase: Threats, Identity Work Types, and Remedial Goals

Table 7.3: Post-Bullying Phase: Threats, Identity Work Types, and Remedial Goals

Table 9.1: Response Frequency, Effectiveness

Table 9.2: Responses and Bullying Acts

Table 11.1: Solo or Multiple Harassers

Table 11.2: Harassers' Supporters

Table 11.3: Solo Harassers' Supporters

Table 11.4: Bully Position and Sources of Support

Table 11.5: Organizational Responses After Reports

Table 12.1: Bully-Focused Sensemaking Themes

Table 12.2: Organization-Focused Sensemaking Themes

Table 12.3: Target-Focused Sensemaking Themes

Table 12.4: Workgroup-Focused Sensemaking Themes

Table 12.5: Society-Focused Sensemaking Themes

Table 13.1: Goals Motivating Conflict Management Tactics

Table 13.2: Conflict Management Tactics

Table 13.3: Target Profiles, Motivations, Tactics

Table 13.4: Bystander Profiles, Motivations, Tactics

Table 13.5: Aggressor Profiles, Motivations, Tactics

Table 16.1: Key Question: How does workplace bullying come about?

Table 16.2: Key Question: How do employees and organizations respond?

Table 16.3: Key Question: Why is bullying so harmful?

Table 16.4: Key Question: Why is workplace bullying so often un-addressed?

Table 16.5: Key Question: How can workplace bullying best be addressed?

Table 16.6: Directions for Future Research

CHAPTER 1

Introduction

Pamela Lutgen-Sandvik

The purpose of this book is to translate scientific research about workplace bullying to interested, non-academic audiences. Too often the people and organizations that researchers hope their research will help, have no access to their research studies. When people can access the studies, the studies are written in such an inaccessible way (my work included) that making heads or tails of the findings and applying them can be challenging if not impossible. To make my research accessible beyond academic settings, what people call the "ivory tower," I have compiled the work in this volume and revised most of it to reduce the jargon, terminology, and so forth that scientists so favor. I hope I have met this goal in my rewriting of these studies. In what follows, I define workplace bullying and its potential causes (or at least contributing factors to its presence), explain the features that mark bullying as a unique type of aggression at work, and provide an overview of the chapters in the book.

Workplace Bullying as a Unique Occurrence

One of the things that make workplace bullying so difficult to explain and understand is that we lack an agreed-upon name for the experience. Some call workplace bullying harassment of a non-sexual nature, employee emotional abuse, psychological terror, mobbing, and so forth. A review of research on the subject suggests that all of these terms describe roughly the same phenomenon—repeated, long-lasting aggressive abuse at the hands of other organizational members. I use the term *workplace bullying* as a short-hand to represent all of these terms. Using a common term helps bullying targets, targets' loved ones, professionals, and other organizational members more easily speak about and address the problem.

Workplace bullying is persistent aggressive interactions that escalate in severity and hostility over time and against which targeted

1

workers ("targets") are unable to defend themselves or are otherwise unable to stop abuse. Research terminology denotes abused workers as *targets* rather than victims, and abusers as *bullies, bullies,* or *aggressors.* I follow these conventions throughout. In what follows, I explain the various markers or features of adult bullying at work.

Features of Workplace Bullying

* **Repetition.** Bullying is recurring and frequent. The hammering and chipping away is laced throughout target stories and represents abuse that often occurs on a nearly daily basis [1, 2]. Repetition differentiates the phenomenon from infrequent negative workplace interactions [3].

* **Duration.** The long-term nature of bullying is a prominent feature giving bullying its corrosive character. Researchers usually adopt the minimum of six months [4], but targets typically report that bullying lasts much longer [5, 6].

* **Escalation.** Bullying intensifies over time if left unchecked [4, 7]. During early phases, targets may have difficulty translating their experience to others aside from describing feelings of unease or heightened discomfort [8, 9]. In later stages, they may not have the language to label their experiences *bullying* but are unmistakably aware of being under attack [10].

* **Harm.** Bullying is exceedingly destructive and is associated with targets' impaired physical, mental, and occupational health; deterioration of personal relationships outside of work; and economic jeopardy. An audience of coworkers also live in fear of being the next target [11].

* **Attributed intent.** Targets and witnesses typically believe bullies' actions are purposeful--that bullies know exactly what they are doing and even work at it. Researchers generally omit intent in definitions [discussed in 3], but people on the receiving end are *convinced* that bullying is intentional and find it impossible to believe that such egregious acts are inadvertent [12, 13].

* **Hostile work environment.** Bullying constitutes, and is constituted by, hostile work environments [14, 15] marked by pervasive fear and dread of workgroup members. Bullying is both an outcome of hostile work environments and a building

2

block of hostile work environments.

* *Perceived power disparity.* Bullying at work is marked by a (perceived or actual) difference in power between perpetrator and target [e.g., 10]. Power inequality exists prior to the onset of bullying (e.g., abusive supervision) or arises as a result of ongoing harassment (e.g., peer-to-peer abuse) [16].

* *Communication patterning.* Bullying is typically a constellation of verbal and nonverbal acts that constitute a discernable, recurring pattern to targets and witnesses [17]. Targets believe their experiences cannot be understood outside this contextual patterning, which makes bullying difficult to describe in a simple straightforward way [2].

* *Distorted communication networks.* Communication networks are typically blocked or stifled in bullying environments. Open day-to-day communication is risky and, in some cases, even forbidden and punished [13]. The situations "that scare a bully most are the possibility of more than one person getting together to complain and [thus,] ... their behavior becoming public" [18, p. 26].

As is apparent, bullying is more than simply a list of aggressive behaviors. It is a complex pattern of negative communication and behavior identified by these features. The features differentiate bullying from one-time aggressive or discriminatory acts. The features of workplace bullying identify it as a unique experience more than do the forms of bullying (e.g., yelling, criticizing, eye rolling).

The Extreme End of a Toxic Continuum

Workplace bullying is extremely aggressive abuse perpetrated on the job. If you can imagine a spectrum or range of destructive communication in the workplace, with occasional rudeness or incivility on the lower end and workplace homicide on the upper end, workplace bullying would be toward the upper end. (Credit goes to Gary Namie for the continuum idea, see [19].)

3

Destructive Communication Continuum [19]

Low-Level		High-
Level		

Incivility & --Workplace------------- Insider		
rudeness	bullying	murder

Workplace bullying is frequent, repetitive, and ongoing. Some believe if the abuse is infrequent, the abuse is not bullying. I do not subscribe to this fixed repetition rule because one bullying act, (for example, moving the target's desk to an overheated, cramped room in the basement) can have severe, ongoing negative repercussions. Others argue that for people to consider abuse as bullying, the abuse must have continued for at least 6 months.

Potentially, the aggression in the early months could be called *pre-bullying*, but similar to the repetition argument, I don't subscribe to a hard-and-fast 6-month rule for duration; I believe bullying can escalate in very short time spans. On the other hand, bullying can take years to fully emerge as targeted aggression. So, what's workplace bullying? Simply put, adult bullying at work is frequent, ongoing aggressive communication and behavior that harms targets and organizations, and which targets cannot easily defend against, prevent, or end.

Explanations for Workplace Bullying

The complexity of workplace bullying is rivaled only by the many explanations for it. To fully understand the phenomenon one must "take a broad range of potential causes of bullying into account, which may lie with the organization, the perpetrator (bully), the social psychology of the work group, and also the victim" [20, p. 166]. Globalized economic environments, professional norms, and social-cultural traditions also contribute to bullying. There are a number of explanations for workplace bullying, to which I now turn.

Types of workplace bullying. Explanations for bullying origins differ depending on the types of bullying that occurs. The types of bullying are dispute-related [21], predatory-bullying (authoritative-, displaced-, and discriminatory- [22]), and organizational bullying.

4

* *Dispute-related bullying* begins with interpersonal disagreements that build into extremely escalated, entrenched conflicts [21]. Bullies may begin to objectify their opponents and "the total destruction of the opponent is seen as the ultimate goal" [21, p. 19]

* *Authoritative-bullying* is the abuse of power granted through organizational position and is the most commonly reported [19, 23, 24]. For authoritative bullies, serial bullying is usually present, in which many workers are bullied, usually one after the other.

* *Displaced-bullying*, or scapegoating, is aggressing "against someone other than the source of strong provocation because aggressing against the source of such provocation is too dangerous" [25, p. 197]. It occurs when increased frustration or stress caused by workplace factors result in employees taking frustrations out on others.

* *Discriminatory-bullying* is simply abusing someone out of prejudice, usually workers who differ from, or refuse to accept the norms of, the rest of the workgroup or "belong to a certain outsider group" [10, p. 19].

* *Organizational-bullying* indicts organizational practices that are oppressive, exploitive, and over-controlling as seeding abuse [14] (e.g., corporate downsizing, outsourcing jobs, forcing uncompensated overtime work, closing entire plants to relocate for low-cost labor).

Book Overview and Style Explanations

This book represents more than a decade of my research about adult bullying at work. One hope I have for this work is that targets might feel better about their situations when they see that bullying is *never* their fault. I also hope reading the book will lead them to discover they are not alone: Sadly, nearly a third of all working adults in the United States suffer at the hands of aggressive bullies sometime in their careers. Another goal for the book is to provide organizational decision-makers research-based approaches to recognizing and taking quick action when bullying occurs. In fact, some chapters focus entirely on interventions for building respectful workplace climates.

Chapters, for the most part, are in the chronological order of when I completed the study or article on which the chapter focuses. One exception is Chapter 2, which I placed in the beginning of the book to set the stage for the subsequent chapters. Some the chapters represent adapted work from previously published pieces in scientific journals, others are appearing in print for the very first time. In all cases, chapters represent information I have updated, revised, and extended, information that does not appear in the previous versions. Additionally, readers will find citations updated, so cited work is often times more recent than what was in the original pieces. As such, this book represents what I believe is a fresh look at older ideas and a first look at issues yet to be considered in current research.

"Yes, It Really *Is* Happening ..."

Many have asked me, "Do adults really get bullied at work? Isn't bullying something that just happens at school with children?" and I have answered resoundingly, (and sadly), "Yes" and "No." Sadly, workplace bullying is relatively common; it touches the lives of nearly half of the working adults in the United States—by either being targeted or being forced to witness one's coworkers and colleagues bullied. Adult bullies are far more astutely strategic than children, more likely to use indirect aggression because indirect is easy to deny, and are excellent at *managing up*—appearing completely innocent to upper-managers or other organizational authorities.

I became interested in this subject before entering academia, while I served as non-profit organization's executive director. In that capacity I intervened in many cases of what I now know was workplace bullying, but for which at the time I had no language to describe. Given my management background, my commitment to do research that contributes to creating respectful workplaces, and the issues I have faced intervening in adult bullying cases, the driving goal of my research is,

✳ *How can we make the workplace more humane?*

My research spans a decade plus, is extensive, and crosses a number of topics: US prevalence, effects on bystanders, harm to employees and organizations, worker resistance to abuse, effect on target identity, and why women tend to bully other women rather than bully men. I have theorized about the spiraling, silencing effect of persistent abuse on workgroups and the communication types that likely lead to creating employee-abusive organizations. Some of these published articles or chapters are collaborative; I believe researching in teams results in exceedingly rich studies and have a number of co-authors with whom

I continue to work. (See original publication citations at the end of the book for titles of the solely authored and co-authored pieces from which the book is drawn.)

The studies reported here are social science, so were initially written using the conventions of social science writing. Some studies are based on quantitative (numerical) survey data and statistical analysis, others on qualitative (transcripts) and theme analysis. On one hand, qualitative interview studies use smaller samples and produce pages and pages of detailed rich explanations and experiences. Quite often when others read the qualitative studies, they realize that they have had similar experiences. This similarity is what researchers call *transferability*. Survey studies, on the other hand, use larger numbers of people, and produce thinner yet more specific data. Survey data allows researchers to draw conclusions from the research and apply them to other similar groups of people. This similarity is what researchers call *generalizability*. Neither approach is better or stronger than the other, they simply answer different kinds of questions.

Social Science Writing and Reading

Scientific writing conventions require researchers to structure the write-ups of their research using the following format: (1) a review of related past research, (2) a description of the method used (if the study depended on collecting data), (3) a section reporting the findings followed by a discussion of the findings, and (4) a glance at the study's limitations and areas where future research might be needed.

Readers who just want to know, "What did you find out?" can skip to the Findings (for qualitative studies) or Discussion-Implications (for quantitative studies) and start reading there.

To ease reading, I have removed much of the statistical analysis language and numbers because readers rarely have much interest in the actual statistical tests used. I have retained sample size (signified by letter "n"), means or averages (signified by letter "m"), standard deviation (signified by letters "sd," which explains how big the differences were (larger numbers mean bigger differences), and the alpha-level (statistical significance signified by lower letter "p").

For readers interested in the statistical tests and analyses, they will want to read the original scientific publications, see First Publication Citations at the end of the book. I have reduced the Methods sections for most studies; these sections talk about how data was analyzed, sampling controlled, and so forth. Again, I direct interested readers or researchers to the original publications.

Another change I made was reducing in-text citations in terms of how much space these usually take. Scientific writing typically includes many, many citations, which show up in the text as (parenthetical) information about the author, year of publication, pages (if directly quoting the other author). Citations in this book have been reformatted into an endnote-number style, which means a number replaces the citation information, and the reference list at the end of the book provides the full citation material—names and publications of hundreds of studies—the numerous dedicated professionals and researchers who are concerned about workplace bullying.

For smoother reading, I use a numbered citation format. If readers are interested in learning more about ideas in the book, they have only to look at the number in the text [#] and then go to that number in the Reference pages at the end of the book. I have also reduced the number of citations from Chapter 11 to 17, as many of the later chapters discuss studies cited a number of times in the earlier chapters. Therefore, for readers wishing to extend their reading on the subject, Chapters 1 through 10 will provide the majority of cited work. Chapters 11 through 17, for the most part I cite the newly introduced research or sources with directly quoted material and page numbers. Occasionally, I refer readers back to earlier chapters. I also use the abbreviations H1, H2, and RQ1, RQ2, which mean Hypothesis 1, Research Question 1.

Because scientific writing conventions do not translate easily to non-scientific audiences, I have provided chapter summaries of the studies, which precede the chapters and a glossary of terms for quick reference, which is at the end of the book. Readers can skim the summaries to see which studies are of the most interest and then go back and read the study more closely. Because each piece in the anthology was a stand-alone research project, readers can read the papers in any order they wish. The studies were presented, published, or are under review (for potential publication) in a variety of venues. As such, the pieces do not depend on each other for explanation. That is, each addresses an aspect of the workplace bullying phenomenon, explains the harms, provides definitions, and so forth. As such, introductory sections have some repetition.

Chapter Overviews

In what follows, I briefly summarize the contents of the coming chapters. As a communication scholar, my focus throughout is on the communicative features of workplace bullying in organizational and social life. Chapter 2 reports on the prevalence of workplace bullying in the US workplace. The piece compares US prevalence with the UK and Scandinavia (places about which workplace bullying research is abundant). The chapter also compares three employee groups in terms of the degree of negative treatment they report experiencing, their job satisfaction, and their rating of their jobs overall. Chapter 3 explains how serial bullying works. I argue that with serial bullies, bullying never stops just because the aggressor has driven the current target out of the organization. The cyclical model explain how witnesses are silenced, how upper-managers turn their heads, and how new targets are chose after the current target or targets are driven out of the organization.

Chapter 4 describes how targets and witnesses fight back against bullying. Employees affected by workplace bullying do many, many things to try to stop abuse. The piece also explains the resistance that appears to be more successful than other approaches. Chapter 5 was written to publicize how painful bullying is and how targets talked about the pain in terms of metaphors such as bullying is poison, bullies are evil dictators, and being targeted is like being a child in a dysfunctional home.

Chapter 6 compares the experiences of younger and older workers in terms of the type of abuse they report experiencing and their responses to abuse. Chapter 7 deals with the trauma and stigma of being targeted at work. The chapter presents three stages of bullying, the threat to targets' identity or self-image, the types of identity work or identity repair targets report using, and how people learn to "live around" the experience once they are out of the toxic environment.

Chapter 8 is a conceptual piece about the forces that set the stage for workplace bullying in terms of organizations and their structures. (Fair warning: This chapter can be a bit challenging to understand.) The piece looks at the individual-level (personalities and work processes), the organization-level (policies and practices), and the societal-level (worship of aggressive business people). Chapter 9's focus is twofold and makes two arguments: (1) Workplace bullying is fundamentally a communication phenomenon. (2) The most common employee responses to bullying are fundamentally communicative.

9

Chapter 10 specifically takes up the women-bullying-women pattern in US research and explains why this pattern may occur. The chapter also suggests questions that women and their coworkers (bosses, peers, upper-managers) might consider to figure out why bullying is happening and what might be done about it. Chapter 11 is a refinement of a study looking at the various people who appear to be the aggressors' allies in bullying. The piece also reports national prevalence of adult bullying and examines the legal or policy-related actions targets take when bullied at work.

Chapter 12 looks at supervisory bullying and how targets make sense of why bullying started and why it has continued. It offers suggestions for thinking and talking about bullying that can feel and be more empowering. Chapter 13 looks at the three groups of employees involved in bullying—targets, witnesses/bystanders, and bullies. The piece explores the different motivations members of each group usually have in bullying and the tactics employees use because of the motivation. Additionally, the chapter presents the common profiles for the three types, and the subtypes if applicable.

Chapter 14 combines ideas from *positive organizational research* (research focusing on what's good in organizations) and bullying. Specifically, the chapter asks and answers the question, "Does positive phenomenon buffer or reduce the negative effects of workplace bullying. Chapter 15 explains how workplace bullying affects workers, workgroups, workforces, and workplaces. The chapter also suggests interventions for organizations that involve upper-management, middle-management, workgroups, and individual employees. Chapter 16 is a review of the communication research about workplace bullying. The chapter looks at why bullying is so harmful and so difficult to address, but looks at these issues from three perspectives: individual-level, organizational- level and societal-level.

The final sections of the book are general rather than specific and include references, publication permissions, glossary, author biographical notes, and first publication citations. A full list of referenced articles, books, and book chapters follows Chapter 16. Citations are extensive and reflect national and international researchers who have contributed to what we currently know about adult bullying at work. Permissions for reconceptualizing and re-releasing my previously published research studies are included in an abbreviated form. Typically, this information matters little to readers; I include it solely for my publisher's copyright requirements.

All of the research in this book is original work that I have written, most of which I am either the sole author or the first author. The glossary of terms is a quick reference tool and an explanation of familiar and unfamiliar terms and phrases. A short biographical note about the author follows. The book ends with a list of first publication citations if readers should wish to reference the original publication upon which I have based particular chapters.

I hope the research I report here is helpful for readers, whether they are wondering if they're being bullied, wondering if they're bullying others, pondering how to report bullying to upper-management, or trying to build more respectful workplaces and needing some pointers.

I wish you "good reading" and hope you will talk to others about what you learn here. For workplace bullying to end, we need common language, understanding of how complex bullying can be, people talking about it, and the courage to face those who verbally abuse and psychologically terrorize others in organizations.

✹ NOTE: For this book, I used a publisher that I have not used in the past (ORCM Academic Press). If while you're reading you find proofreading or typographical errors, would you take a moment and send an email to the publisher with the error and the page number? Thank you in advance.

✹ orgcommpress@gmail.com

CHAPTER 2

Prevalence, Perception, Degree, & Impact of Adult Bullying in the American Workplace[A]

Pamela Lutgen-Sandvik, Sarah J. Tracy, & Jess Alberts

Chapter Summary: This chapter reports how often workplace bullying occurs in the US workplace. We used the most common measure of workplace bullying (Negative Acts Questionnaire, NAQ) so we could compare the prevalence rates with those from other bullying and aggression studies. We open by defining bullying and contrasting it with other negative workplace actions and interactions and then look at bullying frequency, job satisfaction, and stress for US workers. We then compare these to similar studies and analyzed the negative acts leading to someone actually feeling bullied. The chapter also introduces the idea of *bullying degree* because bullying can range from bad to horrifying. We also looked at how bullying affected others who witness their coworkers being bullied (but who were not bullied themselves).

Keywords: bullying prevalence, mobbing, employee emotional abuse, workplace aggression, job satisfaction, witnesses, targets

---

"Right now, there's two open positions under [the bully], and whoever gets them is doomed. That's all we know ... whoever gets those positions are doomed." *Witness to coworkers' bullying in a large US restaurant chain.*

Bullied employees look forward to work with dread and a sense of impending doom. They steal through the workplace in a state of high alert, fearing the next attack. Privately, they are ashamed of being victimized and confused at what feels like their personal failure when they can't end abuse [26].

Workplace bullying is interpersonal aggression on the job [27] that goes far beyond incivility or rudeness [28]. Bullying occurs frequently, is intense and ongoing, and leaves victims feeling powerless [10]. Bullying is a sort of hammering and chipping away at those targeted. This hammering away results in victims feeling isolated, demoralized, and unable to escape or stop the terrorizing tactics [4]. In the language of researchers, workplace bullying is "harassing, offending, socially excluding someone or negatively affecting someone's work tasks.... repeatedly and regularly over a period of time" [10](p. 4).

Bullying causes widespread damage. Victims of bullying, called *targets* in research on the subject, suffer long-term often permanent psychological, physical, and professional harm [18]. The experience is *crippling and devastating* [29]. Being the target of relentless attacks at work erodes people's self-esteem, mental performance, and emotional strength [30-32]. It can lead to depression [5], alcohol and drug abuse [33], posttraumatic stress disorder (PTSD), and even suicide [4, 34]. Being treated unjustly at work leads to chronic stress, high blood pressure, and increased risk of coronary heart disease [35]. Some targets are so damaged they cannot return to work once they have escaped the bullying, even when they go to different jobs where there is no bullying. Other targets can only return to their work lives after considerable counseling [1, 36].

Witnesses or bystanders working with the targets also suffer. They watch what's happening to the targets and rightly wonder if they're going to be next in line. Coworkers who see their colleagues bullied are more stressed and more likely to quit their jobs than are employees who work in settings without this kind of aggression [11]. And bullying has disastrous effects on interpersonal relationships and family communication [37, 38], both for targets and for witnesses who bring the anxiety home.

This chapter reports on the prevalence of bullying for working adults in the United States and compares this prevalence to the experiences of adults in other nations. During the course of the study we realized bullying occurred in gradations, sort of like a continuum of abuse. When we made this discovery, we developed a measure of what we called *bullying degree* and then looked at how *bullying degree* affected stress levels, job satisfaction, and overall job rating. We also examined witnesses' experiences to determine how seeing others being abused harmed the witnesses. To provide some background for the study and for the chapters that follow in this book, the following section gives a brief history of the bullying research and its national origins.

Background of Bullying Research

Research on workplace bullying began in Sweden in the 1980s, following the country's attention to school yard bullying [reviewed in [39]. Heinz Leymann [4], a German-born physician and psychiatrist working in Sweden, was a pioneer researcher of bullying. He was initially interested in school bullying and became concerned about workplace bullying (what he termed "mobbing") when he saw that his adult patients had very similar experiences at work.

Leymann's work sparked interest in Norwegian [40] and Finnish [41] researchers, who began to research mobbing and work harassment in the late 1980s and early 1990s. In 1990, a British freelance journalist named Andrea Adams [29] brought the issue to public attention through a series of BBC broadcasts. She called it *workplace bullying*. Andrea is deceased but her legacy has lived on, first in the Andrea Adams Trust, and more recently in the Andrea Adams Consultancy in England and Wales. The Trust worked to raise awareness of adult bullying and provided a national helpline for targets. The Trust closed in 2009, but concerned professionals still work at the Consultancy and have similar goals. Charlotte Rayner, a professor at Portsmouth Business School in the UK, conducted one of the earliest studies of workplace bullying. Since that time, many other UK researchers have conducted and published studies about adult bullying [3, 42].

Since the initial work in Sweden, Norway, and Finland, research about bullying has spread to Australia [43], South Africa [44], Austria [45], The Netherlands [46], Germany [47], Bangladesh [48], and numerous other countries [49]. The topic continues to receive considerable attention internationally, particularly in the fields of organizational-industrial psychology and business-management. This growing interest can be seen in the increasing attendance at the biennial International Conference on Workplace Bullying.

In the US, Carroll Brodsky, a psychiatrist who interviewed over 1,000 persons filing workers' compensation claims in California and Nevada, published *The Harassed Worker* [30]. This book is one of the earliest examinations of workplace harassment but raised very little interest at the time. Brodsky's research was revived in the early 1990s when interest surged in Britain. The book is now considered a central manuscript on the topic, even though it is out-of-print. In the early 1980s, Helen Cox, a professor of nursing in Texas, began studying nurses' experiences of verbal abuse. She became interested when one of her most gifted nursing students threatened to quit school as a result of continued abuse [50]. At about the same time, others were studying the similar experiences of medical students [51].

Since this early work in the US, researchers have explored a wide range of "hostile workplace behaviors [that] can be found in a variety of literatures...and under a variety of names" [52](p. 42). The US interest in workplace hostility has grown since the early 1990s, in part due to workplace violence and murder (reviewed in [53]). The research can be found under a variety of terms such as *workplace aggression* [27], *emotional abuse* [7, 54], *generalized harassment* [55], *perceived victimization* [56], and *counterproductive* [57] or *antisocial* [58] *workplace behavior*. In the next section, I explain how these topics and terms are similar and different.

Workplace Bullying and Other Names for Negative Workplace Experiences

To understand where workplace bullying fits within the various studies of harmful communication and behavior at work, we organize the terms into a layered list or hierarchy. The terms are organized from large to small—sort of like Russian nesting dolls. The hierarchy begins with the general over-arching types of negative communication and conduct. It moves to mid-range acts and ends with narrow-range acts. Over-arching terms span a wide range of harmful interactions, of which bullying is only one. Key experiences at this level include workplace aggression, counterproductive workplace behaviors, workplace injustice, and so forth. (See Table 2.1 for terms; the bracketed numbers indicate the studies cited in References at the end of the book).

Mid-range terms fall under overarching types of negativity and include both general and specific types of workplace abuse. General types of abuse include bullying, emotional abuse, and mistreatment—highly similar phenomena. Specific types of abuse include acts targeted at specific groups of people, such as sexual or ethnic harassment and particular types of discrimination (e.g. age, race, disability, etc.). In actual workplace experiences, these often overlap. Sexual harassment frequently includes abusive actions that are not explicitly sexual, and bullying can be sexually discriminating. For example, people might be targeted for failure to act according to accepted gender roles or targeted because they are different from the rest of the workgroup [21, 59].

At the third level, narrow-range terms include behaviors or elements of intermediate behaviors. These include victimization, incivility, and verbal aggressiveness. Thus, bullying and sexual harassment usually include acts of incivility and a sense of being victimized. Phenomena at each level include most behaviors below them. For example, *workplace bullying* is a type of *workplace aggression*. Bullying could also be classified as a type of *antisocial work behavior* that includes verbal/physical and active/passive dimensions and produces harm or injury [58].

Table 2.1: Hierarchy of Terms

Over-arching Terms

Counterproductive workplace behavior [57, 60]

Organizational injustice [61, 62]

Organizational misbehavior [63]

Workplace aggression [27, 64, 65]

Workplace deviance [66]

Antisocial work behaviors [58]

Workplace violence (broadly defined) [67]

Mid-range Terms

General forms	Specific forms
Emotional abuse [7, 17, 68]	Discrimination (multiple authors) [race, age, religion, ethnicity, disability]
Mobbing [69, 70]	
Social undermining [71]	Ethnic harassment [76]
Workplace bullying [3, 72]	Sexual harassment [77, 78]
Workplace harassment [73]	Abusive supervision [79]
Workplace mistreatment [74]	
Victimization [75]	

Narrow-range Terms

Incivility [80, 81]

Petty tyranny [82]

Social ostracism [83]

Verbal abuse [50, 84]

Verbal aggressiveness [85, 86]

Features of Bullying

Adult bullying at work has four specific features: intensity, repetition, duration, and power disparity. First, bullying involves intensity—multiple negative acts make up abuse of this type [21, 32, 87]. Second, bullying occur frequently, usually weekly or more often. *Hammering and chipping away* at targets is a hallmark of bullying. Most research does not consider one-time incidents of aggression as bully-

17

ing [4, 88]).

Third, bullying occurs over an extended period of time. Researchers usually apply a six-month criterion to differentiate bullying from lower-level negativity [49, 88], but target experiences point to far longer durations of abuse. Finally, power disparity between perpetrator and target is "central to the definition of bullying" [10](p. 21). Most definitions of workplace bullying include the targets feeling unable to stop or prevent abuse. That is, a power disparity either exists at the onset of bullying or develops over time [89].

Based on these features we determined that bullying was occurring by using the following criteria:

* at least two negative acts occurring

* weekly or more often

* for at least six months

* where targets feel less powerful than bullies

Prevalence Comparisons Across Studies

International researchers have compared prevalence rates across national samples, but these comparisons usually do not include US data. Studies have also used different measures for bullying, which make clear comparisons challenging [49]. As of 2009, the publication date of the original study reported in this chapter, there had been no US studies assessing the prevalence of bullying using a tool designed to measure bullying. There were, however, several US studies of similar mid-range and over-arching phenomena.

Hypotheses

In order to assess US workers' experiences of bullying so we could make comparisons to international studies, we used the Negative Acts Questionnaire (NAQ). Past research on bullying, emotional abuse, and workplace aggression guided the hypotheses about bullying in a sample of US workers.

Bullying Prevalence

Studies typically have used one of two methods to determine prevalence. Researchers have identified bullying by (a) counting the occurrence of negative acts over a specified period of time using a checklist; and (b) participants' self-identification as a target (for a discussion of bullying measurement, see [90]). These measures have produced very different prevalence rates [42, 91].

Prevalence based on counting the number of negative acts results in higher rates than counts based on a person self-identifying as being bullied [87]. A UK study, for example, found that only one-half of respondents who reported long-lasting, frequent negative acts self-identified as bullied [92]. Similarly, a Finnish study had similar results. There does seem to be substantial overlap between the two methods, however. Most employees who self-identify as bullied also reported frequent, intense attacks [91].

As is true for self-identifying as a target of sexual harassment [93], there are a number of reasons people will avoid identifying as being bullied. Some may not think their treatment is bullying. Others may simply want to avoid identifying as a "victim" because being a victim implies weakness. Because people want to avoid thinking of themselves as victims, assessing bullying prevalence based on self-identifying as bullying leads to under-estimating the frequency of bullying.

Moreover, self-identification may be less important than experiencing the persistent kinds of negativity at work researchers "count" as bullying. Employees who report persistent hostility also report negative health effects, regardless of whether they self-identified as bullied [94]. Given these issues, we hypothesized the following in this study:

H1: Bullying prevalence based on researchers counting the number of reported negative acts will be higher than bullying based on people self-identifying as being "bullied" at work.

We were also interested in finding out which sorts of aggression or combinations of aggressive acts separate people who feel bullied from those who do not. Current research points to the negative acts that targets experience at higher rates than non-targets [94]. Evidence also exists pointing to particular negative acts—false allegations, hostile communication, intimidation, and threats of violence—evoking amplified target self-defense responses. Other forms of abuse—work overload, working below one's competence, excessive work monitoring—do not appear to evoke amplified responses [95]. Thus, we hypothesized:

H2: Certain kinds of negativity, particularly threats to identity, economic stability, and physical safety, will increase people's perceptions of being "bullied" at work.

Bullying prevalence also varies by national culture and "appears to be less widespread in Scandinavia than in countries such as the UK" [87](p. 407). Lower rates of bullying in Scandinavia may be due to the low power-distance and egalitarian cultural norms there [87, 91, 96]. In low power-distance cultures, people in different social positions experience smaller differences in power and status [96]. Because perceived power disparity is a feature of bullying, we expected to find lower levels of bullying in Scandinavia than in UK or US [49, 87]. Furthermore, as Scandinavian cultures are more egalitarian, people in these cultures might generally be more concerned with the quality of interpersonal relations [97]. Very likely, bullying is less tolerated in Scandinavia than in more competitive cultures, such as the UK and US, "in which there is a greater focus on individual assertiveness and achievement" [87](p. 408).

Certainly, US companies stress market rivalry, individual achievement, managers over workers, and the "competition between individuals" (p. 91) [98]. Stressing competition and individual achievement and reward reduces collaborative efforts. Moreover, favoring management over workers creates an uneven playing field for subordinate staff—enabling powerful organizational members to bully others with relative impunity. Thus, we hypothesized:

H3: Bullying prevalence will be higher for US workers than for Scandinavian workers.

Bullying Degree

Bullying occurs in gradations—*degrees*—which includes abuse frequency, intensity, and duration [7, 99]. Bullying degree is the combination of intensity, frequency, and duration of aggressive acts. Bullying intensity is usually a collection of hostile tactics rather than a single aggressive action. Also, frequency and duration are linked. Targets "who are frequently bullied ... report a longer duration of their problem" [100](p. 192). The sheer number of different negative acts associated with bullying and the effects of frequency and duration on targets indicate that bullying is not a simple yes-or-no experience.

Rather, bullying may best be conceptualized as a continuum of negativity. Davenport and colleagues [99] for example, argue that bullying could be characterized by degrees of harm, similar to first, second and third degree burns, a model we extended in this study. More importantly, intensity, frequency, and duration—*degree*—are linked to seriously negative outcomes for targets. US workers persistently exposed to aggression showed greater signs of harm than those occasionally exposed. For example, employees exposed to five or more persistent aggressive actions report more harm than employees exposed to fewer than five [101]. This research led our fourth hypothesis:

> *H4a: Increased bullying degree will be associated with increased stress.*

> *H4b: Increased bullying degree will be associated with decreased job satisfaction and overall job rating.*

Witnessing Your Coworkers Being Bullied

Bullying results in a ripple effect indicating that the phenomenon does not involve just a few 'problem' employees [102]. Rather, bullying is a dynamic process harming everyone in the workgroup. Witnessing coworkers are secondary victims—"employees who themselves [are] not violated but whose perceptions, fears and expectations are changed as a result of being vicariously exposed to violence" [103](p. 35). Witnesses report increased levels of stress, "excessive workloads, role ambiguity, and work relationship conflict" [104](p. 495). In toxic work environments where some are bullied, witnessing bystanders likely experience more frequent aggression targeted at them than do non-exposed workers, even if witnesses do not feel directly bullied. Thus, we hypothesized:

> *H5: Coworkers who witness others being bullied will*

> *a) have lower rates of personally experienced aggression than the targets ... but ...*

> *b) have higher rates of personally experienced aggression than people who work where no bullying is present (non-exposed workers).*

Research also suggests that bullying not only negatively affects targets' work quality outcomes (e.g. satisfaction, stress), but also adversely affects those outcomes for non-bullied witnesses [11, 104, 105]. Wit-

21

nessing bystanders have "significantly more general stress and mental stress reactions" than non-exposed workers [11](p. 65). Additionally, witnessing bystanders more often "leave their jobs as a result of their contact with bullying" than do non-exposed workers [3](p. 56). As such, we hypothesized:

> H6: Witnesses of bullying will report
>
> a) better work-quality outcomes than targets
>
> ... but ...
>
> b) worse work-quality outcomes than non-exposed workers.

Method

Data Collection and Sample

We used an online survey (Survey Monkey) hoping to draw a variety of US workers spanning age groups, industries, and locales. All communication on the website or in conversations referred to the project The American Workplace Survey. We simply asked respondents to "Tell us about your job."

Participants. We drew 403 US workers to the survey from various methods (268 women, 135 men). Respondents worked in 18 industries, lived in 33 states, and ranged in age from 18 to 57. The majority of respondents (76%) worked in administration, health and social services, education, service sector, professional and scientific fields, finance and insurance, and public administration.

Persons aged 35–44 years and white-collar industries were somewhat over-represented, and 6 of the 17 US Department of Labor industries were somewhat under-represented (accommodation/food, construction, manufacturing, public administration, retail, transportation) [106]. On the other hand, the sample was representative of all other age groups, five industries (agriculture, arts, information, real estate, utilities), and included workers from more than two-thirds of the 50 states.

Similarities and differences of samples. Because we wanted to make comparisons to international bullying studies, it is important to note how the sample compares to other NAQ samples. Our sample was weighted towards white-collar professionals, similar to Denise

22

Salin's [91] Finnish study and a significant portion of Mikkelsen and Einarsen's Danish sample [87]. Our participants represented a wide range of ages, as was the case in the Scandinavian studies [87, 91]. The broad spectrum of industries represented in the current sample, however, was less comparable to the Danish study that focused on only four organizations [87]. Women were over-represented, but this sex characteristic was also apparent in the Finnish [91] and Danish [87] samples. In sum, our sample was similar in age and sex distribution to the studies to which we made comparisons. Our sample also reflected a similar industry distribution to Finnish [91] and Norwegian [100] studies.

Measures

The study's procedures measured bullying, frequency and intensity of aggressive acts, bullying degree, whether participants had witnessed others being bullied, and work-quality outcomes.

Operationally-defined bullying. Respondents were asked how often they experienced (behaviorally defined) negative acts over the past six months. Response categories for each negative act were:

0, never   1, occasionally (less than monthly)

2, monthly   3, weekly   4, daily

The list of aggressive acts came directly from the NAQ, the standard measure of workplace bullying [88]. None of the NAQ items specifically referred to *bullying*. We used the NAQ because it had established reliability and we could compare our findings with other studies using the NAQ [23, 87, 88, 94]. We changed one NAQ item asking about being sent to "coventry," a British term associated with the silent treatment or shunning. We altered the original wording, "Being ignored, excluded, or being "sent to Coventry" to "Being ignored, excluded or isolated from others."

Self-identified bullying. We also measured respondents' perceptions of being bullied at work by presenting a definition and asking respondents to state whether they identified with the definition (taken verbatim from the NAQ):

We define bullying as a situation where one or several individu-

23

als perceive themselves to be on the receiving end of negative actions from one or more persons persistently over a period, in a situation where the targets have difficulty defending themselves against these actions. The current study does not classify one-time incidents as bullying.

Response categories were: No; Yes, but only rarely; Yes, now and then; Yes, several times per week; Yes, almost daily.

Intensity and frequency. To determine the number and frequency of aggressive acts experienced, we used two continuous measures of intensity and frequency. Intensity was the cumulative number of different negative acts experienced. Frequency was the cumulative number of aggressive acts experienced with high regularity (daily, weekly). We used frequency to categorize operationally-defined targets (e.g. two negative acts at least weekly).

Bullying degree. Frequency and intensity were also components of the bullying degree construct. Past research suggests that as *frequency* (how many negative acts repeatedly occur daily or weekly), *intensity* (number of negative acts experienced), and *duration* (how long bullying went on) increase, so do the harmful results from bullying [21, 107]. Therefore, *bullying degree* included intensity, duration, and frequency of experienced aggression.

Witnessed bullying. Respondents who reported they were not currently bullied were asked if they had witnessed bullying at work during the past six months. Answers choices were "yes" and "no."

Workplace outcomes. We measured three outcomes related to bullying: job satisfaction, overall job rating, and perceived stress. Job satisfaction: "Overall, how satisfied are you in your job?" Answer choices ranged from 1 (very dissatisfied) to 5 (very satisfied). Overall, job rating: "Overall, how would you rank your experiences at work?" Answer choices ranged from 1 (very negative) to 5 (very positive). Job stress: "How stressful do you find your work environment?" Answers ranged from 1 (not at all stressful) to 5 (very stressful).

Other survey measures. The study from which these data were drawn explored a wider range of workplace dynamics than bullying or witnessing bullying. The NAQ was embedded into the online survey as one part of the study. Other measures omitted from this chapter included frequency of positive acts; responses to being bullied; and in-depth, open-ended items about target and witness experiences.

Results

Correlations and descriptive statistics for all continuous measure dependent and independent variables are summarized in Table 2.2. As indicated, variables are significantly related to each other. That is, job satisfaction, rating one's job, job stress, and bullying are all linked in the workplace—one affects the others.

Table 2.2: Key Variables and Their Relationships to Each Other

Variable	Average	Degree	Satisfaction	Rating
1. Bullying degree	8.9			
2. Job satisfaction	3.8	-0.6*		
3. Job rating	3.9	-0.6*	0.9*	
4. Job stress	3.5	0.3*	-0.3*	-0.3*

Degree ranged from 0 to 41. Average of satisfaction, ranking, and stress ranged from 1 to 5 (higher score = more or greater). *Two items significantly correlated (minus sign means as one increases, the other decreases).

Prevalence Rates with Two Measures of Bullying

H1 proposed that "Bullying prevalence based on the number of negative acts will be higher than bullying prevalence based on self-identification as targets." Nearly a quarter of the respondents (n = 113, 28%) were classified as *bullied* by their responses on the negative acts check list. Only 38 (9.4%), however, said "yes" when asked if they had been bullied during this time frame—a little over 1/3 (see Table 2.3). The size of the two groups differed considerably, but the two methods did have some consistency. People who self-identified as bullied also reported experiencing significantly higher rates of all but one of the negative acts in the NAQ. This finding was similar to Denise Salin's work with Finnish employees [91]. Thus, researcher-classified prevalence was significantly greater than self-identification prevalence, supporting H1.

25

Table 2.3: Prevalence Comparisons, Workplace Bullying and Aggression

Population (sample size)	Negative Acts Questionnaire			
	1 neg/act weekly past 6 months	2 neg/acts weekly past 6 months	Self-identified last 6-12 months	Self-identified work history
Current study: US workers (403)	$46.8_{a,b}$	28_c	9.4_d	29.8_e
1. Danish workers (765)	15.8_a	4.8_c	3.2	8.8_e
2. Finnish workers (377)	24.1_b		1.6_d	
3. UK workers (5288)			10.6	

Population (sample size)	WAQ-R and other measures		
	≥ 1 neg/act weekly past 6-12 months %	6 neg/acts weekly past 6-12 months %	Bullied sometime work history %
Current study: US (403)	46.8	7.7	29.8
4. US Michigan workers (689)	18.4		42
5. US Michigan workers (433)	14		56
6. US VA WAQ-R (4801)	36	6	

Notes: Same subscript (a,b,c . . .) in the same column indicates statistical differences between groups. Studies' referenced see bracketed reference in References pages: 1. [87] 2. [91] 3. [23, 94]. 4. [108] 5. [109]. 6. [101, 110] 7. [65]

Self-Identification as Bullied

H2 stated that "Certain negative acts, particularly threats to identity, economic stability, and physical safety, will discriminate between those who self-identify as targets and those who do not." First, compared the frequency of the 22 negative acts experienced regularly (monthly, weekly, or daily) between the two groups. That is, we contrasted self-identified targets (38) and non-targets (n = 365). Only one negative act failed to meet statistical significance: violence or threats of violence—a rare occurrence for both groups. Self-identified targets reported all other negative acts at higher rates than non-targets. Table 2.4 summarizes comparisons between the two groups.

Table 2.4: Negative Acts Compared for Targets, and Non-Targets

Negative acts associated with bullying	Experienced monthly, weekly, or daily	
	Targets	Non-targets
1. Had information withheld that affected your performance	60%	18%
2. Been exposed to an unmanageable workload	57%	28%
3. Ordered to do work below your level of competence	51%	27%
4. Given tasks with unreasonable or impossible targets or deadlines	49%	17%
5. Had your opinions and views ignored	46%	12%
6. Had your work excessively monitored	41%	13%
7. Reminded repeatedly of your errors or mistakes	41%	8%
8. Humiliated or ridiculed in connection with your work	41%	4%
9. Had gossip and rumors spread about you	38%	7%
10. Had insulting/offensive remarks made about you (i.e. habits, background, looks, etc.), your attitudes or your private life	35%	4%
11. Been ignored, excluded or isolated from others	32%	8%
12. Received hints or signals from others that you should quit job	30%	3%

13. Intimidated with threatening behavior such as finger-pointing, invasion of personal space, shoving, block-ing/barring the way	27%	2%
14. Experienced persistent criticism of your work and effort	27%	4%
15. Been ignored or faced hostile reactions when you approached others	27%	4%
16. Had key areas of responsibility removed or replaced with more trivial or unpleasant tasks	27%	4%
17. Had false allegations made against you	24%	4%
18. Subjected to excessive teasing and sarcasm	24%	5%
19. Been shouted at or targeted with spontaneous anger (or rage)	24%	5%
20. Pressured into not claiming something which by right you were entitled to (e.g. sick leave, holiday entitlement, travel expenses)	16%	4%
21. Been subjected to practical jokes carried out by people you don't get along with	8%	Less than 1%
22. Experienced threats of violence/ physi-cal abuse or actually physically abused/ attacked	3%	Less than 1%

Notes: Targets and non-targets reported experiencing all of these at statistically different rates (targets more often than non-targets), except violence/threats of violence, which were low for both.

To determine which negative acts made people feel bullied (differen-tiating between self-identified targets and non-targets), we used a statis-tical approach called a multiple discriminant analysis. Basically, the analysis looks at the negative acts most commonly reported for the group of employees who said the felt bullied at work. These six nega-tive acts were

✳ Being humiliated or ridiculed in connection with your work

* Having important information withheld

* Being faced with threatening behavior (finger-pointing, invasion of personal space, shoving, blocking/barring the way)

* Being pressured not to claim something to which entitled (sick leave, vacation pay)

* Being ignored or faced with hostility when approaching others

* Hints to quit your job

US Bullying Prevalence
Compared to Scandinavian Prevalence

H3 proposed that "Bullying prevalence in the US sample will be higher than in Scandinavian samples." We compared as many forms of bullying and aggression prevalence as our data allowed. Using NAQ data, we found that US workers reported being bullied at significantly higher rates for nearly all points of comparison. For example, 47% of the US, 16% of the Danish, and 24% of the Finnish employees reported experiencing one negative act at least weekly.

Comparison with the Danish study [87] also indicated significant differences between the two groups. Specifically, 28% of US and 5% of Danish employees reported experiencing two negative acts at least weekly. For self-identification as a target, 9% of US, 3% of Danish, and 2% of Finnish employees reported that they had been bullied— significant differences. Finally, 30% of US and 9% of Danish employees self-identified as bullied sometime during their work history. Taken together, substantial support was found for H3. (See Table 2.3 for summary of these percentages and comparisons that were significantly different.)

Bullying Degree and Work Quality Outcomes

H4a and H4b stated that "Bullying degree will be positively correlated with stress and negatively correlated with job satisfaction and overall job rating." To test this, we analyzed respondents' degree scores and their correlations with three work-quality outcomes (stress, overall job ranking, job satisfaction). Bullying degree positively correlated with stress, and negatively correlated with job satisfaction and overall job ranking/rating (see Table 2.2). These findings were consistent with previous research. Increases in the number of bullying acts experienced weekly increases the extent of harm [107]. H4a/b were supported.

Witnessing Bullying

H5 stated that "Witnesses to bullying will report overall workplace negativity at rates lower than targets but higher than non-exposed workers." We used *bullying degree* as an indicator of overall workplace negativity. We compared bullying degree across three self-identified groups: bullied workers (n = 38), witnesses to bullying (n = 44), and non-exposed workers (n = 321) to see if experiencing workplace aggression differed between groups. We found significant differences. Self-identified targets experienced the highest degree of bullying aggression (average = 20), followed by witnesses (average = 12) and then non-exposed workers (average = 8). Thus, H5 was supported. Table 2.5 summarizes these comparisons. Our interpretations of these results are as follows:

❋ Certainly bullied workers experience the highest level and frequency of abuse at work when bullying is present.

❋ However, even when employees do not feel personally bullied, if they work in environments where they witness their coworkers being bullied, those witnesses personally experience higher levels of aggression than do employees in workplaces where no bullying occurs.

H6 hypothesized that "Witnesses to bullying will report work quality outcomes that are better than target outcomes but worse than non-exposed worker outcomes." We compared the three groups in terms of their job satisfaction, job stress, and overall job rating. Results indicated significant differences for all three work quality outcomes among all three groups (see Table 2.5). Job satisfaction was highest for non-exposed workers (average = 4.0), followed by witnesses (average = 3.1), and then targets (average = 2.9).

Similarly, non-exposed workers rated their overall work experiences highest (average = 4.1), followed by those who saw others being bullied (average = 3.5), and then targets (average = 2.9). The same pattern was evident in reported stress levels; targets reported the highest stress levels (average = 4.1), followed by witnesses (average = 3.6), and then non-exposed workers (average = 3.2). Thus, H6 was supported.

Table 2.5: Averages – Bullying Degree & Work Quality Outcomes for Three Groups

Worker Group	Bullying Degree	Stress	Satisfaction	Ranking
Targets (38)	19.6 d	4.1 a	2.9 b	2.9 c
Witnesses (44)	12.1 d	3.6 a	3.1 b	3.5 c
Non-exposed (321)	7.6 d	3.2 a	4.0 b	4.1 c

Bulling degree scores ranged from 0 to 41. Averages of satisfaction, ranking, and stress range from 1 to 5 (higher scores = more, greater amounts).
Averages with same subscript (a,b,c. . .) differed significantly.

Discussion

The central contributions of this study include (a) assessing the prevalence of bullying in a US sample, (b) exploring US workers' perceptions of being bullied, (c) introducing the bullying degree construct, and (d) examining the impact of witnessing others being bullied. According to the analyses, one quarter of US workers experience bullying at any given 6-month period, but only 1/3 of them self-identified as targets. This difference suggests that US workers experience high levels of aggression, but they do not always equate that negativity with bullying. The reason could be that respondents have come to accept bullying as a normal part of their jobs.

Maybe the "bullying" terminology has not made its way into popular American language. Alternatively, US workers may associate the term with weakness so avoid self-labeling. The competitiveness of the US dominant culture may contribute to perceptions that being bullied reflects weakness. Alternately, US workers may successfully defend against aggression so do not feel like their experiences match the definition of bullying as a "situation where the targets have difficulty defending themselves."

Comparing bullying prevalence across samples is complicated, because bullying has been measured so many ways and over different lengths of time. Despite these differences, findings suggest that preva-

31

lence of bullying and aggression in the US studies and UK bullying study are similar. Given that the UK and US share many cultural similarities, this perhaps should not be surprising.

This similarity was not present between the current study and Scandinavian research, however. Comparisons suggest that bullying is significantly higher in the US than in Scandinavia. Approximately 35–50% of US workers experience one negative act at least weekly in any 6–12 month period, and nearly 30% experience at least two types of negativity that frequently. These numbers suggest that bullying for US workers is 20–50% higher than for Scandinavian workers. US workers believe their workplaces are more hostile than Scandinavian employees. Such beliefs could indicate that US workplaces actually are more aggressive, that US workers are more likely to perceive actions as aggressive, or both.

As we anticipated, there appears to be a cluster of negative acts associated with *feeling bullied*. Unlike work-overload and impossible deadlines (common pressures in many jobs), the aggressive acts that differentiate between self-identified targets and non-targets are serious threats to identity (humiliation and ridicule), economic stability (information withheld and hints to quit), and physical safety (threatening behavior, faced with hostility). These are more outrageous and disrupting, seriously transgress professional norms, and threaten essential life domains (professional-personal identity, ability to provide for oneself, security of physical safety). Thus, these acts are more likely to incite fear, dread, and flight-fight-freeze responses [95].

Findings also underscore that witnessing bystanders experience elevated negativity and stress and decreased satisfaction and overall rating of their jobs. This insight is consistent with what we know about the effect of seeing others being abused [11, 104]. The negative effect on witnesses reminds us to look beyond the bully-target dynamic to the broader negative effects of bullying on workgroups and organizations. Bullying is not simply a personality conflict; it is an organizational dynamic that affects all who are exposed.

Finally, exploring the features of bullying (intensity, frequency, duration) supports the notion of bullying degrees. Bullying is a complex phenomenon most effectively thought of as a continuum. Extending Davenport et al.'s metaphor of being burned by degree, our findings provide evidence that as bullying degree increases, so does the associated harm. Low levels of abuse are similar to first-degree burns (e.g. sunburn). Like sunburn, low levels of bullying can cause damage over time, but are common, potentially superficial, and usually quick to heal. More intensive, frequent, and persistent bullying is similar to second-degree burns, because this level is more painful and often requires professional treatment and intervention. Last, extremely escalated bullying is like getting third-degree burns. Such serious burns often result in deep scarring and permanent damage. Likewise, high degree bullying may result in permanent psychological damage, post-traumatic stress disorder, and even suicide [4, 35]. Bullying degree affects workers in fundamental ways; being bullied is not a unitary experience but one that occurs on an escalating continuum. In the last section, I recount the central findings in this study.

Findings Summarized

* Nearly 30% of US workers are bullied sometime during their work histories.

* In any given 6 month period, 1 in 10 (10%) US employees *feel bullied* at work.

* In any given 6 month period, 1 in 4 (25%) US workers experience aggression at work that is persistent and harmful, whether or not these workers *identify as targets*.

* In addition to the 25% of US employees who are directly bullied, another 11% witness their coworkers being bullied.

* In any given 6 month period in the US, workplace bullying harms nearly 40% of US working adults.

* Bullying is far more common in the US than in Scandinavia; rates in the US and UK are similar.

* Witnessing bystanders, even though they do not feel directly bullied, experience more aggression personally targeted at them than do employees working in settings without bullying present.

* As bullying increases, job satisfaction and overall job rating decrease and job-related stress increases—for targets and for witnessing bystanders.

CHAPTER 3

Serial Bullying: How Employee Abuse Starts, Ends, and Restarts with New Targets[B]

Pamela Lutgen-Sandvik

Chapter Summary: This chapter describes a 6-stage cycle explaining serial bullying by supervisors. The cycle illustrates how abuse begins when a target comes to the negative attention of the aggressor, escalates, drives the target from the workgroup, and then starts up again when a new target emerges. Stage 1: Initial Incident—Cycle Generation. In this stage a target come to the negative attention of the manager. Stage 2: Progressive Discipline. Stage 2 is when the aggressor uses organizational policies and procedures to create a "paper trail" that supports firing or otherwise punishing the target. Stage 3: Turning Point. In this stage, the abuse becomes increasingly negative, personal, and overbearing. Escalated repetition, reframing, branding, and support seeking mark hostile communication. Stage 4: Organizational Ambivalence. In this stage, other managers including upper-management join with the abuser to redefine the abusive situation in ways that diminish or disregard targets' experiences. Stage 5: Isolation-Silencing. During the final stages, fear and intimidation effectively silence both targets and witnessing bystanders. The abuser continues to manipulate the target's reputation through rumor, slander, and ridicule. Stage 6: Target Expulsion-Cycle Regeneration is when bullying drives out the target. After the target is driven out, workgroups can experience a short lull in aggression, only to find that someone new comes to the bully's negative attention and the cycle regenerates.

Keywords: serial bullying, employee emotional abuse; mobbing; verbal abuse; job harassment; injustice; aggression

Nearly half of all US working adults experience or witness workplace bullying—persistent, harmful psychological and emotional abuse—from their bosses at some time during their careers [111]. *The supervisors who inflict psychological abuse on subordinates represent one of the most frequent and serious problems confronting employees in today's workforce* [112]. The media are quick to report the rare but sensational incidents of "going postal." Rarely does the media report the far more common episodes of employee humiliation and psychological terror perpetrated by direct supervisors.

Humiliation and psychologically beating someone down can set the stage for the shocking acts of workplace murder and violence. These lower-level kinds of abuse and harassment can push some people to the point of hopelessness, driving an obsession to even the score [113]. Bullies grow increasingly aggressive and violent [4], and abused employees may express their anger and outrage in subtle and not-so-subtle retaliating acts against their employers. Retaliation includes work slowdown, sabotaging the abuser, destroying expensive equipment, and so forth [114]. "The cost to employers is untold hours and dollars in lost employee work time, increased health care costs, high turnover rates, and low productivity" p.2 [115].

Serial bullying is a repetitive, targeted, destructive form of bullying directed by direct managers toward their employees. This is a bit different from general bullying, which is hostility toward many employees at the same time. Serial bullying, also called merry-go-round bullying [116], is when a bully picks one person at a time to terrorize and moves on to another person, usually after the initial target is driven from the workgroup.

Sadly, "intimidating, mean-spirited, manipulative, and sometimes high-decibel behaviors are not unusual workplace occurrences, especially from supervisors and managers" [112](p. 477). In the US and UK, direct supervisors are most often the perpetrators of bullying [6]. Some estimate that one in four managers abuse their employees [115]. In some industries, bullying and verbal abuse are simply a way of life: more than 97% of nurse managers report experiencing abuse [84], 60% of retail industry workers [117], 23% of faculty and university staff [118], and 53% of business school students [42] report abuse at work. Evidence of employee abuse was found in a wide variety of organizations, including hospitals, universities, manufacturing plants, research industries, and social service agencies [41, 54, 74, 82].

Serial bullying, like all forms of bullying, is costly—it ...

* Refocuses employee energy from productivity to self-protection [119, 120]

* Results in staff turnover and burnout [121, 122]

* Intensifies the use of sick leave [123]

* Increases medical and workers' compensation claims due to occupational stress [124]

* Results in hiring costly consultants (author's experience)

* Leads to out of court settlements, legal fees and litigation [125]

Serial bullying also breaks down coworker communication and teamwork and leads to organizations losing credibility and positive reputations [99, 126]. Considering the high incidence of serial bullying, the costs to employees and organizations, and the potential for abuse to become aggression or violence, it is a crucial area for research and theoretical development.

Past research has examined the forms, characteristics, effects, and extent of bullying in an assortment of organizations. Investigations explore areas such as organizational position of abusers, incidence of abuse in specific populations, organizational response to abuse, and effects of abuse on targets and organizations [50, 51, 127]. What is lacking is a framework for serial bullying, one representing an entire process rather than a collection of parts. Providing such a framework is the primary objective of this chapter. The cycle I describe offers a way to look at serial bullying as a progression that develops, intensifies, and regenerates through identifiable phases of abuse. The model comes from current research and my experience as an organizational administrator.

Research indicates that workers are at times abusive to their peers and subordinates sometimes bully-up, but supervisors perpetrate the overwhelming majority of abuse in US workplaces (from 60% to 90%) [6, 128]. The model explains top-down serial abuse of subordinate employees. I organize the chapter in the following manner. First, serial bullying is conceptualized and discussed in relation to muted group theory. Second, I explain Leymann's linear depiction of mobbing, which he described as repetitive, psychological workplace abuse. Third, I present a developmental, cyclical model of serial bullying and its progression and regeneration.

Conceptualizing Serial Bullying

Serial bullying is managers' or supervisors' targeted abuse of subordinate staff. This form of abuse focuses on one employee at a time and then moves to another employee when the first is driven from the workgroup or otherwise removed from the aggressors' reach. In such cases, abuse is repetitive, unwelcome and unsolicited, violates standards of appropriate conduct, and results in harm [68].

Sometimes the targeted employees are unsure what to call the hostile treatment and how to explain what's happening to others. Muted group theory (MGT) helps to understand the difficulties targets and witnesses have when trying to talk about serial bullying. This perspective describes the communication barriers traditionally marginalized groups such as women [129] and African American men can feel when trying to relate their experiences to others [130]. I believe many of these barriers also exist for subordinate staff. According to this theory (rephrased for the workplace):

> The language of a [workplace] does not serve all [members] equally, for not all [members] contribute in an equal fashion to its formulation. [Non-supervisory employees and others without organizational position] are not as free or as able as [supervisors and upper-managers] are to say what they wish, when and where they wish because the words and the norms for their use have been formulated by the dominant group [managers or owners]. (p. 1)[129]

MTG initially explained the difficulties women have speaking in a man's world. However, the theory makes three basic assumptions that are applicable to superior-subordinate communication in workgroups. First, due to the experiences particular to managers and employees "that are rooted in the division of labor" [147] (p. 3), subordinate employees experience the work world in very different ways than their managers.

Second, because of their role as a dominant group, the commonly held managerial world view stifles and minimizes employees' alternative representations of work. Typically, the manager's word is taken as true and subordinate's word is taken as subjective and questionable. Third, in order to participate in organizations, employees must reframe their own experiences into the accepted managerial way of talking about work, framing that usually fails to include ideas adequately describing subordinate employee experiences.

This perspective does not mean the muted group is silent. For employees, the issue is whether workers can freely say what they want at any time or place, or whether they must translate their thoughts to make them more acceptable in the domain of work [131]. People organize and structure their experiences, interactions, and social realities through language [132]. In the workplace, those with access to structural (hierarchical) power often dominate organizational language and what language means. The dominant language in workplaces, for example, often reflects productivity and other organizational goals and may gloss over or ignore entirely other issues affecting subordinate employees.

MGT is particularly helpful for understanding the power differences inherent to interactions between superiors and subordinates. For example, human resource managers, guided by organizational management directives, create and enforce the language of personnel policies and employee handbooks. Such documents guide and are the basis for evaluating subordinate behavior. When subordinates fail to perform within these guidelines, the superior's version of reality is primarily spoken or formally documented while the subordinate's is secondarily considered, if at all. As such, the subordinate's experience remains muted and sometimes silenced all together. In fact, when subordinate employees argue or fight back about their evaluations, persons in power label them trouble-makers or problem-employees. Subordinate employees who argue back are "damned if they do and damned if they don't," so to speak. In this and a number of other ways, management's language becomes the final word—the "truth"—as it were.

I believe the workplace mutes all employees to some degree. They enter the organization in a relatively muted state and wait for directions (indirect or direct) from more powerful or experienced members about appropriate actions, communication, and behaviors. New employees learn these through formal orientation and hundreds of informal interactions or observations. Muting subordinate employees occurs in most supervisor-subordinate communication and may be used as a means of control, even if supervisors are unaware that they are doing so. The most egregious kind of silencing is when employees experience targeted abuse. Drawing on the ideas from MGT, the following model describes how serial bullying begins, escalates, and regenerates once the initial target leaves the organization.

Developmental Model of Serial Bullying

I began developing this model after looking at Leymann's [4, 69] research about mobbing. He defined mobbing as:

> hostile and unethical communication [that] is directed in a systematic way by one or a number of persons mainly toward one individual. ...These actions take place often (almost every day) and over a long period (at least for six months) and, because of this frequency and duration, result in considerable psychic, psychosomatic and social misery. (p.120) [4]

Leymann developed a linear model of workplace mobbing that includes four phases. In Phase 1, the original or critical incident, some triggering event brings the target to the negative attention of powerful organizational members. Phase 2, mobbing and stigmatizing, is characterized by consistent, repetitive manipulation of the target by attacks on reputation, social isolation, criticism, and threats. In Phase 3, personnel administration, targets go to upper-management with their concerns, and upper-management further victimizes the targets (e.g., branding the target as a troublemaker). Phase 4, expulsion, is self-explanatory: The abuser fires or transfers the target or the target quits.

My reconceptualization of serial bullying comes from published research on bullying [111, 119, 120, 133-136] and my experience as an organizational administrator. My experience includes eight years as the executive director of two organizations in which I dealt with a number of relevant cases. Over that period, I intervened informally in over 30 supervisor-subordinate disputes and formally interceded in six major occurrences of what I now know was serial bullying (I did not use the term at the time).

I handled the situations using a variety of problem-solving methods that included bringing in outside consultants or personally mediating the employee's complaint of mistreatment. I began to recognize a cyclical pattern in supervisors' mistreatment of subordinates. As soon as I thought a situation resolved with one target, the abusing supervisor singled out a new target.

By coupling published research with an analysis of my past work experience, I extended Leymann's model and created a six stages of serial bullying:

* Initial incident—cycle generation

* Progressive discipline

* Turning point

* Organizational ambivalence

* Isolation and silencing

* Expulsion—cycle regeneration

The following describes each stage, illustrates the stage dynamics with targets' experiences, and clarifies the conditions that move the process to the next stage. Each stage is a level or degree of serial bullying, as aggression and the effects of aggression intensify over time. The stages are meant to be descriptive rather than a hard-and-fast rule of exactly what happens in all cases. Certainly cases can vary depending on the situation. I present the stages as an illustration of the progressive and escalating nature of serial bullying. Additionally, some targets may experience serial bullying for years in their jobs [4], but other targets exiting the organizations before reaching later stage abuse is not uncommon [137].

* Stage 1: Initial Incident—Cycle Generation

Superiors and subordinates generate models of the work world, but when there is a discrepancy between the two the issue is most likely resolved in favor of the superiors' view [132]. We can see this dynamic in the initial incident, an event that triggers or starts the cycle of abuse into motion.

Triggering events can be starting a new job or getting a new boss [42], conflict over work goals or processes [4], clash of beliefs and values, increased pressure on managers [111], or changes in parties' personal lives [119]. Triggering events I saw in my work included an employee arguing or disagreeing with his or her supervisor, failing to carry out an assignment within a required time frame, calling in sick on a crucial day to a supervisor's timetable, or getting caught talking

40

negatively about the supervisor behind the supervisor's back. Triggering events in published research included many of these and two others: a formerly dedicated employee announced her pregnancy; another employee refused to give in to a boss's authoritarian procedures [119]. Ultimately, the subordinate behaves or performs in a manner interpreted as unacceptable in the dominant view of management.

Target experience. The most common occurrence coinciding with the onset of abuse is getting a new boss or starting a new job: "A surprising number (19%) are bullied almost immediately on starting their new posts. The recent job change and a change in manager account for 82% of the offered events relating to bullying onset" [42] (p. 203). The following illustrates the changes for one employee, after his transfer to a new job and a new boss. Ron was a 20-year employee at the time of the initial incident:

> Ron's [new] supervisor, Raymond, was fifteen years younger than the staff he managed ... [and] was on the fast track .... Ron found Raymond to be overly controlling and belittling from the beginning. The supervisor was minutely critical, insisting that work be done over to correct minor errors that would have been acceptable to past supervisors .... Ron could never do the job well enough to suit Raymond. [120] (p. 140)

In this situation, Ron had few performance problems before the initial incident—the arrival of his new manager. After the assignment of his new supervisor, Ron was unable to perform in a manner that avoided criticism.

Increased pressure on supervisors to perform can also trigger the abuse of subordinates so act as an initial incident. The supervisor subsequently translates the pressure to employees by bullying them. For example, downsizing, and the resulting stresses can mark the point where a previously fair supervisor becomes abusive. The following illustrates an employee's efforts to speak with his supervisor about the abuse:

> I described how desperate the situation was, how he had changed since the downsizing and reorganization. He never denied any of it. You know what he said? "Fuck you! I got pressures on me that you wouldn't believe. I'm dying and you're crying. You count who's being kicked out into the street from this place: guys like me. And I've got to cover what I was doing and

41

whatever gets dropped when they disappear. I've got no time for your bullshit. My ass in on the line and fuck you if you think I'm going to worry about your ass." [111] (pp. 25-26)

External pressures on organizations often increase internal pressures and contribute to serial bullying. In my experience, increases in regulatory demands, state or federal funding requirements, and accreditation provisions closely occurred with increases in subordinate targeting. For overworked staff members in service agencies, the added pressure of external auditors (e.g., accreditation bodies, funding sources, third-party insurance carriers, Medicaid representatives) and corresponding increases in reporting requirements triggered frustration and efforts to "pin the blame" on specific employees.

Progression. The initial incident shifts to bullying when the aggressive communication continues, the substance of the incident is unaddressed directly, the issues are not dealt with constructively [120] as is evident in the downsizing experience outlined above. As a result, the emotions related to the conflict linger and escalate. Typically, this phase is short and the next phase develops as soon as the target begins feeling uncomfortable and stigmatized [4]. Serial bullying moves from the initial incident Stage 1) to Stage 2 when the supervisor repeatedly uses organizationally sanctioned disciplinary procedures that are intended to improve performance but are used to camouflage the abuse.

✴ Stage 2: Progressive Discipline

Nowhere is the control of language more apparent than in documenting "unsatisfactory" subordinate performance. Leymann's model of mobbing does not address the dynamics of progressive discipline and due process, but I believe this is a key stage in the communicative process of serial bullying. In the progressive discipline process, the real power of management to create and control the language defining "reality" shows up as the subordinates' experiences are muted and distorted.

In the US, wrongful termination and other employee lawsuits have pushed organizations to follow and document the steps of apparent due process to protect against legal claims. Due process is supposed to provide employees with fair warning and an opportunity to improve performance [125, 138]. Managers and HR professionals are "always very concerned about having justified their actions in terminating an employee" [139] (p. 43). Many are fearful that if a subordinate is fired without such justification, the likelihood of legal action against the organization increases [140]. Because of this concern, "some try to force employees out by adopting psychological torture techniques, such as loss of perks or public humiliation" [141] (p. 52).

Aggressive managers appear to be particularly skilled at *appearing* to provide constructive feedback because the organization formally requires it. The extremes to which managers will go to build a verbal and written case against the target suggest that this is done to "make...action *appear* justifiable and reasonable to all parties" [140] (p. 569). Managers targeting particular employees are inclined to distort due process if they want to get rid of an employee (author's experience).

Because the manager creates the documenting language, they author the formal record of "what occurred." Rather than improve performance, this pattern of persistent criticism more often unnerves targets [126]and results in further poor performance. Sadly, the poor performance further supports the abuser's initial claims of target incompetence [120].

Target experience. Abuse reframed as progressive discipline often begins in a benign manner with casual or offhand comments about work performance. Messages can be framed as continued complaints about work without stipulating the desired changes [142]. Criticism is initially oral and subsequently written and becomes a permanent part of the employee's personnel record [140]. The following from an HR professional's observation is an example of criticism that wears down employees and moves toward their departure:

> He would tell them that their work was of deteriorating quality and needed doing again. Attacking their work went on for some time, during which the individuals would begin to work longer and longer hours, often into the night, in order to produce work that met his approval, though it rarely did...[I]t would be on personal files that they would be supported and encouraged to "get better." [126] (p. 196)

This HR professional goes on to say that the targets of this abuser invariably left their jobs.

When supervisors want to get rid of employees, documentation can be conjured up where it had not previously existed. During my time as an agency director, I intervened with four supervisors who wanted to recreate and document past interactions with an employee (in two cases, managers wanted to go back over the period of more than a year) in order to build a case for employment termination. Supervisors can also secretly document employee shortcomings. The following illustrates such written documentation:

> She [my boss] listened as I explained [why I was] ... upset.... She assured me that I would get it all back together in due time, and that was the end of our chat....Three months later ... I was reassigned to another supervisor. My new supervisor asked me if I was familiar with all the write-ups in my performance binder ... I was shocked to find a write up of my frustrated chat months earlier that stated that I was "angry" and demonstrated a "poor attitude." [111] (pp. 57-58)

Written disciplinary action that managers never discuss with their employees cannot improve work performance. More than likely, such tactics provide justification for future disciplinary actions, should they be needed, and create a "paper trail" used to corroborate punishment or future firing or transfer of the targets. The subordinate's voice is not only muted in this kind of back-door interaction but, in most instances, completely missing in the formal record.

Progression. Continued surveillance via numerous oral threats and written warnings put employees on a state of constant alert or hypervigilance (see Glossary) [68]. The repetitive nature of critical communication emerges in the beginning of stage two, but it escalates into Stage 3 when targets begin to feel fearful, intimidated, degraded, and manipulated [119, 133]. The repeated criticism and misused progressive discipline process pushes the cycle of abuse to a *turning point*.

✳ Stage 3: Turning Point

During Stage 3, the abuser's communication becomes increasingly aggressive, personal, and overbearing. The abusing manager controls the substance and form of communication with the targeted subordinate employee. The central features of communication in Stage 3 are escalated repetition, reframing, branding, and support seeking. Repetitive criticism changes the focus of disciplinary communication from performance improvement to targeting employees for removal [126]. As any small error becomes the subject of further correction, criticism

44

or negative attention, the target becomes even more alarmed [143] and hypervigilant [120].

When targets attempt to give voice to their experiences, abusers often reframe the former exchanges and describe the situation very differently than targets' experiences. Reframing challenges the target's view of reality and reinforces the dominant language of management. Abusers also couple reframing with branding—blaming the target for the target's abuse. Branding shifts the blame for abuse by labeling the target as troublemaker, mentally ill, or a problem-employee [133].

To defend against the over-whelming negative messages from more powerful organizational members, targets seek the support of people they trust. Peer support seeking is not exclusive to this stage, but as supervisory attacks amplify, targets increasingly share their feelings with others to gain emotional support and emotional release [144], make sense of their experiences [145], or diffuse some of the emotional intensity of the situation [146].

Target experience. The following illustrates a target's experience of chronic criticism and how she became aware that things at work had taken a negative turn:

> You become aware that something is wrong. You don't seem to be able to do anything right. Though you continue to do the same good job as before, your good ideas are not recognized. Soon, you are questioning whether or not you have the capability to do your work at all. The more you try and improve, the more your boss ... gets angry at you. [147] (p. 127)

Other examples of repetition include frequently calling targets at home to discuss work-related issues that do not need immediate attention [62], regularly expressing the abusers' dissatisfaction with targets to the targets' peers [99], habitually berating targets or the targets' ideas in group or staff meetings [68], and persistently scrutinizing targets' work to find small errors [120].

Reframing the situation in the language of the abuser is also a characteristic of Stage 3 serial bullying. In two different cases during employee-supervisor interventions, I witnessed supervisors' outright denial of the targets' viewpoint (e.g., "That's not what happened at all!"). Research parallels my experience and indicates that abusers minimize the target's concerns [62], implicitly question the target's ability to see reality [68], and reassert the abuser's organizational pow-

45

er [82]. One woman's experience illustrates reframing:

> He [boss] dismissed [the employee's] concerns regarding his bul-
> lying behavior by denying having yelled at her in front of other
> staff "to get the fucking photocopier fixed or get it removed!"
> and telling her, "if *I* say I wasn't talking to you, I wasn't talking to
> you!" [62] (p. 110)

Reframing undermines the target's ability to make sense of what's
happening. Targets can start to question their own view of reality,
which essentially distorts and mutes their experiences. Sadly, the language managers use to describe the target's behavior does not include
or recognize language the target uses to describe that same behavior.
As one target explains, "I tried to [explain to my supervisor] but she
just told me that I was ... not seeing it in the way I should be seeing it,
and in her opinion, I was wrong and she was right" [68] (p. 244).

This woman's experience shows how a manager can not only
disregard but also totally discount a target's explanation. When the
target's view of what happened and the manager's view of what happened chronically diverge, it can be disturbing because we "typically
think an event is real if two or more people see it happen and agree
that they saw it happen" [148] (p. 5).

Typically, abusers also negatively brand the target in some way.
In the following example, the CEO of a nonprofit describes his
branding experience from the vice president on the board that directly supervised him. "The rumor had been spread that I had had several small strokes and was in the beginnings of Alzheimer's disease and
was no longer competent and able to lead the organization" [99] (p.
42). The audience of the board member's message included other
board members and key staff members. Potentially, the vice president
uses this tactic to gain support for the CEO's eventual removal.

In addition to building support for eventual firing, branding destabilizes and discourages the targets because people usually come to
see themselves as others reportedly see do. One of my experiences
with an abusive supervisor in a clinical (therapeutic) setting was similar
to this example. When a female employee claimed mistreatment
from a specific clinical director, the director reframed the issue by
branding her as emotionally unstable. (e.g., "She has unresolved issues with her mother and is projecting that on me.")

The combination of repetition, reframing, and branding plagues
targets and, as a result, they tend to seek support from their workplace
peers and family members [62, 120]. As a female target explained,

"You're only supported by other people who are sympathetic to your situation because they've been there themselves" [68] (p. 241). I have heard many, many targets echo this sentiment in the years I have studied workplace bullying.

Targets also deal with and determine the meaning of their experiences in interactions with people in personal social networks (e.g., family members and friends). "Most people make sense of dialogues in light of and in contrast to dialogues from other parts of their lives" [149] (p. 120). Allan, a male target, explained how he left the abusive workplace with his wife's help. "I could not have done this without my wife. She was very helpful and supportive, and she had some good ideas. I was very fortunate that she was in my life--and that she still is" [99] (p. 125).

Progression. When social support is not enough, some targets feel compelled to report the abuse to upper-management despite the dangers of speaking out [68]. When they can no longer tolerate the abuse and have some idea that upper-management might help, deciding to report to an authority in the organization shifts the cycle of abuse Stage 4.

✳ Stage 4: Organizational Ambivalence

The point at which upper-managers above the abuser in the organizational structure—becomes involved marks a new stage in the cycle. Bringing in upper-management ups the ante, so to speak, and increases the potential losses or gains for all involved [99, 150]. In Stage 4 managers and upper-management often join sides with the abusers and do so in ways that minimize or disregard target complaints. Most targets blame the organization as much as they do the abuser for continued bullying [151]. When upper-managers respond by preventing further abuse, targets feel supported and valued. They may even return to a more optimistic state.

Formal complaints mark a crucial point in the escalation or de-escalation of abuse because upper-management can interrupt the cycle if they give credence to target grievances. Certainly, not all targets experience this stage since not all targets take their complaints to upper-management. Most research indicates that only a small percentage inform upper-management [62, 126, 133], believing either nothing will be done [84], or they will suffer retaliation [62].

Typically, upper-managers are quite hesitant to intervene be-

47

tween supervisors and subordinate staff [68, 143]. Circumventing a bullying boss by speaking directly to the boss's boss breaks the convention of following the "chain of command." Upper-managers worry if they intervene, it might set a precedent, and then all disgruntled employees will complain directly to upper-management and bypass their direct supervisors. Additionally, complaints about an abuser can imply criticism of upper-managers who hired the abuser [133].

Target experience. If upper-management successfully intervenes, however, the cycle may subside. However, most often upper-managers take no action or action that fails to stop the abuse [42, 62, 99]. In an especially cruel twist, they often suggest changes in the target rather than in the abuser [73]. Responses include (1) taking no action; (2) admitting there was a problem with the manager but doing nothing about it; (3) promising action but with no discernable outcome; (4) attributing the problem to a personality conflict; (5) asking the target to work around the problem; (6) directing some change in the target's behavior; (7) minimizing the target's complaint, while building up the abuser's abilities and value to the organization; (8) branding the target as a trouble maker or insubordinate; (9) retaliating against the target; and in some cases, (10) formally disciplining or removing the abuser.

The following target voices a common feeling for those who complain:

> No one would do anything about him. He's been promoted more than once since this, despite the fact that he has an entirely negative reputation with anyone who is his direct report .... But he is carried along by this Mafia of bosses who just defend him .... So all the feedback and complaints from workers are dismissed by these people. [111](p. 112)

A female target explains upper-management's efforts to make targets rather than aggressors change their behavior:

> Constant appeals were made to my boss's superiors for help .... Finally, were all called to a meeting ... when our boss was away ... But were shocked, [the consultant the organization hired] was going to help us think through ways of dealing with difficult boss. [111](p. 117)

Progression. If upper-management does nothing or their actions fail

48

to end abuse, the cycle progresses to Stage 5. Targets feel as if the organization does not want to hear about the problem. Thus, targets and witnesses decide to either stop speaking if previously vocal, or remain silent if yet to voice concern [120, 152].

When the power structure has reframed the situation and branded the target as insubordinate, a troublemaker, a problem-employee, or mentally ill, coworkers may also come to believe that the target's deviant personality is the root of the problem [4, 99]. As the ongoing emotional dialogue wears out those close to the target, a decrease in social and family support may also accompany the loss of workplace alliances. A culmination of support loss, isolation, and silencing moves the cycle to Stage 5.

✳ Stage 5: Isolation and Silencing

During the final stages of serial bullying, fear and intimidation effectively silence both targets and an audience of bystanders. My experience suggests that abusive managers continue to manipulate the target's reputation through rumor, slander, ridicule [99] to maintain upper-management support. At Stage 5, serial bullying can become highly volatile, and the abuser's efforts to drive the targets out can escalate into overt aggression and even threats of violence [69, 137].

As abuse escalates, so does fear. Public forums for resistance and sense-making shrink or disappear entirely [36, 120]. Fear of becoming a victim silences witnessing coworkers who try and ignore the problem [133]. In a study of hotel chefs and support staff, "what was striking was that as the bullying took place, the rest of the kitchen staff carried on as if nothing was happening" [36] (p. 222). Alternately, if audience members do speak up, the cycle can be interrupted [112]. When employees collectively, purposefully, and vocally reject abusive managers' and upper-managers' framing of the situation, employees can change the status quo [129].

Speaking out can be terrifying, however, so coworkers rarely do so. The silent audience furthers silence and segregate targets from support [99]. Colleagues may withdraw their support out of fear of jeopardizing their employment [9], a fear that may be reinforced by the abuser [99]. Additionally, giving social support takes effort. Coworkers can become emotionally exhausted so withdraw support from colleagues they see as too demanding or too needy [144].

Target experience. In Stage 5, employees learn it is not safe to

49

express their views. Upper-management's response and peer support withdrawal reconfirm this conclusion. To feel safer, other employees may side with the abuser or withdraw from workplace relationships and interactions. Increasingly, these social factors create a climate of fear, cynicism, and distrust. Here is a support services manager's observation of an abuser, responses to abuse, and the resulting workplace climate:

> [Employees said little about what was occurring but when they did, they did so with] the proviso that they would deny what they had said, if [the abuser] found out. Staff relations as a group had completely broken down. No one trusted anyone and communication generally was abrupt and confrontational--a culture of defensiveness. New staff came and went, each one attempting to challenge what was happening only to either be singled out for more humiliation and personal, professional insults, or to become one of the "in" gang ....The staff suffered in silence, feeling powerless to do anything about it. [126](p. 195)

In another study, a female target described her and others' decisions to stay silent: "He [the manager] would question everything and turn it around this way and that. It was like an interrogation of criminals, trying to get us to confess things. We'd get exhausted. We didn't even want to answer anymore" [62] (p. 110). In my experience, when targets have argued or tried to tell their side of the story, abusive managers cut them off, raised their voices to silence targets, and threatened employment termination. (When I pointed out their aggressive communication later, the aggressors typically looked puzzled, as if they had no idea that their behavior was aggressive or had any negative effect on the employees.)

Abusers may also challenge the rare coworker who continues to communicate with and support the target, implying that associating with the target might be detrimental to the supportive coworker. Here is an example of an abuser's response when a coworker sided with the target:

> I was asked by my boss [the abuser], "Why are you talking to her? You show compassion for her," is the message I got. He ridiculed her. They would all laugh, roll their eyes. Dehumanizing. Demoralizing. I was a basket case. She was a basket case. [99] (p. 133)

Coworkers and family members can also become emotionally exhausted and withdraw support, as illustrated by this example from a target's wife:

I emotionally supported him for many years, and then I couldn't do it any longer. I started to ignore him. I wanted to run away. When he was at home, he just sat on the sofa, writing down these incidents .... It made me crazy. He became invisible to me because I could not stand to look at him like this. Every day he went into a crazy workplace. And every day I wanted to run away. [99] (p. 124)

Whether from emotional exhaustion, self-interest, or fear, coworkers and family members commonly distance themselves from the target—both socially and literally. Targets report feeling "trapped and alone in their experiences with no help or understanding from inside or outside the system" [120] (p. 13).

Progression. When targets can no longer tolerate the situation—peer support has fallen away, voices of resistance are silenced, and upper-management fails to intervene—they leave the workgroup [62]. Co-workers may even urge targets to leave so that targets can be safer or because coworkers mistakenly believe abuse will end when the "problem-employee" leaves.

Exit can be involuntary (suspension, employment termination) or voluntary (quitting, transferring, taking extended sick leave). Of course, this sort of "voluntary" separation is not voluntary at all. Rather, it is a type of *constructive discharge* (see Glossary)—intolerable working conditions drive the target to quit [138]. When targets voluntarily or involuntarily exit the organization, the cycle moves to Stage 6.

✳ Stage 6: Expulsion and Cycle Regeneration

Stage 6 starts when targets exit. Leymann's model ends with expulsion, but there is good reason to believe target exit is not the end of aggression. Research, witness reports, and my experience coaching serial bullies suggest that aggression does not end with target exit [62, 99, 126]. One employee's exit may temporarily relieve the tension, but serial exits worsen silencing and increase already high levels of fear. The lull after a target's exit is short and the abuser slowly shifts his or her focus, aggression, and criticism on another target. When the bully focuses on a new "problem employee," the cycle regener-

51

ates.

The cycle regeneration suggests that the problem does not reside in targets. Rather, aggression is likely to be a directly or indirectly supported norm in the organizational culture. The norm reflects the organization's failure to listen to alternative voices and deal directly with aggressive communication. Individual aggressors perpetrate abuse and some can be innately verbally aggressive [66], but workplace aggression "will only occur if the offender believes he has the overt or more usually covert support from supervisors for his or her behavior. Tolerance for or lack of sanctions against bullying ... gives permission for the bullying to continue" [153] (p. 269). Without serious change, the cycle regenerates after a brief reprieve or calm period.

Target experience. At this point, targets are out of the workgroup where abuse occurred. Many, however, maintain contact with workplace friends so hear what happens after they left. One explains her colleagues' beliefs that once the targets were removed, the abusive treatment would cease:

> Eventually, I think most were sickened by [the abuser's] behavior. But initially they thought it was the CEO's style, and it would change after some of the victims were out of the organization .... After a calm period, though, he started in on others. [99](p. 61)

Similarly, a human resources staff member in a public organization described expulsion and the regeneration of serial bullying:

> If ... the individual did not somehow manage to recover his/her [formerly favored] position with [the abuser], then disciplinary action would always be started .... Invariably, the individual would go on long-term sick leave, be demoted, fired, or moved. The department would *watch and wait to see who would be next.* [126] (p. 196).

Thus, the regeneration of the cycle of serial bullying seems quite common, despite employees' hope that abuse will end with target exit. My experience coaching aggressive managers mirrors this—I nearly always saw a period of calm inevitably followed by a new target's emergence.

Discussion

The *generation and regeneration* of serial bullying draws on current research, my conversations with hundreds of targets and witnesses, and my work as an administrator coaching aggressive managers. From these sources, I have developed a model of serial bullying as a communicative process that evolves, escalates, and moves to new targets when the initial target is driven out. The model speaks to a growing concern about employee abuse at the hands of aggressive organizational members.

Practical Implications

The model suggests a number of practical applications. First, we must attend to the psychological climate of workplaces, especially those spawning persistent employee abuse. In part, change means opening up and listening to subordinate employees' silenced voices. I have made a number of suggestions about how to do this in the book's final chapter. What we know is that the abuse cycle typically repeats until one or more of the following occurs:

* The workplace is restructured [154],

* The abusing manager is removed or coached successfully to reduce verbal aggressiveness [99],

* A concerted audience gives voice to the abuse, usually by circumventing the bullies [152],

* Upper-management effectively intervenes

* Upper-management reevaluates its human resource management philosophy—both real and espoused [115]

Effectively interrupting the cycle requires more than just removing, coaching, or disciplining the abuser [111, 154]. Ending the cycle means encouraging rather than obstructing the expression of employees' alternative workplace experiences, despite the likelihood that those voices will differ from management's. Without honestly dealing with aggressors and the climate that spawns and supports aggression, organizations are doomed to repeat the cycle. With each cycle, the workforce will be further beaten down and become impoverished

53

(See Glossary) until organizational functioning falters or fails completely.

Organizations must examine workplace values and norms, coach or remove abusers, and develop new pro-social forms of communication [153]. "Simply firing managers without changing the corporate culture does little to prevent their successors from also being abusive" [115](p. 6). From upper-management to all levels of the organization, members must transform the environment from which such abusive behavior emerges.

The serial bullying model provides a powerful tool for managers. It illustrates the early warning signs of abuse (e.g., repetition, reframing, branding). Awareness of the signs can help managers detect and prevent the spread of employee abuse. The model also identifies the dangers of progressive discipline practices—legal requirements for due process can set the stage for workplace bullying. It illustrates how isolation and silencing occur in late-stage serial bullying.

The model underscores the critical role of open-minded upper-managers, especially those who will entertain circumvention should circumvention occur. Sending targets back to the bullies to problem-solve can be disastrous. As importantly, the model shows that serial bullying will not stop just because a particular employee exits. If the organization is dealing with high-aggressives or promotes aggression, serial bullying will regenerate in a new cycle with new targets.

The model also points to the importance of listening to and encouraging subordinate-employee voice. Managers and coworkers alike need to accept targets' experiences as valid representations of experienced reality. Coworkers' and targets' concerted voice has the power to alter workgroup climates in significant ways.

Theoretical Implications

Academics are far more concerned with theory than is the general public, but I do include some thoughts in terms of theory. The chapter extends muted group theory by applying it to the language of dominant and non-dominant workplace groups. The theory suggests that language is developed by and used in a manner that serves management but rarely expresses or gives credence to subordinate-employee experiences [129]. The theory suggests various ways that power can be enacted through language to create and maintain an environment that supports workplace abuse.

The model builds on the theory's basic assumptions in terms of superior-subordinate communication. Specifically, subordinates observe and experience the workplace differently from management because of subordinates' distinctive positions and tasks rooted in the division of labor and in the hierarchy (i.e., pyramid-shaped organizational chart). Management's view and expression of "reality" can and often does mute and obstruct the free expression of subordinates' alternative perceptions. Muting occurs because of management's organizational, political, and economic dominance and their power to secure or deny subordinates' livelihood. Employees will not speak up if they fear retaliation, punishment, or loss of employment security.

To participate safely in workplace conversations and teamwork, subordinate employees usually have to reframe their unique experiences into an accepted language. The accepted language typically is management's system of expression, even when employees' reframing fails to express accurately their experiences and perceptions. Only when organizational members at all levels can safely and openly question the dominant culture can the cycle of serial bullying be interrupted. This is no small feat.

Conclusion

Employee emotional abuse is not just something that happens in a few workplaces. It is quite widespread and likely mirrors the external environment's adversity and aggression. "Given the widespread exposure to trauma and adversity that exists in the general population, ... workplace environments should be inherently therapeutic—restoring health and promoting healing" [153] (p. 268). When work is a safe and nurturing place to be, employees can give their best efforts while growing ever healthier as they do so.

Creating humane workplaces and providing just, fair treatment of all of the people tasked with carrying out the organization's mission are likely to result in positive processes and outcomes. The call for humane workplaces may not compel all managers to action, but the negative effect of serial bullying on the economic "bottom line" at least should be persuasive. There will be no meaningful change in either the occurrence or consequence of abuse unless the structure of the workplace is reformed according to a new social and legal contract, one that encourages cooperation, justice, and a heightened and broadened sense of community.

CHAPTER 4

"Take This job and Shove It": How Targets and
Witnesses Fight Back When Faced with Bullying [c]

Pamela Lutgen-Sandvik

Chapter Summary: Adult bullying on the job is an unbelievable, shattering, shocking experience for targets and witnessing bystanders. This chapter reports the findings in a study that examines the experiences of 30 workers, some of whom were targeted and those who saw others bullied. Their stories tell a chilling tale of power in bullying situations that reframes the "power-deficient target" into agents who galvanize a variety of resources on their own or others' behalf but also place them at considerable risk of job-loss and retaliation. In some cases, employees evaluate the abusive situation and quickly resign. Others protest, but if resistance fails to stop abuse, they also leave organizations. In many cases, employee exit is a way to say in essence, "Take this job and shove it!" The chapter discusses the processes of resistance, outcomes of each case, and dialectic character of resistance and control.

Keywords: workplace bullying, verbal aggression, organizational communication, resistance, power

----

This chapter looks closely at how people fight back against bullying on the job. There is a considerable body of research on bullying [69, 101, 128, 155] but one of the weaknesses of this work is its one-dimensional depiction of power. Research usually frames organizational control (bullies' power/influence) as pervasive and somewhat

56

fixed—you have it or you don't. In fact, research labels abuse as *bullying* only in cases of targets' inability to defend themselves [49, 156]. As such, the push-and-pull features of power remain under-examined. Additionally, research has predominantly focused on the individual rather than group-level features of bullying. Despite the social nature of workplace communication, researchers have done little to explore the communicative nature of bullying in workgroups or the impact of bullying on observers [6, 11, 104]. Up until the mid-2000s, limited research had examined US workers' experiences. Most continues to come out of Scandinavia (e.g., Bergen Bullying Research Group http://www.uib.no/rg/bbrg), the UK [3] and the European continent [47].

Studies of resistance, on the other hand, rarely investigate struggles against hostile, abusive treatment at work [134, 157]. Rather, this research typically examines meanings, rules, or directives against which people resist identifying or complying [158-160]. Moreover, research gives only a cursory look at the contentious character of resistance and very real risks to resisters. Rather, studies of resistance often frame power and control as overwhelming and inescapable [161-163] or resistance as simply a choice without ramifications [164-166]. Moreover, this research rarely examines resistance as a process or its power over time to affect meaningful change (See for exceptions [167, 168]). To speak to these issues, the study reported in this chapter explores resistance to abuse from US workers' perspectives (witnesses and targets). It considers how control and resistance can intersect to "produce complex and often contradictory" meanings [169] (p. 21). Further, it examines the course of resistance and resistance leading to change.

Bullying, Power, and the Push-and-Pull (Dialectic) of Resistance and Control

Adult bullying at work can include public humiliation, constant criticism, ridicule, gossip, insults, and social ostracism—communication that makes work tasks difficult or impossible, and socially isolates, stigmatizes, and discredits targets [2, 101, 170]. Only the organizational potential for aggressor punishment limits this type of abuse [41, 64]. Important to this chapter is that bullying usually involves interactions where targeted workers feel unable to stop abuse or adequately defend themselves [2, 72].

In the previous chapter, I talked about Giddens' dialectic of power and control, a theme I underscore a number of places in this book. Power relations between bully-target are often unequally weighted, but no absolute power situations exist in modern workplaces [171-173]. "In all social systems there is a dialectic of control [with] ... continually shifting balances of resources, altering the overall distribution of power" [173] (p. 32). Human agency enables all organizational members to create or capitalize on "spaces of control" in day-to-day interactions [174] (p. 16). Even those who appear to be powerless retain the capacity to resist processes that can feel dominated by persons with considerable control or influence [173].

Increased aggression and controlling efforts incites and escalates target resistance because control and resistance are an ongoing tension at work [175]. Thus, targets' acts of defiance are not surprising. Given the tension between resistance and control, we should also expect countering forces. That is, aggressors often reframe resistance and the situations that trigger resistance as pathological and problematic (e.g., talking about resistance as mental illness; calling resisters *mentally ill*). As such, bullying-affected workers might push back by framing their resistance as a moral imperative, essential defensive responses, or efforts to be treated with basic human decency. Bullies and their supporters, on the other hand, push back to frame these same messages and actions as insubordination, disloyalty, and troublemaking. Abuse and resistance produce an ongoing struggle to stress different agendas and push them to the forefront.

Thus, the study reported on in this chapter investigates the following interrelated questions: What resistance do bullying-affected workers use to counter abusive treatment? What is the processual nature of resistance? How are case outcomes related to resistance? How does the dialectic tension between control and resistance produce contradictory meanings?

Method

Participants

One hundred fifteen persons volunteered for the study. These potential participants were drawn in two ways: (a) from conversations with personal and professional contacts and (b) from a link on the Workplace Bullying and Trauma Institute website (WBTI; www.bullying institute.org). Participation required that workers had witnessed bullying, whether or not they had personally experienced it, because I wanted to explore instances where bullying was common to a workgroup rather than an individual experience. This choice eliminated 31 volunteers. I also chose an equal sex distribution.

In total, I interviewed 37 people. Three were omitted, because their experiences did not match the key features of bullying (frequency, intensity, etc.). I conducted four other interviews after data analysis to be sure I hadn't missed any types of resistance [176]. Core data came from 30 participants: 10 witnesses (5 male, 5 female), 20 target-witnesses (10 male, 10 female). Target-witnesses were people who had been or were being bullied and also saw others being bullied. Witnesses saw others being bullied but were not directly bullied. Of the 30 participants, 21 were married, 3 were divorced, and 6 had never been married. Twenty-eight were heterosexual and two were gay/lesbian/bisexual. Mean age was 38.5 and ranged from 24 to 53. Twenty-eight were Caucasian and two were Hispanic. They worked in not-for-profit, for-profit, and government settings, and lived in 30 different US states.

I sought persons who had *witnessed* bullying, so all participants, whether targeted or not, had to have seen others being bullied. As such, bullying was a shared experience in the social life of the workgroup rather than a situation in which one person was individually targeted. Bullies usually target more than one person at a time [3, 7, 94], but choosing people for which bullying was a common experience drew specific types of employees. Persons who collectively experience bullying may have more opportunities to join in collective voice and resistance. Collective agreement potentially leads to discussions about abuse, gathering support, and fighting back. In workplaces where one person is bullied, the targets may feel less validation and more fear, resulting in less resistance.

Furthermore, over half of the sample was drawn through a bullying website created in the late 1990s by Gary and Ruth Namie, considered by many to be US pioneers in the field. A simple web search (Google, Bing, Yahoo) for "workplace bullying" pulls up their site in the first page of sources. Moreover, the Namies' work has also appeared in numerous trade magazines and newspaper articles [177-180]. Thus, workers may read articles leading them to the website or search the site directly. It is possible that those seeking help and finding the website are at the peak of the bullying episode and so are motivated to *do something*. As a result, the sample may represent more resistance than might be found in isolated cases of bullying. The current sample is, however, well poised to examine resistance when bullying is a communal experience.

Interview Protocol and Follow-up Contacts

I used semi-structured, in-depth, telephone interviews for data collection. For the most part, participants' experiences directed interviews, which began with a general question asking participants about their jobs. They proceeded with little other guidance. I asked for specific demographic information (age, marital status, ethnicity, etc.) if not mentioned spontaneously. On average, interviews lasted 2.25 hours and ranged from 65-180 minutes. Over an 8-month period during data analysis/writing, I maintained contact with those who were still at the jobs where bullying occurred (n = 18). Follow-up contacts were mostly through email, and I conducted four follow-up interviews that ranged from 30-45 minutes.

Data Analysis

All interviews, including follow-ups, were recorded and transcribed. I read through the transcripts numerous times to assure accuracy. I then categorized data using QDA (qualitative data analysis software program) based on answers to the question, "How do workers respond to bullying?" I marked (i.e., coded) all *employee responses* in interview transcripts. Employee responses were the verbal/nonverbal reactions to seeing or experiencing abuse. Once I excerpted responses to abuse from the interview transcripts, I read through the data, created names or codes for response types, and labeled responses with codes, a process called "open-coding." This resulted in 83 types of responses or open-codes. From the 83 open-codes, I removed responses that failed to meet the my definition of resistance: *Any behavior (direct or indirect) that tries to counter, disrupt, or defy the bully or erode the bully's influence* [168, 181].

For example, *praying for relief,* failed to meet the definition's criteria. This step resulted in 44 resistance types. I further examined codes for redundancies and combined responses initially coded separately. After removing redundancies and consolidating similar codes, I further collapsed data based on relationships among resistance types. (e.g., "Is X a kind of Y?" "Is X a way to do Y?" "Is X an expression of Y?") Through semantic analysis, resistance strategies clustered into five core types: (a) exodus, (b) collective voice, (c) reverse discourse, (d) subversive (dis)obedience, and (e) confrontation. I then conducted four interviews with others who'd resisted bullying to see if I had missed any examples (a process called "saturation") [176]. Saturation interviews revealed no new forms of resistance. Table 4.1 lists types and related tactics.

Table 4.1: Types of Resistance and Descriptions

Type/ *Sub-types*	Description
1. Exodus	
	Quitting, transferring, helping co-workers find work, intentions/threats to leave, talking to one another about quitting, encouraging each other to quit, championing stories of those who left
2. Collective Voice	
Mutual advocacy	Agreement bully is unfair, cruel, crazy, collective knowledge—bully known among many inside, outside workgroup; collegial reassurance about bullying, consolation, support, talking with co-workers about what to do, defending co-worker, subordinate, withholding actions that would hurt others, talking in peer networks regardless of bully's admonishment not to
Contagious voice	One person's voice encourages others to speak, target becomes advocate, people start going to advocate when experiencing abuse; co-workers groups plan or take action against bully
3. Reverse Discourse	
Embracing pejorative labels	Co-opting-adopting labels, epithets, reclaiming "troublemaker"; stories of revolutionaries, labor heroes; satisfaction, moral superiority at fighting "good," righteous battle
Influential allies	Developing powerful allies, accessing current powerful allies, finding managerial support, figuring out who to talk to in supervisory ranks, external professionals' advice to "fight" bullying, using expert power as an element of voice (research, newspaper, website)
Grievance	Informal, formal complaints (to upper managers, HR, union, board, etc.)
Documentation	Recordkeeping to support reports of abuse or protect against attack

Table 4.1: Continued

---

4. Subversive (Dis)Obediance

Labor withdrawal	Refusal to comply, doing just what's required; nothing good enough to deflect abuse, trying then giving up, withdrawing creativity, problem solving, anything "above and beyond"
Working-to-rule	Over-adhering to delegated tasks (working to rule), especially when mocking bully
Resistance through distance	Avoid or avoid talking to bully, especially withholding information bully may want
Retaliation	Retaliating or responding to "even score," hostile gossip, fantasy discussions of hurting, killing bully; intentions to hurt bully in retaliation

---

5. Confrontation

	Direct confrontation with bully, using humor to publicly (covertly) ridicule, parody bully

---

Considering Resistance:
Bullying and the Risks of Fighting Back

To contextualize participant actions and introduce resistance, the subsequent section provides a sample of bullying experiences and perceptions of the risks in fighting back.

> [*Mental health HMO*] She came in and told everybody she was the boss, and we would all now do things her way.... [or] be brought up on charges of insubordination...[She was] intimidating—right in your face—less than an inch away from your face, where her spit would hit you in the face. She would scream at us, her face getting all red and her eyes watering. It was almost like she wanted to reach out and choke you.

> [*Women's multi-service agency*] Staff came and went ... fast when they saw how crazy she was.... She screamed and ranted and raved at us in front of battered women and anyone else who was there in the waiting room.... She had big manila envelopes stuffed in the back of her filing cabinets, all taped up, filled with hundreds of notes on scraps of paper ...—we found them af-

ter she was fired—of secret files on people.... She slammed doors, threw papers ..., even furniture when she was pissed, and boy you better *never* argue with her!

[*Sports fishing industry*] The actual office environment was all glass, so he could see into all of the offices. Constant surveillance was deliberate and apparently part of his strategy of control. He could *see* through every office.... He'd scream and yell every day. Veins would pop out of his head; he'd spit, he'd point, he'd threaten daily, all day long to anyone in his way, every day that I was there. *Every single day.* Oh, yelling! ... [From my office,] I could see his eyes bulging, his veins and everything, spitting, and pointing his finger.... That was daily, with many people, all the time. He...would yell in the speakerphone at his general managers.... He'd swear profusely, "You fucking asshole, you don't know *anything.* You fucking idiot! You couldn't run a fucking peanut stand. Goddamn it! You were brought up with a silver spoon shoved up your ass."

[*Private security business*] He would call people to the fifth floor conference room.... where he "held court." Summoning people to the conference room occurred every single day...with just a string of people. The intercom would be going off all the time, "So-and-so to the fifth floor conference room. So-and-so to the fifth floor conference room." I'd see people *running,* literally *running,* down the halls... It's just *bizarre!* .... He'd *scream,* oh yeah, *screaming!* You'd never know why he called you [to the conference room], so you couldn't prepare yourself, so you'd stand there with no answers to his questions, and that made him even madder. So his face would get beet-red, and he'd *slam* his hands down, stand up, and start shaking his finger at you, and *screaming "Get out of here! Get out of my sight!"* Everyone waiting outside heard all of it, and you'd go out, and the next person went in for the kill.

[*Children's cancer hospital*] She screamed at everybody, but I saw her screaming at Grace, another one of the nurses, and couldn't believe it. Grace was ... vulnerable, because she had lost her son about two...weeks before. He died of cancer, and so we treated him here, and he died. She [bully] knew Grace's son had just died; she knew; she didn't care. She had her finger [pointed

63

in] Grace's face less than a quarter of an inch away from her nose. She was just totally bullying her into her face, and Grace just stood there and...turned bright red.... I couldn't believe anyone could treat another human being in that manner. I mean, her son had just died, for god's sake.

[*Adult Education and Training*] I watched her run over person after person ... Then she was after me for over two years, driving me crazy, constantly picking at [me]..., telling coworkers about my private medical problems and medication I was on, taking away my travel [credit] card, moving my office. She told a new supervisor that I was mentally ill and when that didn't work [to drive me out], she accused me of using work resources for personal use.... [The investigation] went on for two months,... and they found one 41-cent phone call where I called my daughter at college instead of using my cell phone.... Since I've filed the [EEOC] suit, she leaves me alone, but now she's starting in on Keri. She's doing the exact same thing to her that she did to me. She tells you one thing, and then she gives you a note, and she tells you to do something else or she sends you an email...It's just the gouging—the verbal one thing, the written another thing— it's a vicious circle.

These provide a sense of participants' perceptions of their day-to-day experiences. Given that they reported experiencing and witnessing this abuse on a nearly daily basis, it is not surprising that they also reported fighting back. In fact, only three people in the study reported doing nothing in response. Resistance was collective, where workers organized efforts to stop abuse, or disorganized coaction, where workers individually spoke out and later discovered that they were one of many who also complained. "Disorganized coaction ... [is,] fragmented, dispersed, and uncoordinated individuals doing somewhat similar things without explicit coordination" [182](p. 317).

Whether resistance was organized or disorganized, participants perceived it as high-risk. All but two of the alleged bullies were in higher positions (e.g., managers, owners, majority partners). As such, participants believed abusers had or had access to considerable organizational resources, not the least of which was the power to fire them. Resisting workers feared losing their jobs in economic environments with scarce alternatives. Job loss was a constant fear based on stories told and retold of others the bullies had fired or driven from jobs.

Participants reported that bullies also had direct access to upper-managers and thought bullies likely undermined their versions of the story by reframing what happened in ways that harmed targets and witnesses.

Participants believed their resistance triggered more abuse and retaliation. They explained that the more they spoke up, the more the bullies stigmatized them to regain lost ground, similar to what happens to whistleblowers [183]. Retaliation included having reputations impugned, integrity attacked, and mental health questioned and threatened. Nine participants (7 target-witnesses, 2 witnesses) said that due to exposure to bullying, they were undergoing mental or medical health treatment, some taking antidepressants. They claimed that bullies used this medical information to further attack their competence and mental health.

Despite the risks, many told me of many forms of resistance, saying they felt a *moral imperative* to fight back:

* "I have a responsibility to speak up.... If somebody says, 'Did you try to do anything?' I can say, 'You bet I did, and I've paid a hell of a price for it.'"

* "How could I live with myself if I just stayed quiet?"

* "I can sleep at night, because I've done the right thing.... I didn't just stand by and let her steamroll people."

* "How could I face myself if I didn't say something?"

* "I couldn't just take it lying down. Somebody had to stand up to this guy."

* "Somebody's got to speak up, you know, uncover this cancer that's growing here."

For these people, their principles overshadowed their fear of speaking up. Even in their discussions of risk, however, I saw the tension between resistance and control. Participants neither perceived dissent as romantic nor removed from organizational controls. Systems of control, while frightening and powerful, were neither absolute nor unchangeable. Their experiences underscore the claim that where there is power abuse there is likely some form of resistance.

Forms of Resistance to Workplace Bullying

Resistance was complex, and workers were resourceful. Most tactics appeared in both organized action and disorganized coaction. The tension between resistance and control was evident as target-witnesses, witnesses, and perceived bullies "attempted to shape the ... meanings of interactions" [169] (p. 23). Workers reported gaining and then losing ground as countering bullies politicized and reframed their efforts to stop abuse. The following outlines the various forms of resistance and presents them as if distinct from one another, which is not how they occurred. Indeed, resistance typically included many different tactics.

Exodus

Exodus included quitting, intentions or threats to quit, transfers or requests for transfers, and helping others leave. *All* participants told stories of coworkers quitting and talked about wanting to resign. When asked what advice they would give others, most recommended leaving the organization (similar to findings in [184]). Counting quitting alone (excluding transfers and firing), the 30 narratives included stories of 224 workers who had quit due to bullying. (This suggests that for every person who speaks up about bullying, another seven have left their jobs because of bullying.)

When they talked to their coworkers trying to make sense of bullying, conversations were filled with tales of "escaping." They also reported talking to peers about quitting, encouraging coworkers to leave, spreading information about job opportunities, championing those who had "escaped," and helping colleagues find jobs. *If bullying-affected workers had a theme song, it was David Allan Coe's "Take This Job and Shove It."*

Many quit in ways they hoped would communicate their disgust and anger (e.g.. "noisy exits"): Steve left his 15-year position as a highly trained, technical specialist giving three days' notice. He explained, "I did everything I could...; nobody did anything except not give her [bully] the promotion.... I spent two days training my replacement ... and was out of there. Let 'em go down in flames! Maybe this will open their eyes." In Steve's case, many others had filed complaints about the woman's bullying.

Amy, in the sports fishing industry, also wanted her resignation to "send a message to the bully.... He crossed *my* personal line in the sand ... so I quit." She explained,

> I left because two of my executives—the hardest working people
> in the company, the most honest, the most direct, the most
> trustworthy, ethical—and he bullied them, and he bullied them.
> He'd debase them, and blame them, and debase them, and
> blame them, and he chipped away at them, and chipped away at
> them, until they both found other jobs.... It was just *morally*
> *wrong!*

These experiences suggest that quitting represented a form of defiance. At the point participants reported leaving the organization, they were *extremely* angry, resentful, and hurt. Even in cases where bullying had occurred years before, accounts were marked by acute emotion: bitterness, distrust, antipathy, and incredulity.

Participants presented turnover as "proof" of their claims about bullying. Brad, a substance abuse treatment counselor, explained, "Many people here have left for lower paying jobs." Terry, an adult education trainer, said, "When she [bully] was promoted all hell broke loose ... 8 people left out of an office of 24." Michelle, an office assistant in a large restaurant chain, claimed that all the bully's subordinates left within 12 months, since she was "impossible to work for." Diane, a hospital nurse, also noted, "Good nurses don't last under this woman. They've lost so many, I'm surprised the unit's still functioning."

Collective Voice

Collective voice was when several employees talked amongst themselves about their experiences and organized plans for what they could or should do to stop abuse. Participants reported seeking out colleagues to confirm their perceptions, provide emotional support, brainstorm solutions to stop the bullying, and discuss plans to find other jobs. Collective voice provided a sense of connection and a shield against stress [185], but had a distinct *action-orientation*. Two kinds of collective voice came from participant accounts: mutual advocacy and contagious voice.

Mutual advocacy. Mutual advocacy was what Andy called "having each others' backs." Nine participants reported backing up their colleagues. This included developing shared action plans, backing up peers (e.g., countering abusers' accounts that allegedly blamed workers for mistreatment), and protecting coworkers or subordinates. Participants described mutual advocacy with metaphors of connection, struggle, and survival:

* "It's like a badge of honor to say we worked for this guy and survived."

* "We all felt like survivors of a shipwreck."

* "It's like we're war veterans."

In an elementary school, teachers talked about a bullying colleague. These conversations reinforced their decision to report the abuse, softened the impact of the bully's attacks, and made it difficult for the bully to turn teachers against one another. In a sports fishing business, protecting subordinates was reportedly upper-managers' "code of honor." Amy explained that protecting staff was "an absolute given. The guy with the highest rank takes it ... under all circumstances!" In a business where the owner humiliated and ridiculed vice presidents, these department heads went to great lengths to shield their staff from him.

Contagious voice. Another aspect of collective voice was contagion, similar to emotional contagion [186], in which bullies "influence the emotions or behavior of [others] ... through the ... induction of emotion states and behavioral attitudes" [187](p. 50). Eleven participants reported initially questioning their perceptions (e.g., "At first, I couldn't believe it.") but then speaking out after seeing that their colleagues had similar experiences. As Rick, in city government, explained, "At first I thought it was just me.... [but] when Karen [coworker] said something... I knew I wasn't the only one." Levina reported that after a group of teachers spoke to a school board member,

> It's like when the little boys who are sexually abused by the priests ... when one of them speaks out, all the others come out of the woodwork? Well, it was like that. Once we talked to Bob [on school board], a lot of other teachers got up the courage to join in and say, "Hey it's not okay." You know what I mean? They weren't so scared anymore.

Spreading agreement was "an enormous relief," "the thing that encouraged me to go to HR," and "what made me strong enough to come forward." In this way, coworker voice was infectious.

Reverse Discourse

Reverse discourse turned tyrannical practices and name-calling to liberating advantages. Not surprisingly, resistance got its momentum from the oppression that generated the resistance [162]. Workers coopted these controls by providing alternative interpretations. They reversed the abusers' discourse, their abusive treatment, by creating alternative meanings: (a) embracing pejorative labels, (b) accessing influential allies, (c) lodging grievances/complaints, and (d) documenting abuse.

Embracing pejorative labels. This form of resistance occurred when workers embraced negative names as an aspect of how they wanted to be seen. In four cases, participants reported embracing the label "troublemaker." For example, Ben, in the telecommunications industry, explained that he was part of a group labeled "troublemakers." He recounted, "I grew up in a union household.... I'm a union activist through and through. I'm used to being called a troublemaker, and troublemakers are standing up and saying 'this is what we're going through'." Employees who report or fail to go along with abuse are often labeled troublemakers or insubordinate [19, 69], but bullies' name-calling was not always effective at silencing dissenters.

Accessing influential allies. Participants connected themselves with influential others and used expert knowledge to reinforce their claims. The did this in a way that shifted the relations of power toward subordinate employees and away from bullying managers. Twenty participants ($2/3^{rds}$ of the sample) reported speaking with union representatives, EEOC staff, board members, physicians, mental health counselors, attorneys, trusted managers, an agency funder, and a state legislator. Levina's case with the school board member is one example. Mary, in public safety, spoke with a lawyer who encouraged her to document abuse. Brad allied himself with a consulting board member. Rick spoke to a city grant funder. Aligning power-holders and securing influential support also encouraged action.

Participants also recounted using expert knowledge about workplace bullying to support resistance. Nine participants said they "discovered" the bullying phenomenon and examples of others' experiences in newspapers, magazines, and online sources. Mark, in a nonprofit social service agency, read a New York Times article and shared the information with coworkers and an upper-manager. The workgroup agreed, "This is *exactly* what's happening to us!" Mary read "about workplace bullying in our newspaper....[,] sent it to our personnel manager," and distributed it to her colleagues. Similarly, Diane found an article about "bully-busting... in *Nurse Week*," and a coworker copied and distributed it to all the nurses in her workgroup. Diane also took the article to HR when she filed a complaint against the abuser. Participants described using expert knowledge to corroborate their claims, as well as to name the bullying phenomenon and educate others about it.

Grievance. Workers protested abuse using formal and informal complaints. Grievances were often coupled with *accessing influential allies.* Fourteen participants reported lodging or supporting complaints or filing formal or supporting grievances against the bully. Diane, Rick, Mark, and Carmen filed complaints with HR. Terry and Sylvia filed EEOC complaints. Steve and Ben filed unfair labor practice complaints with unions. In five cases, resisters later discovered that others had filed complaints (disorganized coaction).

Documentation. Another tactic was keeping written records of abusive interactions, usually on the advice of an outside expert (e.g., lawyer). Doing so helped subordinate employees to appropriate managerial "retention and control of information" [174](p. 94) to their advantage. Thirteen participants used the recordkeeping bullies developed to monitor them, as a tool to monitor-the-monitors. Participants reported documenting abuse to support their claims or defend against ongoing attacks. Brad said he kept records so that "if I ever...have a confrontation, I can go back and look at what actually happened." He explained that keeping records was "fighting fire with fire." In Brad's case, the bully used documentation as way to control and oppress targets. Targets and witnessed believed their documentation of events turned the bully's control tactics back on the bullies.

Subversive (Dis)obedience

Subversive (dis)obedience involves disobeying and obeying and included well-documented tactics in which workers altered output or communication in ways that disadvantaged the bullies. In combination with other tactics, participants reported labor withdrawal [160], working-to-rule [188, 189], resistance through distance [162], and retaliation [114, 190].

Labor withdrawal. Labor withdrawal was withholding effort as an initial response to abuse, or initially increasing work and then withdrawing output. Working harder and then retracting effort emerged in 12 accounts. When abuse persisted despite working harder, participants reported giving up. Working harder resulted in a brief respite but was inevitably followed by more demands and further demoralization. Greg, a police officer, reflected this sentiment, "There's times where you're so beat down by it that you realize that you can't accomplish everything and even if you do, it's not going to be to his satisfaction, so you just give up."

Four participants reported withholding labor and doing "only enough to get by" as an initial response to abuse. Ben explained, "When you attack or bully an employee, it has a negative effect. Productivity on the job suffers. You push me hard like that, and I just stop putting out." He claimed that when the men in his shop were creative or independently solved problems, they were punished or humiliated. As a result, they slowed down, stopped, or masked these efforts. Kurt, in a law firm, said, "we do day-to-day tasks... but when it comes time to doing things that are above and beyond, we don't do them anymore. The firm loses, but when the partners don't intercede with this guy's tirades, what can they expect?" Thus, abuse engendered noncooperation rather than cooperation and consent.

Working-to-rule. Doing exactly what's required or the minimum required is working-to-rule and creates spaces of control that provide workers with plausible deniability ("I was just following orders.") [191]. If failing to follow directions is insubordination and grounds for firing, doing exactly as directed provides an indirect way to resist. Eight participants reported using this okay-you-asked-for-it tactic when following bully's directives—perceived as highly controlling or insulting—to the letter. For example, Mary said,

> I was out of my office and didn't answer my phone once [and was punished], and after that, every time I went to the bathroom, every time I left my office, I was to call her secretary.... So if I had to send a fax, the fax machine ... is right across the hall from my office, by god, I was leaving my office, so I'd call the secretary.

Before the new supervisor's entry, Mary reported 10 years' success at her job overseeing grant funds. She ridiculed the bully's demands by exaggerating allegedly menial, insulting directives.

Resistance-through-distance. This resistance strategy removed workers physically and communicatively from bullies. Twenty-seven participants (90% of sample) reported avoiding or withholding information from bullies in ways that masked the action or actor, apparently to protect themselves from retaliation. Vice presidents in a sports fishing business figured out how to "duck" the owner. As Amy put it,

> You learn to duck; you learn to just avoid.... You learn not to show up at work too much. You make arrangements to go to meetings. You're just too busy to go to the office;... you lie, and you scheme, and you're not there.... You just learn to not come to work.

Vice-presidents prided themselves in creative ways to "duck." Amy and her coworkers talked about ducking as a near art form. Ducking, like working-to-rule, also provided plausible deniability.

In addition to physical distance, participants reported withholding valued information from bullies. In the private security business, high-level staff earned substantial salaries—what Lynn called "golden handcuffs." Because of the owner's reputation for abusive volatility, "no one would tell him anything. They knew he'd detonate, and so you learned to just keep your head down and then laugh all the way to the bank." Participants withheld information for self-protection, but also felt some satisfaction because they withheld information the bullies probably wanted.

Retaliation. Many participants verbalized desires for vengeance or reciprocation of injury in kind. Relation took the form of hostile gossip [166, 192] and fantasies or plans for physically harming or killing the bully. The most common was character assassination—talking behind the abuser's back. This was done to support individual's reports to others and counter the gossip and rumors bullies perpetrated. Eighteen persons reported speaking to many, many others inside and outside the organization about the bully's "bizarre behavior." This tactic was often embedded in *accessing influential allies* but also appeared in numerous incidents where the central purpose of the conversation appeared to be derogating the bully.

Workers also reported fantasies or plans to harm bullies physically. Four participants recounted workplace or family conversations

72

focused on desires or plans to retaliate physically for bullies' cruelty, up to and including *murder*. Amy explained that after particularly trying days, "all we did was plot to kill him ... [as a means to] debrief and de-pressurize." They discussed poisoning his tea, wiring a bomb in his car, and "hiring a professional hitman."

Linda, in a publishing company, explained that her husband became so angry at the ongoing abuse that "he was going to wait for Ira [bully] after work with ... [her husband's] brother and beat the bejesus out of him." Linda said she talked her husband out of confronting the bully, but only dissuaded him after promising to quit. These violent fantasies and intentions suggest another dangerous potential of unchecked bullying.

Confrontation

Confrontation was face-to-face conversations with the bully or public challenges through humor. Ten participants reported talking to the bully to defend against unfair accusations or explain to the bully how his or her actions had hurt participants' or others' feelings. Confrontation usually occurred at or near the onset of abuse and ostensibly "made matters worse." For example, Ted, in the mining industry, occasionally intervened when Dirk (abusive coworker) bullied him or others. Ted believed these confrontations infuriated Dirk. He based his assumption on Dirk's subsequent sabotage of Ted's equipment that reportedly endangered Ted's life, and Dirk's increasingly aggressive attacks that included threatening the lives of Ted's family members. Despite Dirk's aggression, a few years later Dirk was promoted and fired Ted soon afterward for "failing to follow orders." Ted nonetheless defended his actions. "I couldn't just take it lying down. Somebody had to stand up to this guy."

Another form of confrontation was using humor to counter bullying acts [193]. Sandy, a bullying manager, publicly accused a targeted employee of fund misappropriation during a team meeting. Rick, a witnessing colleague, said, "I just started laughing and said, 'what are you talking about? She can't even go to the bathroom without your approval.'" His humor ridiculed the bully's controlling tactics in a setting where staff was allegedly responsible for processes over which they were given little or no authority. Rick's story was one of the few examples in which workers used humor as defiance, but there were ample dark jokes made about bullies' mental states and participants' experiences.

Research Interview as Resistance

In an interesting development, many interviewees framed their involvement in the research project as a type of resistance. They may have even used the research process as a channel for speaking out, since many said they were willing to talk about and relive their experiences if doing so might stop bullying or help others. They characterized participation as "spreading the news." As Ted said, "it gets my heart going and it makes me feel, have bad feelings ... but if it's beneficial to somebody, you know, it's all right." Thus, the research interview itself served as a sort of political forum for affected employees [194]. Rick explained,

> Somebody's gotta speak up, you know, uncover this cancer that's growing here. So many good people have left and the rest of us want to go, and I'm telling you it's *downright criminal!* I'm just not going to take it from that bastard anymore. Maybe your research can expose the stuff that's happening behind closed doors in this place.

Participation may have also encouraged acts of resistance after the interview and served as another motivated "tactic" in resistance paths. I take this up further in the discussion.

Target-Witness and Witness Experiences

The previous discussion combined the reported experiences of target-witnesses and witnesses. Here, I explore the differences and similarities between these two groups in how bullying affected them and their subsequent responses. The overall experiences of target-witnesses and witnesses differed in some ways, but their reactions were quite similar. Target-witnesses were allegedly treated more brutally than were witnesses so they understandably described intense fear at work. Then again, witnesses also described being very fearful of speaking out and coming to the bully's negative attention. Seeing what happened to others communicated in no uncertain terms what would happen if witnesses became targets. There was no question that bullying environments were marked by profound fear within entire workgroups.

Target-witnesses reported higher rates of directly confronting bullies than did witnesses, most likely because they felt they were under direct attack. Both groups, however, reported informally lodging complaints with organizational authorities at approximately similar

rates. Target-witnesses were more likely to report filing formal grievances, EEOC suits, and unfair labor practice complaints, while witnesses were more likely to support others' grievances. Target-
witnesses talked about being extremely traumatized; of the seven under medical care due to exposure to bullying, five were target-
witnesses.

On the other hand, witnesses were also deeply disturbed by their
experiences. They said the workplace experience took over their entire lives—they worried about it at work and away from work, they
talked about it continually to family and friends, they spent large seg-
ments of work time speaking with others or figuring out how to deal
with or avoid being abused. Witnesses and target-witnesses reported
that the failure of organizational authorities to stop abuse destroyed
their belief that "good prevails over evil." As Ken, a witness in the
retail industry, claimed, "I felt robbed .... I felt violated .... I felt like I
go through life with the basic assumption that people are ... good to
people, and that has been stripped away."

Members of both groups were evenly represented in collective
and individual resistance and reported distancing themselves, withholding information, and accessing expert knowledge at similar rates.
In sum, target-witnesses understandably reported greater injury and
more often used formal communication channels and face-to-face
confrontations as redress, but the two groups' emotional reactions and
resistance were remarkably similar. Thus, it appeared that when bullying was a shared experience, the shared nature of the experience extended to how workers fought back.

Paths of Resistance

Whether witness or target-witness, participants reported using multiple tactics to (re)create a workplace environment marked by respect,
dignity, and justice. Participants' described experiences that included
an average of seven forms of resistance (range 0 to 10). They gave up
only after numerous efforts and reportedly being disappointed and
disillusioned again and again. The temporal order of resistance tactics
was unique for each participant; I found no two people whose resistance sequence mapped the same.

The following describes five randomly selected paths providing a
sense of how resistance unfolds, is met by control or punishment,
shifts to different tactics, and results in different ends. Each path illustrates the resistance-control dialectic and risks of resistance in an al-

75

ready risky environment. For example, Shelly, in a consulting firm, reported initially talking with the bullying partner-owners to defend against allegedly unfair accusations. Abuse escalated, and she started avoiding the partners and keeping crucial information to herself. The partners intensified public criticism of her in staff meetings and talk behind her back, so she again spoke to them privately. Eventually the partners "counseled her out" of the consulting firm, offering her a substantial buy-out package, and Shelly exited the firm.

Terry spoke directly with the bully after hearing rumors the bully had supposedly spread about Terry. The bully denied spreading rumors but soon after, canceled Terry's credit card for travel, making her pay all expenses out-of-pocket and then request reimbursement. Terry appealed the credit card decision. When the appeal was denied, she spoke confidentially with an upper-manager. Later, the upper-manager hired an outside consultant to problem-solve staff issues. In a meeting without managers present, Terry discovered that others shared her experiences so began talking with them about what to do. Terry and a group of coworkers went back to the upper-manager. In the meantime, the bully apparently escalated abuse by moving Terry's office to a hot, cramped space across the hall from the restrooms and divulging Terry's private medical information to coworkers. Terry began avoiding contact with the bully and keeping detailed records of interactions. The bully launched an exhaustive investigation of Terry's "unauthorized use of department resources," so Terry went to her union steward. She subsequently filed an EEOC complaint and after settling left the organization.

Ted reported intervening on numerous occasions when the bully "raged, swore at, and cornered" his coworkers. In response, the bully sabotaged Ted's equipment, and Ted reported the sabotage to the supervisor. Ted continued to stand up to the bully in the face of abusive, humiliating treatment of him and others. When the bully threatened Ted's family members' lives, he again reported the threat to the supervisor and avoided all contact with the bully. Ted recounted that the aggression died down for over a year, after which, management promoted the bully. A month after the promotion, the bully fired Ted.

Brad was shocked by the insulting, humiliating messages from the new agency director and immediately went to her with his concerns. When she continued to criticize and micro-manage his work, despite over 20 years' experience in the substance abuse treatment field, he again spoke with her. Afterward, the bully's insults escalated, her micro-management became an unswerving response to his efforts, and she repeatedly altered his treatment programs and outreach plans. He then spoke with a consulting board member. When little changed, Brad began documenting demeaning interactions, reducing work output, doing exactly what she asked, withholding information, and talking to community members about her.

Karla worked in an organization that ironically operated a battered women's shelter. She explained that four managers began talking in her office one afternoon about what they could do to stop the bullying director. Eventually, seven program managers secretly went to the home of a board member and explained the extent of the problem. They reportedly stated, "we just can't take it anymore" and were ready to find other jobs if the agency director was not removed. (The board had sanctioned the agency director numerous times without effect.) Program managers each prepared written documentation for the board member, to be used in case of a lawsuit. As much as possible, they all avoided contact with the director, but spoke with many others about the director's abusive behavior. The board eventually fired the bully after an protracted, seven-month process in which the resisting workers were terrified of discovery.

Unlike general acts of resistance against managerial [195] or corporate interests [196], or even specific resistance against pressure to increase output [160], in cases of bullying, resistance was a systematic series of actions directed to an end: stopping abuse. None mapped entirely the same, but some underlying patterns were discernable (I take these up in the discussion). The form of resistance (collective, individual) affected the case outcomes, a point to which I now turn.

Case Outcomes

In many cases, bullying continued unabated. In others cases, abusers were punished (fired, involuntarily transferred, denied promotion, driven to quit) and bullying stopped. When workers resisted collectively, even in the absence of organized labor, they reported outcomes that were more positive. Twelve (40%) participants collectively resisted and workers were fired and quit at lower rates than those who individually resisted. Collective resisters reported that their organizations more often took punitive action aimed at bullies' behavior. At the study's completion, seven were still at their jobs, three quit, one transferred within the organization, and one filed an EEOC suit, settled with the organization, and subsequently quit. Four of the bullies in the collective-resistance situations were fired, three were transferred, and five remained at the job, and one failed to secure a desired promotion.

Fifteen (50%) participants individually resisted; of these, six remained at the job, six quit, and three were fired. Eleven of the bullies in the individual-resistance situations remained at the job, three were fired, and, in one case, an employee filed a formal grievance against the bully, and the bully subsequently quit. For those who resisted collectively, in over 58% of the cases, organizational authorities meted out negative sanctions for the abuser, and none of the employees was fired. For those who resisted individually, in 27% of the cases, the bully was negatively sanctioned, and 20% of these workers were fired.

In addition to the collective-individual dynamic, certain communicative tactics were more often reported in cases where organizational authorities took action to ameliorate the problem. Overall, 11 bullies were reportedly sanctioned, and 1 quit after an employee filed a formal grievance. In these cases, the most common tactic reported was informal or formal complaints (grievance) to organizational authorities. Complaints were particularly effective when substantiated with written documentation and expert opinion (e.g., research on workplace bullying). Intervention took months to materialize, but in cases where workers channeled resistance through organizationally legitimized systems, they more often said that upper-managers took action against the bullies.

Two tactics were common in cases where organizations failed to intervene—confrontation and withholding information. The former reportedly fueled more than resolved the situation (finding similar to [184], and the latter was likely invisible to all but the resister. Thus, it appeared that communicating directly with organizational authorities, that is, working within the organization's system of grievances, was most often associated with organizational interventions (whether or not interventions were successful at ending bullying). Organizational authorities also appeared to respond favorably to documentation and substantiating expert opinion.

Discussion

The study's findings suggest a number of valuable insights for understanding resistance and workplace bullying. Specifically, findings suggest (a) the meanings people give to resistance are contentious and other people can interpret resistance in unplanned ways, (b)workplace bullying is social and communal, (c) resistance leading to change is a slow process, (d) power as characterized in bullying research is limited, and (e) participation in research can be a form of resistance.

Arguments About What It Means to Resist

This study specifically draws resistant acts from extensive narratives. As such, it may paint a picture of resistance that, although complex and processual, appears cleaner or more effective at exacting change than experienced. In fact, change took a considerable amount of time to transpire; the time-lapse is potentially one of the dynamics that leads workers to report feeling impotent in the face of bullying. It was in follow-up contacts that participants reported organizational changes, and often by that time, both interviewees and many more of their coworkers had suffered more abuse, left their jobs, or were fired. And sadly, despite resistance, bullying continued in many cases. Moreover, resistance may have hurt resisters more often than it contributed to organizational changes.

Resistance is risky business for workers, and there is always the potential for unintended consequences: they want change but are punished; they report abuse but are stigmatized for reporting; they fight back and are called insubordinate. The inherent risk is why most resistance is covert. Resistance always holds risk for workers, but the risk is even more pronounced in environments where employees are systematically abused. Resistance is high-risk because all such acts have the latent potential for multiple interpretations and meanings, depending on who is doing the interpreting. The meanings of resistance are never fixed. Rather, the essence of the control-resistance dialectic is "the ongoing tensions and contradictions that constitute the process by which organizational bullies attempt to shape workplace practices" [169](p. 23) and fix the meanings of those practices.

To illustrate the various ways that people can interpret and label resistance, I provide three reinterpretations. These demonstrate how resistance, usually carried out with a desire for humanizing organizational communication, can be reframed in ways to neutralize resistance, or worse, re-stigmatize and punish resisters. These examples suggest that resistance is anything but straightforward in workplaces. Rather, resistance is ambiguous—it can mean various things—as bullies or bystanders interpret and assign meaning to fighting back.

First, resisters say exodus is a form of defiance and evidence that there is something seriously wrong—proof of bullies' abusive communication and actions—workers also note that bullies' goals often include desires to drive certain workers from the organization. Indeed, worker exodus can be interpreted as a triumph for both the abusers and for the exiting workers. Moreover, if those with compelling voice resist, then lose hope and leave, this does two things: provides evidence that something is seriously wrong and mutes the remaining employees' voice.

Exodus may also leave the organization blameless in a sense; once the resisting worker leaves, organizational authorities may see no reason to act or examine the departed person's reports of abuse. Writing off the departed worker as disgruntled can neutralize the essence of that worker's past complaints or grievances. Thus, bullying-affected workers may perceive exodus as successful escape and valid proof of wrongdoing, but it can also mean that abusive supervisors/coworkers "won"—it can be effectively framed as both control and resistance.

Second, collective voice and reverse discourse give credence to affected workers' claims, bolster their courage to speak out, and encourage them to plan pooled resistance strategies. Conversely, these workers can then be labeled insubordinate, troublemakers, mentally ill, disgruntled employees, and anti-team players. Workers who speak out against organizational power and control can be depicted as disloyal or blamed for making things worse for those silently hoping that abuse will go away. A rare few can co-opt pejorative labels, but in most cases resisters find that coworkers avoid them, upper-managers discount their complaints, and abusers increase pressure against them. Apparently, bullies are quite successful at reframing these resistant activities as anti-organization and the resisters as deviant [68].

Third, resistance such as subversive (dis)obedience—well-documented, widespread resistance tactics—most likely discredit rather than empower dissenting workers. Withholding labor, working-to-rule, and withholding information can provide resisters a feeling of control and an element of personal satisfaction but are easily reframed as production deficits and suitable grounds for punishment, up to and including firing. Targeted workers most likely feel justified using these strategies, particularly when they are persistently abused. However, such actions place them in precarious positions and, as such, fail to encourage critical reflection of organizational dynamics. Thus, any form of dissent has the potential for numerous interpretations, both intended and unintended.

Nonetheless, in some cases, resistance changes the bullying situation. When targets and witnesses collectively resist, work through the formal problem-solving systems available to them, and provide decision makers with documented evidence of abuse, this combination moves decision maker to action. Using research and other published material (print or electronic) about workplace bullying also supports workers' complaints and serves as educative tools for decision makers. This points to the importance of published studies on the topic.

Beyond One-on-One Interactions

Much of bullying research usually frames it as an individual issue or dyadic interaction between target and bully. However, communication at work, including workplace bullying, is always social and public. Bullying and related stress reactions are not confined to targets, but often affect the entire work unit. When workers suffer at the hands of bullies, their abuse negatively affects the entire workgroup and bullies' actions may serve as a model for others' behavior.

A principal concentration on targets or bully-target dyads conceals the communal impact of bullying and makes it far easier to explain the phenomenon with individualistic assumptions such as individual pathologies, personality conflicts, or problem-employees. This serves a political function by blaming the victim and discursively removing organizational responsibility to provide for worker safety. As William Ryan, author of *Blaming the Victim*, [197](p. 8) aptly notes, "the generic process of blaming the victim is applied to almost every American problem," and workplace bullying is no exception. Examining the impact of bullying on the broader work unit limits overly simplistic blame-casting, since bullying affects and is affected by all workplace relationships to some degree.

Coworkers play a crucial role in the development of and intervention in abusive workplace dynamics. Bullying injures, stigmatizes, and questions targets' character and performance, but does not have this effect on witnessing bystanders. Consequently, organizational authorities are less likely to respect or heed target complaints. Because witnesses are not directly stigmatized, they may have voice and believability that targets lose due to victim-status.

This suggests a crucial role for coworkers. Witnessing coworkers corroborate targeted workers' perceptions, build toward collective efforts at change, bring issues to the attention of organization decision makers, and interrupt abusive communication. When witnesses collaborate with target-witnesses to report bullying, it also reduces the

81

likelihood of individual workers being pejoratively labeled. Of course, joining resistance efforts is not without risk. Collective efforts at resistance are more protracted than individual efforts. Thus, witness substantiation may lead to intervention, but witnessing coworkers will also spend more time dealing with bullying and less time on other more pleasant tasks and social interactions at work.

Process of Resistance

Targets and witnesses told their stories in chronological order. This made it possible to map the process of resistance and how it unfolds over time. That is, resistance forms a sort of motivated trajectory. Employees use one tactic, assess its effect, use another tactic, assess its affect, use another tactic, assess, and so on. They also use different strategies in combination. That is, resisting workers do not give up or silently "take it." They continue trying to end abuse until exiting the organization or bullying ends. As such, bullying may be ignored or minimized by organizational authorities, but its impact persists as workers continue to seek justice.

The paths of resistance are as unique as each person in the study, but two underlying patterns are discernable. First, resistance, for the most part, shows the following pattern: private, private, public, (punishment), private, private, public, (punishment), and so forth. It appears that the private conversations and plans prepare for the public forms of resistance. When public resistance fails to stop abuse or results in retribution, resisters "regroup" in multiple private conversations with trusted others. Second, when help from internal organizational authorities fails to end abuse (formal grievances/complaints, informal talks with upper-management, HR, etc.), two types of responses commonly develop: seeking help from external authorities (e.g., legal redress, unions) or pushing resistance down into subverted, covert tactics (e.g., working-to-rule). Both responses are marked by negatively charged emotions and neither bode well for the employing organization.

Power in Workplace Bullying Research

Findings also suggest that power should be presented in a far more complex manner in bullying research, since current literature typically reifies organizational control. I talked about this issue quite a bit in the previous chapter and repeat some of those ideas here. The power-as-commodity frame presents power as something bullies "have" and targeted workers do not, glosses how affected workers defend themselves and others, and, as such, overlooks circumstances in which workers resist and eventually alter organizational systems. The powerful-versus-powerless contrast hides the resources of power available to workers—resources that they actually report using to defend themselves. Power is better framed as fluid and shifting in which all people involved have access to certain sources of power [173], albeit at greater or lesser degrees depending on the source.

Re-theorizing power means looking at the nuanced push-and-pull of the control-resistance tension. The situations where workers "fight back" can provide clues to fruitful paths of communication for intervention in abusive workplaces. Thus, it is both naïve and short-sighted to study workplace abuse without attending to the resistance such abuse engenders. Since discovering or formulating solutions is the implicit if not explicit goal of bullying research, failing to explore the forms of resistance that contribute to organizational changes is a serious omission. A marriage of sorts between the bullying and critical communication perspectives might provide just such a multifaceted lens through which to analyze and find solutions.

Research Participation as Resistance and Political Act

The findings in this study reflect a collaborative project of knowledge building between participants-researcher. Moreover, numerous participants framed the research interview as a form of "fighting back." It is imperative to recognize that, as with an anthropologist's presence in another culture, the qualitative interviewer's presence in the life of research participants alters the dynamics and trajectory of the situation. That is, researchers may record something as having happened in the field when the researcher's presence contributed to what occurred. Interpretive researchers understand the final product—the written research report—is a text that weaves together the native and researcher's subjectivities to better understand native's life experiences. Interpretive researchers are sensitive to and aware of themselves as being part of the research they are doing. Despite believing this, researchers may or may not have evidence of how or when their work intervenes in research subjects' lives.

I cannot report the subsequent responses of workers as if my interviews with them had no intervening effect, particularly for those still in the bullying environment. The full extent of this effect is unknown but as one woman explained in a follow-up email, "Thank you so much for offering me the support and encouragement I desperately needed. Speaking with you really helped me commit to a course of action." She spoke during the interview of her plans to file a report with HR. Evidently, she did along with a number of others unbeknownst to her. The bully was ultimately removed. This statement suggests that the research participation intervenes in some participants' experiences of workplace bullying.

Conclusion

Resistance to abuse at work is a complex, dynamic process in which workers fight to have a voice and are often punished for their efforts. If organizational authorities finally intervene, many have already left the organization or suffered years of abuse. The human cost is staggering and workers' stories heartbreaking. Neither is resistance straightforward; those for whom the resistance is threatening easily reframe worker dissent as deviant behavior. Nonetheless, workers faced with bullying at work say they have a moral imperative to act against the injustice and in some cases actually alter their situations. Furthermore, workers often collectively organize against abusers, even in the absence of formal unions. Organizations would be well informed to heed these voices. Resistance and the emotional communication that springs from it are warning signs that "act as signaling devices when expected appropriate norms of communication are violated" [136](p. 72). These should not be ignored. Organizational authorities must learn to "read the traces" of resistance to bullying, diagnose the problem early, and construct effective interventions.

CHAPTER 5

Explaining the Unexplainable: The Painful Experiences of Workplace Bullying[D]

Sarah J. Tracy, Pamela Lutgen-Sandvik, Jess Alberts

Chapter Summary: Considerable research has linked workplace bullying with harms and costs, but the emotional horrors of bullying are largely untold. This study examines targets' metaphor to articulate and explain the emotional pain from workplace bullying. Their metaphors etch indelible representations of abuse and translate its devastation to readers and organizational members to encourage change. Based on focus groups with targets, interviews, and drawings, this chapter describes how bullying can feel like a battle, water torture, nightmare, or noxious substance; bullies can appear to be narcissistic dictators, two-faced bullies and devil figures; targets can feel like vulnerable children, slaves, prisoners, animals and heartbroken lovers. These metaphors encourage and discourage possibilities for target resistance, agency, and action. Metaphors also serve as diagnostic cues or shorthand for intervention.

Keywords: Workplace bullying, emotion, metaphor analysis, work feelings, harassment

---

When people bullied at work try to describe the depth of pain and suffering at the hands of aggressors, others are less than convinced. Even when researchers who study bullying talk to professionals, journalists and other researchers about the issue, people often say things such as, "This is the real-world, not school, and these people should just toughen up," and "Are you sure they're not just problem employees?" or "Is it really that bad?"

Targets and witnesses readily admit that bullying can sound unbelievable. Indeed, Amy, an employee in the sports industry, explained that the bullying at her office was so strange that when new people applied for jobs, "I withheld the truth because the truth seemed surreal... To tell anybody the truth in 15 minutes—they would look at me and say, 'She's just a disgruntled employee. It can't be.'"

However, bullying should not be disregarded as a childish problem or simply a reaction of overly sensitive workers. From 25% to 30% of US employees are bullied and emotionally abused sometime during their work histories—10% at any given time [6, 198]. If one in ten workers currently suffer at the hands of workplace bullies, then bullying is a pervasive problem and not just the rare experience of a few "thin-skinned" employees.

Increasingly, organizations are beginning to recognize the costs associated with employee stress, burnout, and depression. Research on health and wellness in organizations establishes that workplace stress has significant harmful effects. Stress results in poor mental and physical health as well as increased employee sick days and workers' compensations claims and decreased productivity [199]. Workplace stress is also connected to psychological strain [200, 201] and to decreases in "social health, ... the quality of an individual's network of professional and personal relationships" [199](p. 549). The emotional responses to adult bullying are linked to a host of physical, psychological, organizational and social costs. Better understanding those emotions is important for attending to the harmful effects on personal and organizational wellness.

This chapter reports a study of bullied workers' in US settings spontaneously use metaphors as they explain their experiences. Metaphors compare unlike, less understood things (e.g., workplace bullying) to better understood things (e.g., war, nightmares) [202], and provide vivid verbal images of emotional experiences [203]. This dense, intense shorthand [130] is powerful and convincing at communicating the very real threat of workplace bullying to important stakeholders (e.g., researchers, consultants, mental health providers, managers, policymakers). These stakeholders typically are familiar with sexual harassment and discrimination but largely unacquainted with adult bullying. Identifying the material effects of adult bullying is an important step in persuading organizational decision makers and elected officials to pay attention to the issue.

However, little research fleshes out the emotional aspects of bullying or answers questions like, "What does it feel like to be bullied?" and "Is it really that bad?" Answering such questions is vital. Even the strongest argument based upon measurable costs of bullying is unlikely to move people to action without an engagement of emotion [204-206]. Understanding what bullying feels like might be necessary for motivating change [207].

Additionally, employee emotion serves an important signal function [208, 209]. Negative emotion serves as a warning sign that organizational interaction is askew. Indeed, negative emotional responses can be the first sign of smoke signifying fire that can tear through organizations and workgroups. Attending to, uncovering, and publicizing emotions associated with bullying might be required to push organizational intervention, change, and prevention.

This study explores the emotional experiences of targeted employees. Popular books include anecdotes describing devastating bullying experiences, but abused workers' emotions are essentially missing in most scientific research. This is due, in part, to traditional writing styles and scientific conventions to present research in rational language that typically "writes out" emotion [210, 211]. Nevertheless, an appreciation of abused workers' subjective experiences is integral to understanding how and why bullying is so costly.

The chapter opens with a review of the definitions, characteristics, and costs of workplace bullying. Then the piece discusses the results from focus groups, interviews and participant drawings, and describes how metaphors turned out to be a good way to make sense of these complex emotion experiences. The heart of the chapter details the metaphors targets used to explain the bullying process, perceptions of bullies, and themselves as targets. The chapter concludes with practical and theoretical implications, limitations, and future directions of research.

Workplace Bullying: Terminology, Characteristics, and Costs

The term *workplace bullying* is similar to a wide array of other terms (see Chapter 2); we made a conscious choice to use the term for several reasons. The term *workplace bullying* appears to be more practical and accessible to the working public than academic terms (e.g., generalized non-sexual harassment). Quite simply, targets can identify with the term. As researchers noted in a study of women's bullying experiences, "naming experiences as bullying was important.... Identifying an external problem may have enabled them to maintain or recover a sense of their own value and competence" [212](p. 40). Indeed, the term highlights the role of the perpetuator of aggression (the bully).

Relatedly, research refers to bullied workers as targets. As one of the participants in the study reported in this chapter said, "I saw myself as a victim of verbal abuse. When [a friend]...said, 'You're not a victim, you're a target'... talk about self-esteem! Suddenly, there was this change of 'Dadgonit, I'm a target.'" In short, the terms *workplace bullying* and *target* appear to be useful to the broader public and help affected workers name and make sense of their experiences in preferred ways. In using these terms, the study follows the lead of international researchers aiming toward a common language [72].

So, what does workplace bullying look like? Adult bullying at work is perpetrated through a variety of tactics or negative acts that can be verbal, nonverbal, and physical [68]. In contrast to workplace incivility, which is defined as "low intensity deviant...behaviors [that] are characteristically rude and discourteous, displaying a lack of regard for others"[28](p. 457), workplace bullying is escalated and can include screaming, cursing, spreading vicious rumors, destroying the target's property or work product, excessive criticism, and sometimes hitting, slapping, and shoving [49]. Regardless of the aggression used, attributed intent is central to workers' judgment that they have been bullied [17, 29]. Bullied workers typically believe that abuse represents intentional efforts to harm, control, or drive them from the workplace [170].

Understanding bullying at work is crucial considering its devastation to individuals' physical and psychological health and to organizational functioning (See Chapters 2 and 16 for in-depth discussion of harms). Bullying terrorizes, humiliates, dehumanizes, and isolates targets. It draws attention and energy away from and interfere with task completion [207].

Most research that pinpoints these harms glosses over targets' emotional pain. A number of factors contribute to this. First, collecting and analyzing target stories can be emotionally exhausting and time-intensive. Second, abused people often have trouble telling their stories and making sense of what has happened to them. Indeed, many norms and beliefs discourage stories of victimization and weakness [191]. Similar to victims of domestic violence [213] and sexual harassment [214], targets can minimize abusive treatment, blame themselves, and have trouble telling stories that persuasively and succinctly convey their situation.

Nevertheless, measuring emotional experiences using things such as prevalence, causes, and effects provides only part of the picture regarding abused employees' pain. In this study, attention is turned toward what bullying *feels like*. Examining these emotional experiences clarifies what occurs between the beginning of bullying and the measurement of costs associated with it. Such an approach examines how targeted people make sense of being badgered and humiliated at work, why they react the way they do, and the devastation caused by persistent abuse. This study started with the question: What does workplace bullying feel like?

Methods

The findings in this study come from ten, in-depth interviews and two focus groups with nine and eight participants respectively, so 27 bullied workers. Participants self-identified as bullied and fit the characteristics of bullied workers. The sample is small, which is common for qualitative, interpretive research (see Chapter 1 for explanation of research-study types). The purpose of this study was to figure out the breadth and depth of emotional responses to being targeted.

Participants

Participants came to the study through a series of media releases and a link on the Workplace Bullying and Trauma Institute website (www.bullyinginstitute.org). The overall sample was similar to other studies examining bullying in professional worker cohorts [91, 215]; and sex, ethnicity, and age were similar across the focus groups and interviews. Of the 27 participants, 17 were women and 10 were men. The ethnic diversity was similar to past studies of bullying [23, 42, 216, 217]; 24 participants were White, 2 Hispanic, and 1 identified as White/African American. Average age at the time of bullying was 45.3 (range 26-72). Participants reported the following industries as the site of abuse: education (n = 7), services and sales (n = 7), local/state government (n = 6), and professional/ technical fields (n = 3), mental/medical health (n = 2), construction (n = 1), and recreation (n = 1).

The primary difference between focus group and interview participants was that 4 focus group participants were being bullied in their current job and 13 reported bullying in a past job. For those interviewed, half (5) were still in the abusive work setting. Potentially there were more interviewees currently being bullied than in the focus group because confidentiality could not be promised to focus group participants. That is, focus group participants could talk about the experience outside the study. Thus, employees bullied in their current jobs may have felt more comfortable in a one-on-one interview than in a group. Despite this current-past bullying difference, the emotional pain of the two samples was remarkably similar. Even after decades since the abuse, people still vividly recalled the painful, shattering, life-changing experience [1, 3, 218].

Data Collection Procedures

Focus groups are an effective method to explore the emotional experience of bullying for at least three reasons. First, the power of focus groups is similar to that of therapy groups. A *synergy* (see Glossary) occurs when participants hear others' experiences that stimulate memories, ideas, and experiences in themselves. This is the *group effect*– "a kind of 'chaining' or 'cascading' effect; [in which] talk links to, or tumbles out of, the topics and expressions preceding it" [219] (p. 182).

Second, bullied workers discover a shared language to describe common experiences and use a form of "native language" unique to the experience. This is especially relevant for experiences that victimize and blame the victim (e.g., domestic violence, sexual assault, workplace bullying) and experiences for which there is no agreed-upon language to label the experience.

Third, focus groups provide an opportunity for disclosure among similar others in a setting where target experiences are validated, have voice, and learn they are not alone. Given participants' lack of voice in the bullying situation, their feelings of isolation at work, and their missing emotional stories from most past research, focus groups were an effective and ethical way to study bullying-linked emotion.

I facilitated focus groups with two other professors in a university setting (i.e., a private meeting room), each of which lasted for about four hours, had two breaks and lunch, were video- and audio-recorded, and later transcribed. The focus groups included an informal environment with food and conversation. An interview guide structured the focus groups and included questions such as, "When did you first know something was wrong?"; "What did a single bullying situation look like?"; "How has this affected to you, the organization and your family?" and so forth.

Creative drawing was also used. This approach can gather important information [220, 221] but can also be healing for people experiencing trauma and pain [222]. The creative process evokes emotions and provides an outlet for expressing complex and subtle feelings that are difficult to put into words [223]. During the creative drawing exercise, participants visualized a bullying episode and focused on how they *felt* during the episode. They drew pictures that expressed the identified feelings—a scene, a face, an abstract object or design—and wrote five to ten words or phrases they felt described the drawing. After drawing, participants presented their portrayals to the other group members.

In addition to the focus groups, I conducted ten in-depth interviews to include targets that did not want to participate in the more public focus group process. Interviews were helpful because targets wanted to tell the whole story of their experiences, but focus group time constraints made telling them a bit difficult. Face-to-face interviews provided the time necessary to talk about the experiences in an uninterrupted manner from the start to the current state.

Interviews averaged over 1.5 hours, ranged from one to three hours (56 to 180 minutes), and totaled 27.5 hours of interview interaction. Interviews were loosely structured, allowing the stories to spontaneously unfold [224]. I began with a with the question, "Why don't you begin by telling me where you work, what kind work you do, and when you started noticing that things weren't quite right." Interviewees needed little prompting to talk about the experiences. I asked about coworker and supervisors reactions, how abuse affected work tasks, and for specific instances of general statements at various places in the interview.

The focus groups were professionally transcribed, resulting in 103 pages of single-spaced type-written data. Transcripts included interactive discussions as well as the creative drawing dialogue. I transcribed the interviews, which resulted in 201 single-spaced typed pages. The recordings were reviewed and transcripts corrected when necessary.

Metaphor Analysis

Bullied workers experienced intense emotional pain, but they had a difficult time summing up their suffering. Even when editing and attempting to connect participants' stories coherently, most were much too long to report in an abbreviated form (e.g., journal article, book chapter). This perhaps should not have been surprising, given that victims of tragedy and sexual harassment often face difficulty in tidily organizing their stories into clean plot lines [225]. Thus, the challenges were feasibly attending to the research questions, staying true to target accounts, and doing so in an efficient manner.

In the early transcript readings, the research team noticed that participants used colorful, expressive metaphors to describe what they said was indescribable. Looking more closely at the metaphors provided the most promising avenue for understanding how abused employees framed and made sense of the complex, confusing emotions associated with adult abuse. Past research suggests that metaphors give people with a way to "express aspects both of themselves and of situations about which they may not be ... able to express analytically ... or literally" [226] (p. 156). As such, metaphor analysis turned out to be an especially worthwhile way of understanding adult bullying, an experience that is yet in a state of *denotative hesitancy* (see Glossary) [214]. Metaphors provided a rich "way of thinking and seeing" [227] and served as "linguistic steering devices that guide both thinking and actions" [228](p. 33). Metaphors do not simply "dress up" speech, they fundamentally guide how people experience their world [229].

Past literature on metaphor and the emotional tenor, length, and complexity of participant stories suggested that metaphors could be a meaningful way to explore and understand the intense emotions associated with adult bullying. After noticing the rich metaphors and the potential for them to "unlock" the targets' emotional experiences, we approached the data analysis with the question, "What metaphors do participants use to describe the emotional experiences of bullying?"

We examined data and created several descriptive analysis tables [230] summarizing metaphor themes in participants' words and drawings. Subsequently, we used QDA software to identify and isolate metaphors from the transcribed data and categorize metaphors into three central themes in targets' experiences:

✳ Bullying feels like...

✳ The bully seems to be like ...

✳ Being a target of bullying feels like...

We examined these three metaphors in terms of how they logically "hung together," so to speak. Some presented a continuum (e.g., bullying as "game" was similar to, but less intense, than bullying as "war"), while others were topically connected (e.g., feeling like a "child," a "slave" or "chattel" expressed weakened humanity and agency).

Bullying Feels Like ...

With several exceptions, including comments such as "I was fearful, vulnerable, isolated" and "this is emotional shit," participants used few actual emotion words to describe bullying. However, their metaphorical language and creative drawings vividly told of their emotions (see Table 5.1).

Metaphors of the Bullying Process

Adults bullied at work compared the bullying process itself to a game or battle, nightmare, water torture, and dealing with a toxic substance (e.g., "being fed garbage").

Table 5.1: Bullying Feels Like ...

Themes	Examples
Game/battle	Bullies "play dirty" and "make their own rules."
Nightmare	"It's the Matrix. live in two different worlds."
Water torture	It is a "hammering away," "drum beat" or "pressure screw."
Noxious substance	"It just kind of drips on down, just festers." (The bully would) "feed us a whole line of garbage."

Game, battle. More than any other metaphor, narratives and drawings characterized bullying as a contest or battle. This metaphor continuum ranged from playing a game to outright war, including killing and death. On the less destructive end of the spectrum, targets described feeling as if bullying was a matching of wits with an opponent who played unfairly. They talked about bullying as strategic attack, defense, and a set of shifting rules. Targets said, for instance, that bullying was "playing a game," "playing their game," and "I had no rights...and they played on that." Dale, who worked in a security business, said the bully was "up to his old tricks." These metaphors of play and game suggest a less-than-serious issue that all organizational members should also be able to negotiate. However, targets saw the rules of the game as unfair and playing the game as dangerous and threatening.

Targets characterized the game as fixed, unfairly weighted in the bully's favor. They said bullies created the rules and changed rules without notice or input. Ben, an aircraft mechanic, explained that bullies made and changes the rules "behind closed doors." Dolly, a dental office administrative assistant, said that bullies "make their own rules." Stephanie, a call-center employee, recalled that the only way the bully would win was "to play dirty." Jack, the director of an online university program, said that bullying "really has to do with making up the rules as you go along."

Sadly, this metaphor of a game that is difficult to win extended to targets' seeking external help through the courts. Going to court was a gamble and "a crap shoot." Furthermore, in this "game," abused workers could see themselves as the "prey" of the hunt. Dale explained, "everybody's fair game" for bullying. Hunting, of course, can result in significant and even lethal injury.

Indeed, metaphors of beating, physical abuse, and death saturated target accounts. Wendy, an educator in a parochial school, said, "I have been maimed... I've been character assassinated." Others expressed feeling "beaten," "abused," "ripped," "broken," "scarred," and "eviscerated." The battle metaphor is perhaps most complexly illustrated in a drawing Stephanie completed. The drawing depicted a professional wrestling match in which she was a champion wrestler fighting her manager—the "heel" or "bad guy who pulls tricks." Her manager and the company's vice president were shown holding her down and taking jabs at her face. She portrayed a disloyal employee as a small dog biting at her leg and the human resources (HR) manager as a blindfolded referee. As such, Stephanie considered HR as "in on the game" and, in fact, prolonging the bullying by appearing to intervene but actually ignoring the situation. She also included two written signs: "Will her posse come to help?" and "Kill." These reflected Stephanie's feeling that coworkers (posse) refused to come to her aid and actually turned on her (kill) when it became clear that she was losing the fight. (See the original publication for actual drawing; the full citation in References).

When bullying is viewed as a fight in which the target can be "killed," "destroyed," and "annihilated," it becomes clear why targets characterized their defensive communication and other behavior in fighting terms such as, "I'm gonna stick to my guns." Whereas the bully's actions were viewed as deceitful and underhanded, many targeted employees framed fighting back as a "righteous battle" and "standing up for what's right." Diane, a children's hospital nurse, said she stayed because "I have a mission that I want to make this right. This is wrong."

In standing up for their rights, abused workers also reported feeling anger at an extreme injustice and wanting revenge. However, their efforts at fighting back often failed and reinforced the unfairly matched battle. Abby, a post-secondary school librarian, told us,

> The other librarian...[quit], but I was gonna stay and fight it out. I said, "This isn't right," so, I went to the new Dean and the new HR person. ... Not only weren't they helpful, the HR person ... helped to sabotage me. I eventually lost my job. I had been there six years.

Laura, a state employee, said, "You get so exhausted with the fight...it's not worth the time or the energy to go on [to]...make the wrong a right." Indeed, some targets became so exhausted and overwhelmed with the fight that they viewed bullying as an uncontrollable nightmare.

Nightmare. Similar to a nightmare from which one cannot awake, many participants described how their work worlds did not make sense. There was a feeling of instability and "crazy-making." Targets felt as though something "real" would happen in the organization (e.g., their supplies would disappear, they would be excluded from a crucial meeting, or the bully would scream and rage), and the bully would deny its occurrence. Lydia, an electrical sales accountant, said that it was so difficult for others to believe her that she almost did not believe herself: "It's so crazy I don't know if I can tell you all these details.... I almost thought I was going crazy. I taped one conversation just to show my husband I wasn't making it up." Similarly, Terry, employed in an education training firm, exclaimed,

She literally made me feel like I was *going crazy*! She would tell you to do things. She would tell you that she didn't say what she just said. She would write me notes. She would tell me one thing, then she would tell me something else, then she would question what I was doing.

By likening bullying to a waking nightmare, the complete lack of control targeted workers felt became starkly visible. Indeed, Wendy said that she was only able to make sense of the experience by equating it to the movie The Matrix, in which the main character lived in a fabricated world that was distinct from the real world where his oppressors lived. In comparing her experience to the hero of The Matrix, she explained,

> It [the movie] was like an epiphany.... It's the Matrix. We live in two different worlds. Two different understandings. Two different world views. For the most part, that helped but, again, you've seen my vulnerability. I need to watch the movie again. The Matrix has really helped me to understand. I'm not nuts. He doesn't think he's nuts. We're just in two different worlds.

For Wendy, framing bullying as a different alien world appeared to make her feel better about her inability to change the situation. However, many abused workers felt trapped in a torturous experience from which they could not escape.

Water torture. Many had difficulty picking out one incident, on its own, that was egregious or ultimately typified their bullying experience. Rather, they described it as "hammering away," a "drum beat," being "under the gun," and "water torture." As such, bullying often felt like a never-ending process that gradually intimidated and wore down the targets. These metaphors underscore the nature of bullying; it usually consists of numerous, seemingly non-serious negative acts that comprise a relentless pattern [32]. Moreover, the wearing down process often accounts for the emergence of power disparity between bullies [10].

On the milder end of the spectrum, respondents likened bullying to being picked on, saying, "Anything they could find to pick on, they would write it up;" "It's like...kids decide to pick on so and so;" and "do I set myself up to get picked on?" The word "picking" refers to tearing off bit by bit, like pulling meat from a bone. This metaphor illustrates how and why bullying is so difficult to identify, especially in its early stages [29]. The metaphor also summons feelings of childhood and vulnerability. Skylar, a sales consultant, described his picture by saying, "Like I tried to draw myself bigger like the Hulk. I think it's all ... it dates back to high school. My last name is Bird so everybody is like 'Big Bird' whatever, picking on me."

This juvenile "picking on" then became code for describing grown-up, relentless abuse. Bullied participants explained, "He would always come by my desk and hound me and hound me" and "It's stuff that chips away and chips away." Kristie, in a state department of labor, described the relentless nature of the attack as "gouging me about another project... she was just really gouging me, gouging me, gouging me." Many comments, like these, illustrate the use of *reduplication*—the repeating of certain words or phrases (e.g., hound me and hound me)—in which "more of the form [hound me] stands for more of content [more hounding]" [202] (p. 127, see Glossary). Thus, the use of repetitive phrases when describing the process of bullying is not accidental but indicates that targets experienced bullying as chronic, repetitive, and relentless.

For some abused workers, repetition was akin to torture. Greg, a police officer, suggested that bullying was like "pulling the wings off a fly." Brad, in a nonprofit substance abuse treatment center, described the constant criticism as, "Chinese water torture"— a means of driving a prisoner mad through the practice of dripping water on the captive's forehead. (The actual practice is traced to 16th-century Italy [231]). Targets described ongoing pressure, like a "pressure screw" and slowly ticking "time bomb." It is unlikely that workers in these environments are working to their potential or finding satisfaction at their jobs. Most likely, they are merely surviving.

A sense of inescapability marked abused workers' stories. Stephanie disturbingly portrayed how she felt when experiencing the repeated infliction of pain, inability to escape, and resulting numbness:

> You're with a serial rapist. You know, you're clinching your teeth. So, I just sat there, and I took it and then when we're done, I just got up, because I was just in a zone somewhere. I just kind of numbed myself so I wouldn't react.

Similar to a victim of torture, Stephanie felt as though her best defense was tuning out. Tuning out appeared as a common response to workplace bullying that helped targets to manage in the short-term.

Elizabeth, a school teacher, described being "like a zombie." However, becoming numb in the long-term, may serve as a barrier to overcoming bullying, an issue taken up in the Implications.

The "water torture" metaphor speaks to the difficulty targeted workers (or researchers) have in answering succinctly the question, "What is bullying?" Brad explained how he kept notes and said, "When I look over some of the stuff I'd say to myself, 'that in and of itself isn't that big of a deal.' It's when you start putting all the stuff together that you start saying, 'okay that was kind of crazy.'" Indeed, single horrific events are rare. Rather, bullying is often perpetrated through many small barbs and jabs coupled with other hostile acts.

Noxious substance. Abused employees characterized bullying as a rotten, corrupt substance they were forced to "suck up" at work and "get out" in order to heal and move forward. This metaphor characterizes bullying as a material, toxic matter that makes its way into or out of the person. As such, the noxious substance metaphor highlights how targets feel that bullying can suffocate, smother, foul, or obstruct them. Comments include, "Here I have been through two years of this shit"; "[The bully] would sit there and feed us a whole line of garbage;" and "It just kind of drips on down, just festers." These images present bullying as a form of excrement that rots over time.

Participant language characterizes bullying as a harmful substance that is forced into them against their will. They spoke of having to "take it," a metaphor that has sexually-violent undertones. Participants said, "It's just force feeding, and that's a form of abuse"; "He was being the aggressor and I'm just kind of sucking it all up like a sponge until finally I can't take it anymore"; and "You don't want to dare to let them see you cry, so you're just sitting there holding everything in and you're shaking inside." Holding in the toxic substance did not come without a price. Being fed "shit" and "garbage," understandably not only leaves, as Dale noted, "an awfully bad taste in my mouth," but also can lead to many emotional and physical illnesses. A mining equipment operator named Tim compared bullying to a malignancy, suggesting that "organizations should cut [bullies] right out and just get rid of them...because some cancers are incurable."

Abused workers describe coping with bullying as a noxious substance by "getting it out." Some reported taking years to heal from and "get over" their bullying experience. However, targets often feel constrained from letting it out until they are outside organizational boundaries. Participants spoke of trying to "let it out" through venting with family members. This process can amplify the negative effects of bullying by bringing the "shit" and "garbage" to other areas of life. When abused workers can only "empty the garbage" of bullying when they go home, it can and does negatively affect family life [37]. Only those who had left the bullying workplace spoke of trying to "close the door on" and "get over" bullying. Leaving the organization doesn't necessarily lead to instant happiness [95], but in the short-run exit might be the quickest path to regaining emotional and physical health [137].

Bullying can feel like a fight or battle, a nightmare, water torture, and a noxious substance. These metaphors serve to sum up conceptualizations of bullying as an active process apart from specific bullies. Nevertheless, they also begin to hint at the most common metaphors used to describe bullies.

The Bully Seems To Be Like …

The three central metaphors that emerged for describing the bully were "narcissistic dictator/royalty" "two-faced actor," and "evil/demon." Together, these represent a continuum that included viewing bullies as self-centered (self-)crowned heads, fraudulent bullies, and outright devil figures.

Table 5.2: The Bully Seems to Be Like …

Themes	Examples
Narcissistic dictator, royalty	"You literally have a Hitler running around down there."
Two-faced actor	Bullies put on "a good show for the boss," or they would "be real sweet one time one day, and the next day...very evil, conniving."
Evil, demons	Bullies were "evil," "devils," "witches," "demons," and "Jekyll and Hyde."

Narcissistic dictators, royalty. Abused workers discussed bullies in terms of privileged crowned heads. They said that bullies "lord" over meetings like "knights at the roundtable" and use meetings for "public floggings." Jack drew a picture in which the bully was wearing a crown and giving the thumbs down sign to a small, confused-looking man confined in a straight jacket (Jack). These images suggest that targeted workers perceive bullies as thinking of themselves as better, greater, and more important than others. Targets felt undeniably trapped and threatened by bullies they compared to evil dictators. Ted said, "You literally have a Hitler running around down there who's a mile and away from the management who can't see it."

Two-faced bullies. Targets felt frustrated in their attempts to report bullying because the perpetrators were skilled performers, who were excellent at "acting" nice when doing so would advantage them or impress organizational superiors. Lynn, a senior accountant for a defense contractor, said, "She could be real sweet one time one day, and the next day...she was very evil, conniving." Others explained that bullies could put on a "good show" for the bosses. Diane described the bully as a manager who screamed at people so close that "her spit would hit you in the face." However, in a meeting with doctors, the bully was "kissing the floor... and kissing the guy's [doctor's] feet.... It's like the Emperor has no clothes." Marilyn, a corporate IT manager, drew the bully as "Superman," because, when the bosses were around, he would come in with his cape on "to save the day." These metaphors vividly illustrate that abused workers view their oppressors as powerful (if fake), and thus feel frustrated when trying to convince others or defend themselves.

Evil demons. A bully as evil demons corresponds to the nightmare metaphors of bullying. Participants described perpetrators as "evil," "devils," "witches," and "demons." Bob, the city engineer, even referred to the bully's children as "the devil's spawn; ...they are just evil, evil children." Marla, a sale administrator for an industrial corporation, drew pictures of the bully with demon horns. Cheryl, a university secretary, drew a devil with a pitchfork and explained, "It felt like the devil was sticking the fork into me." During a particularly volatile incident, a male bully reportedly "threw his chair back and his whole face contorted, his body was contorted. It was like he was going through this epileptic seizure of some sort." Marla recounted an experience when the bully's "eyeballs looked like they were going to bulge out. His face contorted, and he starts screaming at the top of his lungs.... I mean he even flung the chair back, and he was like a demon." Evil characters from the "dark" side provide clues to targets' difficulty explaining and understanding bully behavior. Wendy likened the bully to a Jekyll/Hyde character who was extremely unpredictable and against whom she had little defense.

Characterizing bullies as deluded narcissists, evil spirits, and cunning actors means that targets view bullies and bullying as surreal, shocking, bizarre, and inexplicable. Metaphors of the bully portray aggressors who feel superior to others, possess dark powers, and convincingly shape-shift into whatever façade is necessary given the audience. Such mythic characters are impossible for mere mortals to engage with and emerge triumphant.

Being a Target of Bullying Feels Like...

Feelings of being a target of workplace bullying were explored. Abused workers feel like slaves and animals, prisoners, children, and heartbroken lovers.

Table 5.3: Being a Target of Bullying Feels Like...

Themes	Examples
Slave/animal	"You're a personal servant to the owner and his will"; "He considers you his property."
Prisoner	"I feel like I'm *doing time*." "I felt like I had a prison record."
Child	"I felt like a little girl." (It) is like having an abusive father."
Heartbroken lover	"My heart was broken." (I felt) "sad, confused, exposed, unworthy, and broken-hearted."

Slave, animals. At the more extreme end of the dehumanized spectrum, abused workers feel as though they are "a piece of property," "slaves," and "chattel." Participants explained that, "He treats you just like slaves"; "She acts like she owns me"; "You're a personal servant to the owner and his will"; and "He considers you his property 24 hours a day, seven days a week." Similarly, participants feel degraded—like insects, animals, and beasts of burden. Recall that Greg characterized bullying as "pulling the wings off of flies." Lynn explained that the bullying, "kept on an on and I felt like dirt; I felt like a dog."

Bob said he felt like "a caged animal" and Dale indicated that the bully "treats us like his personal chattel."

Targets also used mixed animal metaphors describing themselves in relation to the bully. In doing so, they characterized the bullying situation as dehumanizing. Wendy suggested that targeted workers were like llamas that had to protect each other from the wolves. Amy and her coworkers labeled an unfortunately mild-mannered newcomer as the bully's future "chew-toy." These comments paint bullies as ruthless animals and targets as defenseless prey in one-down situations—whether that is as the bully's entertainment (chew toy) or quarry. As such, these metaphors accentuate feelings of vulnerability and degradation.

Prisoner. Many reported feeling they were imprisoned in their jobs and cut off from important networks with friends and family. Abby explained, "I felt disconnected; disconnected from my job, disconnected from my life." Laura summed it up saying, "I've been blackballed." Respondents talked about "doing time"; "I feel like I'm *doing time* for the next three months"; "I felt like I had a prison record"; and "I was so tied to my job." Indeed, bullying could result in the horror of feeling forever isolated and ensnared. Abused workers said they felt "alone," "black," "empty," and "suffocated." Stephanie explained, "I had a lot of people who supported me, but when things started happening all of a sudden they backed away and denied everything."

Isolation can serve as a punishment and further complicate targets' efforts at collective resistance [137]. Isolation is also a double-edged sword. It oppresses targets by disconnecting them from others, while shielding them from continued abuse. As Bob said, "It's a trap. A caged animal trapped-type feeling. Because a lot of times you just want to hide." Targets repeatedly discussed how they would purposefully isolate themselves to try to avoid negative attention. They spoke of trying "to fly under the radar" and "not to fly too close to the sun." The next metaphor intensely illustrates this desire to hide.

Child, children. Numerous participants said they felt treated like a child. Several described feeling "scolded," "shrinking," and "small" when bullied. Terry likened her bullying boss to a "babysitter." Lynn drew a picture in which she was much smaller than the bully and explained, "I felt like a little girl and [the bully] was up higher, she was working on a stepladder. She was shouting down, 'Now, be sure to do this.'" Being treated as a child reflects the bully's dismissal of targets' adult status and, for some targets, brought back painful childhood memories. Lothar, a flight technician, explained,

> When I was kid, my old man was a little hard on me. This guy reminds me so much of my old man, it starts dragging up crap from when I was a kid and I'm sitting there going, "I've got to feel like ten years old again."

Abused workers felt righteous indignation in response. As Bob said, "I'm a forty year old man, you don't scold a forty year old man. It's just ridiculous!"

Some expressed feeling like being the unpopular kid at school, being targeted by numbers of "nameless" tormentors, and trying to avoid bullying "like when you're a kid on the schoolyard." Abby, trying to hold back her embarrassment, said, "It sounds totally silly but the two people involved would whisper. It sounds like junior high school." Feeling like a child led to mistrust and humiliation. Bob said he felt as though someone taped a "kick me" sign to his back.

Others said they felt like a child in an abusive family, saying, "I thought this woman was going to hurt me. The way I felt at the time, it was very, it pushed me into a role of being a child." The following comment from Amy vividly captures this sentiment:

> Working for Hal is like having an abusive father and all the children—when they're dressed up on Sunday afternoon and guests come visiting to the house—everything is wonderful and perfect, and we have this *deep dark* secret about the abusive father that *nobody* will tell about.

Like children in abusive families, bullied workers felt depressed and sad, explaining that they cried, experienced extreme dread, and, at times, screamed and wailed when they considered their situations. They also felt conflicted. They were angry about being treated as an incompetent and shameful that they allowed bullies to push them into a child role. They felt confused—wondering what they had done to bring bullying upon themselves.

As with abused children, many admitted having a fleeting sense of relief when the bully targeted others. Relief was coupled with guilt, however, for feeling the relief and failing to defend colleagues. Some characterized the inevitability of being targeted and thus the pointlessness of intervening on another's behalf. Dale frankly noted that when someone was bullied, "It was just your turn in the barrel." However, most still felt as if they were somehow to blame and that they *should* have done something different to prevent the abuse.

Heartbroken lovers. A number of the female participants described feeling betrayed and broken hearted by their experiences. The loss of a job they loved was paramount in their stories. Terry poignantly described how much she loved her work before the bully drove her from the job:

> What bothered me the most out of all of this, I loved my job. I could not wait to get to work in the morning, and I hated to go home at night. I loved everyday. I loved every minute. It was so enjoyable for me. I liked what I did; it made me feel good; it made me want to get up in the morning. That's really hard to find, and I just keep looking at it, and I keep thinking *why? Why* did that happen? *Why? Why* did it have to happen? *Why* was someone so *deceitful* that she wanted this to come down? I mean, I did nothing but make her look good, so *why?*

Her description echoes how one might feel about a lost love affair and reiterates the vital importance of work to identity and social relations [232]. Other women noted similar sentiments about their work stating, "I loved that job"; "I loved those people I worked with"; "I actually loved the job and everybody else there"; "I loved the company; I loved the work"; and "I enjoyed the people in that company. I enjoyed my job. I loved it." It is not surprising, then, that they also connected bullying with broken hearts and betrayal.

Three pictures, each drawn by women, prominently featured their damaged "hearts." Wendy actually ripped her paper, showing the heart torn apart and explained, "My heart was broken." Laura drew three figures, each progressively more upset and confused, the last with a large "X" scrawled through the red heart. She described her feelings as "sad, confused, exposed, unworthy, and brokenhearted." Similarly, Mandy, a school media specialist, drew a series of stick figures, each one smaller than the last, but each with a bigger, blue heart. She said, "I'm a small person with a heavy heart." The heart has long been thought to be the center of emotion. The heart "skips a beat" when we are excited and in love, and we get a pang in the heart or feel heartbroken when we're sad. This imagery illustrates how abused workers feel the weight, scarring and betrayal of abuse, and the loss of a beloved job, to their very core.

Discussion

Adults bullied at work compared the bullying process to a game or battle, a nightmare, water torture and a noxious substance. They talked about bullies as narcissistic dictators, self-appointed royalty, two-faced bullies, and evil demons. Targets likened themselves to abused children, slaves, animals, prisoners, and heartbroken lovers. Indeed, the study provides qualitative evidence provides a sad answer to the questions, "What does bullying feel like?" and "Is it really that bad?"

Implications

Metaphorical language provides linguistic shorthand to describe long, difficult-to-articulate and devastatingly painful feelings associated with workplace bullying. Metaphors are an important tool for better explicating a phenomenon such as workplace bullying that is in a state of denotative hesitancy [214]. Knowing these emotional stories is integral because "it is through such stories that we make sense of the world, of the relationship to that world, and of the relationship between ourselves and other selves" [233] (p. 249). Understanding what the bullying process feels like serves to contextualize, enrich and augment the past survey-based research that statistically links bullying and negative outcomes [234, 235].

In highlighting abused workers' metaphors about bullying, this study also uncovers the frames within which targets place themselves, providing insight not only into individuals' communicative construction of their experience, but also into their cognitive processes [236, 237]. These interpretations play a role in future interaction and point out the range of difficulties targeted workers encounter when trying to name, describe and manage their situation. In short, the metaphors analyzed graphically suggest why bullying feels so devastating and why targets believe as though there is little they can do to change their situation. These consequences were largely teased out within the previous section, but the following outlines the implications of several metaphors in detail.

First, let us consider the implications of viewing oneself as a child. Children who are abused day after day, by a parent or by mobs of other students, are likely to try to isolate themselves, try to be invisible, and if visible, be ingratiating. Doing so might decrease the abuse, but it is also likely to serve as an obstacle if targets want to increase their status in organizational settings. Certainly, "fleeing" a bully may assist small children from being hit. However, if a person consistently escapes interactions with a workplace bully, then the target may decrease his or her own options for organizational advancement. In short, the child metaphor fleshes out a sense of powerlessness in alleviating the maltreatment. Targeted workers can try to be good, try to fit in, but most often avoid abuse by escaping the situation.

Likewise, a tortured prisoner has limited options for changing or feeling better within the circumstances. Someone who is tortured or imprisoned can try to black out or become numb, both of which participants reported feeling. This lack of focus, while it may ease the torture, is likely to have problematic ramifications in the workplace. Becoming emotionally numb effectively prevents an important way of knowing the world [207, 208].

If bullying is viewed as a nightmare, complete with uncontrollable plot lines and perpetrators from the dark side, efforts to control the situation are usually perceived as fruitless. Those who view themselves in a nightmare are likely frightened and, as identified through a number of metaphors, feel as though they have little control over the circumstances or actions of their evil oppressor(s). As such, they may try to focus on the very small parts of the situation that they can control. Or, they may become withdrawn and disengaged, feeling as though there is nothing that can be done. Again, this may help the abused worker (having the nightmare) feel better, but ultimately, the most efficacious way to change the situation is probably to wake up and escape the scene.

The most common metaphor, that bullying feels like a game/battle, is perhaps the most liberating because a fighter has some control over the outcome of a battle. Soldiers can psyche themselves up to fight hard, do more damage to the bully/enemy than the bully does to them, feign an injury to save themselves from further pain and, at least, "go down swinging." Targets often report that the decision to fight back is a turning point at which they begin to feel better [147]. However, the outcome of fighting back can lead to retribution, and targeted persons can quickly become so damaged that they are non-functioning at work and at home. Many talked about fighting back, but none said they won the fight.

Furthermore, the more employees are abused, the more they resist and push back [157], which has ominous implications. As Waldron [136](p. 79) suggests from hundreds of interviews with abused employees, "the resulting desire for revenge and the potential for physical violence...is alarming." And, of course, in a workplace setting, a subordinate *fighter* can easily be labeled a *problem employee* or *troublemaker.*

Considering these metaphors helps flesh out why researchers and practitioners find that once workplace bullying has become an entrenched pattern of negative interactions, the pattern can be difficult or impossible to disrupt [3, 184]. A target's best recourse may be quitting the job and moving on. Metaphors also explain why employees feel such significant pain and despair. They feel suffocated by a toxic substance that is difficult to manage, powerless to control nightmarish evil-doers, and crazy because of two-faced performances. At the same time, they fear being trapped, and feel lonely, isolated, desperate and broken-hearted about their disconnection from important others at work.

Focusing on the subjective experiences of bullied workers spotlights the way targets themselves struggle to make sense of their abuse. This is in contrast to the rather large body of bullying literature that has focused on outlining academic definitions over what counts as workplace bullying, aggression or discrimination [90, 238]. Targeted persons' metaphorical images of bullying notably shift the focus from how researchers label workplace abuse, to how those targeted perceive and make sense of abuse and its impacts. The latter is likely a more crucial issue for attention.

Additionally, the analysis extends research on the role metaphoric analyses can play in examining employees' experiences at work, especially bullying. Past organizational research has been critiqued for its neglect of analyzing spontaneous emergent metaphors in organizational talk [239]—although communication researchers offer some important exceptions [203, 240, 241]. Indeed, previous work analyzing bullying targets' metaphors is limited because of a forced-metaphor approach. Sheenan, Barker and McCarthy [242] relied on a method that specifically asked targets to describe their bullying experiences in metaphorical terms. Although expecting rich metaphorical data, the researchers found that respondents were uncertain what metaphors were, and the data produced was "less valuable information with respect to metaphors than was expected" (p. 30).

In contrast, the current analysis was subjective and inductive, and found a wealth of organically occurring metaphors. The current study aligned with some findings in Sheenan et al.'s forced-metaphor approach. Their participants also described the bully as insincere and two-faced, characterized their own feelings as trapped and vulnerable, and described the organization as blind to the bullying situation. However, the current study provides many more examples of these feeling and additionally uncovers a number of other complex and less obvious metaphors for the bully process (e.g., bullying as noxious substance), some of which grouped together as a range (e.g., from "picking on" to "torture"). As such, the current analysis suggests that an inductive approach is especially worthwhile for making sense of messy interactive processes, such as bullying, which have no definite "face." Such an analysis serves to name and make tangible a process that can be invisible.

Practical Applications

The analysis suggests that abused workers could profit from identifying and reflecting upon the metaphors they use to frame the bullying experience. The mere recognition and identification of metaphors-in-use allows individuals to better understand how they are framing, limiting, or constraining their perspective [226]. At the same time, metaphors also can have a *generative quality* [243]—they create new meaning so can be liberating—allowing individuals to learn and see the world anew [239].

The grounded analysis uncovered outlying metaphors for making sense of bullying that are more hopeful than the primary ones explored here. For instance, Laura explained that when she thought about leaving, her colleagues said, "No, be our Rosa Parks, please stay here. Things are gonna be better." This metaphor of target as survivor or hero figure was not as common in the data. However, it suggests the possibility that targeted workers could choose to frame themselves in different ways—perhaps as survivors of a shipwreck, revolutionaries, war veterans or as the resistance. Each of these metaphors, albeit in different ways, highlights promising ways of framing and transforming the bullying experience.

In differentiation from the self-help thrust of popular press books about bullying, the current study underscores the emotional experiences of targets so that managers, colleagues, and others can "feel their pain." As such, various stakeholders may be more inclined to believe abused workers' stories and perhaps be moved to prevent or intervene. Studies that engage emotion are fundamental to motivating ethical change. Understanding the emotional pain of workplace bullying can serve as a warning device for managers and potential bullies alike, identifying the onset of problematic interactions and providing a window for early interventions.

One of the key ways to avoid the damage associated with bullying is early intervention before bullying escalates into an established pattern. Unfortunately, most bullying interventions are reactive if they occur at all. For instance, national and international health professionals have developed specialized services to treat the injuries resulting from bullying at work. Such clinics are important and needed, but workplace wellness research suggests organizational social health may be most dependent on employees' perceptions of camaraderie and communication with peers, supervisors, and family [199]. We need to proactively maintain and protect these through everyday practices.

One difficulty in early intervention is that most subordinate voice, resistance and complaints in particular, occurs in hidden conversations [244]. Explicit stories of pain and victimization are particularly likely to happen behind closed doors. Metaphors, though, are subtler. And, because metaphors express issues about which individuals may not be consciously aware, metaphorical language is likely to seep into the public and private talk of employees. In ongoing informal conversations with bullied employees, their talk is peppered with many of the metaphors we found. The picture drawing exercise was designed specifically to get at the emotional pain, but the nondirective questions in the research, such as "tell us about your bullying experience?" are not unlike those that might be posed by human resource professionals, colleagues, or family/friends. Employee emotion expressed metaphorically can provide a signal to managers for the need of organizational involvement and change. As noted by an audience member listening to a presentation of this research, "Seeing the pictures and hearing these metaphors makes me realize that I once bullied someone. I didn't think about it at the time, but I remember her looking like a frightened child." Understanding targets' metaphors can also assist organizational policymakers and human relations professionals to identify links between negative social interaction at work and the toxic effects such behavior can have on individuals.

Target metaphors not only graphically detail the pain they endure but also point to two specific types of workplace stress and illness identified by Farrell and Geist-Martin [199]. Metaphors reveal that targets experience deep *psychological pain* (they must live in a world that is unstable and crazy-making, they experience psychologi-

109

cal torture, and they are heartbroken,) and *a loss of important social networks* (they lose beloved friends when they are driven from their jobs, their work feels like a dysfunctional family, and they experience guilt over their inability to defend coworkers). This, in turn, leads to costly organizational repercussions.

Conclusion

The current study provides an important step in understanding the emotion and pain associated with workplace bullying. Whether empowering or disempowering, the metaphors pinpointed through this analysis provide targets with words to explain their situation to others—an important move considering that one of the main problems targeted employees face is that their plight is largely invisible. Similar to how the term "sexual harassment" allowed recipients of the behavior to better make sense of their situation [129], the respondents appreciated the terms "bully" and "target" in helping them to make sense of a situation for which many had previously found no words to adequately describe.

People understand their lives through the language available to them [245]. Therefore, it is important for researchers to provide venues in which abused workers can make meaning of their experience and engage in analysis practices that articulate the devastating effects of bullying. Indeed, "people make sense of their lives through the stories that are available to them and they attempt to fit their lives into the available stories" [246](p. 213). Metaphors act as mini-stories, and thus "act as a compass, which serves to orient us" [237](p. 1). Attending to the metaphors of abused workers serves to not only lay bare the feelings associated with workplace bullying, but also to diagnose current interpretations and provide cues for potential intervention and change.

CHAPTER 6

Does Age Matter? Older and Younger Employees'
Experiences of Workplace Bullying[E]

Pamela Lutgen-Sandvik

Chapter Summary: This chapter reports on a study comparing the experiences of older and younger bullied workers. I contrast bullying prevalence, perpetrators' organizational position, types of abuse, and responses to being bullied in the two groups. What I found suggests that young workers experience abuse more frequently than older workers. Both groups reported that the most common type of bullying was something that obstructed their work and the least common was physical aggression. Young workers said they were verbally abused at higher rates than older workers. Older workers more often made internal and external reports, and young workers more often quit in response to bullying. For both groups, bullies were most often managers or supervisors; however, older workers also said they experienced peer-to-peer bullying at higher rates often than young workers.

Keywords: workplace bullying, verbal aggression, employee abuse, generalized workplace harassment, organizational communication

----

Workplace bullying—the kinds of attacks and how targets repond—differ depending on target age and time in the workplace or profession (i.e., tenure) [247]. Because age and tenure affect our work experiences in so many other ways, they also affect workplace bullying dynamics.

We spend ever-increasing amounts of time at our jobs—more

111

waking hours than we spend in any other setting. As such, aggressive verbal and nonverbal communication at work has the potential to be far more detrimental than negative interactions in other environments [216, 248]. This negative effect of what happens at work happens for several reasons. First, our workplace communication is public, social and takes place on the communal stage of working relationships [136]. As such, abusive messages can be particularly stigmatizing, isolating, and shaming. Second, negative interactions at work are embedded in situations with power and status inequalities between ourselves and others that, at times, make it possible for highly placed bullying to justify their actions as part of "getting the job done" [30](p. 118).

Third, what happens at work doesn't stay at work. The quality of our work lives affects communication with our family members and friends. Quite simply, abusive treatment at work stresses our interpersonal relationships [37]. Fourth, because we have to go to work because daily attendance is usually mandatory, most of us cannot easily avoid hostile workplace communication if it is present on our jobs [216]. Finally, being able to provide for ourselves and our families are usually basic adult responsibilities [216], and work is often a central aspect of our image or identity [9, 249]. These features of working suggest that we're particularly vulnerable if faced with abuse on our jobs.

Despite a growing body of research on the subject, little of it indicates whether older and younger employees experience the same types of abuse when bullied at work. This gap is why I conducted the study reported in this chapter. As such, my findings fill a gap in current research by comparing the types of abuse and responses to abuse by younger and older US workers. For brevity in what follows, I refer to the older workers as Mature and the other younger workers as Young.

The chapter is structured in the following manner: First, I review the current research regarding four issues: prevalence of emotional abuse, bully-target position, the nature of negative acts associated with bullying, and workers' responses to abuse. At each point, I pose related research questions (RQs) or hypotheses. Second, I outline the methods I used to collect and analyze data and then report the findings for the two groups of employees.

Prevalence

US workers are far more likely to be bullied than they are to be sexually harassed [250]. I wondered as studying workplace bullying if age or tenure changed the dynamics in bullying situations since there wasn't much research about that at the time I did this study. Bullies may think younger workers are easier targets than older, seasoned workers, but current research had not explored whether or not this was the case. Thus, I posed the following RQ:

> RQ1: Are Young and Mature workers equally likely to report being bullied at work?

Abusers' Organizational Position

Another key issue is the organizational position of persons most often reported to be abusers. That is, I wondered if people with formal authority bullied others more often than people without such authority. Bullying research suggests that abusers are found in all organizational levels and can be organizational authorities, peers, and even subordinates.

Differences are apparent between national studies of bullying. In Scandinavia, peer-to-peer bullying is slightly more common than managerial bullying [251]. In the UK and North America (NA), aggressors are more often people with more formal power than targets [6, 54, 62, 94]. In UK/NA research, targets say bullies are organizational authorities in 48% [118], 67% [54], and 71% [5] of cases, depending on the study. UK/NA targets identify coworkers as abusers in 17% [5] to 31% [118] of the cases and in only 8% to 12% of the cases say bullies had less formal power than themselves ("bullying up") [118, 128].

US research points to bullies being in higher positions than targets, but worker age remains unexplored in these studies. There is some research that points to the issue of age. Comparing one study of a young student employees [54] and another study of older employees [23] suggests that both groups report higher-placed people as the chief abusers. However, younger workers seem to report top-down abuse at higher rates than older workers. In fact, older workers report higher rates of peer-to-peer and subordinate bullying than do younger workers. Based on the comparison of the two studies I posed the following hypotheses:

H1: The majority of perpetrators in both Young and Mature samples will be persons of higher rank than their targets.
H2: Young workers will report a larger proportion of higher-ranking bullies than will Mature workers.

Negative Acts Associated with Bullying

Research on adult bullying often looks at the forms of abuse that targets report. In research vernacular, these are called *negative acts*. Negative acts are limited only by bullies' imaginations and the chances that they might be discovered and punished [18, 41, 64]. Not surprisingly, bullies prefer using negative acts in a way that "disguises their identity and leaves the victim uncertain as to whether the harm was planned or deliberate" [64](p. 449). In descending order of frequency, negative acts (1) obstruct targets' ability to succeed at work tasks, (2) verbally abuse targets, (3) socially exclude and isolate targets, and (4) come in the form of physical violence against targets [64, 73, 252, 253]. As might be expected and despite sensational press stories, physical aggression is the least common form of adult bullying [64]. In fact, physical aggression is not bullying—it is *assault* and is against the law!

Despite knowing generally which negative acts occur most and least often, past research reveals little about how bullying differs between older and younger employees. Potentially, younger workers have less social and occupational capital than older workers, which could make them easier targets for blatant open abuse. To find out if negative acts differed by target age, I asked the following RQ:

RQ2: Do Young and Mature workers report similar forms of workplace abuse?

Coping and Responding to Adult Bullying

My work and the work of others confirms that targets respond to bullying in a variety of ways; they use many different strategies to cope with and resist abuse [68, 137]. In terms of frequency, target responses include (1) talking to family or friends, (2) talking with coworkers; (3) speaking to the abuser, (4) talking to other authorities; and (5) changing behavior in some way, including quitting [252, 254]. Again, past research does not look at how responses to abuse may vary based on age of the working cohort. There is a study suggesting that quitting and finding another job might be easier for young, entry-level employees than it is for older, established workers with years invested in an organization or career. The authors explain,

> Quitting a job as a fry cook at McDonalds means the person can go to another fast food place whereas quitting a job as an engineer at McDonnell-Douglas often means a longer period of unemployment.... [As such,] the experience of abuse, effects on the individual, and ways of coping are likely to be different. [54](p. 355)

I also thought it likely that having some knowledge about employees' legal protections and having access to legal resources would vary by age. Older workers may better understand legal protections and so may seek legal remedies more often than younger workers. This was conjecture on my part, however, because little was known about seeking legal help at the time I conducted this study. As such, I asked the following RQ:

> RQ3: Do Young and Mature workers respond similarly to workplace bullying?

Method

Sample

People in the study were US workers who volunteered to participate in research about workplace bullying. To compare younger and older employees, I separated the people into two groups. Younger were those 25 to 18 and Mature were those 26 and over. The Mature group included 395 people (262 females, 133 males). Respondents worked in a wide range of organizations, both public and private, spanning 17 industries. Seventy-six percent worked in the following industries: administration, health and social services, education, service sector, professional and scientific fields, finance and insurance, and public administration. They lived in 32 states, and ranged in age from 26 to 57 (average 37.9). Their positions at the time of reported abuse were: 60.8% (n=73) staff/regular employees, 20% (n=24) middle managers/line supervisors, and 11.7% (n=9) upper-managers. In nine cases, respondents did not report position.

The Young sample was 354 university undergraduates (200 fe-

115

males, 154 males) in a large US university ranging 18 to 25 years old (M 21.2, SD 1.8). Of the Young respondents, 75.7% worked in the service sector and retail sales. Their organizational positions at the time of bullying were: 83.8% (n=129) staff/regular employees, 15.6% (n=24) middle managers/line supervisors, and .6% (n=1) upper-manager.

Measures

People in the study either completed pen-and-paper surveys (young) or responded to an online questionnaire (mature) entitled The American Workplace Survey. The survey included questions about age, position at the time of abuse, and frequencies of 22 negative acts drawn from the Negative Acts Questionnaire (NAQ, see Chapter 2) [88]. I also asked if they had ever felt like they'd been bullied and by whom (bully's organizational position in relation to the target). Choices included subordinate, peer or coworker, direct supervisor, and other manager.

To determine how bullied employees in the Young and Mature groups responded to abuse, they were presented with a list of 12 common responses and asked to report how often they took each action. The response list came from research appearing in academic journal special issues about bullying and aggression at work. Responses included talking to the aggressor, slowing or increasing work output, talking with trusted others, leaving jobs voluntarily (quit) or involuntarily (fired), and so forth. Employees ranked their responses from *0-never* to *4-four or more times*. Finally, the people in the study expanded on the list by writing in other responses.

Findings

RQ1 asked, "*Are Young and Mature workers equally likely to report being bullied at work?*" A larger percentage of the Young employees reported being abused than did the Mature employees. Over 43% of the 354 Young respondents (n=154) and nearly 30% of the 395 Mature respondents (n=110) reported being bullied sometime during work histories. In addition, 39% of Young employees (n=139) and 23% of Mature employees (n=90) said they were targeted by two or more negative acts weekly or more often over the past six months.

H1 and H2 proposed, "*The majority of perpetrators in Young/ Mature samples would be persons of higher rank than their targets, but Young workers will report higher-ranking bullies at higher per-*

centages." For Young workers, 85% (131 of 154) of their perpetrators were higher ranking, 13% (20/154) were peers or coworkers, and 2% (3 of 154) were lower ranked. In the Mature sample, 60% (72 of 120) of their perpetrators were higher ranking, 28% (34 of 120) were peers or coworkers, and 12% (14 of 120) were lower ranked. Both groups most often said that bullies were higher-ranked people, but younger workers reported this position-difference at significantly higher frequencies. Thus H1 and H2 were supported.

RQ2 asked, *"Do Young and Mature workers report experiencing similar types of abuse?"* To answer this, I conducted a factor analysis, a statistical approach that groups items together based on their similarity. The process resulted in four groupings (called factors in statistical language) of similarly related hostile acts. I labeled the four factors using terms from past workplace aggression research [21, 64]. The factors were as follows: *verbal abuse*: primarily verbal or symbolic acts (e.g., belittled or put down in front of others, continued harsh criticism, insulting jokes, yelled or shouted at); *work obstruction*: acts that hindered the ability to perform jobs successfully (e.g., work overload, impossible deadlines, failing to pass on information); *social exclusion, isolation*: acts that deliberately segregated or separated targets from others in a publicly embarrassing way (e.g., deliberately excluded or left out, given little or no feedback, silent treatment, shunning or social ostracism); and *physical aggression*: acts associated with workplace violence (e.g., threats or actual physical attack, destruction of property, pushing/shoving). (In Tables 6.1.A and 6.1.B, "no" and "yes" indicate *statistically significant difference* between groups.

Work obstruction was the most common and *physical aggression* was least common for both groups. Average scores for *social exclusion, isolation* were higher for younger workers, but the difference was not statistically significant (failed to meet scientific norms for meaningful differences). Mature and Younger workers differed significantly in terms of *verbal abuse*. Younger workers' experienced more of *all forms of verbal abuse* than Mature workers. More specifically, Younger workers were subjected to insulting jokes and were harshly criticized, yelled and shouted at, and put down in front of others far more frequently than Mature workers.

117

Table 6.1.A: Sample Comparisons Abuse Factors

Abuse Type Factor	Young	Mature	Difference
Work obstruction	1.5	1.5	No
Physical aggression	0.4	0.5	No
Exclusion, isolation	1.1	0.9	No
Verbal abuse	1.5	0.7	Yes

Numbers under Young, Mature headings are the frequency at which they experienced the type of abuse, ranging from 0=never to 4=daily. "No" and "Yes" indicate whether or not there was a *statistically significant difference* between groups.

Table 6.1.B: Sample Comparisons Verbal Abuse

Frequent Types of Verbal Abuse (Weekly/ daily)	Young	Mature	Difference
Harshly criticized	47%	6%	Yes
Jokes at your expense	27%	3%	Yes
Put down in front of others	40%	12%	Yes
Yelled or screamed at	29%	10%	Yes

Numbers are the percentage of Young and Mature employees who said they experienced the type of abuse very frequently—weekly or daily. "No" and "Yes" indicate whether or not there was a *statistically significant difference* between groups.

RQ3 asked, *"Do Young and Mature workers respond similarly to being bullied?"* To answer this, I again used factor analysis to find clusters (factors) of similar responses to abuse. Factors included *making an internal report*: reporting or speaking to someone within the organization (e.g., abuser, personnel, abuser's boss, upper-management); *making an external report*: reporting or speaking to authorities outside the organization (e.g., union representative, legal professional); *seeking social support*: talking to others in order to feel better, find agreement, or develop plans of action (e.g., talking to family, friends, coworkers); and *adjusting behavior*: responses that tried to reduce bullying or to retaliate against bullies (e.g. work slowdown or

118

speed up, sabotage, defiance, leaving organization). See Table 6.2.A.

Table 6.2.A. Comparisons of Responses to Abuse

Response Cluster	Young	Mature	Difference
Support, help seeking	3.5	3.6	No
Behavior adjustment	1.3	1.5	No
Internal report	1.0	1.8	Yes
External report	.05	.5	Yes

Figures in the 2nd and 3rd columns indicate the average number of times Young and Mature employees took particular actions, ranging from 0=never to 4= four or more times. "No" and "Yes" indicate whether or not there was a *statistically significant difference* between groups.

The most frequent response for both groups was seeking social support by talking to family, friends, or coworkers. Both groups did this at about equal rates. Both groups adjusted their behavior at about equal rates, most often saying that they initially worked harder to try and prevent further abuse. In terms of differences, Mature employees reported abuse to internal and external people more often than did Young employees. Mature employees more often spoke with the abusers, talked with union representatives, and sought legal advice than did Young employees. Older workers more often sabotaged the abuser. Younger employees reported quitting, subtly defying the abuser, and working harder more often than did Mature employees. (See Table 6.2.B.)

Table 6.2.B: Comparisons of Response Factors that Differ Between Groups

Internal, External Report	Young	Mature	Difference
Talked to abuser (3 + times)	15%	34%	Yes
Talked to union rep (3 + times)	2%	10%	Yes
Talked to legal professional (1 + times)	2%	15%	Yes
Behavior Adjustment			
Sabotaged abuser (3 + times)	9%	24%	Yes
Worked harder (3 + times)	81%	36%	Yes
Quit job (at least once)	65%	26%	Yes
Subtly defied abuser (3 + times)	71%	23%	Yes

Numbers are the percentage of Young and Mature employees who said they experienced the type of abuse at the frequency in parenthesis. Yes" indicate that there was a *statistically significant difference* between groups in terms of taking the action.

Discussion

More Young workers reported being bullied at work than Mature workers. Possibly, younger workers are more sensitive and inexperienced [255], and thus feel like interactions are more abusive than older more seasoned workers do. That is, as workers get older and experience more of worklife, they may be less likely to feel as if others' actions are personally abusive; they might be more likely to see aggressive communication as a normal part of working. The difference between the groups is an indication that over time, worklife socialization brings people to agree with sayings such as, "That's why they call it work," "Capitalism depends on competition," and "Grow a thicker skin."

Findings indicate that by a wide margin supervisors and managers are the most commonly perceived perpetrators. The proportion of peer-to-peer abuse is higher in the Mature worker group. This finding is similar to a Veterans Administration study where the majority of interpersonal aggression came from peers[101]. Possibly, peer bullying increases as non-managerial employees gain experience and expertise. They might be aggressive to maintain what they perceive as their earned status, power, or influence. More seasoned workers also might have become aggressors because of being abused when they were younger workers. That is, being bullied during the onset of their worklife might contribute to becoming a bully toward their peers. Or they may develop an aggressive stance to avoid being targeted by others, a sort of self-preservation response.

Peer bullying for older workers might also be a consequence of overall upsurges of pressure as organizations become "leaner and meaner" [256, 257], pressures that younger workers probably have yet to face. Given the link between downsized organizational structures, politicized workplaces, and increased incidence of bullying [258], it may be that older, better-compensated workers are being pushed out of organizations seeking to cut costs [259, 260]. As a result, these workers may respond with increased displays of verbal and nonverbal aggression in response to perceived injustice [261].

Both groups reported covert forms of abuse most often and physical violence least often, but younger workers more often reported being the targets of cruel, humiliating, public forms of verbal abuse. Bullies might justify abuse as legitimate control to mold young, inexperienced workers, but verbal abuse and aggression reflect a serious loss of civility in workplace communication, deprecation of young organizational members, and frightening potential to mold young workers in the image of their tormentors.

High rates of young workers' verbal abuse may also be linked to abusers' perceptions of their minimal social and occupational capital. The perceived (or actual) repercussions for bullying a younger, less-valued employee may be far less. No doubt, it is riskier to bully older, established workers who have organizational knowledge, legal knowledge of worker protections, or network centrality.

In both samples, respondents frequently reported "working harder" in response to being bullied. This finding should be interpreted cautiously. There is a compelling body of research, both in the US and in international settings, suggesting that abuse and aggression reduce the productivity of not only targets but also of witnessing coworkers or bystanders [101, 252, 254]. The relationship between abuse and productivity is most likely sort of up and down, that is, employees try working harder to avoid abuse and then give up the tactic when they see that harder work does not end bullying [137] so start working less. For example, a Young respondent explained, "At first I started working harder and trying to get more done. At the end, I started working slower and getting less done. I also started being late more. I just gave up trying to please her." Similarly, a Mature respondent reported,

> Because many people in the project group reacted negatively to the bully's attitude, lies, and ineptitude, they most often circumvented the bully and relied on me to bring sense and order back. This artificially buoyed the productivity level for a short time, while I silently dealt with the initial threat, but it seems when my results waned, everyone else got fed up and disengaged too. Productivity slowed to a crawl, and I left soon after.

Potentially, abuse initially increases workers' efforts as they try to please the bully and prevent future abuse. However, when the abuse continues unabated or escalates, which is often the case, workers discard efforts to please. Despite scientific research, the belief that bullying makes employees work harder is pervasive and stubborn; popular press authors and work gurus continually make this erroneous claim [262]. (A journalist interviewing me reported later that bullying pushes people to work harder, even though I *never said this during the interview.*) Thus, aggressive organizational members may rationalize their abuse of others with "bottom-line" arguments.

Considerations

Given the criticism of using undergraduate students in scientific research, I wanted to talk a moment about the strengths and limitations of the Young sample. The specific purpose of this study was comparisons by age, but using mainly white, middle class undergraduates limits the ability to generalize research findings to other young workers. The young sample is suggestive, however, of what entry-level employees might experience and definitively presents an estimate of bullying for working undergraduates. This cohort is no less important than other worker groups; as university tuitions increase, so will the percentage of working university students who are being bullied on the job. Moreover, there are expanding ranks of temporary employees taking jobs that used to be considered the domain of working students. As such, the undergraduate sample may have even more relevance as older workers fill these jobs. If bright, college-educated young people are being abused at high rates, what might be the experience of young, poorly-educated people?

Conclusion

Research on bullying needs to take its place beside the rich tradition of theoretical and conceptual critical organizational communication studies to which it is fundamentally coupled. Critical studies uncover the ways that human interests are overshadowed by economic interests. Indeed, "research concerned with oppressive work conditions, authority relations, processes of coercion, dominant ideologies, work rules, and various other forms of manipulation and oppression must be continued" [263] (p. 151). This is changing over time, but too few communication studies explore verbally aggressive or abusive workplace environments.

Exposing the overtly abusive, aggressive, damaging forms of organizational communication that are the material manifestations of ideologies that support abusing employees is as important as any type of critical theory. There are fledgling dialogues among communication researchers regarding destructive communication in organizations, and the field has much more to offer. Currently, the predominant disciplines studying workplace bullying are psychology and business/management—fields with somewhat circumscribed perspectives. The former tends to focus on the individual, psychological subject and the latter on economic business interests. Research exploring the relationship among messages, meanings, and power explicitly questions the political discourses of individualized psychological subjects and "bottom-line" language. Specifically, critical research is fundamentally concerned with both enlightenment and empowerment. Since workplace bullying is a material manifestation of these underlying meanings, communication researchers can recognize and expose it in concert with theoretical and conceptual critical work.

CHAPTER 7

Trauma and Stigma of Being Bullied: Reconciling Crushed Beliefs and Salvaging Self-Image[F]

Pamela Lutgen-Sandvik with Lisa Farwell

Chapter Summary: This study investigated how people save face and restore their images in response to the trauma and stigma of adult bullying. The study analyzed the narratives of 20 workers who reported being bullied at work, in which they talk about persistent emotional abuse and shifting, intensifying identity work in response to abuse. The following specific questions are explored: (a) what threats to identity does workplace bullying trigger?; (b) what are the types and remedial goals of identity work?; (c) what is the processual nature of this identity work? Analysis resulted in seven inter-related types of identity work: first-and second-level stabilizing, sensemaking, reconciling, repairing, grieving and restructuring. Each of these was associated with specific identity threats and a constellation of remedial goals. Comparative analysis among self-narratives suggested that identity work occurred in three approximate phases associated with abuse onset, escalation and cessation. Findings extend understanding of intensive remedial identity work in the face of persistently traumatic and stigmatizing organizational experiences.

Keywords intensive remedial identity work; stigma; trauma; workplace bullying

----

Although identity and its relation to organizational life is widely studied in academic research, for most people, "identity only becomes an issue when it is in crisis" [264] (p. 43). When faced with workplace bullying, identity work grows progressively more intensive, acquiring a crisis-like quality. As a result, everyday identity work or face-saving can become acutely painful and shift to what researchers [265] call *intensive remedial identity work*. Notwithstanding the extraordinarily pejorative character of adult bullying, little is known about the specific identity threats it poses, how identity work seeks to remedy these threats, or the progression of such identity work.

Even though bullying and identity are not often examined in tandem, the psychological and physiological harms associated with bullying suggest that one influences the other (see Chapter 2). The range of damage is indicative of the threat to identity bullying poses. Thus, those affected likely perform intensive identity work when faced with this destabilizing experience.

Defining identity as a instinctively created narrative about one's life [249, 266], this study investigates identity work in response to persistent abuse that threatens people's identity. It frames workplace bullying as an experience constituting both trauma and stigma and expands current understandings of identity work in these situations. Specifically, the current study analyzes the narratives of 20 bullied workers, paying particular attention to their shifting, intensifying identity work in the face of ongoing identity threats. The chapter is structured in the following manner: First, it examines different perspectives of self-identity and explores the literature on identity work, trauma, and stigmatization. Second, the chapter describes the traumatic, stigmatizing character of workplace bullying. Finally, it outlines the genesis of the current study and details the guiding research questions, methods/analysis, findings, and implications.

Identity (Image) and Identity Work

In societies that emphasize achievement from paid employment, like the US, our workplace experiences have an especially significant impact on how we define ourselves and on the identities we claim [267]. The concept of identity reveals itself in the existential question, "Who am I?" Our responses to this question include not only who or what we believe ourselves to be but also our beliefs about how we should respond to others and how we should be treated by them.

For most of us, our intuition tells us that we do have some sort of an authentic self. This is a kind of grand narrative or story of ourselves that we create from our past and our past patterns of acting and reacting across various experiences and through our life histories. In sociological terms, the grand-narrative perspective assumes that our self-identity has "an intrinsic, essential content, defined by a common origin or a common structure of experience, and often, both" [268](p. 385). Yet some researchers and even mental health professionals question the assumption that we have such a fixed, organized, enduring identity. There are those, researchers in particular, who believe identity formation is more of a chaotic process, that our identities develop based on with whom and how we interact and can change accordingly. They critique the idea that people have a stable, unified, authentic identity. Rather, they view the maintenance of identity as an ongoing process "characterized by confusion and conflict, inconsistency, complexity, and ambiguity" [269](pp., 2, 5).

Other perspectives fall between the extremes of the grand narrative and chaotic process views, and it is this middle-ground approach that I take here. For example, Anthony Giddens[174, 249], a sociologist from the UK, describes self-identity as "the self as reflexively understood by the individual in terms of his or her biography." From this perspective, the process of *identity work,* is "the capacity *to keep a particular narrative going*" [249](pp. 244, 54). This perspective acknowledges the possibility of sustaining a sense of an authentic self and also acknowledges the challenges of doing so. From this perspective, the development of a preferred self is an ongoing task, but not necessarily a confused and conflicted task.

One of the challenges to this ongoing task of maintaining a particular self-narrative is that we can only do so when we personally believe it to be authentic and when it's authenticity is endorsed by important others [270-272]. In our workplace life, the important others are usually our peers and supervisors. Under normal conditions, identity work is reasonably automatic and instinctual [249] and "comparatively unselfconscious" [265](p. 626). But in the face of traumatic, stigmatizing experiences, identity work shifts dramatically. At these times, we become acutely self-conscious and identity work can be, at times, painful [273], as we try to re-create a coherent new self-story [271].

Trauma, Stigma, and Identity Work

Despite the essential nature of the workplace (and other organizations) to the personal and social identities of many of us, I found little previous research focusing on identity work in response to trauma or stigma in the workplace. For the most part, social science has focused on unexpected, serious life changes such as death, divorce, or illness diagnosis [273, 274]. Identity work in these circumstances often

126

requires substantial shifts, as people revise their personal biographies to fit within a dramatically changed set of life circumstances. When research has focused on organizations, it has addressed the extraordinary but highly visible occurrences of violence and homicide [67, 275] yet rarely has it explored identity work per se.

Likewise, research on the relationship between stigma and identity predominantly deals with life outside the workplace or organization [276, 277], while recognizing that stigma can certainly affect workplace performance and opportunities that are available to the stigmatized [278, 279]. In general, stigmatized persons may manage their identity work using strategies such as concealing their stigmatized status through "passing", or through discretion in disclosing their status to others, or through more open activism to change others' perceptions of their stigma [276, 277]. Whereas identity work following trauma focuses on readjusting to a deeply changed set of life circumstances, identity work linked to stigma focuses on image repair and escaping the negative judgments of others.

From reviewing the literature, it appeared that more work was needed to explore the connections among trauma, stigma, and organizational identity because work life is so central to our identities while, at the same time, posing various threats to maintaining them. One of the most significant challenges to preserving a coherent and stable sense of identity is the experience of workplace bullying.

Workplace bullying is profoundly traumatic as well as socially stigmatizing. It is traumatic because it is unexpected and *always* perceived as undeserved and unjustified [101]. The abuse is perceived as unwarranted because it is not included among legitimate work duties and is irrelevant to job requirements. Research with those singled out for repeated abuse shows that this shocking experience can be as traumatic as a divorce or death of a loved one [235], resulting in anxiety and psychological pain severe enough to require psychotherapy [26]. What makes this experience especially corrosive is that it is ongoing, frequent, enduring, and escalatory—typically worsening over time. The trauma is exacerbated by the intensive fear and dread bullying creates [69]. In fact, bullying (by individuals or groups) is often called *psychological terror.*

Bullying is also profoundly stigmatizing because the abuse and public humiliation buzz through the workforce and "linger in a hundred conversations as members of the original audience re-encounter one another and negotiate the meaning of the original event" (p. 71] [136]. Whereas stigma caused by a visible difference may lead an

127

individual to be "discredited," [280], persistent abuse socially defines the targeted worker as "discreditable" (p. 4). In cultures that value individual achievement, bullying triggers questions about the merit of targets themselves more frequently than it raises questions regarding the competence of the perpetrator(s) or problematic organizational features. Targets are often blamed because others think the targets must have done something to deserve mistreatment [21]. Persistent abuse also creates the impression that targets are incompetent and relatively weak or child-like, probably because it is reminiscent of schoolyard bullying. Indeed, targeted workers frequently feel shame about being bullied and about their inability to stop it. Thus, they experience self-blame, even while challenging the blaming responses of others.

In addition to blaming by witnesses, targets are stigmatized by the content of the abusive allegations themselves. Bullying demeans the targets' personal lives, beliefs, values, personalities, or physical characteristics, effectively portraying them as undesirables [21]. It can interfere with, or prevent successful job performance thus contributing to actual reductions in the targets' effectiveness [137]. When the stigmatizing directly and indirectly paints targets as incompetent, morally flawed or deviant, ostracism can result, a dynamic that further casts the target as socially undesirable. Given the range of harm, the psychological pain, and the identity threats posed by bullying, it is vital to understand how workers steer their sense of self through these treacherous waters.

Methods

The impetus for the following study was an academic journal's request for contributions to a special issue on identities in organizations. Having studied workplace bullying for years and hearing how the experience challenged and at times destroyed targets' self-perceptions, I saw the special issue as an opportunity to explore the problem of identity threat and mistreatment in the workplace. In the following, I try to present a faithful narrative of the research process as I explored this phenomenon.

Participants

I have interviewed or otherwise communicated with (email, telephone, letters, etc.) over 500 persons affected by adult bullying from the US, Canada, the UK, The Netherlands, and South Africa. Of these, most were targets; the others were coworkers, family, friends, and bullies, in that order. I chose as materials for the study, transcripts from interviews with 20 bullied workers, selecting an equal number of men and women to achieve some diversity in participant narratives. Of these, the average age was 32.4 years (range, 18 - 62). At the time of the interviews, 6 were working in, and 14 had left, the bullying environment.

Procedures

My approach was guided by the assumption that humans make sense of their experiences through the process of recounting those experiences and so I collected data through in-depth interviews. The starting point for the research was each participant's willingness and ability to articulate the experiences they had with workplace mistreatment [219]. These in-depth interviews were particularly useful for studying the complexities of how targets of workplace bullying experience identity threat and then attempt to remedy those threats.

Of the 20 interviews, 15 were via the telephone and 5 were face-to-face. For the most part, I simply asked participants to tell me about their workplace experiences, and then audio recorded them as they proceeded with little other prompting. They chose both the content of their stories and how their stories unfolded. Most participants told stories in a fairly chronological way marked by occasional backtracking to clarify certain story elements. Their choice of a chronological sequence was helpful to me in understanding how their identity work developed over time. On average, interviews lasted 2.5 hours. All interviews were transcribed and then double-checked against the original audio recordings to ensure their accuracy.

Analysis

Using a computer data analysis system called QDA (Qualitative Data Analysis), I approached the data without any preconceived ideas about how to categorize the participants' responses [281]. Rather, the first question I asked of the data was: "How do targets of bullying use identity work to maintain a coherent, personally acceptable self-story?" I should mention that the participants themselves did not use the term "identity" or "identity work"; but these social scientific terms are the labels I gave to specific aspects of their personal accounts. .

The participants' concerns with issues of personal identity were frequently revealed by the use of personal pronouns and the expression of emotions. Personal pronouns (e.g., I, I'm, my, mine, etc.) point toward the importance of the self in one's experiences. For example, phrases like "I'm usually not," or "I'm the kind of person who," are revealing of the significance of identity and identity work within the narrative. Expressions of emotions are likewise revealing because "emotions are a sign of the 'I' ... provide strong cues for the construction of identity" (p. 101] [282], and because "negative emotions stem from ... inability to convey an image that is consistent with a salient self-conception" [272](pp. 78-81). For example, phrases like, "I was outraged," or "I cried the entire vacation" pointed to identity work in response to abuse. The two categories (emotions and pronouns) often appeared together in a single individual's narrative.

All personal experiences are, in some ways unique, but I wanted to identify types of identity-related concerns that were common across different people. After identifying multiple types, I reviewed them and combined together those that seemed quite similar or appeared to be subtypes of other, more general concerns. I retained only those types of concerns that appeared to be truly distinctive. For example, I combined "I've always been a stellar employee" and "I was trained to kill people" into a larger category I termed: being treated differently than one expects based on a past professional identity.

I returned to the social scientific literature on identity and found the term "intensive remedial identity work" [265](p. 626), which seemed to capture the participants' struggles to maintain or reconstitute their identities in the face of bullying. The word "remedial" inspired the next stages of my data analysis. Since remedial means to correct or resolve, the second question I asked of the data was: "What are the threats to identity workplace bullying poses?" and the third: "How do participants attempt to remedy the threats to their identities?"

It was clear that descriptions of specific identity threats and attempts to remedy them were often found adjacent to participants' accounts of their emotional reactions and their use of personal pronouns. In light of this, I applied the "Find" feature of Word to the original transcripts. I then read the transcript sections immediately before and after the pronouns or emotional reactions. In some cases, participants directly stated the identity threat and then alluded to the identity remedy. For example, Brad said, "He [the bully] forced my hand when he accused me of slackin' off on the job.... I couldn't let it go." In this example, Brad states the stigmatizing threat to identity was

130

the accusation of sloth and suggests the remedy was to correct the original accusation to resolve the threat. But in other cases participants combined their descriptions of the identity threat with the attempts they made to remedy it. For example, Rae explained, "I was so stunned, I finally had to see a counselor to get my head wrapped around it." Here Rae states that her remedy included making sense of the trauma and stabilizing her sense of security. Her description of her remedy (i.e., identity work) also helps us understand how she perceived the threat to her identity: bullying challenged her most basic sense of feeling secure in her environment. Bullying also tested her belief in the accuracy of her perceptions and ability to anticipate the future.

The participants' responses suggested that their identity work tended to follow an unfolding process over time. I returned once again to the data with a fourth research question: "What is the process of identity work?" To explore this question, I closely re-read the transcripts to find common elements in how the "story" of the identity work unfolded. This analysis was aided by participants' tendencies to "start at the beginning" and tell their stories in a mostly chronological manner. I read each interview multiple times to identify breaking points or points at which identity work seemed to shift, be resolved, or change in nature. Noticeable breaks in the stories occurred at two points: when targets acknowledged bullying, and when the bullying ended, producing three "phases" to the process. Finally, I identified the types of identity work that were prevalent in each one of the three phases by counting the number of times specific types of work were mentioned within each phase of the narratives.

Identity Work: Phases, Types, and Remedial Goals

I labeled the three phases of abuse: pre-bullying, bullying, and post-bullying. Some types of identity work tended to occur in only one phase but others were found in two or all three phases. In what follows, I describe these three phases, the threats posed to the participants' identities during each phase, the kinds of identity work they felt they needed to resolve the threats, whether identity work was mainly in response to feelings of trauma versus feeling stigmatized, and the remedies sought for each type of threat.

Pre-bullying Phase and Identity Work

Participants characterized the abusive tactics as initially subtle, indirect and immensely difficult to describe. During the pre-bullying phase, participants felt increasingly uneasy but were unsure whether they were being targeted or were misinterpreting what was happening. Participants attempted to maintain their sense of self through two types of identity work, *stabilizing* and *sensemaking*. These tended to occur together but served somewhat different goals.

Table 7.1: Pre-Bullying Phase: Threats, Identity Work Types, and Remedial Goals

Identity Threat	Identity Work	Remedial Goals
Disturbance to psychological comfort and day-to-day predictability	*Initial Stabilizing* (Response to trauma)	✳ re-establishing sense of safety, security ✳ rebuilding comfort; reducing discomfort ✳ increasing stability
Challenging mental perceptions; crazy-making; threats to cognitive ability to accurately perceive environment	*Sensemaking*, continues in all phases (Response to stigma & trauma)	• confirming perceptions • identifying causes of abuse and remedying • validating self and value of self

Initial stabilizing. In the Pre-Bullying phase, participants attempted to address threats to their sense of comfort and predictability by initial stabilizing. They had previously taken it for granted, but the uneventful nature of their day-to-day organizational activities was easily disrupted. As Giddens [249] suggests, "the slightest glance of one person towards another, inflection of the voice, changing facial expressions, or gestures of the body might threaten it" (p. 52). Al-though they were not yet able to identify exactly what was happening, participants nonetheless reported feeling "uneasy," "weird," "nervous," and "uncomfortable."

For example, Bea started feeling uncomfortable when she first heard rumors circulating about her at work, rumors the sender denied. Her team manager, the alleged bully, reportedly praised Bea in face-to-face interactions but told others Bea had an inflated sense of herself. Bea explained, "It was hard to describe at first.... Things didn't feel right." Bea's experience was ambiguous, difficult to interpret, and could have had any number of meanings. (Who was telling her the truth?) This ambiguity made the experience difficult to "put into words." However, the experience created increasing concern that disrupted her sense of day-to-day stability.

Bea pursued the remedial goals of initial stabilizing to reduce her discomfort, increase her sense of predictability, and reclaim the relatively uneventful nature of her day-to-day worklife. For example, Bea stopped telling her manager when she received praise from others. That is, she attempted to stabilize the situation by making small modifications in how she presented herself to this threatening team manager. Indeed, such selective disclosure is a common stigma-management strategy for members of marginalized groups [276, 277, 280].

Table 7.2: Bullying Phase: Threats, Identity Work Types, and Remedial Goals

Identity Threat	Identity Work	Remedial Goals
Targets' response to abuse dissonant w/ identity and experience of being abused dissonant w/ past identity	*Reconciling* (Response to stigma & trauma)	• reducing conflict about being someone but acting differently • highlighting preferred identity and past success • neutralizing, countering accusations • fortifying, reiterating preferred identity
Image seriously damaged by being targeted, others (upper-management) believe bully, blame target for being abused, minimize or disbelieve target	*Repairing*, also in post-bullying (Response to stigma)	• convincing others of one's value and truthfulness • moving others to action based on one's own value to organization • overcoming, reducing shame/stigma •
Image seriously damaged by being targeted, others (upper-management) believe bully, blame target for being abused, minimize or disbelieve target	*Repairing*, also in post-bullying (Response to stigma)	• convincing others to treat one according to valued identity • impugning bullies' (characters, personalities)

Table 7.2: Continued

Identity Threat	Identity Work	Remedial Goals
Disrupting, on a deep level, one's basic sense of security, including shaking/destroying important values and beliefs about the world in which one lives	*Second-level Stabilizing,* Also in Post-bullying (Response to trauma)	• recovering from trauma, shock, surprise • coming to grips with unfair world • recreating/regaining sense of equilibrium • rebuilding self-narrative to include converted beliefs

Reconciling. In the Bullying Phase, participants experienced a mismatch between their personal identities and being targeted for abuse, or between their identities and their reactions to that abuse. On reflecting upon their reactions, participants often perceived them as foreign to their real selves. These perceptions of inauthenticity triggered attempts to reconcile the mismatch. For example, Kay explained,

> I heard [the bully's] footsteps to the upstairs door, and I *ran* to my computer with my heart thumping. I remember thinking, "I am a highly educated, respected professional woman, and I am *running* to my desk like a child. *What is wrong here?*" I was physically sick at the thought that I'd be *caught* looking out a window.

The terror she experienced conflicted with Kay's perception of herself as a "highly educated, respected professional woman." As a result, she attempted to reconcile being an educated professional with reacting like a scared child. Many others reported fear-dread emotions and the challenges such emotions posed for their senses of self. Participants were deeply uncomfortable discovering that others could arouse such fear—even terror—and had believed, before the experience, that this would not have been possible.

Participants' previous beliefs about themselves, including being valued, successful, or powerful and in control, were also threatened by the abuse. For example, Kim noted, "I've had exemplary evaluations from all my other supervisors, ... until [the bully] came in. ... After that, I couldn't do anything right." Ben, on the other hand, had served in the US military's special forces during the Viet Nam conflict where he said he was "trained to kill people." As such, he reported being a person others "shouldn't fuck with." The mismatch between his previously valued (and lethal) identity and current evidence of his devalued (and victim) identity demanded some type of reconciliation.

Reconciling was intended to achieve the goal of reducing the discrepancy between the bullying/responses to the bullying and participants' identities, as well as helping them regain a sense of stability. In interviews, individuals recounted bullies' accusations about them. To "prove" the inaccuracy of these charges, they repeatedly told me of their past successes. For example, Mack noted, "I had a number of successful careers in risk management and insurance before coming to this company." Others defied the demeaning accusations by highlighting certain aspects of their biographies. Ben claimed, "If I can jump out of the sky ... for the government, I'm damned well not going to be abused by some foreman." Ben's self-identity centered on maintaining power/control; his repeatedly summoned "soldier" narrative was evidence of this identity. Despite this show of strength, Ben reported seeking psychotherapy, suggesting that "stigmatized persons sometimes vacillate between cowering and bravado" [280] (p. 18).

Repairing. Participants experienced a significant identity threat as a result of damage to their professional reputations. Their diminishing sense of their social selves occurred through many, often innocuous negative interactions that together comprised a pattern of humiliation and degradation. Each negative act, whether passive or active, called into question their competence, commitment, honesty and even social desirability. Ann explained that the bully started "this tag team attack to underhandedly get rid of me." Others reported being screamed and sworn at, ignored in meetings, having doors slammed in their faces, and other nonverbal forms of demeaning behavior (e.g., rolling eyes, refusing eye contact, glaring).

In many cases, others avoided targets, allegedly out of fear of becoming tainted by association or because they were acting as the perpetrators' "henchmen." As a result, participants also experienced the pain of social ostracism. Ben described the following after defending an abused coworker:

The people who all joined in the beating and the mobbing were

136

considered friends of the foreman [alleged bully] so now [a targeted coworker] was isolated with a couple of us other pariahs, so to speak, and we had to stand on the other side of the garage by ourselves. ... We were treated like sub-humans, like we weren't even there.

Sadly, avoiding the stigmatized is a typical social response due to "the tendency for a stigma to spread from the stigmatized individual to his close connections" [280](p. 30).

Despite feeling impassioned to repair their threatened identities, participants also described acute shame. Researchers have noted that "Shame bears directly on self-identity because it is essentially anxiety about the adequacy of the narrative by means of which the individual sustains a coherent biography" [249](p. 65). Shame was linked both to being targeted and to being unable to stop the abuse. Participants reportedly "began to doubt" or "second-guess" themselves, and to "wonder if there's something really wrong with me." Indeed, stigmatized persons at times begin to believe their detrbullies and "agree that [they] do indeed fall short of what [they] really ought to be" [280](p. 7). Especially shaming was when participants failed to alter important others' perceptions and they were then fired or driven from jobs.

The goals of repairing were distinctively social. Targets focused on altering others' perceptions of the situation by convincing them of the reality of the target's pain, of their truthfulness or value to the organization as well as by discrediting the bullies themselves. Numerous accounts revealed a need for listeners to believe the participants' stories. Initially, many found that others doubted their claims, but "serial bullying"—when bullies attacked others—apparently decreased disbelief as well as reduced the shame participants experienced. Brad echoed a frequently cited reaction to the abuse of others and the guilt felt regarding that reaction:

As bad as it sounds, ... I was glad when [a coworker] was cornered. Then at least I knew it wasn't me, ... After that, [coworkers] would come to me and say, "Man, you were right, we should have believed you."

As the bullies targeted more people, disbelief among peers dissolved, yet decision makers remained reluctant to intervene. Participants typically said that upper-managers doubted them, believed the bully, minimized their claims, or blamed them for being abused. A few reported that with peer support, upper-management finally took action. Ann explained, "I had to convince the owner this was bogus.... I was saved by having a few friends at work that believed and supported me." Ann's comment points to the social nature of identity and resistance to bullying; both need support and validation from important others.

Participants also attempted to repair by discrediting perpetrators [265] (p. 634). I am discussing the discrediting of bullies under the heading of *repairing*, but I should point out that participants interjected derogatory labels throughout our interviews. Good-versus-evil story lines cast bullies as malevolent demons and organizational authorities as those duped by evil bullies. Labels for bullies included "evil," "crazy," "power-hungry," "insane," "lunatic," "narcissist" "Type-A," "control freaks," "devil," and "demon," to name only a few. Targeted workers attempted to repair their identities with derogatory labels that implied, if there is something defective about my attacker, then I am all right.

Second-level stabilizing. Participants attempted second-level stabilizing when confidence in their assumptions about themselves and their social worlds was profoundly disrupted. This was accompanied by damage to or destruction of core values and beliefs. Commonly reported lost beliefs included believing (a) people would, in most cases, do the right thing; (b) hard work would be rewarded; (c) employing organizations would protect employees from abuse; (d) bullies would be punished or removed for aggressive behavior; and (e) targets could effectively stop abuse. By the time participants had been bullied for many months and fully recognized additional episodes of abuse, what seemed, in the pre-bullying phase, as a slight disruption to security, was now felt as an existential crisis.

Ongoing bullying continued to destabilize the targeted, and over time, many reported being unable to rebound fully between attacks. Bill noted, "I'd no sooner start to get over one of [the bully's] rampages, and she'd go off on me again." Ted explained, "It was brutal... I was coming home almost in tears.... I couldn't believe it had happened." Bea too recounted, "I was so hurt and surprised, that it got to the point that I just could hardly breathe. I just couldn't believe this could happen at work." Bill, Ted, Bea, and others told stories of lost resiliency, lost beliefs, and downward spirals, all of which made maintaining a sense of identity even more taxing and less effective. Thus, workplace bullying disrupted participants' predictable workplace routines, derailed their habitual activities and normal self-definitions and

138

gutted the self- and social beliefs through which they had constructed their personal identities.

The goal of second-level stabilizing was dealing with trauma: regaining a sense of balance, coming to grips with injustice, and rebuilding a personal biography to include a set of altered beliefs. For example, Mary explained that after she "recovered from the shock ... [that] no one was going to do anything about it [abuse], I changed the way I work." She went on to say, "I *never* work overtime anymore.... I used to be an A+ employee, and ... now I just do enough to stay under the radar ... C- mostly." Since organizational authorities failed to intervene despite multiple reports, Mary's reduction in effort helped restore a sense balance and reciprocity between her and the organization. Mary's second-level stabilizing was centrally concerned with self-identity, as illustrated when she asked me, "What kind of person just lets others walk all over them and keeps taking it?" On the other hand, her reduction of effort created an identity tension; Mary had to sacrifice her highly-valued "A+ employee" identity to "even the score." Others also claimed that they would never again commit as deeply to or sacrifice as much for an employing organization.

Post-bullying and Identity Work

Post-bullying identity work occurred after participants or bullies had left the workgroup or organization, either voluntarily or involuntarily. (The target or bully may have to exit the organization to reach post-bullying stage.) Targeted workers described two interrelated types of identity work in this phase, *grieving* and *restructuring*. More than in any other phase, post-bullying identity work was concerned with integrating one's damaged self-identity and weaving the experience into one's personal biography. In the absence of continued abuse, targets began a more enduring healing process, but they vividly recalled the painful humiliation decades later.

Table 7.3: Post-Bullying Phase: Threats, Identity Work Types, and Remedial Goals

Identity Threat	Identity Work	Remedial Goals
Loss of valued position, career, identity as professional and "good worker," Long-term loss of belief in justice, fairness, personal power, etc.	Grieving, also in late bullying phase (Response to trauma)	• working through/processing the loss • accepting the loss • incorporating loss into self-story
How to permanently merge the experience into restructured life story and self-perceptions	Restructuring (Response to stigma)	• recreating valued self-identity • rebuilding work-related identity aspects • learning or transforming from experience • reaffirming specific aspects of identity • converting evil to good • healing from trauma, "putting oneself back together again"

Grieving. Post-bullying, participants faced challenges to their identities including perceived loss of professional reputations, organizational identities, self-confidence, and core beliefs in justice or fairness. Ted explained the loss of his reputation by saying: "It's a small community, and [the bully] just character-assassinated me... It's going to be hard to find another job now." Rae described her loss of organizational identification; "I believed in the company. I believed the company ... was a good company to work for ... like you can really accomplish something in your life. That has just been ripped away from me, and it really hurts." Kim described a loss of self-confidence: "I just don't know if I have the stuff anymore, ... the stuff it takes to do this kind of work."

Participants also grieved over lost beliefs about the world in which they lived and their relationship to it. Unmistakably, participants had expected worklife to be just, for people to be honest, and for hard work to be rewarded. With these fundamental expectations shattered, participants were unable to "keep a particular narrative going" [249](p. 54). For example, Mack recounted, "I just felt like someone ... tore a part of me away." Ken said, "My anger is related to what this has taken from me. It's as though in order to go outside of my personal space, I need to suit up with a toxic shield." Targeted workers were forced to formulate new—often jaded and distrustful—beliefs about the work world, the people in it, and their future in this threatening place.

The remedial goals of grieving included processing and accepting loss and including the revised beliefs into self-stories. Participants described how they handled losses and came to some form of resolution. Dan said, "I had to process it, you know? Work through ... what had happened and somehow learn to live with it." Repairing such damage to identity may even call for therapeutic help, and such was the case for twelve of my participants [265].

It was during post-bullying grieving that participants most often talked about their identities in other aspects of their lives—particularly home and family. Rae claimed, "my husband has been an anchor. He helped me let go of it and ... see there's lots more to me than just my job. I'd lost sight of that during all this." Grieving meant rebuilding an essential self and a life story that incorporated the bullying experience; this often included drawing more on nonwork domains to construct a post-bullying identity.

Restructuring. As sociologist Paul DuGay [267] aptly notes, "as a fundamental human category, work is represented not only as livelihood, but also as a stable, consistent source of self-identity" (p. 9). Supporting Du Gay's observations, participants reported that their post-bullying challenges included merging this profoundly negative experience into a restructured life story. For example, Rae echoed a common feeling when she said, "I wasn't sure I was anything without my job, and ... it took a long, long time to look at myself in a positive way after it [being bullied and leaving the job] happened." Successful restructuring took months and, for some, even years.

For participants, the goal of restructuring was to recreate a self-story that they could "live with." Such identity work included redefining the experience as an impetus for learning or an opportunity for moral transformation, that is, for converting "evil to good." Stories also included accounts of becoming "smarter" or "stronger" because of the experience. For example, Brad explained, "It was worse than going through my divorce, but, like that [experience], I came out smarter on the other end." Months after the interview, Deb sent an email saying the bully had been fired and claiming, "Complaining and standing up and saying 'no' has given me opportunities to grow stronger!! (more than I really wanted!). Today I can honestly say I am happy I stood up, because the greatest growth came with self respect." As sociologist, Irving Goffman, argues, stigmatized people "may see the trials [they] have suffered as a blessing in disguise, because of what suffering can teach them about life and people" (p. 11)[280]. This theme was present, but only in the post-bullying phase.

For a few, bullying redirected their life "mission" or "purpose." In these cases, abuse was integrated into new self-stories of their personal campaigns against bullying. Deb explained, "Now that I know something about this stuff, it's my responsibility to help other nurses that are being abused at work and think it's their fault." Surviving workplace bullying then developed into a moral imperative that drove new identities and rendered suffering valuable.

Failed restructuring. Some efforts at restructuring failed. Two participants explained that the trauma completely fractured their lives: beliefs in themselves, family relationships, and fundamental notions of who they were in relation to the external world. For Kim and Greg, self-identity was splintered to a degree that felt irreparable. Even months after the situation ended, Kim blamed herself for allowing others to abuse her, finding it even more unbelievable in retrospect. She continually reflected back on when her self-identity included being a "good worker." Kim explained, "My work made me feel good about myself .... I just can't come to grips with it. How could it happen? Why'd it have to happen?" The contradictory threads of her lived history simply could not be woven back together. She went on to say, "I've just been ripped open by this experience." Both Kim and Greg reported being so shattered that they were unable to rebuild a stable self-identity (at least at the time of the interview). Both had been away from the bullying environment over 12 months. Their experiences illustrate the devastating potential of workplace bullying that goes unchecked followed by a failure to recreate a new self-story.

Discussion

This study contributed to the scientific literature on identity and increased our understanding of "intensive remedial identity work" by exploring the types of remedies participants chose and the goals they pursued as they attempted to repair a sense of self damaged by workplace bullying. This study also expanded upon existing bullying research by exploring how its traumatic and stigmatizing nature impacts the personal identities of those who are targeted.

Intensive Remedial Identity Work

Three themes emerge from participants' stories. First, the unique characteristics of work life demand that this type of identity work be described as intensive. Our work lives fulfill both our basic human needs (e.g., clothing, shelter), and also satisfy higher-level needs (e.g., self-actualization, social status). When confronted with threats to such a broad range of needs our responses tend to be passionate ones. Moreover, our work lives are public, collective experiences. Unlike unpleasant experiences at home, mistreatment at work is often a matter of common knowledge, since others witness or hear about negative, shaming, or punishing episodes. Furthermore, work is generally mandatory. Most of us *have* to work to earn a living, so if we are targeted we cannot easily avoid abusive work interactions.

Second, this kind of identity work is consciously directed toward the goal of remedying the effects of bullying experiences. Workers feel compelled to justify themselves and their behavior in the face of accusations, threats, and/or social ostracism. The goals of identity work are to reinforce positive, coherent self-beliefs, to repair and restore one's image, to counter messages that one "does not belong" and to stabilize beliefs about oneself in relation to the world. Unlike everyday, unselfconscious identity work, this type of identity work mindfully seeks to improve significant others' perceptions as well as self-perceptions.

Finally, social science often describes identity construction as "work" or "struggle," but identity work in response to trauma or stigma requires far more effort than identity work under normally challenging conditions. It takes substantial exertion; persons engaged in this process spend an inordinate amount of time on the three interrelated tasks of making sense of the situation, defending themselves and managing their identities. Given the effort required, the physiological effects targets report (e.g., exhaustion, insomnia) are not surprising.

Trauma and Stigma in Organizational Settings

Because working adults spend the majority of their waking hours in organizations, understanding trauma/stigma and identity work in these settings is essential. Except for particular occupations (e.g., hospitals, police), workers rarely anticipate being devastated by workplace experiences. Nor, when embarking on a job, do employees expect to be singled out for ridicule and degradation. However, the idea that organizations can be abusive, alienating, hurtful places is not new [280: 11], despite the fact that bullying comes as a considerable shock to those targeted. Indeed, globalized capitalism likely contributes to trauma/stigma in organizations. Capitalist economics typically value profit/efficiency over human concerns [283] and thus promote workplaces marked by "alienation, degradation, powerlessness, ... abuse and aggression" [284](p. 170).

What this study reveals is that identity work in response to workplace shock or degradation is quite similar to identity work that takes place after trauma or stigmatization outside organizations. In such cases, targets are also forced to restructure identities within a strange, threatening landscape[273]. Targeted workers grieve the loss of their jobs and reputations in the same way others grieve losing good health, loved ones, or marriages [273, 285-288]. They persistently recollect pre-trauma/stigma times in their lives [249, 286, 289] and employ "progressive narratives" [271](p. 166) to convert bad to good. Like other stigmatized persons, targets reject tainted identities, develop moral imperatives that drive social activism, help others, and raise awareness [276, 290]. Targets also struggle with self-blame while fighting the stigmatizing actions of others [280].

Addressing the Tension Between Concepts of Identity

Identity work, whether within or outside organizational settings, underscores the human drive for stability, balance, and predictability. The experience of fragmentation, disconnection, and insecurity [273, 285] creates psychological pain—pain clearly evident in bullied workers' self-stories. Our identity work is considered successful only to the degree that it maintains a consistently perceived self with which we are relatively comfortable. Despite the challenges, human bullies strive for and often achieve a stable self-identity despite attacks on

144

their cherished beliefs, affronts to their personal dignity, increasing lifestyle options, diminishing traditional authorities, and rapid social change through the experience and practice of identity work—saving and repairing face.

Methodological Implications

The current study moves us toward a better understanding of identity work in workplace settings. Yet like any single project, the results must be viewed in light of the limitations of the research approach used. Two of these are my use of in-depth interviews and stage-models. Interviews do not render objective "truths," but they do provide a window for understanding experiences from the perspective of other persons. I cannot objectively know whether participants were bullied; I know only that participants *believed* they were bullied. However, the perception of bullying was sufficient, since the issue at hand was participants' attempts at identity work in response to their perceptions of threat. Moreover, infusing my interactions with the participants was a sense that they wanted information, empathy, and, even more than these, *to be believed.* As result, the interviews provided many examples of how targets managed their identities as competent, truthful individuals as they described their experiences to another human being.

Stage models, like interviews, also have strengths and weaknesses. Applying stage models to human behavior carries with it the risk of glossing over differences and suggesting an unrealistic, orderly progression from one stage to the next ignoring the complexity of actual experiences. On the other hand, participant stories did indicate breaking points that suggested the presence of stages. The movement from a slight perception of "something wrong" to clear recognition of being targeted marked a noteworthy shift in identity work. Similarly, the end of bullying was the beginning of re-storying the post-trauma self. As such, the stage model helped to organize and represent a complex, "messy," long-term experience, though certainly with some loss of detail.

Future Research

This project suggests a number of fruitful areas for future research on identity work. Comparing and/or contrasting men and women's identity work in the face of workplace bullying, trauma, or stigma are important avenues for future research. Whether men's or women's identity work differs in these situations has received little attention. Moreover, identity work likely differs across national cultures. This study specifically looked at the experiences of US workers, and research might explore the similarities/differences in identity work among different national cultures. Finally, identity research suggests that people constitute life narratives by incorporating a variety of lifestyle sectors, in particular work and nonwork domains [272]. This study also suggests that crisis in the worklife domain negatively effects the family domain, reducing the family sector's usefulness for identity work. Further examination is needed to explore the impact of crisis in one identity domain on other domains of identity and what this "contagion" might mean for the reflexive project of the self.

Conclusion

Workplace bullying triggers intensive remedial identity work, especially in individualistic cultures where even respect and dignity are considered things one must earn [291]. For persons who strongly identify with their jobs or professions, the experience can be devastating. This study explains, in part, why bullying is so damaging: it rends asunder targeted workers' life narratives. Self-narratives are, in a sense, anchors that ground human bullies in a world that is in constant flux. When this narrative is deeply disrupted, persons lose their moorings and feel adrift.

CHAPTER 8

Toxic Organizing: How and Why Workplaces Become Toxic ^G

Pamela Lutgen-Sandvik & Virginia McDermott

Chapter Summary: Given the range of destruction linked to persistent employee abuse, understanding how employee-abusive organizations (toxic organizations) come into being, persist, and can change is vital. Looking at system-wide dynamics is essential to understanding the complexity of toxic organizations. This chapter explores how toxic organizations come into being though a various types of functional communication. Specifically, it builds upon a communication-function typology (see Glossary) and creates an extended model for explaining how toxic organizations develop and how they can change. We use a case study to illustrate the model, the relationships among communication types or functions, and the impact of worker resistance.

Keywords: workplace bullying, harassment, mobbing, organizational communication, emotional abuse

---

In toxic organizations, workers experience persistent emotional abuse and hostile communication they believe is unfair, unjust, and unwarranted. As a result of ongoing hostility, workers experience fear and dread and suffer from job insecurity [2]. Communication and teamwork break down as employees become guarded, suspicious, and hypervigilant (see Glossary) [126]. Indeed, some argue that persistent employee abuse is "a more crippling and devastating problem for employee and employers than all other work-related stresses put together" [29](p.13). Such hostile environments are extremely costly for organizations and their stakeholders [292].

   Given the range of destruction created by persistent employee abuse, understanding how toxic organizations come into being and

147

persist is vital. This chapter explores how toxic organizations come into being, persist, and change via different kinds of organizational communication. We give examples of abusive communication to illustrate how organizations are shaped by cross-currents among communication types. The use of case study illustrates the model and the relationships among communication types. The case also shows how change can occur because of worker resistance.

The chapter is structured as follows: First, we present a definition of toxic organizations and describe a case study of a social-service agency. Second, the chapter explains how the case study illustrates abusive behavior and the development of a toxic organization. Third, we give examples of messages in each type of communication, specifically messages that create hostile workplaces. We hope to show how different kinds of communication can combine to bring about the undesirable, unintended consequence: toxics workplaces.

Defining Toxic Employee-Abusive Organizations

For understanding the ideas in this chapter, we use the term *organization* to indicate entire organizations, especially when they are centrally located and have a relatively small workforce. We also use the term to mean divisions or departments of larger institutions or organizations. Thus, we would more likely identify one university department as an "organization" constituted by employee-abusive communication, than claim that one department's communication comprises a toxic university. Additionally, we use the term *organization* as a noun (i.e., something taking an action) to make it easier to talk about ideas, but we means organizational *members* or representatives.

We use *employee-abusive organization* and *toxic organization* to mean the same thing: hostile work environments in which employees experience persistent harassment and fear because of the offensive, intimidating, or oppressive atmosphere. In toxic organizations, workers are subjected to persistent abuse. Abuse can include obstructing work, verbal abuse, social ostracism, persistent criticism, and, although rarely, physical aggression. Abuse can occur in a variety of situations and target multiple employees.

Aggressive, highly escalated conflicts between two organizational members, absent persistent harassment or abuse of multiple people, do not make an organization toxic. Additionally, one-time interactions, regardless of how disturbing, do not make an organization toxic. If, however, many workers are bullied or mistreated (people typically leave because of constant abuse), if aggression is a persistent feature of work relationships, and if more than one type of communication is abusive, then the organization is likely toxic. The following section presents a case study of such an organization.

Case Study: A Toxic Organization

To illustrate the communication-type explanation for toxic organizations, we organize the model around examples from a case study of a nonprofit social service organization (CWC). The case shows the organization's process into, through, and out of an 8-year period in which it was toxic. (Pam worked with a board of directors to conduct an investigation into the increasingly hostile work environment. The investigation culminated in replacing the agency director and revamping of the communication and feedback systems.) The case is neither unique nor rare; many organizations have experienced similarly toxic patterns [9, 18, 59, 102, 293].

CWC is a small, rural, nonprofit agency providing social services to clients. Initially, five local people founded the organization to provide needed community services. They incorporated as a nonprofit, and during the first five years. Community donations and volunteers supported CWC services. The founders then lobbied to create state funding by working with similar-mission organizations statewide to strengthen efforts. Securing state funding required CWC to develop policies and procedures that met state regulations for social service organizations.

The initial structure was a simple hierarchy with one program; the director ran the program and hired and supervised a small staff. The director worked with a board of directors to craft policies, balance the budget, and otherwise manage the organization. Over time programs were added. As the number of programs increased, the director's position shifted to an overall agency administrator and direct supervisor of program managers. Toxic dynamics emerged in the agency's 11th year when the first director resigned for personal reasons. The board found it difficult to replace the director because they were constrained by limited grant funds and were offering a relatively small salary. After a search with very few applicants and without staff feedback, they hired Ken. Ken was a long-term employee in one of the agency's programs. Ken had no managerial experience but was willing to work for the small salary and appeared committed to the mission.

Traditionally, the board had communicated exclusively with the director rather than communicating with lower-level employees. This communication pattern continued with Ken. Unbeknownst to the board, Ken actually prohibited employees from attending board meetings unless they were specifically invited to give reports. As such, the board had no way to speak to or hear from staff. The board discovered much later that problems were brewing when disgruntled employees appealed to the board about decisions to fire employees or brought other issues to the boards' attention. In fact, the board learned later than Ken had had numerous problems with coworkers before the board hired him as the new director.

Initially, employee abuse appeared somewhat sporadically but escalated in frequency and intensity over time. Ken convinced the board that new policies were needed to deal with "problem employees," instituting policies to make firing workers easier. He found various reasons to fire employees who grieved or appealed his decisions to the board, typically quite soon after the grievance. I found no record of the board overturning any of the personnel decisions that employees appealed or grieved. Turnover and grievances to the board increases so the board sent Ken to managerial training. Staff members said that Ken often established even more punitive policies and practices after the mandatory training sessions, and board meeting documentation (minutes) substantiated this pattern. For example, the board extended the new-employee probationary period from three to nine months, after Ken went to a training entitled "How to Legally Fire Employees."

CWC's climate became more and more hostile as time passed. In response to the toxic environment, program managers tried to hire what they thought would be "thick-skinned" employees. They also tried to inoculate new employees, preparing them for the hostile environment by including hidden warnings in employment interviews. Personnel files indicated that job interview scripts started including questions such as, "Tell me about a time when you had to deal with a controlling manager. How did you handle that situation?" and "Have you ever worked with a manager you had trouble getting along with? How did you handle it?"

The records of interviews with staff turned up a strange sort of early-warning system for new hires. When new employees came in, veteran employees told them stories of Ken standing over fired employees as they cleaned out their desks, publicly yelling at employees, and humiliating employees in front of clients and coworkers. The stories included various warnings about what to avoid doing or saying so the new person could "stay out of trouble." Current and past abused workers and bystanders who witnessed their coworkers being abused told people outside CWC about Ken's reign of terror. Eventually, word spread through the small community and CWC had trouble attracting high-quality employees.

As CWC's reputation declined, state funders sent an auditor to review the program. Staff members were so terrified of retribution from Ken that they withheld information from the state auditor. Ken also "gifted" an outspoken employee with a "a few (paid) days off" to relax. Coworkers believed he did this as a strategic move to keep the outspoken person away from the auditor.

Firings, staff complaints, and employee abuse increased over the next seven years, with short reprieves after board warnings to the director. The board came to see that they needed to remove Ken, but they were fearful of him filing a wrongful termination lawsuit. They may have had this fear in part because at board meetings, Ken often reported the organizations' precarious legal position regarding employee lawsuits—information he apparently gained from board-mandated management trainings. Additionally, CWC's attorney stressed the legal liability and warned of the legal dangers in firing Ken.

Eventually, a group of middle-managers clandestinely approached a board member and strenuously protested ongoing abuse. Many were prepared to find other jobs if Ken was not removed. At the board's request, each of them prepared documentation to be used in case of a lawsuit. The board asked Ken to resign after a protracted, seven-month process in which the resisting workers were terrified of discovery and losing their jobs. To ward off Ken's lawsuit, the board offered him a substantial payment to voluntarily resign, which Ken accepted. The payment emptied the organization's reserve fund. (Word of the payment ran through the grapevine, further demoralizing employees who saw the payment as a reward for Ken's "reign of terror," as one employee said.)

After Ken's firing, the board increased the director's salary and hired a new director with staff input. To open communication channels with staff, the board established a staff liaison position that attended monthly board meetings and spoke regularly with the board president. Staff chose this liaison independent of the director. The board and new director developed a 360-degree employee evaluation system, including confidential subordinate evaluations of supervisors.

Over the following year, CWC slowly regained some of its formerly positive reputation in the community. The agency once again started to attract job applicants, including hiring back some of the previously mistreated employees. We revisit the case throughout the chapter to explain how communication created the toxic culture over time. The case also illustrates how messages in one communication type affect communication in other types, often in unintended unrecognized ways.

Interpretation of Case Study

Instead of simply highlighting how Ken's interpersonal communication with his employees was abusive, the case study illustrates how various messages worked together to create a toxic organization. As the case study shows, a toxic organization develops over time and a number of things contribute to its development. On the surface it may seem as if Ken was the cause of the toxic organization. He was the most visible part because of the pain he caused, so was the easiest to blame. Ken certainly did carry part of the blame, no question, but he was only one of many causes.

Other causes of the organization becoming toxic were less visible but nonetheless to blame—poor funding, limited access to resources, few staffing options, a remote location, a laissez faire (hand's off) board, and a staff that repeatedly talked about abuse and magnified abuse. The case helps us consider the various types of communication in organizations and how communication in one functional area affects what happens in other functional areas. *Functional area* means that certain types of communication *do particular things,* they function in particular ways. The next section explains the communication types by function or purpose and how these communication types can create toxic organizations.

Functional Message Types

The idea that different types of communication have different functions is relatively simple. Stretching that idea to say that functional message types create organizations is a different way of thinking about organizations. Communication "produces and reproduces shared meaning" [294](p. 125) among organizational members and provides the starting point for understanding how communication creates or constitutes toxic organizations. Thinking of organizations as a cumulative result of communication—written, spoken, embedded in values and beliefs—shifts our perspective from blaming one person. Rather, such a view helps us to recognize the other forces that contribute to how hostile workplaces are formed and transformed [295]. The shift in view broadens our ideas about employee abuse, allowing focus to move away from looking only at one-on-one communication to looking more broadly at the forces that appear to support employee abuse. This perspective also brings out into the open the social-communal and historical/cultural beliefs and norms that drive much of what we say at work and about working.

Specifically, our functional communication model of toxic organizations builds on an existing idea from Bob McPhee, a communication professor at Arizona State University, and Pamela Zaug, one of his graduate students. Their original model identified four functional message types that constitute organizations. Each functional type carries out a particular task (function) for the organization so the organization can meet its goals and fulfill its mission. Each type is directed toward a specific audience, some inside and others outside the organization, and includes content that is particular to the specific audience [296]. Each functional type and the messages common to that type are described in what follows.

Organizational Self-Structuring

Organizational self-structuring includes the formal communication that functions to establish the organization legally. Content in this type of communication determines how member time will be used, directs the development and allocation of money and other resources, and organizes the formal lines of communication [297]. Typical messages in this type are official organizing documents—bylaws, contracts, budgets, organizational charts, etc.—and any interactions or conversations that draw legitimacy from these formal documents. This communication creates, maintains, and reinforces the concentration of control in an organization [298]. The chain of command is an example of organizational self-structuring, an organizing document that defines who is supposed to talk to whom and who is supposed to have the power in these interactions.

Membership Negotiation

Membership negotiation "establishes and maintains or transforms its relationships with each of its members" [298](p. 8). This type of communication includes recruiting new members, socializing incoming and established workers, and encouraging employees to identify with the organization. Membership negotiation includes the formal and informal interactions among employees that socialize new members and the impressions of the organization communicated to people likely to become organizational members. In the case of toxic organizations, membership negotiation can include *negative anticipatory socialization*. (See Glossary)

Activity Coordination

Activity coordination communication organizes and fine-tunes employees' work activities. Policies and procedures (i.e., formal texts and documents) "can never be complete or completely relevant, are never completely understood, and are frequently amended in an information patchwork of adjustments" [298](p. 14). Messages in activity coordination include conversations that modify work practices, solve immediate problems, and deal with exceptions and unexpected issues. Handling an absent employee's workload is one example of activity coordination. Social interaction and task-related interactions are part of activity coordination. The social–emotional dimensions of work either provide the lubricant that keeps tasks progressing efficiently or create negatively-charged interactions and relationships that freeze up efforts to work together [299].

Institutional Positioning with Other Institutions

Institutional positioning establishes acceptance or a niche within a community of other organizations and institutions. Branding through advertising is an example of institutional positioning communication. These messages are "mostly external communication to gain recognition and inclusion in the web of social transactions" [296](p. 588). Institutional positioning creates or negotiates the organization's legitimacy or uniqueness, establishes acceptability, and communicates agreement with local social norms and demands. This type of communication includes legitimate interactions (e.g., public relations) and non-sanctioned interactions (e.g., employee talk to friends, family).

Extensions Key to Toxic Organizations

The original classification that we extend in this chapter didn't sufficiently account for the cultural and historical meanings, values, beliefs,

154

and norms that inform how we communicate in organizations. However, these cultural-historical norms guide nearly all human communication and point to "how the global affects the local" [300](p. 10).

Even *institutional positioning* that looks at organization-to-organization and organization-to-external audience communication falls short of uncovering the beliefs that we take for granted [301]. Our beliefs about organizational life can feel so natural and normal that we don't even notice or question them. Because so many of our deep-seated beliefs about work and working support employee abuse, we think it's crucial to bring some of these things out in the open. We do so by adding a type of communication to the original model that accounts for these deep meanings. We label this type of communication *Discourses*. Discourses are "general and enduring systems of thought" that drive much of what we say and do [300](p. 7). (See Glossary for *discourse* and *Discourse* definitions)

Discourses (Social-Historical Norms, Values, Beliefs, Ideologies)

Discourses include the durable social and cultural beliefs, norms, meanings, and ideologies that inform how people communicate in organizations. Many of these beliefs are so strong that they seem to be indisputable. That is, some beliefs, such as communicating along the chain of command, seem so permanent and obvious that people rarely question their correctness. Discourses have a sense of permanence, but beliefs and values are really part of an ever-evolving, changing, social amalgam of meanings. Discourses change over time but do so slowly.

Discourses are the meanings, values, and beliefs that drive communication and behavior at work. Beliefs within Discourses tell us what we know, how we know it, and who has the expertise to speak about our shared truths [175]. For example, we place considerable weight on what managerial consultants tell us about how things should work in organizations. Belief in expertise is common in many modern organizations. Our values and beliefs at any given time form a cluster of unwritten rules about (a) what can be talked about, (b) who is allowed to speak, (c) how they are supposed to speak, and (d) what form of speech is accepted as knowledge or truth.

Organizational members rarely recognize how Discourses drive behavior. But deep-seated beliefs and values create unwritten rules that are so deeply socialized into us that we follow the rules without questioning them. We all have ideas about what's right at work, what should and should not be said at work, how people should interact at work, and so forth. What is amazing is that we share so many of these beliefs, even though we may not talk about them.

In this type of communication, rather than specific message types, there are deep-seated meanings, beliefs, and values. For continuity, we call the various beliefs in Discourses *messages* as we do for the other types of communication. What we mean by the term *messages* in terms of Discourses are the deeply rooted beliefs and ideologies that people have in a particular culture at a particular time. Because we rarely recognize the Discourses that drive our behavior, this part of understanding toxic organizations means we have to uncover the beliefs and bring them out into the open. Once in the open, we can make informed decisions about whether or not we still wish to follow the beliefs or practices.

Constituting Employee-Abusive Organizations Through Communication Types

Each communication type has the potential to contribute to constructive or destructive workplaces. What follows describes the types of messages likely to occur in toxic organizations. Each type is different, but there are extensive cross currents. What becomes apparent by exploring the case study is that different types of communication affect each other, and messages in any give communication-type overlap into and transform other types of communication.

That is, communication used for one function can merge with, shape, and influence communication for other functions (usually in unseen, unintended ways). Moreover, communication both *sends* information that reflects particular beliefs about worklife and *reproduces* beliefs about workplace interactions. The following outlines the messages in each communication type that provide a cross-section of indicators, precursors, and factors contributing to toxic organizations.

Employee-Abusive Organizational Self-Structuring

Although self-structuring message types (e.g., policies, budgets, formal documents) and communication guided by formal documents and texts rarely celebrate employee abuse, they can legitimate the use of power without addressing power abuse. Formal documents lay out the respective rights of employer and employee, usually favoring the former or its managers [191]. Two examples of self-structuring messages

156

that have the potential to contribute to employee-abuse are anti-employee policies and laissez faire upper-management.

Anti-employee policies. Personnel policy manuals and handbooks create the tone of the working relationship between employees and the organization. In and of themselves, policies are not employee-abusive, but they can contribute to legitimated abuse and escalated fear of employment loss [258]. Moreover, adversarial policies generate antagonistic employer-employee relations, particularly when those policies increase employment insecurity. Three such policies are progressive discipline, at-will employment, and top-down employment evaluations.

Discipline policies outline the steps managers take to punish undesirable behavior and chart a course for desired performance [140, 302, 303]. Even though progressive discipline is supposed to give employees due process and "assist in the positive development of the employee" [304](p. 10), managers can as easily use the policy to fabricate an impression of due process while really building a case for firing the employee [140].

In contrast, *at-will employment* policies literally strip away employee due process by stating that employers and employees can terminate employment at any time with or without cause or notice—a policy that clearly favors employers [139]. At-will policies generate fear and economic insecurity and increase pressure and stress, uncertainty, and perceived powerlessness [15]. Additionally, such policies can produce aggressive workplace climates where some workers terrorize and undermine others to establish dominance.

Formal evaluations, usually conducted on a yearly basis, also have the potential for being abused, especially when the only perspective in the evaluation is the evaluating supervisor's. The language and form of formal employee evaluations can easily be subverted and distorted in order to fire or punish "undesirable" workers [30, 124]. Since supervisors create the documenting language, they create the formal record of "what happened" [7]. Employee responses can be included in formal records but, in practice, have little or no impact [305].

Relatedly, many supervisors hate the evaluation process, especially when they have to give negative feedback [306]. Reluctance to complete evaluations is exacerbated when supervisors must evaluate abusive, aggressive employees. In these cases, supervisors may tend to "grossly inflate performance appraisals ... rather than giving honest,

157

constructive criticism.... Inflated appraisals may reflect supervisors' fears of reprisal because the behaviors of the would-be avenger may be as intimidating to his supervisor as they are to his colleagues and subordinates. Though the employee's performance may be substandard, the potential avenger might even be recommended for promotion or lateral opportunities in an attempt by the current supervisor to rid himself or herself of a problem employee" [113](p. 210).

An unintended consequence of positive evaluations used to get rid of aggressive employees is that positive evaluations (and promotion to get rid of someone) indirectly reward aggression. Then aggression becomes even more difficult to confront. Furthermore, when positive evaluations and resulting promotions or raises inadvertently congratulate aggression, other organizational members may begin modeling that behavior. Simply put, rewarded behavior becomes repeated behavior.

Laissez faire managerial oversight. Upper-management's "hands-off" philosophy in terms of supervisor oversight can also contribute to environments where employee abuse is ignored and encouraged [307]. Abdicating upper-managers' responsibility to protect employees from supervisor's bullying can occur because management is physically removed, reluctant to interfere and break the chain of command, or unskilled in dealing with aggression [18].

In some cases, upper-managers are socially involved with aggressors (friends, lovers, family) so allow aggressors free rein. When the people whom employees believe represent the organization, fail to intervene or when interventions fail to stop abuse, employees can feel re-victimized. Even worse, upper-managers can blame the abused employee, side with the abuser, or frame the issue as a personal matter (i.e., a personality conflict) [68]—all of which put targeted workers in even more disadvantaged positions.

Employees conclude that the organization does not care about or want to hear about their abuse, and, by association, that employees are of little value [68, 308]. This conclusion contributes to further degradation of working environments because when employees believe the organization does not value them, loyalty, productivity, positive moods, and performance deteriorate [101]. Absent or ineffective upper-management oversight and failure to end abuse are key symbolic features of hostile work environments. What is more, upper-managers' refusal to intervene or to entertain circumvention (going over the bully's head) closes off employees' legitimate avenues for problem resolution.

Employee-Abusive Membership Negotiation

Membership negotiation includes messages that attract (or repel) potential members, assimilate new members, and provide ongoing socialization for current members. These include formal intended messages and informal unintended messages. Messages in this communication type that contribute to toxic organizations include pre-hiring interactions such as hostile interviews, implicit warnings, and negative anticipatory socialization. Post-hiring messages include socialization into aggressive cultures, warnings, and horror stories.

Hostile interviews. In the hostile interview, the "interviewer seems to delight in constantly evaluating the interviewee, often with belittling and embarrassing comments or questions and subtle nonverbal signals" (p. 261] [309]. Such tactics can reflect the current workplace climate but they also contribute to reproducing that climate. Hostile interviews may be used to weed out persons interviewers see as too weak to handle the pressure or toughen up those preparing to enter the organization [310].

Implicit warnings. Recruitment and interviews may also include cautions that communicate and recreate the workplace's abusive climate. A recent recruiting advertisement warned, "The environment is fast-paced, high-pressured, and sometimes unpredictable." Of course, this does not conclusively point to an abusive workplace, but the job announcement forewarns applicants and encourages the "weak-hearted" to self-select out. Indeed, such ads legitimize high-pressure working environments. Subsequent employee complaints can be muted with "We told you," effectively silencing vital warning signals.

Implicit warnings can also be embedded in employment interviews and include asking if interviewees how they would deal with close supervision, difficult supervisors, or aggressive organizational members [310]. Workers often recognize these implicit early warnings retrospectively, after they have been in the hostile environment a while [137]. Both recruitment and interview warnings convey "previews of coming attractions," but more than simply reporting or warning, they legitimize and reproduce the hostile environment they ostensibly present.

Negative anticipatory socialization. Membership negotiation is most often intended to draw in and assimilate workers [311, 312], but messages in this communication type can also repel potential members. This dynamic is *negative anticipatory socialization.* Al-though not explicitly described in the original model, negative anticipatory socialization is an unintended message type unique to toxic organizations. Organizations—where persistent abuse drives away talented employees and organizational authorities fail to intervene—begin repelling potential recruits, because past and current workers openly discuss their negative experiences with others inside and outside the organization.

Socialization into aggressive cultures. Once recruits become employees, the adaptation to and indoctrination into the abusive environment begin in earnest. In hostile workplaces, new members gradually adapt to aggressive workgroup norms [258], and bullying and abuse may become institutionalized and passed on as tradition [313]. Workers who cannot adjust often leave [137]. When norms accentuate toughness and "survival of the fittest," workers may even support or participate in bullying weaker members, or at the very least, ignore [25] or naturalize it [191]. In particular, if the top ranks abuse subordinates, aggression will likely flow downward and perpetrate the bullying norm [82, 314, 315].

Warnings and horror stories. The interdependent, social nature of work ensures that worker conversations will spread and amplify occurrences of workplace humiliation, punishments, and ostracism [136]. When there is a history of employee abuse, cautionary messages abound for newly hired persons [134]. Warnings can be direct by instructing new workers what to do or avoid doing, or indirect by recounting the others' painful experiences. These admonitions communicate the risk of siding with targeted coworkers or getting on the "bad side" of aggressors.

Extreme horror stories, a special kind of warning, are grapevine tales of abuse and humiliation that are told and retold in work groups [104]. Warnings and horror stories are both the outcome of past abusive interactions and the material from which future interactions are organized. They *perpetuate* the abusive environment by both silencing potential resistance and presenting employee abuse as a taken-for-granted feature of organizational life.

Employee-Abusive Activity Coordination

This communication type, in which workers interact with peers and supervisors to carry out tasks and to manage workplace relationships, includes message types that workers perceive as most directly abusive. By a wide margin, most research related to hostile workplaces focuses on this type of communication. Affected workers rarely recognize how institutional positioning, self-organizing, or Discourses contribute to abusive environments. But they experience hostility in activity coordination first-hand: screaming, sarcastic jokes [10], social ostracism [83], ignored requests, failure to pass on important information [110], and so forth.

The bulk of abusive interactions in this communication type are supervisor-to-supervisee [3, 5], but peer-to-peer communication can be abusive [101, 316]. The persistent nature of abusive messages builds an environment of fear, dread, and hyper-vigilance [7]. Additionally, when many people are aggressive, hostile, and disrespectful, others are likely to follow suit due to the contagious feature of human emotions [186, 317].

Abusive supervision. A common theme in hostile workplaces is abuse of power and "emotional tyranny ... of the weak by the powerful" [136](p. 65). Abusive supervision conflates cruelty and mistreatment with legitimate managing yet can be easily explained as part of directing subordinates' work [30]. Abusive supervisors also appear to pass on their aggressive style to others [71]. When supervisors are abusive, over time, workers subjected to those supervisors may also become abusive [79]. Messages typifying abusive supervision include, but are not limited to, excessive criticism, anger and profanity, unreasonable or impossible work delegation, backstabbing, breaches of confidentiality, and discounting or contempt [68].

Personal criticism of this type has little or nothing to do with the subordinate's job performance and includes attacks on appearance, family, and personal interests or values [21, 68]. Excessive work criticism, often combined with micro-management and surveillance, is the " 'hammering away,' a 'drum beat,' being 'under the gun,' and ... 'water torture'" described by targeted workers [2](p. 163). Anger and profanity commonly mark these exchanges. In addition, job goals conflict, unexpectedly shift, or are moving targets—all of which destabilize already beleaguered workers.

Backstabbing, or talking derogatorily about someone to others, usually while appearing friendly to the targeted person, is also a communicative dynamic of toxic organizations [7]. Workers report hearing aggressors say one thing in the presence of targeted workers (praise) and another in their absence (denigration) [68]. Abusers also disclose confidential information with the targeted workers' colleagues, usually in a manner that stigmatizes, demoralizes, or isolates those targeted [3, 318].

Discounting, contemptuous messages, usually communicated nonverbally or through non-action, disregard workers' presence and needs or concerns [2]. Abusers may snort or roll eyes at comments, ignore the target when he or she speaks, or avert their eyes when passing targets in the hall, [7, 68]. Since reciprocity is a key feature of human interaction, these acts can ripple through the organization in waves of retaliation, revenge, and cycles of aggression [25].

Abusive coworker communication. Coworker communication also contributes to toxic organizations and includes many of the same hostile messages as abusive supervision (excluding work delegation), and is more likely in organizations where supervisor-supervisee abuse is widespread [314]. In addition to anger, profanity, backstabbing, breach of confidences, and disconfirmation, four other abusive peer-to-peer messages constitute hostile workplaces: inappropriate authority, sabotage, silent assent, and henchmen [39, 319, 320].

Using inappropriate power in abusive ways brandishes what targeted workers perceive as illegitimate authority. This serves to establish bullying coworkers' dominance over targeted workers and is more likely when workers feel powerless and are competitively pitted against each other [215]. Coworker sabotage involves destroying targets' work, spreading gossip about targets, derogating coworkers' ideas and projects, or taking credit for targets' work, all of which also contribute to toxic organizations [15].

Silent assent [319] and coworkers as henchmen [39] are also widespread in toxic organizations. Both emerge as responses to the pervasive fear in hostile environments. Fear pushes coworkers to stand by mutely, a response most likely for self-preservation rather than an intentional act to harm others [7]. Targeted workers interpret their coworkers' silence as assent, agreement that abuse is acceptable.

Coworkers can also be directly complicit henchmen. Similar to school yard bullying, these members participate indirectly in bullying but rarely take the initiative. They side with the aggressor most likely out of a desire for safety in a high-risk environment. Both issues make

162

employee abuse difficult to expose and eliminate. Silence and henchmen increase fear, make it difficult to gather concerted voices against abuse, and intensify the difficulty of exposing aggressors.

Employee-Abusive Institutional Positioning

Interactions among or between organizations and with the public are the messages in this communication type. There are various ideas about what should happen at work and in organizational life, but toxic organizations adopt and reproduce beliefs that rationalize worker abuse and oppression. Typically, institutional positioning contributes to creating toxic organizations in such indirect ways that organizational employees and authorities may not even recognize how abuse became a feature of the organization. Three dynamics in this communication type linked to hostile work environments are legal environments, market pressures, and institutional isomorphism.

Legal environment. The legal environment in which organizations situate themselves constitutes the organization in specific ways. For example, countries with lower rates of workplace bullying (e.g., Scandinavia) more often have legal protection against such practices [87]. In the US, there is no such legal protection for workers, but there is statutory protection for worker groups who have historically experiences discrimination [112]. Thus, legal discourse is an important factor that constitutes organizations in different ways.

Market pressures. Restructuring (e.g., downsizing) often results in increased work hours and pressure to bring work home [259, 260]. A potential consequence is that hostile environments are marked by incivility and aggressive communication [15, 81]. If the perceived instrumental power of bullying increases in high-pressure environments, managers can intimidate and harass workers to deal with competitive, increasingly demanding work situations. This contributes to "boiler room" environments primed for even more abuse including peer-to-peer bullying [314, 321]. Stress and frustration can trigger the search for scapegoats to relieve tension. Beleaguered workers may protest, usually resulting in retaliation from already-overwhelmed supervisors.

Institutional isomorphism (organizations "copy-catting"). Organizations often imitate other organizational models [322], even with no proof of these models' success [323], and "consulting organizations and benchmarking practices ... encourage the imitation and spread of [an assortment of] management ideas" [324](p. 370). Organizations that are copied can also have different ethical perspectives. Those embracing values of capitalism and individualism model different beliefs about employees and organizational responsibility than do organizations positing public responsibility [325] or servant leadership [326]. Organizations with "competitive, self-reliant, 'survival of the fittest' attitudes" [325](p. 444) place the responsibility for individual success or failure squarely upon the individual. When other organizations appear successful or chic, other organizations can try to establish a presence via imitation. Unfortunately, in cultures where individualism, meritocracy, and aggression are admired and rewarded, competitive, self-reliant, survival of the fittest organizations will predominate.

Discourses

Employee-abusive organizations reflect overarching Discourses that drive employee abuse. Many of the beliefs in contemporary workplaces come from economic theory, religious and secularized ideals of work, the merger of corporate interests and governing bodies, and ideological beliefs such as rugged individualism, meritocracy, and employees as entrepreneurs.

The Discourses that contribute to and support hostile work environments are complex and often difficult to recognize. Because these messages constitute workplaces in often unrecognized ways, they also go unquestioned or considered normal [191]. Recognizing the values and beliefs that support employee abuse is challenging because Discourses can limit what people think and say [327]. We usually take for granted many of the assumptions about appropriate behavior at work.

Given the contextual, cultural character of ideological beliefs, the issues outlined here are more applicable to Western cultures such at the US with capitalistic economies. They may be less applicable to communal, egalitarian societies with socialistic economies. The following presents a few of the unseen, but powerful Discourses contributing to employee abuse: work and religion, individualism, meritocracy, reverence for hierarchical power, and workers as lazy.

Work and religion. As with many ideologies, beliefs about work

164

are rooted in historical religious teachings. For example, John Calvin suggested that God chose certain people as the "elect," suggesting that success and wealth were blessings from God. These blessings were external evidence of internal goodness and righteousness. Business practices often reflect this Calvinist value (usually non-consciously) but also insinuate the opposite. That is, external difficulties seem to be evidence of someone's internal "badness." Thus, if workers are persistently targeted for abuse at work, we might believe they deserve abuse. (See Just World Hypothesis in Glossary)

Individualism. Individualistic explanations for worker abuse are common in US organizations [137]. Blaming-the-victim explanations successfully transmute the issue from an organizational to an individual problem. This subjectification of workplace experiences serves a compelling political purpose by mitigating organizational responsibility for worker harm [191]. Given the ideology of individualism, bullying can be easily classified as a personal rather than an organizational problem.

What is more, bullies and targets can be shrugged off as simply having pathological personalities. As such, aggression is not an issue for which organizations are responsible. The problem becomes the responsibility of individual employees. Indeed, when abused workers complain to upper-management, they are often told not to take it so personally, or the bullying is framed as a personality conflict [68].

Meritocracy. Relatedly, belief in meritocracy works against systemic diagnoses of hostile work environments. Meritocracy is a system in which advancement is based on individual achievement or ability rather than wealth, class, or birth [328]. The reasoning follows that if workers are bullied, they probably deserve it or, at least, should be able to stop it. For organizational members faced with abuse, meritocracy coupled with Calvinist ideology and individualism underscore an overpowering tendency to blame the victim [197, 329].

Reverence for position-power. Embedded in values about work and achievement are revered tenets of classical and scientific management, especially those related to positional power. Despite the emergence of participatory management and servant leadership, hierarchical structures are still dominant [298]. Contemporary organizational bullies behave toward hierarchical structures and their designated lines of communication as sacrosanct, so rarely question things like

165

managerial privilege [195], even by abused workers [137].

Relatedly, we have a near adoration of highly-placed, ambitious, promotion-oriented employees, coupled with reverence of position power [267]. Reverence for top-level organizational members constitutes organizations in specific ways, often by allowing a few organizational bullies astonishing leeway, including the right to harass and threaten workers with impunity [330]. Hierarchy veneration culminates in environments that silence subordinate workers, overemphasize supervisory voice, obstruct upper-management involvement, and tolerate abuse as part of positional privilege. Furthermore, if someone is highly productive, whether or not they have a high position, ums often overlook that person's aggression [18]. Bottom-line thinking overshadows concern about their abusive performances.

Profit as ultimate goal. When organizations' sole or paramount goal is a drive for increased profit, human bullies are easily treated like objects or detriments. The notion that organizations have social responsibility beyond the drive to higher profits has met both mild [331] and severe criticism [332]. Indeed vociferous advocates for profit as businesses' only social responsibility claim that any organizational responsibility beyond simple profit is "preaching pure and unadulterated socialism" [332](p. 2).

In socialist economic systems, this argument has little power. However, in the US (and other nations emulating the US economic model), particularly after the Red Scare that Senator Joe McCarthy's hearings evoked, at a time when socialism was synonymous with communism, labeling an activity as "socialist" easily predicted its failure. Such arguments are still salient in silencing voices and perspectives claiming that organizations have broader responsibilities. Despite an ideology that organizations are and should be profit-driven, "profitability as the primary measure of economic success is often a highly distorted economic indicator" [333](p. 15).

Regardless of the distortion, profit remains, for many organizations and their members, a primary consideration. In such environments, concern for humans is easily disregarded or framed as a danger to the organization's bottom-line. Indeed, many of the beforementioned belief systems work with a drive-to-profit mentality to minimize or render invisible the abuse workers suffer under the drive for profit. (We believe it important to remind readers that workplace bullying *never* improves profit. Rather, when workplace bullying is present organizations *hemorrhage* resources!)

166

Workers as lazy. Another belief supporting abuse is that subordinate workers need micro-management, surveillance, and constant prodding. Despite the overwhelming scientific evidence that increased pressure and aggression decrease employee productivity [308], some organizations still use terror tactics to drive human resources.

Using such tactics operates on the belief "that workers are most productive when subjected to the goad of fear or harassment" [30](p. 145). Captured in the Theory X of management [334], this argument proposes that workers are basically lazy and need constant managerial pressure and oversight in order to get them to work. An offshoot of this squeeze-the-workers approach to human resource management is blaming targeted workers for being abused. The unspoken accusation is, "If you were doing your job, this wouldn't be happening to you."

In these and many many other ways, beliefs about working create workplaces where employees are harassed and bullied. These meaning schemas along with other functional communication types contribute to employee-abusive organizations. The next section revisits the case study and examines the cross-currents among communication types.

Communication Types in the Case Study

As we respond and interact, we create the organizational cultures that we work in each day. It is usually only when looking back during "retrospective sensemaking, ... [that we] can know what we were doing" (p. 24). We are able to see how everything fits together only after it has all occurred [335]. But make no mistake, our communication does create the cultures in which we work. An organization does not simply appear already formed, and a toxic organization does not simply develop because one person bullies another.

The case study demonstrates how one organization with formally positive employee relations became a toxic organization as various communication types changed. CWC did not become employee-abusive simply because Ken abused employees; becoming a toxic organization involved the implicit consent of the board and the recreation of abuse in employees' stories. Over time, the stories changed outsiders' perspectives and sensitized newcomers to potential abuse.

Further, the case demonstrates how an organization can shift back from toxic to a more positive climate. After the abusive director was removed, policies were changed, communication avenues between staff and board were opened, and checks were put in place to

167

monitor potential abuses of power, CWC's culture shifted toward more constructive organizing.

Organizational Self-Structuring

CWC developed a number of organization-versus-employee policies, used a one-way evaluation system, and maintained a board that, for years was reluctant to intervene in director-employee relations despite high turnover and many, many employee complaints. When the board members finally tried to correct the problems, they did so by sending Ken to management skills training classes.

A review of Ken's personnel file suggested that a number of trainings stressed the legal threats to organizations posed by employees. Board meeting minutes indicated that, by and large, anti-employee policies appeared soon after managerial training—usually within a 3-month window. The board's reliance on external technical expertise had at least one unintended consequence: policies aggravating already antagonistic supervisor-subordinate relations.

Board members attended training that frequently instructed a "hands-off" stance regarding day-to-day organizational operations. CWC also subscribed to the monthly *Corporate Board Member Magazine*; many articles warned of the dangers associated with board interference in management. The board members experienced a double bind: feeling restrained from interfering but ethically pressed to do so. At CWC, laissez faire oversight was rooted in beliefs and practices regarding the role of the board in relationship to management.

Member Negotiation

At CWC, job candidate screening eventually included hostile interview questions and subtle warnings. New member socialization more often than not included horror stories of the departed—employees Ken had singled out to terrorize and humiliate. The hostile environment created by repeated incidents of abuse and grapevine rehashing of those events drove out high-quality staff.

Employees in the oldest program said hiring teams often eliminated really sensitive job candidates because they worried these people would be "crushed" by Ken's aggression. The organization's reputation also served as negative anticipatory socialization, and CWC began having problems attracting qualified employees. Moreover, staff members candidly admitted warning others away from work at the

168

agency.

Activity Coordination

Nowhere is the pain and suffering of abused CWC workers more prevalent than in employees' stories of daily work interactions. Abusive supervision was the most common and recognizable message type, and many said they remained silent out of fear when Ken bullied other.

Some explained their silence as self-protection, but they often experienced considerable guilt for the choice. They understood that Ken had formal power, and experiences underscored the board's support for his use of that power. Few believed fighting back was a viable choice and so either distanced themselves from Ken or left CWC rather than speaking out. Abusive supervision, coupled with widespread peer silence, both communicated and reproduced the hostile environment until finally a group of managers collectively fought back by circumventing the chain of command.

Institutional Positioning

We might not associate market pressures with a non-profit agency, but the move toward social service privatization in the 1980s and 1990s affected CWC. The political environment spawned an accountability mindset for state and federal government funders of social services. Accounting for funds increasingly absorbed staff hours, hours that they had used to provide services to clients.

Many personnel files included administrative notes requiring increasing levels of grant-related record-keeping and reporting. Program managers spent more and more time filling out or creating reports for government funders and, as a result, shifted more of the direct service work to employees. Chronically understaffed, CWC members explained that every year each person was doing the work of a larger number of needed, but unfilled staff positions.

Discourses

Individualistic explanations for employee abuse abounded at CWC—mostly that abused workers were to blame. Ken labeled them problem employees who were lazy, inept, or disgruntled and would or could not follow direction. At first, other employees hoped that removal of one targeted worker would end the abuse. Unfortunately,

169

after a short reprieve, Ken singled out another worker whom he identified as the problem.

Because targeted workers were often so disoriented by ongoing abuse, when they appealed up the chain of command and appeared to testify before the board, their stories were often disjointed and highly emotional. Ken's voice, until the final seven months of his time with the agency, was given more weight than grieving workers. The few who sought legal assistance were unsuccessful at winning their cases.

Under-funding for social services and inequity of women's salaries are also important to this case. Despite increased funding for the services during President Clinton's first term, funding for all local social service agencies was chronically inadequate in an swiftly growing area in terms of population. CWC suffered because it could not offer a competitive salary for the director's position. The agency was forced to hire someone with fewer qualifications who was willing to work for a very modest salary.

Compounding this issue was board's continued adherence to a low salary for the director. The majority of the CWC Board was female, and the members (with one exception) worked at relatively low-paying jobs. The board member who earned a six-figure salary often spoke of her difficulty convincing other board members to increase the director's salary.

The Constitution of Toxic Organizations:
A Communications Type Model

The goal in this chapter is to understand how an organization is rebuilt by day to day communication and overarching Discourses that inform communication. Examining the communication types in one organization allows us to understand how small changes in one type can affect change in others, which subsequently affect the overall character of the organization's treatment of employees. Examining how one toxic organization developed provides us insight into the insidious ways that organizations become toxic and points to their complexity. The communication types, messages, and the illustrating case study suggest the following propositions about the constitution of toxic organizations:

Proposition 1: Toxic organizations are likely to develop when abusive, employee-antagonistic messages are evident in two or

170

more communication types.

The more communication types in which employee abusive messages are evident, the more embedded the abuse. Though there are instances when one employee abuses another, and though workplace policies sometimes limit employee recourse, these communicative behaviors, in and of themselves, do not constitute an abusive organizational culture. An organization is employee-abusive when hostile messages occur in two or more communication types and multiple workers are negatively impacted.

In the CWC case, Ken's treatment of individual employees, though harassing, was not sufficient to create an abusive organization. However, when the board failed to intervene, despite years of employee firings and grievances, employee abuse became a regular albeit toxic dynamic. Moreover, as organizational members talked about abusive messages in and outside of the organization, abuse became taken-for-granted.

> Proposition 2: Toxic organizations are likely to develop when organization leadership enacts or condones abusive, hostile communication.

After reading the CWC case study, it would be easy to blame Ken for the development of the hostile workplace. However, the board was complicit in how CWC transitioned into a toxic organization. The communication of organizational leaders often sets the tone of an organization's climate. When organizational leaders enact or condone employee abuse, abusers can feel justified in their behavior, and targets and bystanders can develop a sense of powerlessness [79]. Additionally, leaders create and implement the formal documents of organizational self-structuring, so any changes in official policies require the agreement and action of those same positions.

> Proposition 3: Toxic organizations are more likely to develop when numerous organizational members breech the norm of civil discourse.

When many organizational members breech the social norm by acting aggressively and disrespectfully toward others during day-to-day activity coordination, others are more likely to breech the norm themselves. Indeed, acting aggressively, like other emotional behavior,

171

can be as "contagious" as a social disease [317]. Such contagion may be due to others' beliefs that they can breech the norm with impunity or that they are expected to breech the espoused norm [336]. When many organizational members breech the norm of civility, others are likely to do so as well, constituting an exceedingly hostile climate.

On the other hand, when organizational members see only one or two organizational members breeching a social norm (e.g., civility) but no one else breeches that norm, the deviance stands out and renders the breech more dramatic and powerful [337]. When only one or two aggressors are in a workgroup, their abusive behavior presents a vivid reminder of undesirable interactions, and others will be less likely to replicate bullying behavior—especially if they are punished, or at least not rewarded [338].

Proposition 4: Toxic organizations are likely to develop when Discourses are marked by cultural norms of competition, individualism, and aggression.

Cultural norms strongly affect the level and degree of workplace bullying and the provision of protection for workers [87]. For example, German labor law protects workers and includes statutes against bullying [339]. Additionally, low power distance and feminine and or egalitarian cultures likely contribute to the lower rates of bullying. As such, harassing behavior and a superior's abuse of power is more common in cultures that focus on individual achievement and assertiveness, such as the UK and US, than in Scandinavia, which privileges a more egalitarian style [137].

Proposition 5: Toxic organizations are likely to worsen when abusive, hostile interactions persist over time.

There is considerable evidence linking repeated abuse over a long period to escalated hostility. Continued abusive interactions become more intense, extreme, and personalized the longer they endure [184]. Employee abuse is often a developmental process that escalates—either gradually or rapidly—depending on the bullies, situation, and setting [4] [7]. Both the intensity of hostility and the intensity of toxic effects multiply when no one intervenes.

During the early phases of abuse, targets may have difficulty describing their experience. Abusive tactics may be "subtle, devious and immensely difficult to confront" [29](p. 17). Devious, hidden attacks also make the experience difficult for targeted workers to encode [69].

172

In later stages, however, targets are assailed by more directly aggressive acts, and they are unmistakably aware of being under attack. Over time, "more direct aggressive acts appear. The victims are clearly isolated and avoided, humiliated in public by being made a laughingstock of the department, and so on. In the end both physical and psychological means of violence may be used"[21](p. 19).

> Proposition 6: Toxic organizations always result in harm and negative outcomes.

Toxic organizations are extremely destructive and negatively effect targets' self-esteem, physical health, cognitive functioning, occupational functioning, and emotional health [101]. Abused workers report elevated levels of anxiety and are at higher risk of substance abuse, depression, and developing heart disease than are non-abused workers [33, 340]. Research also associates long-term abuse to posttraumatic stress disorder and suicide or suicidal ideation [1, 235].

Abuse at work also negatively affects those who have witnessed it. Coworkers are *secondary* targets of employee abuse, similar to persons who witness and are psychologically marked by acts of workplace violence and murder [103]. When coworkers witness others' abuse, they make the logical assumption that they could be targeted in a similar fashion; hyper-vigilance becomes a permanent feature of worklife. Organizations are also damaged as fear, emotional exhaustion, and guilt increase the likelihood of staff turnover for those targeted and bystanders. The human costs of bullying [137] are heartbreaking, but bullying also impairs organizations and by extension those served by organizational products or services [124].

> Proposition 7: Toxic organizations can be altered but generally require concerted, collective efforts and the commitment of upper-management.

Organizations, like all systems, are constantly changing and evolving. Toxic organizations are constituted through communication, and as such, they can be reconstituted through shifts in communication patterns—remarkably, changes can take place with even small communication changes [101]. The CWC case study exemplifies how one organization developed into an toxic organization via multiple abusive communication types. The case also demonstrates how changing the communication shifted the organization away from employee abuse.

173

However, transforming a system from negative to positive required concerted effort and time and was not without cost to those who resisted.

Additionally, because the policies of an organization affect how personnel issues are resolved, upper-management must acknowledge the abusive policies and commit to changing the procedures. In fact, the severity of an organization's response to employee harassment is linked with effectiveness in combating the abuse [341]. At CWC, the board eventually recognized the organization's overall deterioration and worked with a new director, employees, and stakeholders to change its policies and improve its communication.

Discussion

A communication types model provides a unique and useful tool that assists in understanding the complexity of toxic organizations. That communication constitutes organizations and organizes human action and relationships are virtually taken-for-granted concepts in communication research. Intuitively, one can grasp that as we talk with others and use cultural messages, impressions and sense-making are shaped and transformed. As impressions and sense-making shift, so do the actions and the way we organize those actions. By association, it stands to reason that communication also organizes human collectivities into larger, complex, goal-oriented organizations and societal institutions that persist over time.

Explaining the power of communication to create our working environments is one of our goals. The challenge is creating an explanation that takes complexity into consideration while also being simple enough to be useful. The framework also provides a way to assess organizational climates in a systematic way. We applied the model to analyze a specific toxic organization, which helped us uncover how different types of communication affected each other and created an organizational culture in particular ways.

CHAPTER 9

Communicative Nature of Bullying and Responses to Bullying[H]

Pamela Lutgen-Sandvik, Sarah J Tracy, Jess Alberts

Chapter Summary: Adult bullying at work is a communication phenomenon, both in how bullies enact it and in how targets respond. Yet, few researchers have explicitly examined it as such. This chapter responds to this gap by analyzing the most common tool used to assess incidences of bullying, the Negative Acts Questionnaire, as well as drawing upon a national sample of US employees regarding their responses to being bullied. Findings indicate that the majority of bullying behaviors are specifically communicative in nature. In addition, this analysis reveals that only a small number of respondents reported that their efforts effectively reduced bullying. Talking about being bullied had a much stronger relationship with improving how targets felt than resulting in substantive change.

Keywords: workplace bullying, communication as creative, bullying cessation

---

As the US workplace has become busier, more complex, and more stressful, the incidence of negative and aversive interactions has become more commonplace. Current organizational dynamics contribute to escalating aggressiveness at work—highly diverse workforces, restructuring and staff reductions, decreased resources coupled with increased productivity expectations, and autocratic management styles [15, 342]. As the communicative complexity increases in changing

175

organizations, so do the occasions for hostile and aggressive communication. This is especially true for organizations in which change has not yet stabilized—where former work norms are no longer valid but new norms have yet to cohere or emerge [258].

Individual acts of incivility, hostility, and injustice may be increasingly common and tolerated, but over time they can develop into more serious and consequential acts. In fact, the central risk of workplace negativity is its escalation [108]. For example, low-level acts of rudeness and negativity, behavior such as sending hurtful e-mail messages, taking credit for others' work, throwing papers, or failing to say please or thank you, can lead to a range of far more serious negative behaviors [81], including social ostracism and spreading rumors up to and including screaming and, though rare, even physical assault [64].

One highly destructive type of negative interaction on the job is workplace bullying. Though far more severe than rudeness or incivility, bullying is often triggered by these uncivil, unjust interactions that contaminate the workplace [28, 64]. Over time, individual acts of hostility develop into bullying as repeated, long-term abuse wears down, demoralizes, stigmatizes, and isolates those targeted. Feeling bullied at work is not just the response of a few oversensitive employees. Bullying is an extreme form of negativity that targets describe as similar to being beaten, eviscerated and heart-broken. They view it as a constant hammering away that relentlessly undermines what they do, what they say, how they look, how they sound, and how they work [2].

Despite the clearly communicative nature of adult bullying at work, few researchers have explicitly examined it as a communicative phenomenon. Moreover, little is known about how targeted US workers' respond to being bullied or whether those responses decrease bullying or improve how targeted workers feel. In the studies that have examined workers responses, persons surveyed are outside the US and the central focus rarely is the phenomenon's communicative character.

This chapter explores workplace bullying as a unique type of negative workplace phenomenon that differs in important ways from other types, but in which communication is central. The chapter underscores the communicative aspects of the most commonly used workplace bullying measurement instrument and reports the results of a US survey that assesses targets' responses to bullying as well as their perceptions of the efficacy of those responses. Key to these questions is the argument that bullying is a communicative experience shaped by specific organizational dynamics.

Communicative Character of Workplace Bullying

Workplace bullying is largely communicative at both the individual- and organizational-level. On the individual-level, it is through interaction and communication that bullying is played out. At the social/historical-level, bullying and abuse at work are normalized, constructed, and constrained through numerous communication types and cultural ideologies about power.

Communication and the Measurement of Workplace Bullying

A close analysis of the most frequently used bullying measurement tool, the Negative Acts Questionnaire or NAQ [88], reveals that the enactment of bullying is measured predominately through individuals' perceptions of communication behavior. The NAQ assesses the frequency with which targets experience 22 negative acts that are hallmarks of bullying.

A review of these reveals that all but five are clearly communicative in nature, that is, involve explicitly verbal interactions. These include withholding information, humiliating, ridiculing, making false allegations, gossiping, spreading rumors, making insulting and offensive remarks, shouting, teasing, criticizing and threatening violence. The five that do not involve verbalization or language, *nonetheless communicate hostility and aggression* (e.g., isolating, excluding, excessively monitoring, ignoring, workplace violence). See "Table 2.4. Negative Acts Compared" in Chapter 2 for communication and behavior associated with workplace bullying.

Typical Responses to Workplace Bullying

Not only is bullying enacted predominately through language, people most often respond to it communicatively [184]. At some point, most targets attempt to manage or stop the bullying by appealing to others, including the bully, within the workplace. However, little research explicitly studies the communicative nature of those responses or the effect of responses on targets' emotional states. Further, and importantly for this study, little is currently known about the nature of US worker responses to being persistently abused at work (for an exception see [5]). A complicating factor regarding response to bullying is the gap between what targeted workers report doing and what non-

177

targeted persons believe they would do if faced with similar situations.

Typically, fewer targets confront the bully or complain to management than non-targets assume they would do if targeted [92]. At the same time, more targets use avoidance tactics such as quitting their jobs than non-target say they would use [247]. In general, then, targets choose more passive/avoidant strategies while non-targets believe they would use more assertive and help-seeking strategies. This is mostly likely linked to the very real risks of speaking out.

Responding to bullying is fraught with difficulty for targets. Expressing anger and aggression is a way of establishing and maintaining one's organizational status; so higher status employees may use it "strategically to intimidate others in the pursuit of goal attainment" [343](p. 301). Furthermore, research suggests that workers in the US expect (and accept) that higher status individuals will express anger and aggression toward lower status workers but that the reverse will not be allowed. Nonetheless, employees report ongoing feelings of anger long after such acts occur. Thus, employees on the receiving end of this aggression *feel* anger, even if they believe constraints exist on how they can express it. Consequently, lower level employees often disguise or suppress their anger [343].

Because of these lingering feelings of anger and the fear of retaliation, targeted workers face a dilemma. How can/should they respond to acts of aggression by those who they perceive as more powerful? Likely they are afraid to respond with aggression or retaliation, but at the same time they seethe with resentment. Indeed, responding aggressively most often exacerbates the situation [184]. Ignoring or avoiding the bullying may be a short-term strategy, but is not an effective long-term response and may even mask [137], or result in increased, bullying [247].

In some cases, employees band together or quit; in others a few targeted employees may respond with violence [344]. However, most research exploring worker responses examines a small number of targets [137] or worker groups outside the US. A large-sample German study [184] found that targets' most common responses were (in order) talking with bully, talking to the bully's supervisor, talking with workers' representatives, and avoiding situations involving bullies. Similarly, a UK study found the three most common target responses were talking to coworkers, friends/family, and the bully [345]. The bulk of these are communicative behaviors. These studies, however, do not explain how US workers might respond when targeted. Therefore, in order to understand more clearly how US workers respond to bullying, the following research question is explored:

RQ1: What are US workers' most commonly reported responses to bullying?

Although understanding how targets respond to their experiences is useful, it is perhaps even more important to discover whether targets perceive their efforts to be successful or effective. In the German study [184], talking with bullies generally made the situation worse, a similar dynamic found in some UK research [3]Talking to bully's supervisors and workers' representatives decreased bullying for about half of targets and exacerbated bullying for the other half. For these workers, avoidance improved the situation in more cases than it made things worse. On the other hand, an Icelandic study found that avoidance and passive responses (doing nothing) were associated with increased bullying [247]. While informative, these studies do not tell us about US workers' experiences, since such study in the US is yet nascent. Since one in four US workers are bullied at work and the harm associated with bullying is so great, understanding the success of various responses in the American workplace is a potentially interesting avenue of research.

Knowledge about which actions reduce bullying is helpful for other targets that must decide how to respond, since response strategies likely vary in their effect on these issues. Such knowledge is also important information for organizational members responsible for managing employee personnel issues and responding to employee complaints of bullying, who often have little understanding of bullying or how targets can/should respond.

In fact, organizational responses to workplace bullying are notoriously ineffective. Because managers and other organizational representatives usually do not understand bullying dynamics, they tend to respond with disbelief or denial when informed of its occurrence or know abuse is occurring but brush complaints aside [68]. Therefore, representatives are commonly dismissive, side with the bully, or even punish the employee who reports being bullied. According to a US survey conducted by the Workplace Bullying & Trauma Institute (WBTI):

Targets who reported their abuse to the perpetrator (bully's) manager and asked for relief elicited positive, helpful responses only 18% of the time. In 43% of the cases, the bully's boss actual-

179

ly compounded the problem. And in 40% of cases, the boss did nothing. Appealing to human resources officers and anti-discrimination officers was equally unhelpful: 17% took positive steps to stop the bullying; 32% reacted negatively, and 51% did nothing. [5](p. 4)

Two qualitative studies of US workers suggest similar dynamics [68, 137] with organizational responses failing to stop abuse or make targeted workers feel any better about their situations.

One must ask, then, what strategies targets should use to seek assistance and to stop the bullying; that is, what strategies do actual targets find to be successful? The Namies' [5] study examined targets' perceptions of organizational responses, but it does not address the specific strategies targets find useful. Neither does it explore which responses improve targets' emotional states. Studies that have examined how targets evaluate the utility of their strategies have tended to be qualitative and focused on a relatively small number of respondents or have examined the experiences of workers outside the US. Therefore, in order to understand how a US group of targeted workers evaluates the effectiveness of their response strategies in stopping the bully, the following research question is posed:

RQ2: What target responses decreased bullying?

Bullying is a traumatic event for most targets, who describe their experiences as a "battle, water torture, nightmare or noxious substance" [2](p. 148). Their experiences result in both physical and psychological illnesses as well as significant emotional pain. Workplace bullying has been associated with increased levels of anxiety, depression, burnout, illness and job dissatisfaction as well as an increased incidence of suicide and symptoms of post-traumatic stress. An incredibly salient emotion reported by nearly all targets is overwhelming fear—even terror.

The wide range of negative effects spontaneously leads targets to try various tactics that help them cope. In addition to decreasing or ending the bullying, targets engage in response strategies designed to make them feel better. Existing research does not reveal how various responses impact how targeted workers *feel* about the situation, a clearly important issue. If a course of action makes someone feel better, even if bullying continues, then some gain has occurred. The limited research that has examined targets' responses to bullying has not explored respondents' perceptions of how successful their responses were in making them feel better. Therefore, the following research question is posed:

RQ3: What responses improved targeted workers' feelings?

In terms of responses to bullying, another area that current research has yet to explore is whether specific types of negative acts are more likely to elicit specific kinds of responses. For example, are people who are subject to ridicule and exclusion more likely to seek assistance from a therapist while those who experience criticism and insults more apt to approach management for help? Likely such relationships exist, but little research actually explores the associations among types of negative experiences targeted workers face and the types of responses they choose. Analyzing the associations among specific bullying tactics and target responses can provide additional understanding of targets' experiences as well as help us understand which negative acts may trigger which types of worker response. Therefore, the following research question is posed:

RQ4: What associations exist among targeted workers' responses and bullying acts?

Methods

Data came from non-student, working adults who responded to an online survey (administered through Survey Monkey) entitled *The American Workplace Survey II*. Respondents were drawn to the survey through network/snowball sampling procedures coupled with online and print advertising.

Sample

Because the bulk of bullying research represents international worker samples, the study specifically sought persons working in the US As such, of 469 people who responded to the survey, 18 non-US responses were deleted during data cleaning. Of the remaining survey responses, 403 were sufficiently complete to be usable in analysis. Sixty-six% of the sample was females; 45% were male (3 missing sex data). Mean age was 35.8 years (SD 9.5, range 18 - 57). Seventy-six% worked in administrative support, health and social services, educa-

181

tion, service sector, professional and scientific fields, finance and insurance, and public administration; the remaining 24% identified with
a large range of industries and positions.

Measures

The online survey measured frequency and type of negative acts experienced *over the past six months* employing the Negative Acts
Questionnaire (0 = never, to 4 = daily/almost daily) and targets' perceptions of being bullied (self-identification). The NAQ was selected
because it is the most widely-used measure of workplace bullying and
has demonstrated high internal consistency, with Cronbachs alpha
ranging from .81 to .92. Cronbachs alpha for the NAQ in this study
was .92. Self-identified bullying was determined by asking respondents
to consider a definition of bullying and state whether or not they had
been a target. The definition came directly from the NAQ and is as
follows:

> We define bullying as a situation where one or several individu-
> als persistently over a period of time perceive themselves to be
> on the receiving end of negative actions from one or several per-
> sons, in a situation where the target of bullying has difficulty in
> defending him or herself against these actions. One-time inci-
> dents are not considered bullying.

The study also assessed workers' responses to being bullied for those
who self-identified as "bullied." Based on published research, a fifteen
item response inventory was developed. Participants indicated whether they had used one or more of the 15 response strategies, including
talking to personnel or human resources, talking to family and
friends, working harder, and so forth (0 = never, to 4 = four or more
times). In addition to asking how workers responded to perceived
bullying, the survey asked how effective respondents perceived those
responses to be at decreasing the bullying and making the respondent
feel better (1 = very ineffective to 5 = very effective). The survey also
provided space for open-ended comments.

Analyses

Pearson correlations were conducted to determine (a) perceived decreases in bullying and reported responses, and (b) perceived im-

provements in feelings and responses—two variables measured at an interval level. Because negative act data were measured at an ordinal level, Spearman's rho correlations were conducted to determine if relationships existed between the (c) NAQ's negative acts and reported responses. Frequency data of the following variables was specifically examined: self-identified as bullied, specific response types, responses considered effective/highly effective, and number of different responses. To control for sex, the study also conducted independent samples t-tests for each response between male/female respondents.

Results

Of the 403 respondents, 120 (29.8%) self-identified as being bullied sometime during their work history (90 female, 27 male, 3 undefined sex). Of these, 99 completed the response-to-bullying section of the survey. To answer RQ 1, "What are the most commonly reported responses to bullying?", analysis examined frequency data of the reported responses. Table 9.1 summarizes these frequencies. Controlling for sex, since previous research suggests men and women respond differently [247], only one response was found—missing work to avoid bully—that differed between the two groups (t = 2.21 [68], $p <$ .05) with women missing work more often than men. As such, further analyses treated bullied workers as an aggregate. See Table 9.1 on the next page.

Table 9.1: Response Frequency, Effectiveness

Response	Effective or Highly Effective	
	Reduced Bullying	Improved Feelings
1. Spoke with family and friends	No	Yes
2. Spoke with coworkers	No	Yes
3. Worked harder	No, worsened	No
4. Talked to bully	No, worsened	No
5. Reduced work output	No	No
6. Spoke to bully's boss	No	No, worsened
7. Spoke with HR	No	Yes
8. Spoke with union representative	No	Yes
9. Sabotage/secretly defy bully	No	Yes
10. Missed work to avoid bullying	No	No
11. Spoke to legal professional	No	Yes
12. Spoke with mental health provider	No	No
13. Spoke with medical doctor	No	No
14. Left job voluntarily	Yes	Yes & No
15. Left job involuntarily	Yes	No, worsened

Targeted US workers report responding to bullying in multiple ways—a pattern also found in international studies [184, 247]. They reported taking anywhere from one to nine different actions to deal with prevent abuse. The four most frequent responses were talking with family/friends, talking to coworkers, working harder, and talking directly to the bully. Three of these are specifically communicative in nature. Looking at the number of respondents who reported response types at any frequency, this study found a similar pattern. The most commonly reported responses were speaking with family/friends (n = 90), talking to coworkers (n = 89), talking to the bully (n = 57), and talking to the bully's boss (n = 51). Bullied workers more often used these communicative behaviors than the other fifteen potential responses.

To answer RQ2, "Which responses decrease bullying?", the relationships between target response and reported effectiveness at decreasing bullying was evaluated. The two right-hand columns of Table 9.2, notes the percentage of respondents who reported that the specific act was "effective" or "highly effective" at reducing bullying. Speaking to the bully's boss (7%), talking with the bully (7%), sabotage (7%), seeking legal advice (5%) and speaking with HR (5%) were reported most often as "effective/highly effective." Despite these reports, the percentages are exceedingly small. Pearson's correlation indicated that only working harder was significantly—but inversely—associated with decreasing bullying.

To answer RQ3, "What responses improve targeted workers' feelings?", the study examined the percentage of respondents who reported that the specific act was "effective" or "highly effective" at improving feelings. Speaking with family/friends (48%), talking with coworker (42%), working harder (36%), and quitting (22%) were reported most often as "effective/highly effective" for helping them feel better. We found that two communicative actions made targets feel better: speaking with family and friends and talking to coworkers. Getting fired made people feel worse but ended bullying. Quitting made some people feel worse and others feel better. Either way, bullying ended when people quit.

Finally, RQ4 asked, "What relationships exist between targeted workers' responses and bullying acts?" A goal of the study was to determine if specific types of bullying were associated with specific communicative responses enacted by targets. We found that four responses to bullying were directly associated with experiencing twelve types of abuse. Three responses were types of communication: (a) talking to human resources, (b) talking to a legal professional, and (c) talking to bully's boss. The fourth response was missing work to avoid bullying—a response carried out more often by women than men.

Table 9.2: Responses to Bullying Acts

Targets Did This	When Bullies Did This
Missed work to avoid bullying	Excluded, isolated from others
	Ignored or faced with hostile reactions when you approach
Spoke to bully's boss	Gossip, rumors spread about you
	Had false allegations made against you
	Ignored or faced with hostile reactions when you approach
	Insulting, offensive remarks
	Intimidated with threatening behavior
Spoke to HR	Excluded, isolated from others
	Ignored or faced with hostile reactions when you approach
Spoke with legal professional	Ignored or faced with hostile reactions when you approach
	Intimidated with threatening behavior
	Threats of violence or actual physical violence

n = number of people saying they took column 1 action in response to column 2 type of abuse. "Yes" indicates that there was a *statistically significant relationship between the type of abuse and the type of action taken.*

We found the following relationships between particular forms of abuse and taking particular actions. Missing work to avoid bullying was related with being (1) excluded and (2) being ignored or facing hostility when approaching others. Speaking to HR was associated with being (1) excluded and (2) ignored or faced with hostility when approaching others. Speaking to the bully's boss was associated with being (1) gossiped about, (2) falsely accused, (3) ignored or faced with hostility when approaching others, (4) insulted, and (5) intimidated in some way. Speaking with a lawyer was associated with being (1) intimidated in some way, (2) threated with or targeted with actual violence, and (3) ignored or faced hostility when approaching others.

Discussion

This study strengthens the significance of communication to understanding bullying and developing effective individual and organizational responses to workplace abuse. An analysis of the Negative Acts Questionnaire, a workplace bullying measure with consistently high reliability measures, indicates that the majority of bullying behaviors are specifically communicative in nature. Even those acts that might not be explicitly communicative—social ostracism and violence—nonetheless communicate contempt, disregard, and disdain. As such, "changing the nature of workplace conversations" and creating "an atmosphere in which people are valued and respected" [101](pp. 363, 366) are primary goals for supportive workplaces. In fact, one of the most promising efforts is a participatory project at the US Department of Veterans Affairs between organizational members and researchers [101]. Some of the most successful ways of reducing aggression are simply changing, in numerous small ways, how people talk to one another.

It also seems apparent that targeted workers take many actions to try to correct their painful work experiences. Assuming that organizational exit (voluntary or involuntary) was the final response to workplace bullying, participants tried many methods of recourse to make sense of, deal with, and try to stop bullying before giving up and leaving the organization. As such, although a larger percentage of non-bullied than bullied workers claim they would not leave their jobs due to bullying, it appears the bullied workers quit only as a last resort. In fact, of the 99 reporting targets in this study, none reported simply quitting. All who did quit their jobs due to bullying (n = 32) reported taking many different actions before this final decision. Indeed, most of the action taken can be classified as "voice": talking to the bully, talking to HR, speaking with the bully's supervisor, seeking legal/union support.

In addition to underscoring the communicative nature of workplace bullying, this analysis reveals that most actions taken by targets had little impact on decreasing the bullying. Of 15 potential response strategies targets invoked by bully targets, only one had any impact on bullying—working harder—and that relationship was inverse. That is, working harder was negatively related to effectively reducing bullying. Similarly, open-ended survey responses, the knowledge of bullying from subsequent research, and published work underscore this in-

187

verse relationship between bullying and productivity. As a survey respondent noted:

> Because many people in the project group reacted negatively to the bully's attitude, lies, and ineptitude, they most often circumvented the bully and relied on me to bring sense and order back in—which I could do. This artificially buoyed the productivity level for a short time while I silently dealt with the initial threat, but it seems when my resolve waned, ... everyone else got fed up and disengaged too. Productivity slowed to a crawl and I left soon after.

What appears to be a common pattern is working harder in an effort to stop or prevent the bullying. However, when bullying continues unabated regardless of productivity level, targets may reduce work, speak to organizational authorities, direct their efforts toward being "invisible," or leave the organization. This is an important finding since there are still some who believe that workers are best motivated by aggression. Indeed, despite the claims to reporters about this negative relationship, some articles alluded to the effectiveness of bullying to achieve higher productivity.

In addition to statistically significant associations between actions and reduced bullying, examining the number of respondents (frequency data) who reported that their actions were effective/highly effective at reducing bullying is also valuable. These were small percentages overall (5% - 6.7%), but they are important. A small number of bullied respondents reported that talking to the bully, speaking to the bully's boss, speaking to HR, and consulting a lawyer effectively reduced bullying. It does appear that taking communicative action (e.g., by talking to someone about the issue) has some perceived impact on the problem.

Talking about the issue had a much stronger relationship with improving how targets felt than with reducing bullying. Indeed, the two responses that made targeted workers feel better about their experiences were communication acts. Talking to friends and family as well as talking to coworkers significantly improved how targets felt about their situations. Frequency data also revealed that nearly half reported that talking to others was effective/highly effective as improving targets' feelings.

On the other hand, voluntarily leaving the job actually made targets feel worse. This finding, like the relationship between reduced bullying and working harder, needs further study and should be interpreted cautiously. An inverse correlation between quitting and improved feelings was found for the entire sample, but nearly a quarter reported that quitting made them feel much better.

Targeted workers very likely have mixed feelings about leaving. Leaving can be framed as success ("take this job and shove it") or as failure ("they've beaten me"). Quitting is not often considered an explicitly communicative act, but people quit in a variety of ways. Quitting can incorporate voice, especially when exit is "noisy" [346]. In the case of noisy exists, departing workers exit the organization but while doing so speak their minds about why they are leaving. Noisy exits are potentially more effective at improving how one feels about the situation. However, when examining the statistical evidence for relationships between responses and feeling better, only communicative strategies positively affected targets' feelings. This suggests the communication plays a central role in managing bullying from targets' perspectives.

Finally, the examination of the relationships between being targeted with particular negative acts and taking specific actions indicates that targets select the responses, in part, based on the bullying behaviors to which they are subjected. For example, two responses, missing work to avoid bullying and speaking to HR, were associated with different forms of social ostracism—being isolated from and ignored by others.

Possibly, when someone misses work to avoid bullying, he or she loses opportunities to build or repair workplace relationships. Equally possible, when workplace relationships are weak or troubled, missing work also provides some protection from being socially ostracized. Speaking to HR has similar potentialities. When employees feel ostracized, they may speak with HR to ameliorate the issue. On the other hand, speaking to HR can place complainants in precarious positions and encourage others to distance themselves from the complainant. As with all the relationships reported, negative acts/responses are more than likely related—regardless of which comes first.

Speaking to authorities (bully's boss, lawyer) was associated with more directly threatening experiences and experiences that challenged workers' reputation and identity. Again, correlations do not suggest the direction of the relationship, only that negative acts and responses positively changed in tandem. As such, gossip, rumor, insults, and intimidation could move targeted workers to seek intervention from the bully's boss. On the other hand, target reports to upper-management about bullying behavior has been found to exacerbate bullying situations [184] and may have resulted in increased gossip, rumors, and so forth.

Moreover, speaking to lawyers was associated with the most egregious negative acts: physical violence and threats/intimidation. This relationship is likely directional, despite correlational data limitations. Physical violence and threats at work are few of the forms of workplace bullying against which US workers have statutory protection. These negative acts may be so blatant that workers believe they "have a case" so take their concerns to legal professionals for confirmation or refutation.

Notably, *being ignored* or *facing hostility when approaching others* was a key factor in all four strongly correlated responses. This suggests that distant or hostile social relationships at work are central factors in targeted workers' responses. The order of events is not clear, but *something* occurred that pushed targets to take action. Indeed, when targeted workers speak out, this often creates fear in bullies and witnessing others. Furthermore, this NAQ item is worded as a double-barrel question making it difficult to draw conclusions. Did respondents report being ignored or were facing hostility when they approached others?

This study makes an important contribution by analyzing and highlighting the communicative nature workplace bullying as well as adding to understanding of negative interaction in the workplace, but it has some limitations. First, due to the structure of the NAQ, data for the frequency of negative acts and response was limited to the 38 respondents who experienced bullying in the previous six months. Despite the fact that only 10% of the sample perceived being bullied in the previous six months is consistent with other studies of workplace bullying [49], the analysis would have been more robust had the sample size been larger. In addition, the network sampling used to solicit participants limits generalizability. When compared to extant bullying studies, the sample included a large range of types of workers. Nonetheless, it was weighted toward white-collar employees. Future studies could enhance understandings of workplace bullying by increasing the range of the sample to an even more diverse group.

Practical Implications

The findings have implications for both organizations and targeted individuals. First, organizational leaders should recognize that behaviors they may perceive as relatively trivial acts of incivility, such as being excluded or gossiped about, significantly and negatively affect targets and organizations. Feeling excluded was associated with employees' missing work while being gossiped about was associated with employees talking to the bully's boss. Thus, even "low level" acts of aggression when enacted repeatedly cost the organization through lowered productivity due to employee absences as well as bosses' investment of time in managing co-worker relationships.

Second, and importantly, the findings suggest that organizations can reduce bullying in response to target complaints, but they do so too rarely. Talking with the bully's boss and speaking to HR were not significantly associated with decreasing bullying, but a small number of respondents did think that doing so was effective and even highly effective in reducing bullying. Not all participants' experiences were so positive, however, when consulting HR staff. Typically, targeted workers are encouraged to seek help from human resources within their organizations as a response to their mistreatment. However, respondents indicated that consulting with human resources about the problem neither resulted in reduced abuse nor resulted in improved emotional states. More specifically, there was a *negative* correlation, albeit statistically non-significant, between seeking help from personnel and the situation improving. Thus, it is imperative that new organizational responses to bullying be developed given the current ones do not appear to work.

Third, since talking about workplace bullying clearly improves how targeted workers feel, organizations can provide venues for affected worker voice. It is not easy to come to terms with being a target and can take considerable time. People vary in this process and often feel embarrassed and ashamed at being targeted. Organizational approaches such as "practical listeners" programs can be highly useful at this junction. These programs create a cadre of peer "peer listeners" who are trained in the dynamics of workplace bullying and will believe and validate targeted workers' stories. Briefly, these trained workers "listen to their colleague and provide [support and] information on the choices that were available to resolve their difficulties" [347](p. 158). Providing space for such conversations can be part of an overall approach to improving the way workers feel. Of course, this must be coupled with honest efforts to reduce aggressive communication and encourage constructive interactions.

The findings also offer guidance for targeted employees as well. First, targets can, and should, seek social support from co-workers as well as family and friends. According to the participants, bully targets interactions with others helped them cope with the negative effects of workplace bullying. Because of the negative associations attached to being "victimized" by bullies, targets may be hesitant to confide in others. However, doing so may be one of the few ways targets can find solace in this difficult situation.

In addition, targets should recognize that two common responses – working harder and quitting – may not be as effective as they expect. Almost 40% of the respondents indicated that one of their responses to being bullied was to work harder. Over time, however, targets often find that working harder does not decrease the bullying as they hoped and, in fact, may increase it. Therefore, in general, targets should pursue other avenues to relieve their situation. Finally, 22% of respondents indicated that quitting made them feel better, but voluntarily leaving one's job made others feel worse. Therefore, targets that are considering leaving their jobs should be aware that how they feel about leaving likely is affected by whether they feel "pulled" toward better opportunities or "pushed" out of the organization before they are ready to leave.

Conclusion

This chapter makes a case for viewing workplace bullying as aggression that is communicative in nature. Bullying, as commonly measured in the NAQ, is largely "about" communication. In short, bullying appears to be an extremely rich avenue of study for communicative researchers. However, as it stands, few have explored bullying as a specific way of communicating.

This research provides significant groundwork, but there is still much work to be done. Communication researchers are uniquely poised to add to this intellectual dialogue, focusing upon the interactional dynamics that make up bullying, the different types of bullying messages that perpetuate it, and discourses that normalize and construct organizational cultures of bullying. For example, at the micro-level (individual-level), workplace bullying is fundamentally interpersonal communication in an organizational setting. Interpersonal researchers could examine the types of messages most like to be perceived as bullying, or how targeted workers seek social support and the types of messages viewed as more supportive.

In addition, organizational researchers are uniquely poised to add to this conversation; they can do so by, for instance, studying the enabling structures are antecedents that must be a place within organizations for bullying to occur, or determining the ways in which bullying behavior is communicatively rewarded in valued in organizational cultures. Health communication researchers can make a significant contribution to the area as well by exploring how various bullying messages are connected to problematic physiological responses or assessing the effects of social support, storytelling, and writing about the bullying experience on target health. Or they might determine ways health campaigns could help control or curb bullying in the workplace.

CHAPTER 10

Attacking Your Own: A Deeper Look at Why Women Bully Other Women [1]

Pamela Lutgen-Sandvik, Elizabeth Dickinson, Karen Foss

Chapter Summary: When women are bullies at work, they target other women more than twice as often as men. This chapter considers reasons for why women might turn on their own by looking at the hidden beliefs and values that might drive this behavior. The chapter encourages women to look at what they are doing or saying at work and why. Women bullying women is rooted in the ways women (and men) think about and manage their professional images, especially an image that values aggression as a way to get ahead or get things done. The goal of the chapter to open up the dialogue about why women might turn on other women in workplace situations. To encourage women to begin talking about aggression, the chapter poses questions for consideration. The questions are two pronged: (1) for women to ask of themselves so they might recognize the hidden forces pushing them toward workplace aggression and (2) for others in the workplace to ask themselves so that they might see and then question the forces driving women's aggression. We close with suggestions to dismantle the aggressive images bullying women have built for themselves.

Keywords: workplace bullying, female bullies, gender, women, feminist, discrimination

----

When women are the identified bullies, most often their targets are other women. In fact, women seem to aggress against other women at more than double the rate that women aggress against men. The media have been keen to point out the pattern, but we have yet to explain why such might be the case. Two relatively recent media reports, *Women Bullies Often Target Other Women* [348] and *Back-*

194

lash: Women Bullying Women at Work [349], focus on women's abuse of other women at work. At least in the United States, in over 70% of the female-bully cases, they target women [198]. The gendered pattern is what *Backlash* called "the pink elephant in the room." Media attention marks an increased interest in women bullying women, and research data provides evidence of this trend.

This chapter examines this gender-based pattern and suggests moves toward more working constructive ways to work together. We uncover some of the hidden beliefs, values, and forces that encourage women to bullying other women, encourage women to recognize and question what they are doing and why, and underscore the unintended consequences of becoming known as a bully. This same-sex pattern is considered a consequence of building a certain kind of professional image. To encourage talking about these issues critically, we pose a series of questions to help women see what's pushing them toward aggression. It is our hope that once women see these usually hidden forces, they can make more informed choices about building their professional image. We also pose questions to other organizational members because the responsibility for change belongs to everyone in the organizations, not just individual women.

Research findings indicate that "women ... bully other women, 2.5 times more frequently than they target men" [198] (p. 8). We found at least six US studies reporting the same pattern. People typically explain this pattern in one of two ways: (1) stereotypes of women getting in "cat fights" and being "bitches" (e.g., J. Doe, personal communication, Montreal Conference on Bullying, June 5, 2008) and (2) women are more likely to work with other women (women are at hand). (We found no US that differed from this gendered pattern, but many studies do not report bully-target gender.)

Beyond occasional mention, however, there is little attention to why women target their own. Sadly, people nearly always place the blame on individual women. Rarely do we look deeper at the organizational or social beliefs, values, or contexts that drive and even reward aggression. We look beyond *bitches* and *availability* and consider the various forces that make aggression look like a good choice for some women in the workplace.

Our perspective suggests a different new way for working women, researchers, and professionals to understand and curb the women-bullying-women pattern. The intent is to put forth an explanation based solid research and theory that explains why the women-bullying-women pattern occurs. Hopefully, a new understanding will provide fresh sights. Our goal is to "look beneath" the surface evidence and expose the ideologies, social pressures, organizational expectations that drive the behavior. Most of these social forces are so taken for granted that we don't even question them. We do things a certain way because "that's how it's done" or "that's how everyone does it." Maybe rethinking what we see and do can open up possibilities for change so that women and men might look at aggressive women's behavior differently. A different look can bring to mind more constructive ways to address aggression than simply firing or demoting the offenders or targets. Additionally, a different look helps women to avoid taking all the blame and others from taking part in witch-hunts. A new view can be especially useful for

* women who are wondering if others see them as *bullies;*

* coworkers or bosses, consultants, and researchers so they can talk about and deal with bullying without demonizing perpetrators or blaming victims;

* women who have discovered that they really do not like themselves and who they have become at work and want to build a different kind of professional image.

Women and Workplace Bullying

Currently, there is not a lot of research focusing on women, gender, and workplace bullying. (For exceptions, see also [350, 351]). Such may be the case because researchers differentiate bullying from sexual harassment. People who do look specifically at gender when studying bullying argues, for example, that refusing to conform to traditional gendered roles (women as nurturers, men as workers) can elicit others' displeasure and even aggression [59, 352].

If researchers consider gender at all, it is as a variable (male, female). This oversight stands in stark relief to social and work life, much of which is built around our ideas about gender—what women or men should and should not do, think, or feel. These ideas are always "running in the background" of our minds when we're interacting at work [353]. We only notice that we have these beliefs when someone breaches a social norm about gender: When a woman is very aggressive others see her as a bitch or a crazy bitch. When a man is affectionate and warm others see him as a wimp or a sexual harasser. Gendered norms are always with us, certainly differing by culture but nonetheless always present.

Gender expectations explain the differing ways that men and women experience and respond to bullying. Women, for example, experience physical violence and ethnic harassment at lower rates, and exclusion by jokes at their expense at higher rates, than men. Men and women who are targeted both need and access social support when bullied, but women seem to do so more often.

Men and women are bullied at about the same rates, differing somewhat based on professional context. They both suffer similar harmful effects [73, 118]. Supervisor-employee gender arrangements seem to affect employee health [354]. In one study, researchers found that women with female supervisors (or supervisor-teams that include women) experienced higher levels of distress and physical harms than women working for male-only supervisors. Men, on the other hand, seemed to benefit from having female supervisors, whether the female boss was an individual supervisor or was as a part of a supervisory team [354]. This points to serious disadvantages for women who have female bosses.

In terms of bully gender, targets most often point to men being bullies [355], which could be due to their organizational positions. In the US, targets mostly identify bosses as bullies, and men are more often supervisors than women. Women in some professions (e.g., nursing), however, say they experience peer-to-peer bullying (i.e., horizontal violence) more often than supervisory bullying [356]. Peer-to-peer bullying is often same-sex aggression.

What remains unexamined is why women most often bully other women. Despite the recurrence of this pattern, research and organizational members rarely talk about why it might be happening. When researchers do mention the women-bullying-women pattern, they typically describe it as a function of *target availability*, as earlier mentioned. They argue that the same-sex pattern occurs because "men mostly work together with men and women with women" [69](p. 175). On its surface the *availability* argument seems to explain why survey numbers on same-sex bullying are the way they are (women bullying women 2.5 times more often than bullying men). What the argument fails to explain is *why* women bully other women regardless of how often they might do so. We believe the answer to the "why" question is more complex and attempt to answer it here.

Contributors to the Female Bully Image

Most women who aggress against other women likely slide into the behavior rather than consciously deciding to become a bully and doing things that demolish other women's professional lives. Rather, bullying other women is more likely an unintended consequence of women's professional image management, their "capacity *to keep a particular narrative going*" [249](p. 244) about themselves in their professional roles. Image management can purposely involve "creating and projecting a particular sort of self to others as well as ... avoiding other performances that are out of bounds" [357](pp. 153-54).

Generally, we build a career and create a professional image at the same time. For most of us, we purposely carry out the task-related work necessary for professional image-building. We also try to control much of the relation-related work, especially with people we see as powerful or influential. Our task and relational communication and behavior with people we see as non-influential or less important, however, is usually done in a relatively unselfconscious or automatic manner. With these people, the image we build comes from many, many day-to-day interactions from which others draw inferences and conclusions about us. For female bullies, the inferences are negative and damaging to our goals.

It is implausible to think that any woman deliberately decides, "I will abuse and terrorize other women so I will not be seen as weak (or as a pushover, too soft, etc.)." Rather, a professional image that includes being labeled a bully likely comes about because of our behaviors. Behaviors, in term, come from deeply held beliefs learned through men's and women's socialization, organizational pressures and structures, definitions of female success in a "man's world," the desire to build influence at work, and so forth.

The concepts of *practical consciousness* and *discursive consciousness* are useful here [174]—unlovely words, I know, but bear with me (See Glossary). Practical consciousness is our unarticulated knowledge and skills. This kind of knowledge informs and guides our day-to-day interactions but does so in a behind-the-scenes way that people rarely recognize so don't talk about. It is non-conscious, so to speak, simply routine and very normal-feeling.

Practical consciousness informs all of our day-to-day communication and behavior, so that what we say and do seem feels automatic and predictable. We give this knowledge little thought unless something occurs that breaches our expectations and triggers an elevated emotion (discomfort, elation). Regardless of the non-conscious way we move through our lives, our day-to-day behavior or practices that come from practical consciousness make up much of social life, including our professional images.

Discursive consciousness is a bit different. It is the knowledge people have about living their lives that they can and do put into words or articulate. Discursive consciousness includes all the stuff we talk about, the stuff we know and can say we know. We believe that to change our behavior, we have to recognize and talk about what encourages or drives our behavior. To do this, we need to move our actions from knee-jerk, automatic ways of responding that we rarely question or talk about (practical consciousness) to talked-about conscious decisions about how we are going to respond (discursive consciousness). That is, what's needed to reduce the chances of becoming a bully is being able to explain what we're doing and why. Although building a bully-reputation takes many, many interactions that are given little thought *(practical consciousness)*, tearing down the bully-reputation and building a more constructive professional image means talking about and explaining what we're doing and why *(discursive consciousness)*.

This shift takes some work. The work pays off though, by helping us build professional identities that better serves our needs. Talking about behavior is vital because the struggle for status among people is going on all the time. "The pernicious effects occur *because we don't talk about it*. Once it becomes an explicit part of a relationship, we have a lot more control over how it plays out" [358](p. 9). Bringing the practice of communicating with others into conscious thought and conversations (in this case about how women communicate with and behave toward other women) means *talking about* the reasons for actions and reactions.

Earning the image of a woman who bullies other women is probably unintended, simply an outcome of building a professional reputation without questioning some of the means and motives. The ideas in this chapter can be useful for questioning bullying behavior without undue blame. The goal is for women to exercise more choice and control over whom they are becoming. Thus, we believe that the bully-identity or image comes about as a result of behaving according to unarticulated unrecognized beliefs, norms, and expectations, many of which fail to serve our best interests. The process of image recreation involves recognizing how we (1) are socialized and treated in organizations, (2) create a specific type of professional identity, (3) experience negative ramifications as a result of being seen as a bully, and (4) change the course of our image. Changing course or dismantling the bully-image means talking about the unproductive, harmful aspects of image work and remaking a more constructive and powerful image.

The ideas in this chapter are grounded in the belief that organizations are gendered collections of people. Generally speaking,

> men will be advantaged in organizational settings over their female coworkers, skills identified with men will be rewarded more than those associated with women, male workers and male-dominated organizations will be constructed as ideals ..., and these gendered advantages will be perpetuated in both personal and impersonal ways, through policy, organizational structure, ideology, interactions among workers, and in the construction and maintenance of individual identities. [359](p. 469)

Reconceptualizing women-bullying-women as a byproduct of social and organizational forces rather than a result of mental illness or pathology keeps us from *witch-hunting*. It provides us with a framework for understanding and then *articulating* what's happening or has happened, while avoiding self-blame about the situations in which we may find themselves. What follows examines the historical and social forces that can encourage some of us to bully other women. At each point we pose questions intended to move bullying away from knee-jerk ways of responding (i.e., practical consciousness) and toward behaviors that we can see and then discuss (i.e., discursive consciousness).

Socialization and Identity Building

The ways that we grow up and what we hear and see during these processes prepares and encourages us to want particular professional images. Many social forces encourage us toward aggression at work: (1) women as oppressed and muted, (2) women as not-men, (3) the women-as-authority contradiction, (4) emotion display rules for women, (5) the women-are-sisters belief, and (6) beliefs that there are limited spaces for women the higher they move up in organizational levels.

An *oppressed group* is a social group (e.g., women, African Americans, persons with disabilities) negatively labeled by some imagined or actual difference that stigmatizes group members. Part of oppressed group behavior can be aggression by group members toward

200

others of the same group—what some researchers in the nursing field call *horizontal violence*. As a few women rise up the corporate ladder, they will "almost always, during the initial stages of the struggle, ... instead of striving for liberation, tend themselves to become oppressors" [360] (pp. 29-30) of others who are similar to them. When the larger society stigmatizes members of an oppressed group, members of the oppressed group can bully each other with relative impunity.

Members of oppressed groups are also *muted*; the members have less voice and less influence than members of dominant groups. In fact the oppressed group members may not even have the language to clearly describe their lived experiences (See Chapter 3 for explanation of *muted group theory*). Especially in organizational structures, most of which have men have historically created, "women's voices ... are rarely heard because they must be expressed in a [preferred way of speaking] ... not designed for their interests and concerns" [361] (p. 24).

And when women do speak, if they fail to conform to historically masculine norms (rationality v. emotion; task v. people), others usually view them as less assertive, less influential, and less powerful than their male counterparts. Some ideas about working may even equate aggression and anger with power, influence, success, and dominance [362]. Being a member of oppressed or muted groups, coupled with associating aggression with power, can encourage some ambitious women to ramp up antagonistic rhetoric in order to be heard or heeded.

Women as not-men means that many women work in organizations and professions historically defined by men and masculine ideals. Thus, women can feel like the encroaching "others" where they may believe they do not "naturally" belong [363]. Women can bully other women in order to distance themselves from other women in order to gain males' support [364]. Crafting a powerful forceful professional identity could easily involve acting more in line with often-rewarded masculine, competitive, aggressive standards—especially in individualistic societies like the US that revere winning, mastering, and dominating.

As one woman described her female bully, "She was one of the guys and them some ... distancing herself from other women in the office by doing things like badmouthing their decisions to have kid. She's a he-male" [442](p. 107). Male colleagues may even reward women who are more like one of the boys. We believe they do so because they feel more comfortable with man-like women, not because of any hidden agenda to put or keep women down. But when people around us reward aggression, we then repeat aggression. This happens because we are *social animals,* and the need to belong and have others' esteem is extremely powerful [365].

Some women fear being perceived as incompetent or unable to cut it in a man's world. Sadly, despite gains for women, some bosses and coworkers *do* have this prejudice, but they rarely articulate the bias, so may not even know they have it. Unarticulated values and beliefs about work imply that women are too soft to handle the tough situations in the rough-and-tumble world of work [366]. The fear of appearing incompetent creates fear and pushes women to try to be perfect. The drive for perfection can be a powerful motivator to bully others, especially other women seen as standing in the way or holding someone back.

For bullies, whether female or male, the fear of being perceived as incompetent "*stimulates extreme aggression designed to defend against the threat of incompetence*" [367] (p. 53). As one female bully said, "I knew I was a bully, but I thought I was justified. It is the perfection combined with the urgency that created a lethal combination" [348]. To discover if these forces are behind aggressive behavior, women might ponder the following questions:

✳ Do women irritate you more or more often than men?

✳ Do you feel smarter or more competent that other women?

✳ Do you believe others won't listen to you unless you apply force?

✳ Does the incompetence of others infuriate you, especially when their work reflects on or affects you?

✳ Does your job constantly press you to do more and more but also do it flawlessly??

Co-workers, organizational members, practitioners, and researchers might to ask in women-bullying-women situations:

✳ Does the workplace support, prize, or tolerate (directly or indirectly) aggressive behavior?

✳ Do highly placed people look at sex-gender or skills first? (Evidence: Men more often receive coveted jobs and positions even though women may be more skilled.)

✳ Could women in the organization use aggression because of fear? If so, what might they be afraid of?

In organizations there is often a *woman-as-authority contradiction.* This means that being female and being in a position of authority presents conflicting demands [182, 368]. In many organizations, the "expectations for how a person in authority should behave are at odds with our expectations for how a woman should behave" [369](p. 179). If women perform like men, they might be respected but not liked. If they perform in line with feminine ideals, they can be liked but not respected [370].

Because this contradiction is typically unarticulated, it creates an impossible situation for women forced with trying to be two opposing things at one time. To survive the contradiction, "many developed thick skins and 'roaring bitch' reputations" [364](p. 109). They may turn their aggression on other women who behave in line with more feminine expectations.

In fact, *emotion rules* socialize women in particular ways in organizations. Though men can get away with being aggressive at work [371] and even have others see their anger as a sign of status, women actually lose status when they display anger [372]. If they get angry and lose control, others believe they're being emotional, hysterical, or unprofessional. Ironically, women may believe they should "never show [they] can't cope" [210](p. 89), which leads to the belief that a sort of belligerent aggression is not only appropriate but necessary.

But if they are aggressive, coworkers and subordinates can question their sanity because aggression represents a deviance from femininity. In other words, women are expected to suppress anger, even when using anger is simply women successfully playing a male game. The following questions help women determine if these forces are driving aggressive behavior:

✳ Do you struggle with feeling you have to be soft with people at the same time you're expected to be tough?

✳ Do you feel like you have to be two different ways at work that conflict?

✳ Are you irritated with women who seem too emotional or soft?

Additionally, others in the organizational might consider:

* Does your workplace have double standards for men and women in terms of expressing emotions?

* Do your coworkers or bosses look down on being emotional or expressing emotion?

* How do people perceive and express emotions where you work?

* What is the common reaction to men losing their cool? How about when women losing their cool?

Another dynamic that can push women to bullying other women is the *expectation of sisterhood* [373]. Muddling the rules that professional women have about expressing emotions is "a prevailing myth that [women] should not express or even experience negative feelings toward other women" [364](p. 53). Thus, when women get angry with one another, they may suppress their feelings rather than talk them out in face-to-face conversations. Even the thought of having such a conversation can feel so uncomfortable that the conversation never takes place [374]. Coupling the sisterhood myth with the myth that female anger is irrational and hysterical means that many women stuff their resentments and irritations with other women rather than talking about them right away. Sadly, stuffing negative emotion can backfire when the emotions build up and then blow up. If this sort of thing occurs over and over with particular women, the women can easily be perceived as bullies.

The belief that there are *limited spaces* for highly placed women is another force that fuels female-to-female bullying. Just hearing how few women run Fortune 500 corporations seems to reconfirm the myth that space for women at the top is limited [375]. As women move up the ladder, they can feel more and more like they're tokens, especially when they see fewer and fewer other women around them. Adding these experiences to often-publicized statistics about the small numbers of highly placed, highly paid women can reconfirm the myth of limited places for women. *But the truth is that the number of places "at the table" is the same number of places available for women at the table.* Why can't women occupy all the places at the table? For no reason other than our belief that women's places are limited.

Despite the limited-space myth, fighting for an apparently scarce resource creates tensions in which some women think they have to bully other women in order to secure or protect their place. Consider the following questions to determine if these pressures might encourage your aggression toward other women:

✳ Do you suppress negative feelings about other women because you feel you need to be supportive? Do you explode later when things pile up?

✳ Do you see other women as potential threats to what you've worked so hard to achieve?

✳ Are you uncertain if you should befriend women or closely watch them to figure out if they're out to get you?

The next set of questions helps co-workers, mangers, practitioners, and researchers contextualize and understand related pressures:

✳ Do your coworkers and bosses look at women in positions of power differently than they do men?

✳ Do you or others think that women should be supportive of each other and show more solidarity than men?

✳ Are there organizational pressures that might make women feel they need to be more severe with women than with men?

✳ How does your organization encourage competition among females?

The Grim Down-Side of Women-Bullying-Women

When others start to see a woman as a bully, a number of unexpected and unpleasant outcomes emerge for female bullies, other women, and organizations. A this point bullying begins to have negative effects on women's professional images. At the organizational and societal levels, when women bully other women, *they ironically reproduce many of the repressive forces, beliefs, and norms that disadvantaged women and pushed them toward aggression in the first place.* The organizational processes reproduced include (1) reinforcing the limited space idea, (2) creating perceptions of female incompetence, (3) fortifying gender-based oppression and female-denigration, (4) strengthening male-dominated norms, (5) disciplining gender, and (6) deflecting attention from deeper organizational issues that feed the women-bullying-women phenomenon.

205

When women bully other women to move up the career ladder because they believe that *space for highly place women is scarce*, their actions recreate the beliefs against which they struggled to find a place. In the competition for a perceptually scarce resource, especially when competition includes bullying similar others, women actually do limit spaces for other women. In these situations, *women can become the forces barring other women from advancement.* That is, women's aggression can restrict both the numbers of highly-placed women and the potential for female networks and woman-to-woman mentoring.

Additionally, women-bullying-women often elicits others' *perceptions of women's incompetence.* If out of the fear of being perceived incompetent women develop a take-no-prisoners professional identity, others in the organization can begin to see the aggressive females as interpersonally incompetent, regardless of their technical competence. In many cases, females bullies lose their jobs, suffer demotion, or experience transfers to less desirable positions [137]. Firing and demotion may even occur more readily for women than men. Thus, the negative outcome women may have feared most—being perceived as incompetent—can occur because of the very behavior the female bully used to deflect others' perceptions of incompetence.

Sadly, women-bullying-women ironically reconstructs *female-oppressive structures* and the *denigration of women* (for both targets and bullies). When women bully other women, they become complicit in reproducing the structures that oppress women—ostracizing themselves, their targets, and women in general. Each aggressive act suggests that abused women deserve mistreatment and disrespect. Rather than women focusing their energy on organizational or societal structures that oppress them, female bullies degrade other women by recreating cat-fight stereotypes and notions of women as bitches, whiners, and emotional inferiors (to men). More specifically, women-bullying-women exemplifies the stereotypes that women are petty (i.e., not serious enough to be in the business world), overly sensitive (i.e., prone to female-to-female friction making them undesirable employees), and irrational (i.e., typically respond emotionally instead of rationally).

Women-bullying-women also *strengthens male-dominated norms*, the beliefs that the masculine is "inherently dominating, superior to everything and everyone deemed weak ... and endowed with the right to dominate and rule over the weak and to maintain that dominance through various forms of psychological terrorism and violence" (p. 18] [376].

Undeniably, men are rarely surprised when women bicker. Gendered infighting is simply viewed as an inevitable downside of having women in the workforce. Men may even point to women-bullying-women as female pathology rooted in pettiness and jealousy, as they woefully shaking their heads. And women are not immune to such opinions. In the *Good Morning America* piece, for example, the reporter says, "sometimes a clash of coworker personalities, *particularly amongst women*, can make for a toxic office" [348].

When women bully other women at work they indirectly *discipline gender*. That is, female bullies groom, chasten, and mute other women by teaching them to perform as an "ideal female" (i.e., subservient). There is no question that witnesses to bullying say they are terrified of being targeted if they speak out and draw the bully's attention. Thus, female bystanders can begin shifting their own behavior toward subservience to avoid being targeting. Entire cadres of women are thus groomed into silence and docility, not by men but by other women. (In fact, male upper-managers who avoid disciplining female employees themselves may delegate this task to mid-level women [339].) And female bullies choose very specific targets to drive from the workforce—usually other women who speak their minds, show exceptional talent, and are well-liked [147]. When these strong women exit the workplace, we lose their voices of resistance and models of powerful females.

Finally, women-bullying-women can be a *red herring*—something that diverts attention from the actual forces pushing female aggression and oppression in organizations. Many organizational forces can trigger, enable, and motivate bullying including poorly planned change, crisis, inadequate management, and reward for extreme competition among organizational members [377]. If females are fighting amongst themselves, focus shifts to the visible fight and away from the organizational forces that incited the fight. Because of the stereotype of the emotional woman, when women bullying other women, upper-managers typically view it as an individual-level gender-linked phenomenon, punish women for acting out, and completely overlook the deeper activating forces in organizational systems.

Recreating a Positive, Differently Powerful Identity

Our professional identities can suffer under the effects of bullying, but female bullies can also reconsider and then cast off aggressive behavior as part of their professional identity. Women who are or have been acting as bullies can change, as can organizational norms that contribute to women-bullying-women. Rebuilding a new, improved image suggests that we can change taken-for-granted assumptions, challenge unquestioned practices, and talk about previously unexamined behaviors. We can take steps to become critically aware, insightful, and productive in ways that positively benefit ourselves and others. However, individual women's actions are more effective when others recognize the organizational and social forces that drive bullying at work [378].

Rebuilding a new identity typically starts when upper-managers demand that female bullies cease their aggressive behavior. Upper-managers make these demands because victims and bystanders eventually rebel, resist, and report abuse. Ceasing aggression means women must improve their communication skills, rethink their management styles, stop alienating people, and so forth. When dealing with charges of abuse and demands for change (or expulsion), female bullies have a chance to reassess their routinize ways of acting and reacting (practical consciousness) and really look at how their past behavior has affected their career trajectories. These interventions mark key opportunities—watersheds—for gradually shedding the bully identity and rebuilding professional identity in a constructive direction. Yet, for women to make and sustain this move, others in the organizational setting must also change.

Recreating a constructive professional identity requires two fundamentally different skills-knowledge bases. The first is recognizing the typically unrecognized (e.g., taken-for-granted) social, cultural, historical, and organizational forces encouraging women to bully other women [379]. The earlier discussions and subsequent questions were targeted in this direction. The second skill-knowledge base includes critiquing and beginning a slow shedding of aggressive day-to-day interactions and responses, especially with other women. Similarly, those who surround and supervise female bullies need to shift the organizational pressures that trigger and enable bullying behavior.

Women who have built reputations as being bullies, even if unintentionally, need to avoid self-blame and recrimination. These emotions are less than useful for affecting change. Gaining the first skill-knowledge base is fundamental. Changing without self-blaming means recognizing the compelling power of social pressures, organizational structures, and workplace norms to drive and guide individual behavior. More importantly, however, is *immediately ceasing the abuse of others*—recognizing and catching yourself in abusive interactions and making a decision to act more constructively. At the same time, it is equally essential for those around female bullies to avoid shunning and retort. Acknowledging and talking about the devastating destruction caused by bullying is usually necessary, and responding with understanding, redemption, and empathy is exceedingly helpful for successful change to occur.

One tactic for all parties to open space for change is articulating how one responds, why, and under what contexts the response occurs, particularly after interacting angrily or aggressively. Women, like all humans, routinely go about day-to-day interactions drawing on stores of knowledge (practical consciousness) that are relatively habitual ways of managing social interactions. These habits form and firm up over women's lifetimes, so become ingrained and frequently automatic. By moving habitual responses and practices from practical to discursive—*talking about what one is doing and why*—women can make changes to their professional identities, and those who surround the women can be open to the change. Talking does not guarantee that women will stop bullying other women, but talking about aggressive interactions does make small shifts possible.

The Growth Leadership Center in California, featured in the *Good Morning America* episode, facilitates round table discussions of "bullying broads" to talk about their "tough" office demeanor in order to redirect and remodel aggressive management. In the Good Morning America episode, featured women from this group expressed hope that by attending the group, they could recognize how their negative behavior affected others and make changes. Articulation, which is at the root of this group approach, can provide the materials for small changes over time, which cumulatively results in professional transformation.

Another key strategy for change is accepting others' perceptions as truth and releasing the *feeble defenses* when asked to change—the "I-didn't-mean-anything-by-it" and "That's-just-the-way-I-am" defenses. One way to accept others' perceptions is to consider Miller's Law: "To understand what another person is saying, you must assume that it is true and try to imagine what it could be true of" [380](p. 40). As research and consulting has found, most bullies have been warned to change their behavior. As such, Miller's Law encourages women facing these warnings to accept that the warnings are true. In the beginning, knowing *why* is less important than simply accepting that one does respond aggressively and building new response skill sets. Miller's Law is an equally valuable tool for those who surround female bullies. Parties must be open to the "truth" of women's claims that they are viewed and evaluated differently because of their gender, that they feel pressure to perform differently, or that they may not know why they are behaving aggressively.

The ability to pause at the moment of aggravation or irritation and consider her own behavior and the structures that contextualize her behavior requires a certain level of vulnerability on the part of aggressors and those who surround them. In working contexts that view vulnerability as undesirable or bad for business, women are placed in a situation where the changes they want to make go against the workgroup norms. The vulnerability itself, however, can provide the movement to another way of acting. Rowe [381] makes use *vulnerability* in terms of building alliances between women who come from different backgrounds. She encourages finding ourselves in the other person and building common ground through mutual places of discomfort and pain.

Targets experience a great deal of emotional pain and negative physical symptoms from the stress of being bullied. Bullies likewise engage in bullying behavior from similar places of fear, apprehension, emotional hurt, and uncertainty based in concerns of proving their competence within masculine organizational cultures. Understanding that female targets and bullies are likely coming from a similar emotional place can be used as a starting point for building common ground. Even when the intersections of gender, race, class, and sexual orientation are operating, and the women's standpoints are very different as a result, women can seek common ground on their femaleness pushing back against the dominant patriarchal organizing structures.

The processes of putting experiences into words (i.e., articulation), critiquing organizational and social norms, reflecting on the self, accepting the truth in others' perceptions, and finding common ground begins to reduce aggression and foster women's and organizations' success. The following questions for female bullies help build these processes:

* What kind of person do I want to be in this organization in relation to men and to other women?

* How can I start addressing the pain and frustration that leads to my aggressive and destructive behavior?

* What kind of new identity can I begin to create and enact?

* What new picture can I build that will reduce dysfunction in my working relationships?

* What immediate behavioral steps can I take to catch myself at the moment *before* lashing out?

Additionally, those working with aggressive female coworkers should consider:

* How can we change how the organization and workgroups see the ideal woman employee?

* How can we move away from punishing women who are too passive or too aggressive (violating this ideal)?

* In what ways does the organization hinder or get in the way of people by creating double standards or placing the blame for organizational problems on individuals?

* How can we make shifts toward more constructive organizing in terms of women and men?

Conclusion

This chapter talks about a specifically gendered sub-phenomenon within bullying research: the tendency for women to aggress against other women. It offers a variety of explanations and a creative way to look at the issue to provide space for women to examine their behavior without undue self-recrimination and those around her to look at her and their own behavior differently. We fundamentally believe that to reduce adult bullying, in addition to examining targeted workers' experiences, we must shed light on bullies' perspectives. Thus, the chapter makes visible the typically unrecognized social norms, biases, and beliefs that press women to bully other women.

CHAPTER 11

Active and Passive Accomplices to Workplace Bullying[1]

Gary Namie & Pamela Lutgen-Sandvik

Chapter Summary: When aggressive organizational members bully others, they rarely do so without accomplices. In the current study, bullied workers (targets) and non-bullied bystanders (witnesses) who observed bullying reported that persistent abuse involved either several harassers or support for solitary harassers. Active accomplices were other aggressors; passive accomplices included upper-managers, HR staff, the bullies' peers, and, in some cases even the targeted persons' peers. Respondents also believed that organizations were complicit in bullying; in over 70% of the cases upper-management took no action or made the situation worse. The study extends bullying research by revealing the involvement of numerous other organizational members, and it bolsters targeted worker accounts by comparing target and witness perceptions and finding extensive convergence regarding others' involvement in bullying.

Keywords: workplace bullying, mobbing, workplace aggression, passive aggression

---

When aggressive organizational members bully others, they rarely do so without accomplices of one type or another. Despite the implicit focus on single perpetrators and single victims in bullying research, some suggest that bullying interactions may well include multiple bullies (i.e., mobbing), social support for bullies, or both. To date, however, few studies have examined whether organizational members believe that bullies are deliberately working together with others.

Popular accounts typically also frame bullying as a problem solely involving bullies and their victims (referred to as *targets* in bullying research). These accounts often criticize the targets and accuse them of being thin-skinned or feeble. For example, a columnist recently advised a bullied woman that,

> the real answer lies within yourself. You've given this woman way too much power over you, so you need to . . . take that power back. I can guarantee that most people would not let this little tyrant dominate their existence so completely. But for some reason, you are allowing her to control you. [382] (p. H2)

Such advice paints the targeted woman as psychologically weak — someone who simply "allows" a tyrant to abuse her — and ignores the power of social, collective organizational communication that often contributes to bullying. Unfortunately, the columnist's counsel (as well as the beliefs behind it) is far too common and leads to the perception that workplace bullying is a rather isolated sort of personality conflict. There is reason to believe, however, that bullying and mobbing are communal experiences [383]. In fact, targets frequently feel ganged up on.

Thinking of bullying as a matter involving only a bully and target contributes to viewing it as a solely subjective, psychological experience. As such, managers may be less likely to believe target reports and take immediate corrective action. Moreover, when bullying involves others beyond the bully and target, and accomplices are parts of the mix, viewing bullying as a private two-person conflict oversimplifies how collective voices magnify bully-target power disparity. Nearly all targets have great difficulty stopping abuse once it has started, despite considerable effort and a wide variety of approaches.

If bullies have accomplices, whether publically involved or privately participating behind the scenes, this might explain part of the reason that targets have such difficulty ending abuse. Accomplices, as opposed to witnessing bystanders, actively participate in abuse or support bullies by siding against targets, making determinations in bullies' favor, ostracizing targets, and so forth. To date, however, the frequency of bullying with accomplices or bullying supporters has received only scant attention.

The ways that organizational upper-managers respond to reports of bullying is also an aspect of the collective character of the phenomenon. These responses typically set the tone for others. When upper-management ignores reports of abuse, this is symbolic in its implica-

213

tions. Organizational members infer from non-response that upper-management views workplace bullying as unimportant or trivial [384]. But inertia supports and encourages bullying [18].

Like a police officer that stands idly by when someone is beaten or robbed, others might consider unresponsive upper-managers as passive accomplices because of a similar sort of dereliction of duty. Upper-management may also be active accomplices in bullying situations by not only siding with bullies but also interacting with targets in a hostile, denigrating manner that blames targets for being abused, casts targets as mentally ill, or accuses targets of being problem employees.

The current study extends workplace bullying research by examining workers' perspectives regarding how often others serve as accomplices in bullies' campaigns. It also compares the perspectives of two worker groups: targets and witnesses. Specifically, we investigated three variables associated with the communal character of adult bullying at work: a) the frequency of multiple perpetrators or active accomplices; b) the frequency of passive accomplices — others who indirectly support bullies without actively bullying anyone themselves; and c) the frequency of organizational responses to reports of abuse that aggravate or ignore bullying.

To determine the prevalence of these features, we queried directly targeted workers and non-targeted bystanders or witnesses. We compared aggregated target and witness accounts from persons in different organizations and found considerable convergence. Targets and witnesses were not reporting on the same events in the same organizations, but the level of convergence between the two groups' perspectives of bullying processes suggests that target reports are likely quite authentic indicators of bullying and others' involvement.

The chapter is organized by discussing the importance of attending to perceptions of abuse and underscoring the value of examining multiple perspectives. This is followed by a review of the current research as it guides the study's hypothesis and RQs regarding active and passive accomplices. The chapter then outlines study methods, presents key findings, and discusses implications. The piece ends by recapping methodological strengths, exploring limitations, and proposing fruitful areas for future research. Following conventions of current workplace bullying research, the following terms are used: *target* to indicate those bullied by others at work; *witness* to indicate non-bullied bystanders who have seen others being bullied at work; and *bully, perpetrator,* or *harasser* to indicate the aggressive person who perpetrates abuse. The terms *upper-management, upper-managers,* and *organizations* are used to indicate system-level authorities or persons seen to personify the organization. The chapter begins by underscoring the importance of employee perceptions of bullying.

Perceptions of Workplace Bullying

In the current study, we measured workers' perceptions of bullying on their jobs. These perceptions are fundamentally important for at least five reasons. First, perceptions of abuse shape workers' sense of emotional and physiological health, public and private conversations, identity work, and relationships with employers. Perceptions are the stuff of organizing and sensemaking, and bullying interactions are inextricably linked to target perceptions and affective reactions to abusive behavior.

Second, perceptions of bullying, rather than researcher-generated lists of negative acts, are typically the processes that trigger organizational action, because upper-managers most often directly deal with perceived bullying rather than either operationalizations or firsthand observations. When workers report perceptions of bullying, organizational authorities (hopefully) investigate to substantiate or refute initial perceptions. When enough people share the perception that bullying is occurring, organizations may even create formal anti-bullying policies and procedures.

Third, it is only through perceptions of abuse that either researchers or organizational members can ascertain the features of bullying beyond prevalence (e.g., duration, perpetrators, supporters, responses, etc.). Without reported perceptions, such dynamics are exceedingly difficult, if not impossible, to detect without direct observation.

Fourth, there is substantial overlap between measures based on perceptions of being bullied and operational methods [385]. Operational methods present respondents with an index of items measuring exposure to negative acts, regardless of whether persons feel bullied. Self-labeling asks respondents to identify with a global definition of bullying and thus measures perceptions of abuse. In studies using both methods, the majority of persons who self-label as bullied are also operationally classified as bullied (See Chapter 2).

Finally, the emotional responses to perceptions of abuse are important signaling devices for organizations. When workers perceive that they or others are being bullied and feel hurt, fearful, or angry as a result, these emotions can serve as warning signals pointing to potentially more widespread problems. Negative emotions typically symbolize the tip of the workplace aggression iceberg, indicating that more widespread hostile, abusive communication is submerged beneath the surface of organizational processes. For these reasons, workers' perceptions, both targets and witnesses, are of vital importance.

The Importance of Both Target and Witness Perceptions

A commonly voiced criticism of bullying research is that it tends to focus solely on target perspectives. There is a small but steadily growing body of work, however, focusing on witnessing coworkers. There is little doubt that watching one's peers being bullied at work is harmful. Witnesses report higher levels of stress and workplace negativity and lower levels of job satisfaction and overall liking of their jobs than do non-exposed workers. These experiences are also extremely draining and damaging for witnesses, reducing their productivity and increasing their incidence of health problems.

Importantly, for the communal character of bullying, is that witnesses also wait and see how organizational authorities respond to others' reports of bullying. Managerial responses — whether effective, absent, or ineffective — encourage witnesses to speak out or stay silent, engender support for or withhold support from targeted workers, and increase or decrease intentions to leave. These issues underscore the ways that bullying is shared, even by workers who are not directly targeted.

To some extent, past research has explored target and witness perspectives of bullying situations; specific to the purposes are studies that compared target and witness perspectives. Some research has examined workers in the same groups, while other studies have analyzed aggregate data from people in various workplaces. Coyne's work, for example, explored target-witness perspectives in teams. His research found areas of convergence in that targets "were nominated as preferred people to work with" [102](p. 301) and divergence, as targets felt bullied at higher rates than peers recognized [386]. Research suggests that target and witness reports have both similarities and differences [3].

Disagreement typically concerned the degree of harm rather than the presence or termination of bullying. That is, targets perceived the situation as more harmful than did witnesses, but both recognized its occurrence and cessation. Many subordinates report that the same supervisors is abusive to a number of employees, even though employees often had unique experiences with these supervisors [82]. S.E. Lewis and colleagues [212, 387] also observed a number of target-witness similarities regarding the more general features of bullying. They suggested that similarities were likely a result of inter-subjective sensemaking: Coworkers talked with one another to make sense of abusive interactions, which may have moved individual viewpoints toward convergence.

Other research has examined aggregated target and witness accounts from persons in different organizations, as did ours. From aggregated target-witness data, researchers have found both agreement and disagreement in these perspectives. In Jennifer et al.'s extensive UK study, both targets and witnesses (what she called bullied/non-victims) reported work overload, workplace negativity, and unwanted physical contact more often than did unaffected workers.

Other research has found that workers in both groups typically expected organizational authorities to stop abuse after someone reported it [388] and even to recognize the evidence of abuse (e.g., turnover) and proactively intervene when unreported. Targets and witnesses have somewhat different expectations regarding the outcomes of interventions, however [389]. Targets often sought an apology from the bully or visible punishment, while witnesses simply wanted the bullying to end, usually by having the bully removed.

The studies suggested areas of both convergence and divergence between target and witness perspectives, but they did not examine the presence of bullies' accomplices or bullying supporters. Nor did they compare whether those directly bullied and those who witness bullying came to similar conclusions regarding these issues. To examine the presence of accomplices and make subsequent between group comparisons, we first assessed the prevalence of being a witness or target of bullying at work. We then explored and compared the perceptions of these two groups regarding others' complicity in bullying situations.

Support for Perpetrators: Active and Passive

Whether bullying is the act of one or a number of persons, from whom (or if) bullies find support, and whether bully position in relation to that of targets involves different sources of support are understudied aspects of bullying. However, researchers have noted the

217

need for such research and even suggested that, in bullying processes, the cases with multiple perpetrators are likely to be as frequent as those with sole perpetrators. Certainly, there is evidence that, in some situations, multiple bullies work in concert. Researchers examining gender, for example, reported that pairs of male and female supervisors (one man, one woman) bullied subordinates. This type of accomplice is active and indicative of mobbing.

The term *mobbing* is more evocative of group-level involvement, but key researchers have defined bullying [10] and mobbing [70] with exactly the same words. Mobbing research explicitly points to multiple coworkers who imitate bullies' hostile communication when interacting with targets [390]. Passive accomplices are also a constitutive aspect of how bullying is collective.

As important as recognizing the frequency of multiple active bullies is recognizing how often bullying includes passive, or at least covert, accomplices. Different from witnessing bystanders, passive accomplices support bullies in less direct ways by, for example, siding with bullies, laughing at the jokes made at targets' expense, or ostracizing targets. Despite past research pointing to these communal features, research has yet to specifically investigate whether organizational members believe bullies are deliberately working together or have indirect support from others. Thus, we posed the questions:

RQ1a: Are bullies perceived to act alone or in concert with others?
RQ1b: Do target and witness perceptions differ?
RQ2a: Whom are bullies' supporters perceived to be?
RQ2b: Do target and witness perceptions differ?

Bullying has a contagion effect, especially when someone with power or influence has spearheaded hostility. Hierarchical position likely affects sources and degrees of support, but past research has not explored this directly. Past research has found, however, that supervisor aggression has a stronger negative effect on targeted workers than does aggression from coworkers or outsiders [391]. The stronger negative effect from supervisory aggression might, at least in part, be due to the support others lend to persons in positions of authority.

Perceptions of such support can exacerbate the feeling of powerlessness, both for those targeted and witnessing bystanders. As types of aggression and harm from aggression differ by perpetrator position [392], sources of support likely also differ. Additionally, bully sex may affect sources of support. We do not know whether male or female bullies have different sources of support, if support is present. Given these issues, we posed the following questions:

RQ3a: Do perceived sources of support differ by bully position and sex?
RQ3b: Do target and witness perceptions differ?

Organizational Responses to Reported Abuse

Of central importance to ending employee abuse are organizational responses and interventions when workers report bullying. Without such interventions, workers must confront bullies alone or search for other individual-level solutions, such as quitting their jobs [393]. In the majority of studies, targets have typically reported that organizational authorities took no action to stop abuse, ignored their complaints, or sided with the bullies. In other words, targets believed that after reporting abuse, upper-managers paid little heed to their reports, or that the actions that upper-managers took made things worse.

We know less about witnessing bystanders' perceptions of organizational responses, but their perceptions should not be taken lightly, as onlookers are less likely to speak out if they perceive inertia or penalizing actions toward others who make reports. Even when management is concerned, but appears to remain silent, worker audiences may read this silence as acquiescence, support for bullies, disregard for targets, or some combination of these. Thus, we posed a H and related RQ:

H1: As opposed to improving the situation, employees will perceive that the most common organizational responses to reports of abuse will be to do nothing or exacerbate the situation.

RQ5: Do target and witness perceptions differ with respect to the character of organizational responding?

Methods

Zogby Survey and Sampling

Determining if target and witness perceptions converge or diverge regarding communal features of bullying requires a large enough sample of workers to detect even small differences. Additionally, to assess the national prevalence of being bullied or witnessing others' abuse, calls for a representative sample of US workers. To access such a sample, the Workplace Bullying Institute contracted with Zogby, a polling and public opinion research center (see Glossary).

The population from which the study's sample was drawn included more than 350,000 participants who represented every state in the United States. (Consequently, the study's findings may have limited generalizability to work settings in other nations.) Respondents agreed to participate in online surveys. Zogby drew a random sample of persons from this panel, whom were then invited to participate in an online survey and asked to follow a link to a secure server hosting the survey. Results were weighted to reflect the target population; in this case, working adults nationwide over the age of 18.

Sample

The sample is one of the strongest aspects of this study and included 7,740 adults. Respondents were screened for age, and only adults (18+) were included. The sample demographics closely reflect current US census data (http://www.census.gov/main/ www/access.html) with a margin error of +/- 1.1%. In subgroups, margins of error were slightly higher, so slight weights were added to more accurately reflect the US working population. After screening for age, two other screens were used. The first was for employment; those employed full or part time, currently unemployed, or retired were allowed to continue. No other information about work history was gathered. This screen eliminated three categories — self-employed (-855), student not working (-293), and other/not sure (-329) — and resulted in 6,263 respondents completing the first part of the survey.

The second screen was for persons who had experienced or witnessed bullying, which we globally defined. This ended the survey for those saying they had never witnessed or experienced bullying (-2,802). The second screen left 3,461 persons to complete the remainder of the survey questions about bullying.

Measures

The online survey ran from August 10 through August 13, 2007. Its completion took approximately 13 minutes. In addition to demographic information, the survey inquired about bullying experiences.

In the current study, we analyzed the following issues: whether one had witnessed, experienced, or perpetrated bullying; primary harassers' position and sex; whether harassers acted alone or with others; harassers' supporters; and organizational responses to reported bullying.

Survey responses resulted in categorical data for all questions. We adapted the questions from the Workplace Bullying Institute's (WBI) past research with more than 3,000 targeted workers, as this organization has extensive experience with bullying in the United States, and past studies of bullying, mobbing, and harassment.

Prevalence. As noted, research typically employs two methods of measuring bullying prevalence: counting negative acts over a period of time with behavioral checklists and self-labeling as a target (See Chapter 2). As we were interested in perceptions, we used the latter and asked, "At work, have you experienced or witnessed any or all of the following types of repeated, persistent mistreatment: sabotage by others that prevented work from getting done, verbal abuse, threatening conduct, intimidation, or humiliation?" Choices for self-labeling were: (a) "Yes, I am experiencing it now or have in the last year"; (b) "Yes, it has happened to me in my work life, but not now or in the last year"; (c) "I've only witnessed it"; (d) "I've been the perpetrator myself"; and (e) "I've never had it happen to me and never witnessed it." In concert with past research, we omitted the term *workplace bullying* from the definition because employees may not have interpreted mistreatment as bullying, may have avoided self-labeling that connotes weakness or childishness, and so forth. Also, in line with past research, the definition underscored hallmark qualities of bullying, including repetition, persistence, verbal and non/verbal acts, hostility, humiliation, intimidation, and mistreatment.

Active and passive accomplices. To determine if employees believed that bullying was solely or collectively perpetrated, we asked, "Did the harasser work alone or were there several people involved in the mistreatment?"

Answer choices were:

1) Solo harasser; 2) Several harassers; 3) Not sure

To determine direct or indirect support for bullying, we asked, "Who supported the harasser, if anyone?" Answer choices included:

1) One or more senior managers, executives, or owners
2) Harassers' peers
3) Human resources (HR)
4) Targets' peers
5) No one
6) Not sure

Respondents chose all that applied. We adapted these choices from WBI's past surveys and qualitative US studies. To determine the position of perceived bullies in relation to accomplices, we asked, "What was the principal harasser's rank?" Answer choices included:

1) Harasser ranked higher (Boss)
2) "Target and harasser same rank (Peer)
3) "Harasser ranked lower (Subordinate)

To explore bullies' sex in relation to accomplices, we asked, "What is the gender of the person primarily responsible for the mistreatment?"

Organizational responses, complicity. We focused primarily on responses to reported bullying, as upper-managers rarely observe bullying behavior. To determine workers' perceptions of organizational responses when targets brought the problem to authorities, we asked, "When the mistreatment was reported, what did the employer do?" Choices included:

1) Completely or partially resolved the problem in a way that helped the target
2) Did nothing
3) Worsened the problem for the target
4) Not sure

We framed these responses in terms of overall perceptions, as workers — both targets and witnesses — typically know little about the specifics of behind-the-scenes employment investigations.

Findings

Prevalence

Of those who completed the survey after the first screen (n = 6,263), 791 or 12.6% reported being bullied during the last year, and 24.2% (n = 1,515) reported being bullied at other times in their career (US workers bullied: 36.8%). Men and women reported being targeted at approximately equal rates (x^2 [1] = 0.65, $p > .50$). An additional 12.3% (n = 773) witnessed bullying, but were not directly targeted. As such, 49.1% (n = 3,079) of adults working in the United States reported direct or indirect exposure to bullying.

The questionnaire also included this choice: I've been the perpetrator myself. We excluded this category from analysis due to questionable reliability and validity, as less than one half of one percent (n = 22, 0.35%) selected this response. (We explore this response in the discussion.)

Men and women reported being bullied at approximately equal rates, but males were more often reported as bullies than were females (males 1,862 [60.05%]; females 1,239 [39.95%]; x^2 [1] = 125.16, $p < .005$). This pattern held for both targets and witnesses. Additionally, bullying was primarily top down; in 72.5% of the cases, respondents reported bullies as someone ranked higher than targets.

Peer-to-peer bullying represented 17.4% of cases, and bullying by someone with a lower organizational rank ("bullying up") occurred in 8.5% of cases. This differed significantly from and equalized distribution (x^2 [2] = 72.2, $p > .5$). Witness and target reports did not differ significantly regarding bully position. The following outlines the key findings regarding support for bullies. For all questions, we compared target and witness reports.

Active and Passive Accomplices

RQ 1 asked if bullies worked alone or in concert with others. Respondents collectively reported, in order of frequency: *solo harassers, multiple harassers*, and *not sure*. Targets and witnesses reports converged, and the majority believed bullies worked alone. Chi-square tests revealed no significant differences between target and witness reports (see Table 11.1).

Table 11.1: Percentage of Targets and Witnesses Reporting Sole Harassers or Multiple Harassers

	Targets (n = 2,306)	Witness (n = 773)
Number of Harassers		
Solo harasser	66%	76%
Several harassers	30%	19%
Not sure	5%	5%

RQ2 asked who supported the bullies. Respondents chose all supporter categories that applied, and in 23.7% of the cases, they reported multiple sources of support for bullies. Collective reports identified bullies' supporters in order of frequency as senior manager/owners, harassers' peers, HR, and targets' peers.

In nearly a third of the cases, respondents said no one supported the bully. That is, unsupported bullies were not one type of actor (i.e., boss, peer, subordinate) more than they were another; they were equally distributed for higher-, same-, and lower-level bullies. When comparing target-witness reports, the only significant difference we found was that witnesses, more often than targets, reported that no one supported bullies. In all other categories, witness and target accounts did not differ significantly. Table 11.2 summarizes perceived supporters and percentages reported.

Table 11.2: Percentage of Targets and Witnesses Reporting Who Supported Harassers

Bullies' Supporter(s)	As Reported by Targets (n =2,689)	As Reported by Witnesses (n =740)
Senior managers	34%	23%
Harassers' peers	25%	21%
HR	11%	8%
Target's peers	7%	7%
No one	24%	39%

We examined cross-tabulated data regarding the two previous RQs (solo harassers and harassers' supporters) to determine whether respondents believed solo harassers had others' support (see Table 11.3). Of those reporting a solo harasser, 60% said the harasser received support. In these cases, respondents thought support for bullies came from the following, in order of frequency: senior manager/owners, harassers' peers, HR, and targets' peers. No significant differences were found between target and witness reports. Thus, even in the cases reportedly perpetrated by solo harassers, the vast majority of respondents assumed others enabled bullies in some way. And it appeared that employees distinguished between active co-bullies and passive accomplices that enabled bullies (see Table 11.3).

Table 11.3: Percentages of Targets and Witnesses   Reporting Who Supported Solo Bully

	Targets (878)	Witness (377)
Who Supported Solo Bully?		
Senior managers	47.9%	46.1%
Harassers' peers	29.7%	31.0%
HR	14.2%	13.8%
Targets' peers	8.1%	13.5%

Note: 2,103 solo harassers

To answer **RQ** 3 that asked if perceived sources of support differed by bully position or sex, we cross-tabulated bully position with source of support and found that support varied based on bully position. Bullies in higher level positions than targets had significantly higher rates of perceived support from higher-level others (i.e., managers, executives, owners) and **HR** than did bullies in peer or subordinate positions. When bullies were subordinate to targets, their support most often came from the subordinates' peers. For persons targeted by peers, bullies gained support from other peer-level persons and senior managers at approximately equal rates. As such, the pattern appeared to be gaining support from others at similar levels in the organization, except for peer bullies, who also found support from higher-level persons.

To determine if sources of perceived support differed by sex, we examined cross-tabulated data for these two variables. No significant differences were found between males' and females' sources of support. Additionally, males and females were equally likely to be reported as receiving no support. We found no significant differences between target and witness perceptions of support in relation to position or sex. Table 11.4 illustrates cumulative respondent data.

Table 11.4: Bully Position and Sources of Support

	Bully Position in Relation to Target			Bully Sex	
Bullies' supporters	Higher	Peer	Lower	Male	Female
Senior managers	31% a,b,d	21% a,e	18% b,g,h	34%	36%
Harasser peers	20% c,d	25% f	31% c,g,i,j	28%	24%
Human resources	10% d	6% e,f	8% h,i	10%	13%
Target peers	6%	6%	9% j	7%	9%
No one	29%	35%	29%	30%	30%

Percentage reported for each supporter group; different subscripts (a, b, c ...) indicates statistical difference between reports. Read subscripts across, then down.

Organizational Responses and Complicity

H1 proposed that inertia or making the situation worse would be the two most common responses to reported abuse. Those who responded to this question said, in order of frequency, that when workers reported bullying, organizational authorities did nothing, completely or partially resolved bullying in a way that helped targets, or worsened the situation for targets. Thus, we found only partial support for H1. Encouragingly, the second most commonly reported outcome, as opposed to worsening the situation, was completely or partially resolving the problem. Witnesses and targets did not differ in their perceptions of organizational responding (see Table 11.5).

Table 11.5: Target & Witness Reports of Organizational Responses, Results of Responses

Response, Result	Targets' Perspective (n = 1,188)	Witnesses ' Perspective (n = 323)
Did nothing	46%	35%
Resolved situation	31%	36%
Worsened situation	18%	20%
Not sure	6%	8%

% = proportion of each group responding in each category

Discussion and Implications
for Organizational Communication

This study extends workplace bullying research by exploring the collective character of adult bullying from the perspectives of those directly targeted and those who see others being bullied. From both perspectives, employees paint a complex picture of bullying that involves bullies, bullies' active accomplices, bullies' passive enablers and supporters, and employing organizations.

Taken together, the converging accounts from a representative sample of US workers provide convincing evidence that the majority of these cases involve many workers beyond the target and bully. Specifically, the cases of multiple perpetrators, combined with cases in which perpetrators who had others' support, represents nearly 70% of the bullying situations. As such, widespread metaphorical depictions of the lone-wolf bully and one bad apple fit less than a third of bullying cases. In most cases, workplace bullying is a social process embedded in workgroup and organizational communication networks. In what follows, we further examine the central findings regarding these communal features and discuss possible implications.

To determine targeting and witnessing, we used a global definition of bullying that underscored the key features (persistent, frequent) taken from past research. The definition also included terms associated with properties of bullying communication such as humiliating, intimidating, and threatening. Like other global definitions, it included a sample of associated negative acts (e.g., mistreatment, verbal abuse, work sabotage), but did not list all possible bullying interac-

228

tions (e.g., social ostracism, gossip and rumors, teasing and sarcasm). As the definition did present the common features and properties of bullying definitions, we have considerable confidence in drawing comparisons between the current study and past prevalence of perceived bullying based on identification with a global definition. For the respondents who identified with this global definition, we then explored their perspectives of bullies, supporters, and organizational responses.

Prevalence

From both target and witness perspectives, we can conclude that while not all bosses are bullies, nearly three-quarters of the perceived bullies are supervisors. This is similar to a number of prior US studies and British studies (See Chapter 2) in which respondents are asked to identify the primary abuser, demonstrating that the bullying-boss stereotype is very real. This is somewhat inconsistent with a US study of the Department of Veterans Affairs [101] in which workers more often reported coworkers as aggressors (47%) than they did supervisors (40%) and with an earlier Michigan study that found bosses and coworkers at equal rates [394].

However, this study's findings parallel four other US studies reporting that supervisors are the most frequently reported bullies. Given the similar pattern in target and witness reports and the study's sample size and representativeness, we believe these findings are generalizable to the US workforce. However, we comment here on potential reasons for the difference, which we believe are linked to sample variations and measurement differences.

The current study included workers in various organizational types (of which government is only one), whereas the VA study predominantly examined the experiences of government employees (working in a wide variety of functional VA areas). It appears, then, the two studies are querying fundamentally different populations: public employees in a large US government division and employees in a broad range of different organizations. Measurement tools also differed. We asked about perceptions of the "principal harasser's rank" — wording that asks respondents to identify the person whom they believed predominantly perpetrated persistent abuse. In the VA study, researchers used an operationalization approach by identifying primary sources of aggression and from that determining the actor who perpetrated 75% or more of that aggression. As different data analysis and dissimilar populations can produce highly variable results, we assume some of the difference regarding primary bullies' positions is attributed to these two issues.

Perceived impact and the leading power of hierarchical position may also push targets to identify supervisors more often as primary abusers. Targets suffer more negative effects from supervisory abuse than they do abuse from other sources. As such, supervisory bullying likely feels worse and has more far-reaching negative ramifications than peer-to-peer aggression, even though it may occur less frequently.

Additionally, targets may perceive supervisors as leading the attack, so to speak, so they more often identify supervisors as the primarily responsible perpetrator. Certainly, research on university professors being bullied suggests that senior faculty members instigate mobbing and then junior members join in [395]. Such cases implicate all workgroup members, but targets likely view senior persons as primary harassers and those who follow suit as secondary harassers.

There is also some question as to whether the elapsed time since bullying occurred alters targets' identification of the primary perpetrator(s). At least one US study found that persons recently bullied (i.e., in the past year) and those bullied in the past (i.e., overwork history) report different perpetrators [394]. In one US study, people bullied in the past year identified bosses and coworkers at equal rates, while those bullied further in the past most often identified bosses as the bullies.

Since supervisory abuse is more damaging than peer-to-peer abuse, it is probably more memorable, which may account for some difference. However, we did not find this elapsed-time difference in the data. Both recent- and past-bullied groups, examined separately and collectively, most often reported higher-ranking persons as principle harassers.

Men were also reported most often as primary harassers, a finding similar to past UK and EU research as well as similar to a number of US studies. Researchers have proposed that this bully-gender pattern is due to men enacting overt (and thus more obvious) aggression because of social norms accepting male aggression and men being over-represented in supervisory positions. We did find support for the latter; a significantly larger proportion of higher-level bullies were male (60.6%) than female (39.4%). It is possible that males are simply in a position to bully more often than are females.

Overall prevalence, however, is quite similar to past studies. Given the representativeness of the current sample and the similarity of findings to past research, we have considerable confidence regarding the prevalence of experiencing and witnessing workplace bullying in the United States. In another study [6], for example, the second author found that 9.4% of workers reported feeling bullied in the past six months, and the current study found that 12.6% of workers felt bullied over the past 12 months. As such, we are fairly confident that, in the United States at least, roughly one in 10 workers have recently experienced persistent psychological, emotional abuse at work. The finding that 37% of workers have been bullied sometime during their careers falls within past estimates that range from 30% to 42% over work histories. I also found in an earlier study that 11% of workers had witnessed, but were not directly targeted; in the current study; 12% of non-targeted workers witnessed bullying.

Active and Passive Accomplices

In nearly a third of the cases, bullying included multiple harassers. This draws attention to at least one of the communal features of bullying: It can occur as mobbing-type communicative behavior involving many active aggressors. Multiple-aggressor bullying underscores others' active and public collusion with bullies. Thus, the findings are consistent with case study research of North American academics, pointing to bullying as concerted efforts to drive out targeted persons. [383] What is equally important, but can make bullying even harder to describe, is the passive or less public support for bullies that both groups perceived.

A third of the cases involved multiple aggressors, but in nearly 70% of cases bullies were solo bullies, which seems to support the notion that bullies are lone wolves or bad apples. However, looking a little deeper into employee accounts, we find that in nearly 60% of the solo-bully cases, respondents believed the bullies received support from many corners of the organization, most often from upper-managers, but also from HR staff, bullies' peers, and even targets' peers. By combining multiple harassers and solo harassers who received support, we find that nearly three quarters of bullying cases were concerted and collective to some degree. It does seem that "bullying will only take place if a bully feels he or she has the blessing, support, at least, the implicit permission of superiors and other coworkers to behave in this manner" [396](p. 119).

Both groups also reported different sources of bullies' support in relation to bullies' hierarchical position, a pattern one might expect, given power allegiances and social dynamics of in- and out-groups in the workplace. For the most part, support came from same-level others. Those in higher positions than targets had more support from their peers (also highly placed persons) and senior-level organizational members. Similarly, lower-level bullies were perceived to be working with the support of their (subordinate bullies') peers. Peer bullies also found support from same-level others, but equally received support from upper-management.

Overall, the pattern of support suggests that persons may side with "their own," so to speak. Bullies found little support from targets' peers, regardless of bullies' position. However, subordinate bullies — those bullying up — most often worked together and garnered a small edge with targets' peers. These patterns lend support to the notion that when workers bully up, they do so with groups comprised of other subordinates.

The degree of convergence in target and witness accounts is striking regarding these communal or collective features. The critique of target-focus research insinuates that the target perspective is limited or narrow, potentially even skewed. Because targets suffer most acutely in bullying situations and as a result can be highly emotional when giving accounts, discounting their perceptions of others' complicity might be easy.

Management and workers alike disbelieve highly emotionalized stories of organizational interactions, as this kind of emotional display breaks with implicit display rules and expectations of rationality at work. As such, organizational members (and some researchers) tend to minimize these perspectives. Agreement between these two groups lends considerable credence to targets' perspectives of bullying situations and could increase confidence in not only this study's findings but other workplace bullying research based on target-report data. Given such convergence, upper-managers and peers might err on the side of believing targets unless there are compelling reasons for not doing so.

We found a target-witness difference on one aspect that bears discussion. Witnesses perceived similar sources of organizational support for bullies as targets. In equal proportions both groups believed that upper-managers, HR, bullies', and even targets' peers were involved. However, witnesses said there was "no support" for bullies more frequently than did targets. This difference might be due to a number of considerations, three of which we address here.

232

First, targets are closer to the situation and may simply know more about the involved parties. The experience often eclipses all other aspects of targets' work lives, and targets spend considerable time trying to alleviate persistent bullying and its effects. Second, targets may less often report that bullies received "no support" because they may interpret witnesses' silence as assent. When targets suffer at the hands of bullies and their coworkers seem to look on silently, targets can feel like this silence is betrayal or even complicity [397]. Witnesses in bullying situations might be less likely to perceive others' silence as a type of support. Finally, "no support" could also mean that others have responded in ways outside of the view of the target that indicate a lack of support for the bully's behaviors. In such cases, witnesses might have more access to these conversations than do targets.

Both groups did point to upper-managers' involvement, however. That perceived support came from upper-managers is disturbing, and two general management styles are associated with a tendency toward employee bullying. A coercive-authoritarian style encourages bullying supervisors and demeans workers who become disadvantaged in peer-to-peer bullying. Laissez-faire managers, on the other hand, are unlikely to respond at all, and by failing to respond, inadvertently support bullying [307].

We were unable to discern these different styles from the data, but it is possible that a laissez-faire leadership style may underlie what we did find. Leadership theory generally characterizes laissez-faire leadership as either benign or simply ineffective; however, it can be particularly damaging in situations where action is needed [398]. If upper-management fails to intervene when employees are abused, such failure makes them complicit in employee bullying.

Organizational Responses, Complicity

Both targets and witnesses had similar perspectives of organizational responses, and in equal proportions, reported organizational inertia, situation improvement, or condition deterioration. In nearly a third of the cases, respondents believed organizational actions made a positive difference — somewhat better than intimated by past research. This is good news and could be a function of having a representative sample versus a self-selected sample. It could also mean that upper-managers' efforts are becoming more evident to organizational members as these members' awareness of the phenomenon increases.

233

Increased awareness of the bullying phenomenon is likely fueled by academic research, press coverage, consulting firms, and Internet sites dedicated to the subject (e.g., http://www.workplacebullying.org/, http://www.iawbh. com/, http://www. kickbully.com/). Regrettably, how-ever, in over 70% of the cases, respondents thought that authorities either made the situations worse or did nothing, perceptions that indict organizations' involvement or impotence. Unfortunately, when employees speak out about bullying and upper-managers do nothing (that is visible at least), organizational climates develop in which bullies can abuse others with impunity.

We can speculate, based on organization research and theory, why upper-managers might fail to act, or why workers perceive a failure to act. First, negative sanctions against or investigations of aggressive workers are veiled to ensure employee privacy while providing for alleged bullies' due process; employment laws often mandate privacy in such matters. Second, upper-management may hold firmly to a classical chain-of-command idea about communication direction in which interfering with line supervisors' decisions or actions can seem practically heretical. And line supervisors trained and socialized with similar values and beliefs will likely cry foul if upper-management does interfere.

Third, some inertia might be due to lack of knowledge about the bullying phenomenon: what it looks like, how to assess it, and what to do about it. US organizations provide training on sexual harassment and protected-group discrimination, but adult bullying is not as well understood and lacks statutory regulation. Bullying is also in a state of denotative hesitancy in the country as a whole. Though not the case in other parts of the world, the US has yet to agree upon a common term to label persistent emotional and psychological abuse at work. Fourth, lack of intervention could result from the aversion to conflict. Most supervisors dislike and avoid even the most pedestrian employee evaluations, including negative feedback, and thus, dealing with aggressive workers could feel overwhelming. In fact, many upper-managers report being as afraid of bullies as are the bullies' targets.

Finally, upper-management is unlikely to witness employee abuse. Especially in highly complex organizations (e.g., government divisions/departments, universities, multinational corporations), many interactions among employees and between supervisors and subordinates are, for the most part, out of upper-management's view and may even strategically be concealed from upper-management. As such, the workgroup space can be a place where formally disapproved practices nonetheless occur. Thus, even in situations where organization's upper echelons frown on or forbid employee abuse, their direct observation of such behavior is improbable. Upper-managers then must weigh accounts from the involved parties, a process that often favors hierarchical position: The bullying boss has a voice, whereas the bullied target's voice is minimized or muted. In accounts of what occurred, targets typically believe bullies are outstanding at managing up, misleading upper-management, and concealing their bullying behavior.

Implications

The findings enhance the viability of targeted workers' perspectives that have framed much of bullying research to date. Despite critiques of target-only standpoints, targets and witnesses report similar perceptions of bullying involvement and complicity. The current findings come from a representative sample that was large enough so we were able to detect even small differences between these two groups. For the one variable that differed significantly, effect size was small. Perception convergence underscores the patterned and shared nature of bullying in the United States and gives rise to a number of implications.

First, convergence suggests that target perspectives of workplace bullying are reliable, valid indicators of the phenomenon and its features. Despite the stigmatization of victimizing experiences, such as workplace bullying, sexual assault, or domestic violence, the abused person likely has the best understanding of the phenomenon (what's happening and whom is involved).

Second, the notions that workplace bullying is an individual, psychological issue or a set of interactions solely between the bully and target are myths. As illustrated in the columnist's remarks in the introduction, the language of individualism and the discourse informing this language is deeply rooted and as deeply flawed. Individualism as a lens through which we perceive the world focuses the conclusions about much of social life. Work — how we talk about work and interactions among people at work — is no exception.

Viewing bullying dynamics through an individualistic lens encourages blaming the victim and expecting the victim to single-handedly resolve what's clearly a collectively communicative problem manifested by multiple harassers, support for harassers, organizational inaction, or upper-managers' exacerbation of the abuse. These fea-

235

tures explain why individual efforts rarely end workplace bullying. Undoubtedly, multiple perpetrators make resistance, reporting, and responding far more difficult and risky.

Third, one of the features of workplace bullying is power disparity, typically represented as uncomplicated differentials between bully and target. However, power disparity appears far more complex and involves numerous strata of discursive power beyond, but implicative of, hierarchical position. We are able to see from the findings that this disparity is not simply a bully-versus-target dynamic but is multifaceted and layered. One stratum is the interpersonal level. The study and a number of others have found that bullies often hold higher organizational positions than targets, and managers can quite easily justify their actions as necessary supervision or surveillance [30]. Targets on the other hand, face a number of biases around the notions of victimization that stigmatize and cast their accounts as suspect. And peer bullies with informal, charismatic power often attract into the aggressive cliques, those very coworkers who would otherwise support targets .

Another layer of power disparity is within the workgroup. Workgroup members' responses to bullying, such as fear-induced silence, victim blaming, or siding with abusers, forecloses the potential for collective resistance and engenders feelings of being mobbed. Targets explain that allegiances easily shift, and someone who had supported them in the past suddenly sides with what may look like a dominant actor or group. A third stratum is organizational, as inferred from upper-managers' responses. Organizational responses compound power disparity because when those with fiduciary responsibility fail to intervene or even support bullies, workers' legitimate avenues of redress are closed off. Of course, this also exacerbates the feeling of being abused and increases not only perceptions of, but very real, impotence. The stratified character of power disparity intensifies the feelings that bullying comes from all sides, which from the study appears to be the case.

Other Thoughts

A central strength of the current study is the representative nature of the sample. It is large enough to comfortably state there is great similarity in how targets and witnesses see the bullying phenomenon. Although sampling for an online survey is not random, we argue, based on the sample demographics, that it is one of the most representative US samples to date in the study of this topic. Despite the representativeness and size of the sample, the findings are limited to US workers' experiences and have only limited generalizability to settings in other nations. Research does suggest that US workplaces are similar to UK workplaces since these countries have a number of similar cultural features. UK studies generally find the majority of bullies are bosses, which was also the case in the study surveying a representative sample of US workers. However, generalizability of the findings to Scandinavian workers, for example, is problematic because these cultures are quite different.

Another issue is that data come from witness and target aggregates rather than from witnesses and targets reporting on the same situation. The findings do little to flesh out the shared perspectives of workers when colleagues talk with one another and move toward perspective convergence (or divergence). Potentially, when there is an opportunity for intersubjective sensemaking, target-witness perspectives converge even more than what we found. As Schaller noted [399], "It is not difficult to perceive a narrative discourse between employees . . . where labeling of deviants and the moralizing of bullying in the face of inadequate voice and representation becomes a norm" (p. 80). On the other hand, the perspectives of these two groups were remarkably similar, even without intersubjective sensemaking, and go far to reduce marginalizing and minimizing targets' reports. Future studies of targets and witnesses in the same workgroups might be compared to this study to determine these groups' convergence or divergence in perceptions.

Additionally, survey responses to the bullying definition did not permit identification of those who had witnessed and were also bullied. Rather, if targeted workers also witnessed the abuse of others, this was subsumed in the target-only category. Future research might provide for more extensive categories to include target only, witness only, witness-target, and neither target nor witness. Differences between those who witness only and those who are witness-targets are possible in terms of how they perceive bully supporters, targeted worker actions, or organizational responses.

We inquired about the most commonly perceived sources of support for bullies, but we did not ask about bullies' or targets' subordinates. We omitted this due to the rarity of bullying up; however, there is evidence from this study that when subordinates are identified as bullies, they find support from other subordinates. However, since lower-ranked colleagues might join in the mobbing process of more senior people, we likely missed part of the communal character of

237

bullying through this omission. Future research should include subordinates as potential collaborators in communal bullying (mobbing) or even act as bullies themselves. Understanding how the bullying-up process might be intertwined with peer-to-peer or supervisory bullying is a crucial step toward gaining a full picture of the communal character of adult bullying at work.

A final concern is that getting input from the bullies' perspective is exceedingly difficult. In the current study, less than one% of respondents reported abusing others, a highly questionable figure (12 men, 10 women; 13 peers, 8 bosses, 1 subordinate). As Rayner and Cooper, two UK scientists, [355] have imaginatively explained, "finding and studying the bully is like trying to study black holes — we are often chasing scattered debris of complex data and shadows of the past" (p. 47). Some researchers and practitioners claim that managers are unaware of how often others perceive their interactions as aggressive and harmful.

Despite the difficulty of getting to the bully perspective, new research is beginning to shed some light on the issue. Fast and Chen's [400] study, for example, found that organizational members with formal power most often revert to aggression when they feel incompetent. Additionally, creatively designed research could get to the bully perspective. For example, one might interview professionals called in to resolve or mediate bullying to access bullies' accounts. Alternatively, researchers could interview persons others identified as bullies and talk with them about their working or management styles and philosophies.

Conclusion

This study explicitly considers the frequency of bullying accomplices. Findings underscore the communal character of bullying (implicating perpetrators, targets, witnesses, and upper-managers) and emphasize the importance of viewing the phenomenon as collective patterns of communication. As important, we looked beyond target reports, queried those who witnessed bullying, but were not directly targeted, and found striking convergence between these two groups' perspectives. The study underscores the importance of upper-management's responses to bullying. In one-third of the reported cases, organizations took action that improved the situation, which is very promising. However, in the majority of cases, workers perceived no or ineffective action. Inertia and ineffectiveness at dealing with bullying are fundamental problems, whatever the reasons. Doing nothing is not being neutral when workers ask for help; when nothing is done, organizations inadvertently becomes bullies' accomplices. When left unattended, bullying can spread like a contagion, becoming the accepted, albeit painful, norm for interactions

CHAPTER 12

Making Sense of Supervisory Bullying[K]

Pamela Lutgen-Sandvik & Virginia McDermott

Chapter Summary: The current chapter reports a study we did about supervisory bullying, which is the most common type of bullying in US workplaces. We were specifically interested in how targets made sense of why it happened. We looked at the ways people talked about supervisory bullying and the framing vocabularies that seemed to drive these conversations. Targets' explanations seemed to create at least partially how powerless targets said they felt. Most of them thought bullying happened because the perpetrators were mentally ill, evil, and power-hungry. Nearly as frequently, they believed bullying happened because of upper-management's failure to stop it. The ways targets made sense of the experience drew heavily on ideas of individualism and in the belief that upper-managers were all-knowing and all-powerful. Other explanations involved targets, coworkers, and society. We suggest conversational shifts that targets might use when making sense of bullying, shifts that could frame bullying and their responses to it in more empowering ways.

Keywords: workplace bullying, sensemaking, framing vocabularies, emotional abuse, powerlessness

----

When faced with bullying from supervisors, workers struggle to make sense of why it is occurring and what might be done about it. Typically, targets feel like bullying is something they have great difficulty stopping or protecting against. Most targets say that bullying ends only when they leave their jobs. As employees talk about or make sense of experiences, they partially create the reality of the experiences. How people talk about experiences also directs how they respond. Being bullied by a boss places employees in a power-down situation. How employees explain the situation can intensify power-less feelings.

Understanding the ways people make sense of bullying suggests places where they can gain leverage because "to change a group, one must change what it says and what its words mean" [335](p. 108). That is, understanding how targets make sense of abuse can provide hints to how they might make sense differently in ways that are more empowering.

In this chapter, we examine US workers' sensemaking for supervisory bullying, how they explained bullying. Our focus was supervisory bullying because even though coworkers can and do bully one another, and subordinates are known to "bully-up," in the United States supervisors and managers are most often reported as perpetrators.

We examined the accounts of 246 US workers and found that sensemaking ranged from individual to societal. Targets believed bullying came about because of evil perpetrators, complicit coworkers, and norms for US business. The two most common themes pointed to bullies as deviant and upper-managers as incompetent. Targets explained bullying drew on individualism and the ideal of upper-managers as parental caretakers. Typically, each person's sensemaking incorporated multiple themes. Looking at how people make sense of bullying explains part of why targets report feeling powerless to stop abuse.

Bullying breaches the norms of civil conversation, and this breach it can mean many things. Targets and organizational members tasked with intervention spend a lot of time talking about it to understand why it is happening and what to do. Looking at the explanations for bullying, that is the content of sensemaking, sheds some light on why targets can feel so powerless.

Perceived Powerlessness and Sensemaking Content

To understand how sensemaking can cast adult bullying in disempowering ways, we draw upon ideas from social constructionism, sensemaking theory's framing vocabularies [335, 401], and attribution theory [402]. We use these conceptual threads to weave a threefold argument: First, the ways employees talk about or make sense of adult bullying creates the social reality to which they then respond. Attributions play an important role, especially when attributed causes cast the situation as intractable. Second, sensemaking typically depends on a

241

social norms and beliefs, which "appear ... as the natural way of looking at the world" [403] (p. 8). These beliefs usually fail to serve the
interests of targets bullied by aggressive supervisors. Third, understanding sensemaking can unmask certain disempowering explanations, open spaces for conversational change, and provide leverage for
change.

Sensemaking and How Personal
Explanations Can Create a Sense of Reality

Sensemaking happens all the time. We have an experience and then
talk to others about what that experience means and why it happened.
We make sense of things by retrospectively (in hindsight), intersubjectively (talking with others) determining what the things mean and how
or if to respond [404-406]. We do the most sensemaking when we
have equivocal experiences. Equivocal means that what happened
could mean many different things, it's meaning is ambiguous and unclear. We talk to others over and over to many different people to try
and reduce the ambiguity and pin down what the experience means.
Once we think we have it figured out, then we decide how to respond.

We believe that the explanations people create during sensemaking produce a fixed sort of reality to which they then respond. Most of
us need a stable-feeling explanation for what something. An explanation resolves part of the ambiguity about what our experiences mean
and why we're having those experiences. In the case of bullying, if we
explain bullying by saying that bullies are crazy, the problem feels like
it's them (bullies) not us (targets). However, attributing "crazy" to bullies fixes the reasons for why bullying is occurring in a way that makes
it seem more uncontrollable than it is. When our friends and
coworkers agree with us, ("You've got that right; he's a sociopath!"),
other kinds of equally plausible explanations are short-circuited. We
think analyzing "what is being processed" [335](p. 108), the sensemaking conclusions people come up with, give us a way to understand
and then change feeling so powerless.

We can find disempowering language use by discovering the
common attributions we use in conversations that give reasons for
bullying. Uncovering disempowering communication can create opportunities for language changes. When in hindsight we make sense
of something by talking to others, we collectively call upon shared
beliefs about work and people [407]. In the workplace, our numerous
conversations create shared explanations for things, which can build

resistance or feelings of helplessness [408].

Attributions are the causes we conjecture for actions and events that have very real consequences for how we understand and react to bullying. Language use and how we communicate can make what we feel inside (subjective experience) seem as if it were an irreversible reality (objective experience). Quite simply, the way we talk about our life experiences in a sense we creates the reality of our life experiences. We respond to our lives depending on the ways that we interpret life events with others. As such, discovering our commonly attributed explanations for bullying provides a starting point for changing how we feel inside about the experience. When we hear what we're saying and realize we might be making things even worse than they already are, we have a starting point for shifting the power dynamics in bullying.

Attributions have three specific dimensions: (1) causality (internal, external), (2) permanency of experience (stable, unstable), and (3) control over events (controllable, uncontrollable) [409]. Attributing internal causation means we have concluded that some innate feature or trait of a person is the cause, while external causation means environmental pressures were the cause: ("She's basically evil" v. "I was just getting over an illness so was more vulnerable"). Stability is the perception of an event as likely (or unlikely) to endure over time: ("Once a bully always a bully" v. "A few supervisors are just bad apples"). If we believe some action can change the outcome, the situation feels more controllable to us, but if we believe the outcome will be the same regardless of what we do, the outcome is uncontrollable: ("When I complained, the bully was fired" v. "No matter who complains nothing is done").

Sensemaking Slanted Toward
How We Talk About Our Experiences

The ways we think and talk about things is the material for sensemaking [335]. We call these ways of thinking and talking *framing vocabularies,* a term we borrow from Karl Weick, an organizational psychologist at the University of Michigan. For targets of bullying bosses, targets might use framing vocabularies that reinforce their feelings "subordinate" and indirectly bolster bullies' abuse of power.

Weick argues that are at least six different types of framing vocabularies or ways that people explain experiences at work: *ideologies, third-order controls, paradigms, traditions, theories of action,* and *stories*. *Ideologies* are vocabularies of society, relatively consistent interconnected sets of emotionally-charged points of view, morals, and beliefs that filter how we perceive things [410]. *Third-order controls* are vocabularies of organization that indirectly guide what we say and do. Examples are managerial manipulation and peer pressure [411, 412].

Paradigms are vocabularies of work, the "standard operating procedures, shared definitions of the environment, and the agreed upon systems of power and authority" [335](p. 118). Paradigms are usually specific to certain professions or organizations. *Traditions* are vocabularies of predecessors that call upon history and past events to guide current behavior. *Theories-of-action* are vocabularies of coping and are oriented toward seeing cause-effect patterns in events. Finally, *stories* are vocabularies of sequence that create "a history for an outcome .... [Stories gather] strands of experience into a plot that produces that outcome" [335](p. 128).

We usually draw on many framing vocabularies to make sense of the cues regarding our experiences. In bullying situations for example, when aggressors persistently rage about targets' perceived shortcomings (the cue), targets may weigh the outburst against a paradigm of professional decorum (the frame), connect the two and conclude that the actor is incompetent (the derived explanation or sensemaking content). Alternately, the target could connect raging (the cue) to the ideology of individualism (the frame) and conclude that the actor has a personality disorder (the explanation).

Once we intersubjectively agree on what the cue means based on the framing vocabulary, we then choose a reaction that fits the sense made. So for example, understanding the framing vocabularies that drive sensemaking can uncover the beliefs that lead to the conclusion "bullying is just the way things are done around here."

Sensemaking Themes and Possibilities for Change

Workplace bullying is a very real and traumatizing experience, and finding different ways for us to talk about it might ease some of the hopelessness we can feel and provide ideas for change. Some ways we talk about bullying can further paralyze those targeted and aggravate their feelings of helplessness. In my collaborative study of targets' metaphorical language, for example, targets frequently characterized themselves as children trying to avoid abuse by being invisible or acting ingratiatingly [2]. We thought it possible that targets thinking of

244

themselves as children could be counter to their workplace goals. Thinking about themselves as children and trying to be invisible "might decrease abuse, but is also likely to serve as a stumbling block if targets want to increase their status in organizational settings" (p. 172). That particular study pointed to the potential for language choices to close off avenues for blocking abuse at work.

We believe to some degree, "language transformation can be a pathway to behavioral transformation" [335] (p. 109). That means, when we change how we talk about things, it makes it easier to change how we react to things. Looking closely at common explanations and attributions about bullying can explain why targets and witnesses feel powerless to change these situations. Understanding where we are in terms of sensemaking also helps us think outside the box and maybe start talking about bullying more empowering ways.

Methodology

We drew data from interviews, focus groups, surveys, and emails. The participants were targets of bullying and worked in the United States at the time they were bullied. We analyzed the data looking for sensemaking patterns or themes.

Sample Characteristics

Participants included 246 US workers who felt bullied by their supervisors. Of the 246, 28 interviewees came to the study via print and online notices and conversations with persons known to the researchers. A series of media releases drew focus group participants (n = 18) and email senders (n = 53). Survey data came from open-ended questions in two surveys (31 business/communication undergraduates; 115 working adults). In the overall sample, 229 provided sex/gender (57% female) and 188 provided age. Average age was 32, ranging from 18 to 70. Targets worked in 23 industries and lived in 42 different states.

Measures

In interviews I simply asked targets a global question ("Tell me about your experience"), and they told me about their experiences with little other prompting. All of the targets speculated about why bullying happened, from their own and from others points of view. Focus group participants responded to a similar question ("Briefly explain what happened at your jobs").

The people who responded to the survey filled in a "comments" box at the end of items from the Negative Acts Questionnaire-NAQ (see Chapter 2). Journalists' reports of our research led to us receiving many emails in which targets described bullying.

Analysis

We looked for sensemaking themes using a grounded approach (a scientific term that means we didn't use a list or typology from past research to categorize what people said about bullying). We categorized what people said in terms of the frequency of particular sensemaking themes. We then noticed the themes roughly represented different levels of analysis: individual, group, organizational, and societal.

Our first step was extracting from the data the sensemaking passages where people explained bullying, this is called *unitizing* the data or breaking data into specific units-by-theme. We used software designed for this purpose (Qualitative Data Analysis). When unitizing was complete, we linked our participants' demographics to illustrative examples so we could report age, sex, and profession in the findings.

In the second step, we examined the unitized reports and created names and descriptions for each sensemaking theme. We kept a running list of names and descriptions as we went along. We compared each new passage to previous themes to determine if the passage was similar to or different from established themes. If the new passage appeared similar to an established theme, we labeled it accordingly. If not, we created a new theme and description. After we analyzed the interviews, we found no new themes for sensemaking. We did analyze the remaining data, however, for the purposes of triangulation and exemplar range. (*Triangulation* means we looked at all the sources of our data and found similar patterns. *Exemplars* are the illustrating examples that researchers add to reports of their findings.)

Our third step was data reduction-analysis, "a form of analysis that sharpens, sorts, focuses, discards, and organizes data in such a way that 'final' conclusions can be drawn and verified" [253] (p.11). Reduction-analysis included condensing initial themes into more inclusive themes by locating redundancies, combining analytically similar themes, or creating more comprehensive themes for equivalent themes. We ended up with 13 core explanations for bullying.

In the fourth step, we grouped the 13 explanation types into 5 groupings based on each theme's orientation: individual [actor, tar-

get]; workgroup; organization; and society. We counted the undupli-
cated numbers of people who used each explanation theme and sort-
ed themes by frequency. As a final task, we reread Weick's writings
about framing vocabularies and re-examined the explanation themes
to determine which framing vocabularies targets were using to make
sense of bullying.

Findings

Sensemaking as Intersubjective (Meaning is Something People Agree Upon)

The experiences targets told us about really did highlight the intersubjective character of sensemaking. That is, targets' accounts confirmed
that *sensemaking was accomplished in communication with others.*
They repeatedly pointed to the social contexts in which they made
sense: conversations with coworkers, friends, or family members. For
example, a 32-year-old man working in state government said, "Several of us *have spent many hours* trying to determine what, exactly, it
was about him [that made him bully others]." A 41-year-old man in
the insurance industry said, "We have literally spent *hours and hours*
talking about this woman trying to figure out what her deal is" (em-
phasis original). Sensemaking appeared to colonize workplace conversations. A woman working a travel agency said, "I asked someone
at work the other day, 'What did we ever used to talk about [besides
bullying]?'"

Participants said they spoke to family and friends to figure out
bullying but usually characterized these conversations as less helpful
than those with coworkers. A young woman working in a hardware
store recounted, "I told my mother about it, and lots of my friends....
But Jason [coworker] was the one who really knew about what was
going down. I'd have gone nuts without him."

Coworker conversations apparently generated explanations targets found most plausible. As a 41-year-old man in a nonprofit service
agency explained, "No one understands unless they've gone through
it." The intersubjectivity was in focus groups too. When participants
described why they thought bullying occurred, others nodded, mur-
mured assent, and followed up by stating similar beliefs. So what conclusions did targets draw and why?

Sensemaking Themes and Framing Vocabularies

Sensemaking themes focused on what targets believed were the five contributors to bullying, the bullies, organizations, targets, workgroups, and social norms. We present the themes in order of frequency, noting the percentage of participants by theme and explanation type. We also include the data source, sex, and occupation, when known. If unknown, we omitted these without comment. The conclusions (themes) targets drew resonated with different framing vocabularies (frames). We explain both themes and frames in the findings because the frames point to how targets came to the conclusions they did.

Bully-focused sensemaking. Bully-focused explanations identified the aggressor as a principal source of the problem. Nearly all accounts (n = 233, 94.7%) included bully-focused explanations centering on personal characteristics or scapegoating.

Bully traits. A large majority concluded there was "something very wrong" with bullies (n = 223, 90.7%). Explanations for bullying included attributions of aggressors as mentally unstable, evil, and "power-mad," typically employing some combination of these. Labels associated with *mental instability* included "manic," "crazy," "totally irrational," "a serial sociopath workplace bully," "passive aggressive," "delusional" and "type A," "narcissist," "borderline," "schizo" and "antisocial" (all sources). Evidence of instability included capricious oversight, incongruous emotions, and highly changeable moods.

* Capricious work oversight: "She'd say one thing and then send an email saying something else, and then a memo with something else. I never knew what to expect, what she wanted." (female, interview, state government)

* Incongruous emotional displays: "He's completely blown up about himself but, at the same time totally terrified that someone's plotting against him." (male, email)

* Changeable mood and affect: Bullies were in "a bad mood," "pissed off about something," or "furious most the time" and could "change on a dime" becoming "high as a kite," "feeling good," or "on the top of the world." (multiple sources, respondents, occupations)

Table 12.1: Bully-Focused Sensemaking Themes

Theme	Description	Framing Vocabularies
Bully-focused, 95% of explanations for bullying		
Traits	Bullies' personality characteristics, beliefs, values that drive abuse of others	Ideologies: individualism and the psychologized-self Third-order control: mythical evil power invoked; power as zero-sum—bully does not *have* it so must *take* it Stories: socially constructed plots highlighting sequences supporting claims about bully's character
Scapegoating	Bullies "take out" frustrations on others; blame mistakes on others	Theories of action: frustration, error (cause) results in raging at others (effect) Paradigms: managers should be cool and infallible; managers as masculinized Stories: events about bullying plotted to support theories of action and managerial paradigms

Targets also explained bullying by labeling Bullies *malicious* and *evil*. Bullies were characterized as "cruel," "tactless," "mean-spirited," "insensitive," someone who "hates everyone," and "has absolutely no empathy" or "ability to feel remorse." Alternately, targets called Bullies "evil," "immoral," "wicked," "hateful," and "fiendish" (all sources).

✳ Malicious: "Bullies are working at it. We've talked about and think they know exactly what they're doing, that they're hurting somebody." (male, interview, telecommunications)

✳ Malevolent: "He wanted to be rich; we think he made a pact with the devil." (male, email, entertainment)

* Duplicitous performer: "She can turn on a dime. She can be railing on somebody, have a board member walk-in, and there is a complete personality change." (male, interview, social services)

* Jealous: "She only did this to the RNs. She wasn't a nurse, so she envied the RNs' knowledge." (female, email, nursing)

Scapegoating. Targets also believed that aggressors took their personal frustrations out on others and shifted blame to others for their own mistakes and shortcomings (n = 136, 55.3%).

* Personal problems: "[She's] unhappy at work, unhappy at home, and she doesn't like other people that are in a good marriage or anything" (male, focus group, city government)

* Blame-shifting for mistakes: "He verbally jumped all over me and, in a threatening and heated manner, told me I was never to talk to anyone, including my supervisor, about the data problem he caused—deleting thousands of vital records." (female, email, medicine)

* Blame-shifting for shortcomings: "Management needed a reason as to why the problem of her missed calls continued. She found some way to blame me to take the heat off her" (female, email)

Power-hungry. Many believed that bullies wanted *power* and *control* and were "power-hungry," "manipulative," "driven," "control-freaks" who "had to dominate and be in control of every situation," in order to "climb to the top—no matter what the cost" (all sources). The bullies seemed to be very politically astute and effective at *managing up,* performing politely or even grovelingly in the presence of influential others. Relatedly, participants thought bullies were jealous of others' skills, education, or social capital. Aggressors targeted anyone posing a threat to the bullies' aspirations to power.

* Power-hungry: "She would roll over everybody to get whatever she wanted—basically using steamroller tactics. She didn't care who she stepped on, on the way up." (male, interview, federal government)

250

Targeted workers had a rich repertoire of explanations centering on bullies and typically made sense of bullying with attributions of deviance, evil, or mental disease. Because the abusive behavior seemed so far outside of acceptable norms for how people should interact at work, the targets could only conclude that bullies were crazy. The bullies' power-abuse and power-gaining strategies were also consistent explanations. The targets connected bullying to the aggressors' love of position-power, drive for control, and use of "dirty" politics and aggression to achieve power.

Targets also thought bullies bullied to scapegoat others, to hide the bullies' errors. Scapegoating was extremely stigmatizing for targets blamed for something they did not do. In that respect, bully-focused explanations were more empowering than self-blame. Perceptions that bullies "hated everyone" or were "mentally ill" were stable, uncontrollable attributions, explanations that made bullying look unchangeable and left little room for target action.

Bully-focused framing vocabularies. Sensemaking focusing on bullies' abnormalities called on the ideology of individualism. This ideology points to the individual as completely responsible for what happens to him or her. Explanations in terms of individualism suggest that the bully's deviant behavior stems from personal pathology. Interwoven in the accounts of mental deviancy were supernatural threads. Bullies were painted as evil and demonic. This mythical frame explained shocking, bewildering bullying interactions but also served as a third-order control. Evil demons mean that bullying is beyond mere mortals' control. Targets told egregious, shocking stories to support their claims of bullies' unbalanced or evil nature, but these explanations often created a sense of being frozen, being unable to fight back.

Targets also described power like it was a zero-sum commodity, which is a commonplace vocabulary about power at work. Zero-sum means that power is limited; if one person has it then others cannot get it. In other words, targets talked about power as something that was material, something that bullies lacked or coveted so seized from others. Their stories wove together explanations into plot lines highlighting series events in which bullies manipulated or wrenched power away from others.

Targets also said bullies used others as scapegoats in which they blamed their own shortcomings or mistakes. They talked in terms of cause-effect theories of action explaining scapegoating: bullies' frustration, personal pain, or embarrassment (cause) drove aggressors to bully others (effect). Target explanations for abuse also reflected a sort of masculine managerial paradigm or perspective. This paradigm exposed targets' underlying beliefs that managers should always be rational and unemotional, and that good managers were nearly infallible. The paradigm suggested that, above all, managers should *never* blame their mistakes on others. Rather, managers' should care for subordinate employees, never abuse them.

Organization-focused sensemaking. Targets coupled bully-focused explanations with beliefs that organizations supported bullying. In some cases, they believed bullying was *primarily* due to the failures of organizational upper-managers (n = 227, 92.3%). A central theme was upper-managers' reluctance to intervene and punish bullies. Targets believed that upper-managers supported employee-abusive cultures, bullied to cover up inadequacies, used aggression as an HR tool, and feared or had personal relationships with bullies. Table 12.2 summarizes these themes.

Employee-abusive cultures. Many pointed to organizational cultures as the root of bullying (n = 155, 63.0%). In such cultures authorities normalized, allowed, or ignored bullying. Aggressors bullied others because they were bullied or were imitating other bullying managers. In these organizations, subordinate employees were "cogs in a wheel."

✳ Normalizing: "It's such the norm that people look at you like you're insane to think there is something wrong with it." (female, email, higher education) "Within the strangeness of the Postal Service, it is just all in a day's work." (male, email)

✳ Allowing, ignoring: "Every single person in her office has spoken to the manager at least once about similar incidents (yelling, saying rude things, refusing to do her work) and nothing is ever done. She is never reprimanded, so she is getting even worse." (female, email, city government)

✳ Trickle-down: "We think they're [bullies] micro-managed like a bunch of puppets. They're on a string, so if the boss yells at them, they yell at us." (male, interview, consulting)

Table 12.2: Organization-Focused Sensemaking Themes

Theme	Description	Framing Vocabularies
Organization-focused, 92% of explanations for bullying		
Employee-abusive culture	Organizations fail to intervene; organizational dynamics trigger, enable, or reward bullying	Ideologies: divides between labor and capital/management, naturalization of employee abuse Traditions: abusing workers part of how things always done Third-order controls: abusive culture acts as implicit warning to workgroup members Stories: historical accounts of employee abuse and disregard by multiple authority figures
Human resource tool	Bullying used to "fire" or increase productivity	Theories of action: abuse (cause) used as means to drive unwanted persons out (effect) Stories: Events sequenced to link bullying with worker expulsion or managers' efforts to "motivate" employees to work harder
Avoidance, attachment	Upper-management fears actor, has personal relationship with actor	Theories of action: fear or personal relationships (cause) muzzle upper-managers (effect) Stories: plots of fear-ridden upper-management, narratives of social ties between actor-management blocking intervention
Management inadequacies	Management lacks needed skills so abuses staff out of ignorance	Paradigms: managers should be emotion-neutral, highly skilled, infallible Stories: narratives of managers' mistakes and ineptitudes

✷ Imitating: "She was instantly taken under his [actor's] wing, and he trained her in his unique method of employee terrorizing." (female, interview, state government)

✷ Workers as cogs: "We're treated as an object; you're not treated as a human being." (male, interview, telecommunications) "EEOC really doesn't give a shit whether you get justice or not; you're just supposed to keep working." (female, interview, construction)

Human resource (HR) tool. Targeted workers also believed that organizations allowed bullying because abuse indirectly carried out the HR tasks of firing or increasing production (n = 115, 46.7%).

✷ Employment termination: "He's trying to drive out the troublemakers—that's anyone who stands up to him." (male, interview, government)

✷ Increase production: "Bullying bosses try to get you to work at your highest break neck pace. In their hearts, someone believes that behavior and productivity will increase if they discipline you hard enough." (male, interview, telecommunications)

Emotional avoidance, attachment. When upper-managers failed to intervene or interventions were "too soft to make a difference," participants concluded that upper-managers were "cowed" by or "in bed with" bullies (n = 58, 23.6%). Upper-management's fear was especially striking when bullies were exceptionally aggressive or "had friends in high places." In other cases, targets believed some kind of "behind the scenes" relationship hindered intervention.

✷ Avoidance: "We're not the only ones afraid of her; her boss tiptoes around her too." (male, survey, transportation)

✷ Attachment: "She threw herself all over the men to try to get ahead [and] became his [the bureau chief's] little doll, his favored one." (male, interview, government) "His little mafioso of supporters all golfed together and went to some country club. There was no way they [upper-managers] were going to do anything about their little buddy's behavior, so we all just suffered." (female, interview, real estate)

Management inadequacies. In some cases, targets thought that overall management used bullying because they lacked effective leadership skills (n = 46, 18.7%). In these cases, when the managers' lack of skills led to failures or errors, they blamed and punished the workers. This explanation pointed to management as a uniformly incompetent group that shifted blame to the less powerful.

* Managerial incompetence. "No one gets any training to be a manager. So they [managers] harass and wrangle and abuse people instead of being good supervisors who know how to motivate people" (male, email, wholesale)

* Blame-shifting. "They [managers] don't seem to be organized enough so there isn't always some crisis. They project that on someone else, and it's clear that they've had a series of scapegoats, so they don't have to admit what a poor job they're doing." (male, interview, consulting)

In organization-focused sensemaking, participants concluded that upper-managers were scared of bullies so failed to intervene to avoid volatile confrontations or alienating bullies' political allies. They also suspected that upper-managers and bullies shared non-work relationships (sexual, social-class friendships) that protected bullies. Female bullies were most often accused of sexual liaisons with higher-ups, and males of being part of a good-old-boys network.

Targets told stories about organizational cultures where bullying was the norm. Unimpeded bullying led targets to draw conclusions about the organizational values that drove bullying. One was that organizations viewed workers solely as *producers*—objects to incessantly churn out work or be eliminated. They also believed that worklife was grueling and punishing and that wanting anything else either naïve or crazy. As such, they concluded that bullying the norm, something inevitable and impossible to challenge or change.

These comments implicated organizational systems rather than individual bullies but the explanations were similar. In bully-focused sensemaking, participants believed that bullies scapegoated and blamed others for their own incompetence or their personality problems. In organization-focused sensemaking, targets concluded that upper-managers as a group were incompetent. The proof of their incompetence was workplace bullying—its very existence pointed to managements' overall inability to lead. Interestingly, there is quite a bit of research that supports the accuracy of these organization-focused explanations. Sadly, when organizational culture includes employee abuse that upper-managers ignore or reward, employees can believe it's hopeless to try and change things. In this regard, the "organizational culture is one of the fundamental causes of creating learned helplessness" (p. 25] [408].

Organization-focused framing vocabularies. The organization-focused explanations reflected many of the ideological tensions between labor and management, particularly the perceptions of the management as a whole. Targets talked about traditions of worker abuse and expectations that management would forever ride and goad employees. They talked in terms of resignation: Managers abused workers—period. Feeling resigned to abuse was a kind of third-order control that thwarted their action, characterizing action as pointless.

Drawing the conclusion that management condoned or disregarded bullying silenced employees. Targets' stories used past accounts of employee abuse and accounts of many authority figures ignoring abuse when supporting their conclusions. They felt that managers were always favored over workers, and though they felt this favoring was oppressive and abusive, it came through in their stories as inevitable. This was especially true when efforts to stop abuse had repeatedly failed. Paradoxically, underlying their explanations was the belief that the ideal upper-manager was an all-knowing, all-powerful caretaker who's responsibility was to protect employees.

Explanations that bullying was simply a veiled way to carry out unsavory human resource functions brought up theories of action like the means justifies the ends. These layperson theories were based on the idea that low-skill managers used bullying (means) to remove or drive out (end) subordinates they did not like, employees who had challenged them, or employees who were otherwise unwanted.

Stories summarized events into sequences that linked bullying with worker removal, typically contrasting abuse with fair due-process. Targets also talked about upper-manager' avoidance or attachment to bullies using cause-and-effect theories of action. They said that upper-managers were too cowardly (cause) to confront aggressive bullies or too emotionally involved (cause) with bullies to protect workers (effect).

Their stories supported cause-effect theories with plotted narratives of fear-ridden upper-managers or tales of ongoing social ties, both of which apparently allowed bullying. The social-tie explanations also demonstrated a kind of class-based paradigm about power and influence: "It's not what you know but who you know."

Another profession-oriented paradigm in target explanations for abuse was the gendered stereotype of women "sleeping their way to the top" because they lacked legitimate skills. The idea that there was an ideal manager was present in target accounts. Managers should be neutral, detached, composed, favor nor fear anyone—a non-emotional masculine ideal [413]. They should protect employees and provide for their safety, much as a patriarchal parental figure. Stories informed by these paradigms with chronological tales of inept managers filled with performance anxiety, stories that derided managers as far less than the ideal.

Target-focused sensemaking. (See Table 12.3.) Target explanations often included taking partial responsibility for bullying (n = 176, 71.5%). Targets thought that something about them contributed to bullying: their past action or lack of action, their personality characteristics, or their personal-life situations.

Action or lack of action. Targets reflected on past interactions with bullies to explain bullying (n = 168, 68.3%). They believed that their past action had sparked bullying, or their failure to take action contributed to bullying. *Standing up* metaphors emphasized their sensemaking: standing up to bullies, failing to stand up, or standing up too late.

* Standing up: "When he yelled at me in a meeting I just stood up and walked out while he was standing there yelling. [After that] he saw me as a challenge—his challenge was to try to break me." (male, interview, security)

* Failing to stand up: "I'm too easy to get along with, and people take advantage of that. I should stand up for myself and not let him walk all over me." (female, interview, retail sales)

* Standing up too late: "We thought it would go away, so we didn't do anything. I see now that we should have stood up to her in the very beginning."(male, email, travel agency)

257

Table 12.3: Target-Focused Sensemaking Themes

Theme	Description	Framing Vocabularies
Target-focused, 72% of explanations for bullying		
Action, lack of action	Something target said triggered bullying or failed to say allowed bullying	Ideologies: personal responsibility, individualism, capitalism, neo-con economics, Just World Hypothesis, victim blaming
		Theories of action: action or inaction (cause) as reason for bullying (effect)
		Stories: identifying points in time where action was or should have been taken that shifted outcome for the worse
Traits	Target personality traits, beliefs, values that allow abuse or triggers actor aggression	Ideologies: individualism and the psychologized-self
		Theories of action: some trait (cause) reason for being bullied (effect)
		Stories: accounts linking target characteristic as triggering bullying
Situation	Personal circumstance contributing to vulnerability	Stories: socially constructed plots or sequences revolving around targets' external pressures leading to susceptibility and then bullying

Target traits. Some believed that aggressors bullied them because they were different from others, held stricter values, or had social or occupational capital that the bullies wanted. In some cases, targets simply thought that bullies disliked them. Regardless of the reason, over half of the targets partially blamed themselves for being abused (n = 134, 54.5%). As a 38-year-old male working in city government said, "You blame yourself a lot.... I was talking to a friend of mine wondering, what is it about me that enables people? What am I doing

258

to allow these people to bully me?"

* Difference: "These three men didn't like taking orders from a woman. It was that simple.... So they sabotaged me at every turn." (women, email, construction) "He [bully] was by far the most aggressive person in the factory, and he disliked me, who was probably the least aggressive worker." (male, email, manufacturing)

* Beliefs, values: "She hated me because I'm a Mormon. She once said that we were all whores and whoremongers." (male, interview, government) "I wouldn't be party to [the bully's wrongdoing]. I'm sure that's part of the reason he had it in for me." (female, survey, sales)

* Social, occupational capital: "We agreed he goes after anyone who is well-liked in the firm because no one likes him." (male, interview, law office) "She went after me because I'm an RN. We believe it's because she doesn't have the education." (female, interview, nursing)

* Dislike: "For some reason, she just didn't like me.... I wasn't one of her favorites." (female, email, advertising)

Target situations. In a few cases, targets said that extenuating circumstances contributed to their vulnerability, typically related to family and health (n = 43, 17.5%).

* Family: "My mother was diagnosed with lung cancer. I was very vulnerable, and she really kicked me when I was down." (female, interview, government)

* Health: "I was going through a bad time. I was in a car accident; I was taking pain medication. I just couldn't defend myself anymore." (male, survey, social services)

Targets took some of the responsibility for being abused but attributed their vulnerability to external pressures or personal characteristics that were relatively stable (e.g., sex, education, religion). Situational issues, while not causing bullying, rendered targets vulnerable and "made it harder to fight back." Targets also admitted that these issues affected their performance so their reduced performance might have encouraged bullying. In cultures that targets said used employees like "grist for the mill," there was no tolerance for non-performance. Some explanations elevated targets to a higher moral ground than bullies, the explanations that characterized targets as victims of prejudice, bigotry, or envy.

The retrospective (hindsight) feature of sensemaking was particularly striking in these explanations. Targets came to self-focused explanations as one might solve a mystery—tracing what occurred, sifting through clues and evidence, talking to others to gather information, piecing together elements, and deciding how their behavior contributed to the situation. Part of the mystery included personal blame, although none believed they had done or said anything to warrant the level and degree of mistreatment they received. Unfortunately, nearly all target-focused explanations appeared self-defeating because these either internalized the causes for bullies' behavior or focused on factors outside targets' control.

Target-focused framing vocabularies. Participants used theories of action to link their social capital, beliefs, or differences (causes) to bullying (effect). Explaining bullying by blaming oneself invoked tenets of personal responsibility associated with the interrelated ideologies of individualism, capitalism, and neo-conservative economics. Indeed, the notion of personal responsibility has contributed to self-psychologizing and self-blame, even for many things that are rooted in social, cultural, and historical forces, forces that often shape individual psychology.

Their talk about personal responsibility and victim blaming reflected the Just World Hypothesis—the idea that "people ... need to believe that their environment is a just and orderly place where people usually get what they deserve" [414, p. 1030]. Stories supporting self-blame where action was or should have been taken also emphasized Just World beliefs. Targets constructed events with plotted sequences of 1) external pressures, 2) led to susceptibility, 3) capitalized upon by bully, 4) resulted in bullying.

Workgroup-focused sensemaking. Some participants indicted colleagues for contributing to bullying (n = 157, 63.8%). In these workgroups coworker communication was apparently compartmentalized, and cliques became "warring factions." A few coworkers sided with targets, but most remained silent and some gravitated to the bullies. Workgroup explanations focused on failing to speak out (n =

119, 48.4%) or serving as "spies," "infiltrators," or "agents" (n = 96, 39.0%). Table 12.4 summarizes these explanations.

✳ Silent assent: "People would come to me and say they were sorry they couldn't help because they felt she would, in turn, start on them." (female, email, medical)

✳ Henchmen/women: "She [bully] got one of my people that report to me to be a spy for her." (female, focus group, call center) "We were very careful who we talked to around her. We made damn sure *never* to be caught in a huddle by one of her [bully's] hit men." (male, interview, primary education)

Table 12.4: Workgroup-Focused Sensemaking Themes

Theme	Description	Framing Vocabularies
Workgroup-focused, 64% of explanations for bullying		
Silent assent	Witnessing coworkers stand by silently	Ideologies: moral imperative to fight injustice; silence-as-agreement, accomplices' moral weakness
		Third-order controls: silence and accomplices as concertive control;
		Stories: narrated anecdotes about coworkers who failed to speak up or support targets; hero tales of oppressed uprisings led by conspicuous champion
Henchmen-women	Witnessing coworkers directly, indirectly participate in bullying	Third-order controls: coworkers' concertive control supports bullying
		Theories of action: coworkers side with bullies (cause) to protect themselves (effect)
		Stories: sequenced events featuring coworkers as bullies' confederates and spies, bully all powerful, no safe place

Targets knew that their coworkers' were silent because coworkers feared being targeted. However, they also thought their coworker silence encouraged bullies. They recognized, to some extent, that those who sided with the bully probably did so to "play it safe." But they believed that the cliques at work increased everyone's fear and made exposing the aggressors more difficult. Despite efforts to "stay out of the line of fire," the bullies' loyalties and the people they targeted seemed to shift back and forth. No one was really safe, no matter who they allied with because safety was tenuous. ("You could be a silent onlooker when you left for the day and a target the next morning." "She changed mafioso members regularly.") These stories showed that people facing abuse at work can see the power of collective action but didn't really know how to marshal it in an organized effort to end ongoing abuse.

Workgroup-focused framing vocabularies. When targets thought that bullying silenced or co-opted coworkers, they were framing the situation using the third-order control of peer-pressure. Bullies no longer needed first-order control (direct oversight) to hold power over the workgroup. Fear-induced silence led to more silence, whether it was fear of being targeted or fear that coworkers were spies or henchmen/women for the bully. Those who collectively resisted portrayed the silent majority as weak, lacking character, or both. Their accounts called to mind hero stories in which resistance was noble and silence was cowardly. Targets believed henchmen/women were morally weak, akin to what Bird [415] calls *morally mute*, because of their failure to speak up even though they knew what was happening was wrong. Bullying allegedly continued or worsened due to coworker silence, complicity, or both. Stories also attributed mythical power to bullies whom targets portrayed as having the power to hold workgroup members in an invisible but iron grip, even in their absence.

Society-focused sensemaking. (See Table 12.5) About a third of participants mentioned larger social patterns, norms, or values as reasons for bullying (n = 82, 33.3%). These explanations centered on lack of legal protection (n = 57, 23.2%) and reverence of hard-driving achievers (n = 31, 12.6%).

* No legal protection: "I went to an attorney who basically told me I had no recourse. It was not against the law to be an ass-

262

hole." (male, email, securities) "In today's corporate climate, I found no recourse, no laws against their bullying." (male, survey, banking)

※ Veneration of hard-drivers: "This guy is a killer, and when you've got a legal battle, you want a lawyer who's a killer—problem is, he's killing the firm." (male, interview, law firm)

All organizational cultures are rooted in social beliefs, norms and values, but targets talked about social forces less than any other explanation for bullying. They thought the lack of legal recourse was one of the reasons for bullying, but no one spoke of the prevailing US values (business interests) that block such legislation. They articulated the belief that workplace or corporate norms exulted high-producers at any cost. Targets talked about the short-sightedness of these norms, explaining that upper-management failed to see the negative effects of maintaining aggressive workers until profits declined or turnover skyrocketed.

Table 12.5: Society-Focused Sensemaking Themes

Theme	Description	Framing Vocabularies
Society-focused, 58% of explanations for bullying		
Statutory short-coming	No legal protections against bullying	Ideologies: enduring belief in justice and fairness as represented by legal institutions Theories of action: because no laws prohibit bullying (cause) bullies abuse others (effect) Stories: recounted plots of reduced sexual harassment and discrimination due to workers' legal protection, law = magic
Veneration of hard-drivers 52 (20.7)	Society rewards productive people regardless of how they treat others	Ideologies: entrepreneurial selves and relatedly value of instrumental aggression as means of attaining desired ends; capitalism Theories of action: high productivity (cause) shields bullies from negative sanctions (effect) Stories: accounts of bullies who act with impunity because of their productivity, supporting theories of action

Society-focused framing vocabularies. Lack of statutory protection explanations pointed to a value-based belief (ideology) in legal systems to protect workers and ensure them justice and fairness on the job. From this belief targets concluded certain theories of action. For example, because no laws prohibited bullying (cause) organizations failed to take bullying seriously so bullies abused others with impunity (effect).

Law as social-vocabulary underscored explanations, and stories recounted stories about how legal protection has reduced sexual harassment and discrimination. Rarely did they mention or seem to know about the extremely small percentage of such cases that actually prevail against deep-pocket employers. Like the devil-bullies, these framing vocabularies equated law with magical, mythical, powers. Additionally, targets wove threads of capitalistic ideology into their explanations, calling on social beliefs that in a bottom-line world, high-achievers were free to (mis)treat others as they wished. Theories of action informed these explanations: high productivity (cause) shielded bullies from negative sanctions (effect). Stories of unpunished, high-producing bullies supported these theories of action.

Implications of Sensemaking

Workplace bullying, the majority of which comes from supervisors in US workplaces, is a very real experience that nearly 40% of workers experience sometime during their careers (See Chapter 2). Targets' explanations for supervisory abuse are multi-faceted and implicate (in order of frequency) bullies, targets, organizations, workgroups, and society as a whole.

An important caveat: Here we reflect on the implications of the sensemaking themes found but first would like to express a major qualification—*Targets simply thinking about bullying differently will not end bullying or make bullies stop attacking.* In no way do we intend to say something so ridiculous or blame the victims, as they have already been blamed plenty. We don't want to join that *wrong-minded chorus*. Rather, changing how one talks about and thinks about adult bullying might bring to mind different ways of seeing the situation and responding to it, ways that could be more effective at ending abuse but will unquestionably be more effective at making targets feel better.

The analysis focuses on sensemaking content, what we saw as the communicative building blocks that constitute explanations. The content of sensemaking and the framing vocabularies upon which content draws have serious implications for those targeted, those who might be "next in line," and those concerned with building cultures of respect. Of central concern in the current study is how explanations contribute to targets' sense of impotence or lack of influence. The communicative materials in explanations are commonly held ideas of work and working, but they can represent the situation in ways that are paralyzing to affected employees.

Reframing the cause of workplace bullying provides leverage for change and possibilities for direct and indirect resistance. Of particular interest are the sensemaking foci and attributions targets employ and how these can contribute to viewing workplace bullying as impossible to stop. Agreeing about the causes of bullying influences their subsequent actions and ongoing reactions.

In bullying situations, most explanations include attributions about bullies and their behavior, attributions rooted in individualism. Explanations make sense of the experience by attempting to make sense of the bully. Bully-focused explanations in particular lead to dead-ends when figuring out what to do. If the bullies are evil, they have supernatural powers that mere mortals dare not challenge. Similarly, attributions of mental illness provide little or no advantage to targets.

In terms of attribution theory, these causes are internal, stable, and uncontrollable—regardless of targets' action, the bully remains unchanged. Attributing bullies' abusive communication to desire for control, duplicitous performances, and jealousy of others' accomplishments provides a better understanding of bullying behaviors. Recent research indicates that bullies are aggressive because they are fearful, particularly fearful of perceptions of incompetence—both bullies' self-perceptions and others' perceptions of bullies. Explaining bullying as a fear-based response that is far more likely to occur when bullies have *both* hierarchical power (i.e., supervisory status) and feelings of incompetence elicits a different response. If bullies are demons or mentally ill, targets freeze or flee. If bullies are fearful and feel incompetent, targets can figure out different influence-options.

Organizationally focused explanations are quite complex and implicate management as a whole. Certainly upper-management must lead the charge to build respectful workplaces, and targets concur, but explanations in this realm are less than encouraging for target leverage. Organizationally focused explanations cast upper-managers (and thus the employing organization) in parental, caretaker roles. Considerable research suggests that upper-managers typically fear, or lack the skills for constructively dealing with, bullying or otherwise aggressive bullies [416]. If employees' explanations include an understanding that upper-managers' skill deficits, intense apprehension, or both likely stand in the way of their capacity to effectively intervene, employees can recast upper-management as partners and collaborators, albeit frustrated or even paralyzed ones.

Reframing upper-managers as collaborating partners lacking knowledge suggests a different approach to bullying cessation than simply delivering the problem to upper-management and expecting action. Such a recasting generally calls for educating upper-managers regarding the bullying phenomenon, and specifically researching and then suggesting strategies proven effective in similar situations. Educating upper-managers about bullies' perceptions of incompetence by citing relevant research could lead upper-management to reward different indicators of success. Potentially, organizations might move to public celebrations and awards for those supervisors with *outstanding interpersonal communication skills*. This, in turn, could encourage bullies to develop interpersonal communication skills, if only to feel and be viewed as competent.

Workgroup focused explanations underscore the tricky character of social dynamics when supervisors bully subordinates. Attributing silence to assent or acceptance of bullying will likely exacerbate targets' feelings of powerlessness and anger. Explanations linking silence with fear, however, provide change-leverage opportunities. Like upper-managers, workgroup members typically lack the specific skills needed to safely deal with supervisory abuse and, more generally, lack understanding of bullying as a unique phenomenon.

Naming what's happening as *workplace bullying* is a powerful first step for affected employees, so is recognizing that there is power in numbers. Workgroup explanations reflect targets' knowledge that collectives are more influential than one or two persons, an empowering realization even if not initially acted upon. As frightening as collective resistance is, working collaboratively has the best chances of shifting the situation. Thus, recasting silent fearful coworkers as potential collaborators opens space for action.

If targets explain bullying as the result of silent audiences, education regarding the detrimental effects of silence might be in order. If bullying is the result of collaborators' (i.e., henchmen-women) support, education regarding the precariousness of these positions could shift alliances. Both topics are featured in academic journals, trade magazines, and popular press venues and employees could distributed these to encourage potential collaborators.

Social norms and the associated taken-for-granted meaning systems are powerful drivers of communicative behavior and sensemaking about that behavior. Society focused explanations may at first seem even more overwhelming than dealing with someone's mental illness ("you can't fight city hall") but framing bullying as a social issue represents the phenomenon as one amenable to social interventions, particularly grassroots interventions.

Reframing adult bullying as the result of social and cultural processes provides multiple opportunities for employees to increase their perceived influence by aligning with like-minded others. In terms of anti-bullying legislation, for example, targets can work with others at the local, state, and national level in a grass-roots movement initiated by the Workplace Bullying Institute (http://www.workplace bullying-law.org/).

Shifting US organizations' reverence for hard-drivers offers a different point for leveraged change, through joining with those interested in reverence of a different sort of organizational environment. An effort in this direction is the American Psychological Association's *Psychologically Healthy Workplace Award* that rewards organizations for optimizing employee health and well-being in the process of enhancing performance (http://www.phwa.org/awards/).

Developing public health campaigns that communicate the public health risk of psychological abuse at work is another option. By shifting how targets explain workplace bullying these and other avenues for social change open and targets' perceptions of their ability to influence the world around them shift.

Considering whom targets talk to about these experiences is important. Targets report making sense of bullying through conversations with others who have experienced or witnessed the bullying. Speaking only with others who feel powerless might exacerbate feelings of helplessness and hopelessness, creating barriers to receiving more empowering support. If, however, targets' conversations with coworkers constitute collective resistance focusing on organizational change, this shifts language from evil demons to systems and casts bullying as a problem amenable to change.

Because targets often describe bullying as something only someone who has experienced it can understand, they may perceive others in their social networks as inadequate sources of support. But in bullying situations targets frequently need support from their personal networks, so considering that others might have useful ways of looking at the situation is important. Talking with someone with the same sensemaking frame (i.e., colleagues) may serve to solidify further targets' perceptions and even reify framing vocabularies that are less than useful. Though collegial agreement can feel supportive, it may not help the person move through the situation. In some cases, the best source of support might be people who understand but are not experiencing the same stressful event.

CHAPTER 13

Profiles, Goals, and Tactics in Escalated Bullying Conflicts: Targets, Witnesses, and Aggressors[L]

Pamela Lutgen-Sandvik & Courtney Vail Fletcher

Chapter Summary: Workplace bullying conflicts involve a far wider group of employees than simply the bully-target dyad. We distinguish workplace bullying as a unique type of conflict because it involves the markers of routine conflict with the added features of power disparities, aggression, and persistence (i.e., repetition, duration). Specifically, we focus on nine employee groups, detailing their general profiles, motivations (goals), and tactics (communicative actions). By emphasizing roughly three different types of target (provocative, passive, rigidly conscientious), bystander (bully allies, target allies, neutral bystander), and bully (accidental, narcissistic, psychopathic) and noting that each of these types has different motivations and uses different communicative actions or tactics, we provide an idea of how impossible addressing bullying can feel and how these conflicts can be such a *nasty piece of work*.

Keywords: workplace bullying, escalated conflict, targets, bystanders, bullies, conflict goals and tactics

----

Adult bullying can be viewed as a unique type of escalated, entrenched conflict between and among organizational members. This chapter explains bullying conflicts from three standpoints: targets, bystanders, and bullies and show how these types of conflict can be a *nasty piece of work*. Doing so provides a better understanding of some of the forces that constitute the phenomenon and potentially locate leverage points for more effective interventions. The chapter outlines types of conflict motivation and management tactics [417,

418]. It then explains why the factors of focus—profiles, motivations, tactics—are useful for understanding bullying conflicts and subsequently flesh out these three factors for each group. The piece wraps up by suggesting avenues for future research.

Workplace Bullying as a Unique Form of Conflict

Bullying is a *pattern* of ongoing aggressive communication, and the ongoing nature of bullying contributes to why those targeted feel so powerless. Persistent attacks increase stress and decrease coping capacity, which exacerbate feelings of powerlessness making targets even more easily bullied and less able to defend themselves. Bullying is also *escalatory*; initially aggression is passive, circuitous, and immensely difficult to describe; typically increasing in frequency, antagonism, and injury over time. In extremely escalated cases, aggressors may even start to objectify their targets, which enables the use of more aggressive, inhuman attacks. In some instances, "the total destruction of the opponent is seen as the ultimate goal to be attained by the parties" [10](p. 19).

Conflict, on the other hand, involves (a) parties that are interdependent, (b) a perception by at least one party that an opposition or incompatibility (or the potential) exists among the goals or values, and (c) interaction among the involved parties [417, 419]. Bullying includes these general conflict features but has the additional features noted above; thus, bullying is "most like intractable, escalated, violent conflicts between unequals" [89](p. 427). In bullying conflicts the aggressors' goals might be to harm or drive targets out; target goals may be to end abusive treatment and repair identity damage. The aggressive character of bullying conflicts creates hostile work environments affecting many employees, whether directly targeted or not.

The Communal Character of Bullying Conflicts

One of the tendencies, especially in US organizations and popular thought, is to individualize the problem. Supervisors, manager, and bystanders often blame the victims for their own abuse or see targets' reports of abuse as exaggerated, subjective, and questionable. By attending to the experiences of more of the involved, affected employees, we can more readily recognize the complexity of bullying conflicts and avoid, at least partially, such myopic viewpoints. Thinking of bullying as simply dyadic (i.e., a personality clash) glosses over the communal nature of workplace communication and impedes efforts

270

toward resolving this nasty part of work. Because workplaces are sites of collective human interaction, what occurs between dyads or among members bleeds and buzzes throughout the workgroup and affects all in proximity. Thus, under-standing target, bully, and bystander perspectives can shed light on why these conflicts are so difficult to resolve.

Certainly any view of a bullying conflict is partial, and current research on the subject overemphasizes the target perspective. Less research explores bystanders' experiences and bully explanations are nearly nonexistent [for an exception, see [355]. However, interpersonal communication researchers have studied verbal aggression from aggressors' standpoints for decades [420], and psychology researchers have explored aggression and high aggressives for even longer [421]. These findings inform the sections on bullies.

We call attention to the fact that bullying conflicts involve all proximate group members, whether or not they are actively engaged in the conflict. Indeed, bullying conflicts slowly colonize nearly all actions and interactions in workgroups where it is present. To gain a clearer picture of others' involvement, the core material herein explores three inter-related factors associated with targets, bystanders, and bullies: general profiles, motivations to act or withhold action, and conflict tactics. We outline these factors because involved parties may be unwilling or unable to report them. They may not fully understand their motivations; they may feel bound by emotion display rules; they may feel compelled to perform certain image-management work, and so forth. These factors do, however, flesh out bullying conflicts in particularly useful ways.

Motivational Goals, Communicative Tactics, and Group Profiles

Motivational goals and conflict tactics are inextricably linked. Motivational goals fuel action, giving behavior its energy and direction. Motivation is the one of the first links in a chain of interconnected interactions that leads to various outcomes, both intended and unintended. To understand bullying conflicts requires understanding the motives of the involved or affected bullies. Communicative actions or tactics in conflict management are the ways that people approach and engage with conflict; these make sense in light of what motivates parties. Tactics are driven motivations coupled with personality tendencies, social situations, and, especially, "the opponent's message behavior"

271

[422](p. 416). Underscoring different parties' motivations and tactics helps to better understand where to intervene and why certain interventions are less than effective.

In addition to motivations and tactics, experienced subjectivities (what we call *profiles*) can evoke specific motivations and tactics. Profiles are the common markers of persons who report certain personal or social characteristics in interviews or surveys. A few words of warning: On one hand, profiles are over-generalizations and exceptions always exist. As such, those dealing with bullying conflicts will want to avoid using profiles for either witch-hunting or victim-blaming. On the other hand, to ignore personality traits, social tendencies, and the patterns documented in scientific research can be naïve and counterproductive. Rather, profiles can be used as *sensitizing devices* when sorting out bullying, if used prudently as a general guide rather than a hard-and-fast set of rules. We flesh out each of these factors in what follows.

Motivational Goals in Bullying Conflicts

Multiple goals theory proposes seven core motivations or goals in conflicts, two associated with resources and five with relationships [417, 418]. Resource goals are *economic* and *personal*. Economic resource goals include the desire to obtain or protect something of economic value; and personal resource goals are those concerned with maintaining privacy, personal freedom, and choice. Social resource goals include *relationship, power-hostility, identity, functionality,* and *justice.* Social relationship goals are motivated by a desire to maintain or develop high-quality connections with others. Social power-hostility goals include the drive to punish or establish influence and dominance over others. Social identity goals are associated with face-saving, self-supporting, or preserving a preferred image. Social functionality goals "resolve the conflicts in a constructive or socially appropriate manner" [418] (p. 2185). Finally, social justice goals are inclinations toward egalitarianism and restoring social fairness. (Table 13.1, next page, summarizes goals.)

Table 13.1: Goals Motivating Conflict Management Tactics

Motivational Goal	Description
Resource Goals	• *Economic* – drive to obtain or protect something of economic value
	• *Personal* – drive to maintaining privacy or personal freedom and choice
Social Goals	• *Relationship* – drive to maintain or protect good relationships with others
	• *Power-Hostility* – drive to punish or establish influence or dominance over another
	• *Identity* – drive to face-saving, identity supporting, and preserving self-image
	• *Functionality* – drive to resolve conflict in constructive way
	• *Justice* – drive for fairness and the need to restore social justice

Communication Tactics in Bullying Conflicts

An applicable approach to tactical communication in conflicts is Rahim's [423] theory of managing organizational conflict, which categorizes tactics as integrating-problem solving, obliging-accommodating, dominating-forcing, avoiding-withdrawing, and compromising. We also include third-party tactics from multiple goals theory because appealing to third-parties is common in bullying conflicts due to targets' power disparity in relation to bullies. Integrating-problem solving "involves openness, exchanging information, looking for alternatives, and examination of differences to reach an effective solution acceptable to both parties" [423](p. 218). Obliging-accommodating "is associated with attempting to play down the differences and emphasizing commonalities to satisfy the concern of the other party" (pp. 218-219).

A dominating-forcing style is associated with a win–lose orientation in which "a dominating or competing person goes all out to win his or her objective and, as a result, often ignores the needs and expectations of the other party" (p. 220). Avoiding-withdrawing is sidestepping, ignoring, or steering clear of conflicts and the parties with whom conflict is present. In compromising, parties identify and settle on a solution that is partially satisfactory to those involved but not completely pleasing to either. Third-party tactics involve persons outside the conflict; usually someone with formal power, informal influence, or both; to intervene, problem-solve, or protect vulnerable parties.

Table 13.2: Conflict Management Tactics

Conflict Management Tactic	Description
Integrating-Problem Solving	Openness, exchanging information, looking for alternatives
Obliging-Accommodating	Playing down differences, emphasizing similarities for others' sake
Dominating-Forcing	Winning is objective, often ignoring needs of other party, forcing one party's position or opinion
Avoiding-Withdrawing	Ignoring, steering clear of conflicts or other parties
Compromising	Parties identify, settle on partially satisfactory solution
Third-party	Bring someone else into conflict, usually with power to resolve conflict or influence others who have power to arbitrate conflict

Adapted from the following sources: [417, 418]

Group Profiles

Bullying conflicts are social and contextual and a number of systemic contingencies press parties toward particular ways of handling conflict, but bullying-conflict research suggests that certain types of people are

274

more likely to be targeted, to aggress against others, or to remain by-standers. Targets that are provocative may draw the attention of aggressive others, whether that provocation is simply speaking their minds or tending toward aggression themselves. Bystanders most often remain silent hoping they can avoid involvement but may also side with targets or bullies. Bullies typically are high-verbal aggressives and tend to respond aggressively or harshly in most situations, escalating aggressive behavior when perceived pressures increase. We begin by exploring targeted workers.

Targets

Table 13.3 summarizes the target profiles, motivations, and most likely tactics used in conflict.

Table 13.3: Target Profiles, Motivations, Tactics

Profile	Primary Motivational Goals	Most Likely Conflict Tactics
Provocative Aggressive Target	Social Power	Dominating-forcing Integrating - Problem Solving Obliging- Accommodating Third-party
Provocative Assertive Target	Justice Economic Personal	Integrating - Problem Solving Obliging - Accommodating Compromising Third-party Dominating – Forcing
Rigidly Conscientious Target	Social Power	Dominating - Forcing Third-party
Passive Target	Social Functionality Goal	Avoiding - Withdrawing Obliging - Accommodating

Note: * All targets are motivated by Personal Resource Goals, Economic Resource Goals, and Social Identity Goals; Goals noted in Table are those differing among target types.

Profiles. Bullies at work can target anyone, but research on victimization (i.e., being the focus of others' aggression) suggests that certain

275

traits and tendencies situate employees in ways that make them more vulnerable. Victimization research points to three general profiles: provocative, submissive, and rigidly conscientious [424]. The first author's work suggests that there are two sub-types of provocative targets: aggressive and assertive. The *provocative* type is "aggressive, hostile, or irritating and therefore likely to provoke attack from others" (pp. 1025-26). Aggressive provocative targets are conflict-prone, usually less agreeable, and more likely to become involved in conflicts because they often disagree with others and create friction in their interactions. [e.g., 75, 425]

The second provocative target is *communicatively assertive,* typically employees who readily speak their minds, a tendency that can infuriate some bullies. People who are professionally successful or highly skilled are often assertive and can be targeted because their experience or expertise may pose a threat to a less secure bully. Depending on the pressures bullies are facing, the argumentative style of communicatively assertive employees can trigger harsh responses from high-verbal aggressives. The assertive target may also have effective argumentation skills. High-verbal aggressives are often lacking in this area so have considerable difficulty countering skilled peers or "insubordinate" subordinates. When low-argumentation skill employees face conflict situations, they can quickly run out of constructive material so fall back on verbal aggression [420, 426].

The next target type is the *submissive* employee, a person who is conflict-aversive. The submissive target can be "passive, insecure, frequently rejected by peers, and unwilling to defend against attack" (p. 1025] [424]. Submissive targets can be less extroverted, stable, and independent, and they can have an increased dependency on and desire for others' approval [427]. Appearing weak, anxious, unassertive, low in self-esteem, or conflict-aversive can be provocative for high aggressives [20]. Passive inclinations can make the submissive employee an easy target; the "weakling" also can be seen as low-risk—someone who can be bullied with impunity and serve as an example or warning to others. Some high-verbal aggressives even say they use aggression to express disdain of their targets [428].

The final target type is the *rigidly conscientious* worker. These employees are very scrupulous, assiduous, "organized, self-disciplined, hardworking, conventional, moralistic, and rule-bound" (p. 234] [429]. Rigidly conscientious employees can be bullied at work because others perceive them as infuriatingly condescending due to their apparently inflexible, perfectionist approach to work and adher-

276

ence to work-related rules. Rigidly conscientious workers are unlikely to go along with informal group rules if they believe the informal rules to be morally or ethically wrong. When these employees face situations they view as breaking the rules, they can become "rude, suspicious, uncooperative, ruthless, [and] irritable" (p. 234] [429]. They are likely to stubbornly defend their points of view, especially when issues such as work quality, client ethics, or productivity expectations are at stake. What they see as moral or ethical issues are far more important to rigidly conscientious employees than are relationships or others involved in the conflict. Additionally, they may report coworkers who break rules, behaviors making them widely unpopular, increasing their social isolation, and reducing potential allies or supporters. When workers are in such socially isolated positions, they are easier targets; bystanders may even feel satisfaction at seeing them targeted.

In addition to these general profiles, three other factors increase the likelihood of being bullied: organizational position, communication skill deficits, and social difference. First, employees at all levels can be bullied, but typically the higher one's position, the lower the incidence of bullying. Second, persons who lack effective social and communication skills (e.g., some submissives and many high-verbal aggressives) can have great difficulty protecting themselves and thus be targeted quite easily. Third, being noticeably different also increases the risk of becoming an outsider and thus a target [377, 430]. In the United States and Britain, for example, employees of African descent "are victimized more frequently than any racial group" (p. 182) [56].

Motivations (i.e., goals). Most targets involved in an entrenched bullying conflict are motivated by *resource personal, resource economic, social identity,* and *social justice goals.* Resource personal goals are driven by a need to maintain personal freedom, in this case freedom from attacks on their character. Targets go to great lengths to protect themselves and end abuse.

Interpersonal aggression, by definition, is behavior targets are motivated to avoid. Targets are also highly motivated by social identity goals. Targets want to be vindicated; they want to redeem themselves because being victimized is stigmatizing [431]. Especially in the US, being a victim brands someone as weak, childish, or culpable—others often assume targets did something to bring abuse upon themselves.

Most targets are motivated by *resource economic goals;* they want to maintain their jobs, and this motivation is well-founded. Most

277

targets find that bullying only ends when they quit, transfer, or are fired. Targets want to manage face and identity threats and be vindicated; these are social identity goals. *Social justice goals*, based on a drive for fairness or restorative justice, are at play in bullying conflicts. Targets communicatively position themselves as moral warriors fighting depraved enemies and argue that they respond accordingly to restore justice and fairness. Many responses to bullying conflicts are indirectly motivated by what targets call a *moral imperative* to act against what they perceive as corrupt actions and interactions.

Typically all parties are motivated to protect their interests and identity and to achieve a fair or just outcome. All target types share some similar motivations in bullying conflicts, but goals also differ depending on what's personally important. *Provocative (aggressive) targets* are motivated by social power goals. Rather than a drive to punish (often seen with bullies), these targets' power goals are to establish influence and dominance over others in conflicts. Also quick to speak up, the *communicatively assertive* provocative targets are motivated by economic personal goals—they are driven to protect their right to free speech, personal freedom, and choice.

Submissive targets want to avoid conflicts so are motivated by the social functionality goal, the desire to settle conflicts in a socially proper way. They are also motivated by social relationship goals as they wish to maintain peaceful, non-confrontational contact with others. *Rigidly conscientious* targets are motivated by power goals; they want to make other parties see the issue as they do. Specifically, rigidly conscientious targets want others to recognize the importance or moral value of the issue.

Tactics. Bullying conflicts most often involve affective (e.g., threatening identity, values) types of conflict rather than cognitive (e.g., focusing on ideas, tasks). Problem-solving and compromising work well for cognitive conflicts, but such is not the case for affective conflicts like entrenched workplace bullying. Problem-solving efforts in bullying conflicts often exacerbate the conflict [432]. And despite targets' efforts to appease or oblige high-aggressives (e.g., speaking with the bullies about the problem, working harder, cutting off communication with certain peers, monitoring their own messages to the bullies), hostile actions and interactions continue unabated or even escalate.

In line with diverse target profiles and motivations, victimization literature suggests that "conflict styles [tactics] ... [can] distinguish victims from non-victims [, and] ... employees who rely on certain styles more than others may unwittingly present themselves as potential targets of aggressive action" (p. 174] [56]. The provocative aggressive target's tendency to use forcing communication likely elicits aggressive tactics from other parties. Because provocative aggressive targets want to gain influence over bullies in the conflict, they more often use dominating-forcing tactics, but some form of problem-solving typically precedes forcing. Forcing tactics are more often passive aggressive because bullies typically have more power, influence, or both than targeted workers. In fact, "higher levels of bullying [are] predictive of ... behaviors such as purposely wasting company materials and supplies, ... doing one's work incorrectly, and ... damaging a valuable piece of property belonging to the employer" (p. 283] [433].

The *provocative assertive targets* are motivated to speak their minds in disagreements and argue about issues of disagreement without employing verbal aggression. Depending on the parties involved, even their assertive disagreement can trigger aggression, hostility, and behavior framed to "put them in their place." Tactics of *submissive targets* usually are obliging-appeasing and avoiding-withdrawing, although all targets use these tactics to some degree. They hope that if they do nothing to upset anyone, the conflict might go away. Submissive targets are typically amenable to compromising tactics to manage conflict but rarely suggest such tactics themselves [433]. Rather, they are willing to go along with others' ideas regarding compromises if they believe those tactics will end the conflict.

Rigidly conscientious targets use forcing tactics because they feel so strongly about the issues at hand. They will also use problem solving, accommodating, and compromising but *only* when these tactics get them the results they want. If less aggressive tactics fail, rigidly conscientious targets shift to forceful communication, often coupled with third-party involvement [424]. Because they believe they are right—absolutely—they work to involve higher authorities as allies in the conflict. In the next section, bystander types are reviewed.

Bystanders (Non-bullied Witnesses)

Table 13.4 summarizes the bystander type profiles, motivations during conflict, and likely conflict management tactics that each type will use.

Table 13.4: Bystander Profiles, Motivations, Tactics

Profile	Primary Motivational Goals	Most Likely Conflict Tactics
Bully Ally Bystander	Economic Resource	Third Party
	Relationship	Avoiding–Withdrawing
	Identity	Obliging-
	Justice	Accommodating
	Power-Hostility	
Target Ally Bystander	Economic Resource	Third Party
	Justice	Domination-Forcing
	Relationship	
Silent Bystander	Economic Resource	Avoiding-Withdrawal
	Identity	
	Relationship	

Profiles. Because bullying conflicts are so volatile and aggressive, they typically spread fear through the entire workgroup and push members into one of three non-bullied bystander groups: those who cluster around and support bullies (*bully allies*), those who support or protect targets (*target allies*), and those who attempt to distance themselves from the bullying conflict (*neutral* or *silent bystanders*). Bystanders are often considered *secondary* targets because they are not targeted directly, but their "perceptions, fears and expectations are changed as a result of being vicariously exposed to violence" [103] (p. 35). This group often reports "significantly more general stress and mental stress reactions in employees from the workplaces without bullying" (p. 108] [156] and often leave organizations (avoiding) after witnessing bullying.

Depending on the framework, researchers call bully allies "passive bullies, followers, henchmen," [39] (p. 67), patrons, and pawns [434]. Passive bullies and followers are those "who participate in bullying but do not usually take the initiative" [39] (p. 67). These "passive bullies can be equally troubling to the victim ... where others are gath-

280

ered willingly or unwillingly to participate in continuous malevolent actions" [435] (p. 271). Henchmen-women, on the other hand, actively take part in bullying conflicts, loyally following the bully's lead and working to undermine, remove, and sometimes even destroy targets' reputations. Bullies usually have two types of allies: patrons and pawns. Patrons help bullies ascend to positions of power and persons to whom bullies turn to as third-party allies. Bullies often choose these people as a support network. Pawns, who often emerge later as targets, are persons initially loyal to the bullies who side with them in bullying conflicts but later feel or discover they are being used or manipulated.

In other workgroups, bystanders who witness and then subsequently model aggressive communication and become bullies can be of grave concern. Whether bystanders mimic bullying behavior depends, in part, on group norms and cohesion. If workgroup cohesion is high, bystanders' direct observation of bullying can increase their own use of aggression [436]. Additionally, "norms of toughness ... tend to reduce the likelihood that witnesses to workplace bullying will take action against it. On the contrary, such norms tend to increase the odds that witnesses will join in and even applaud the action of workplace bullies" [342] (p. 217). In a majority of cases, emerging active bullies is not as frequent as members becoming more rude and discourteous in everyday interactions, likely due to the reciprocal nature of communication [437]. Some members may become more uncivil over time, and others might empathize with and try to help targets.

Target allies, in contrast to bully allies, are bystanders who witness abusive conflicts and side with the targets. They comprise a second (albeit small) group of bystanders—those who either believe abuse is morally wrong or have long-standing friendships with targets. Ferguson and Barry [436] suggest that directly witnessing another's abuse "affords the observer an opportunity to witness and, accordingly, vicariously experience the emotions of the target (or victim) .... [giving the observer ... an opportunity to empathize with the victim, and perhaps to mentally place themselves in the victim's shoes" (p. 89). Other bystanders may eventually join the target's side of the conflict, especially if they shift from being followers, patrons, or pawns to being targets.

Unlike target or bully allies, *neutral* or *silent bystanders* withhold voice and allegiance to parties of the conflict and take a Switzerland-type position in the conflict, striving to be uninvolved non-combatants. Silent bystanders want to stay out of the conflict because they see targets being "undermined, disenfranchised, and emasculated" (p. 124] [438].

The relative size of bystander groups is unique to each workgroup, bullying conflict dynamics, issues of contention, and personalities of those involved. Regardless of the setting, membership in bystander groups continuously shifts and morphs. Targets' supporters may burn out; non-involved persons can become targets or begin taking sides, and persons in the bully's circle of supporters are ousted. Persons safe from targeting can become targets when bullies' alliances shift, which they commonly do. Depending on the bullies' profile, bullies often redirect aggression to persons who look like a threat or whose actions or words place bullies in a negative light.

Motivations. Nearly all bystanders are motivated by *economic resource goals;* like targets, most want to keep their jobs. The threat of becoming embroiled in the bullying conflict often jeopardizes employment. Further motivations depend on the bystander's profile. *Bully allies* who may passively and symbolically side with aggressors are often motivated by *social relationship goals* and want bullies to see them as allegiant. Some bully allies are motivated by *social justice goals* and believe that targets are in the wrong and bullies in the right. Many are motivated by *social identity goals* and preventing their own potential target status. *Power-hostility social goals* motivate henchmen-women who, like bullies, can be high-verbal aggressives. This type of bully supporter may want to establish their own dominance, strength, and position in the workgroup.

Target allies are often motivated by *social justice goals;* their primary motivation is to restore fairness at work and stop abusive treatment of workers. Some are motivated by a moral imperative to right a wrong and to take action against tyranny. In some cases if bystanders are motivated toward justice, they collectively work with targets and like-minded allies in acts of collective resistance. Target allies are also motivated by *social relationship goals* and want to maintain their friendships and positive interpersonal affiliations with targeted persons.

Silent bystanders, on the other hand, are typically motivated by *personal resource goals;* they want to maintain their privacy and personal freedom, which can be threatened if they become involved in the conflict. Another motivating factor for silent bystanders is the *social identity goal* (face-saving, identity-preserving); they want to avoid

282

becoming a target. Additionally, silent bystanders may be motivated by *social relationship goals* and hope to not alienate bullies, targets, or anyone allied with either side by appearing neutral. Sadly, this strategy rarely works because bullying conflicts are so emotionally charged, mainly because the stakes are high, that both target and bully groups negatively judge those who stand by silently. In all bystander groups the motivations typically drive the tactics.

Tactics. Bully allies side with aggressors and use tactics including spying on targets and target allies and reporting back to bullies (third party, forcing), silently looking on as bullies harass and abuse targets (avoiding), and bending to the bullies' demands (obliging). For allies who also aggress, tactics can include ignoring targets' feelings or needs (avoiding), asserting their influence (forcing), and stressing their position as a bully ally (forcing, appeasing). The latter move is tied with efforts to force outcomes favoring bully allies or bullies [435].

For *target allies* motivated by *social justice goals*, they may speak with upper-management (third party), meet with union stewards (third party), organize group discussions outside the workplace (avoiding). Most tactics have a dominating-forcing thread because target allies are interested in taking disciplinary action against bullies—blocking promotions, countering claims, constructing employment termination— even if third-parties are involved. Target allies motivated by *social relationship goals* provide social support. They offer instrumental support by helping targets with their work and trying to arrange breaks and moments of escape, informational support by telling targets of their redress avenues or about powerful allies who might help in the fight for justice, and emotional support in the form of "empathy, caring, acceptance and assurance" (p. 88] [439]. Supportive tactics are supplementary to conflict tactics but often involve advising targets how to fight back in the bullying conflict. Thus, even social support can be indirectly forcing and advising targets how to win. Tactics of those choosing to remain silent, however, are focused on self-protection.

Silent bystanders try to withdraw into a nonaligned position that appears safe using avoidance-withdrawal tactics. In toxic working environments, however, neutral bystanders may struggle with whether to stay uninvolved or help the targets being persistently abused [440]. It can be difficult "to remain uninvolved in such cases ... due to a seemingly strong need for the target to seek support for their case" (p. 151) [441]. On the other hand, neutral bystanders are often motivated by social relationship goals, so will remain friendly with persons from both sides of the conflict—an obliging-accommodating tactic.

Bullies

Table 13.5 summarizes the different kinds of aggressors likely to abuse others. The Table provides an overview of aggressor type profiles, motivations for each type, and likely conflict management tactics each will use.

Table 13.5: Aggressor Profiles, Motivations, Tactics

Profile	Primary Motivational Goals	Most Likely Conflict Tactics
Accidental Bully	Economic Resource	Dominating-Forcing**
Narcissistic Bully	Identity Justice	Dominating-Forcing** Third party (pawns)
Psychopathic Bully	Power-Hostility Economic Resource Justice	Dominating-Forcing** Third party (patrons)

** Verbal aggression is a hallmark of bullies' communication.

Bullying conflicts involve all affected workers, not simply bully-target dyads, but in bullying conflicts the bully or aggressor plays a crucial role. Unlike other types of conflict that assume mutuality of parties, "workplace bullying ... is characterized as involving a clearly identified bully (bully).... [who is] primarily the provocateur" (p. 52) [52]. Bullies cannot harass, humiliate, and verbally abuse others unless the organization's climate is marked by a "sense of permission to harass" (p. 84] [30], but certain personality types tend toward using verbal aggression more than others. That is, some people are simply more verbally aggressive than others due to having an inborn trait [86] or having socially learned that aggression pays off [342]. These bullies may not always instigate the conflict but are the parties who persistently use hostile, aggressive attacks to press their side.

Profiles. Bullying conflicts occur in relationships of unequal power, so despite coworkers being most common source of aggression in the workplace, when asked to identify a bully targets most often report that the perpetrator is someone with legitimate power—supervisor, direct manager, or upper-manager. Even when lacking legitimate power, bullies tend to have access to more resources than targets, including relationships with persons with influence. In addition to more power and influence than targets, research suggests three general bully profiles based on motivation, tactics, and responses to challenge [442]: the *accidental bully* (under pressure); *narcissistic bully* (vulnerable, insecure); and *psychopathic bully* (grandiose, power-driven) [443]. For the most part, most bullies fall into the accidental category; they bully as a means of goading productivity from others. Other bullies, however, appear to have personality pathologies driven by fear, insecurity, or extreme ambition. Narcissistic and psychopathic traits are tendencies that range on a continuum and are influenced to some degree by contextual, situational factors. However, people who have worked with any bully type will recognize the characteristics to some degree, as they are quite descriptive of observed behaviors.

Accidental bullies are the most common and are (usually) managers with a very tough, even rough, style and way of interacting and directing others.' They demand that others complete work tasks, often within exceedingly tight deadlines, and have little or no perception that what he or she says hurts or disturbs others. The accidental bully typically over-reacts to pressure and passes that reaction on by blowing up, making impossible demands, and otherwise communicating in a blunt, insensitive, insistent manner.

The situational factors that trigger accidental bullies are wide-ranging and can include unorganized or poorly orchestrated changes and demands; organizational conditions such as work pressure, high performance demands, role conflict, and role uncertainty. In their drive toward tasks, they often lose sight of the humanity of others [443]. They frequently act aggressive as a means to an end—to reach higher standards, thrash the competition, protect the company, and so forth. The welfare of people is secondary to task or output goals. Accidental bullies expect others to be resilient; to understand that nothing personal is meant by their tirades. In fact, "such people are often shocked when they are made aware of the consequences of their attitudes and actions" [paragraph 8] [443]. This bully type is the most amenable to intervention, particularly if that intervention is tough and straightforward.

The *narcissistic bully* is charismatic but driven by fear, especially fear of appearing incompetent and so "justifies harm to others for [his or her] own survival" (p. 277] [442]. This bully does not plan to harm others, "he [or she] does so offhandedly, as a manifestation of his[/her] genuine character" [paragraph 10] [443]. They are exceedingly self-absorbed, frequently pretentious, and can have "fantasies of breathtaking achievement" [paragraph 10). They believe themselves to be better than others and therefore should be treated exceptionally, yet feel entitled to treat others as they wish.

Narcissistic bullies are typically shame-prone and exceedingly sensitive to slights or any hint that they are less than competent [367, 400]. Because they have limited impulse control and are fear-driven, their grandiose self-image is easily punctured, and they can respond by acting out in rage and making outlandish claims about their detr-bullies [442]. That is, if they are crossed or questioned, they can respond with cruel fury [444]. Given these tendencies, narcissistic bullies can shift from being very charming to extremely difficult and even vicious. "Their abuse is not cold and calculating and meant to intimidate, it's just an expression of their superiority when they rage against you because they see you as the idiot. Of course they don't have much empathy" [paragraph 8] [443]. The narcissistic bully can alter his or her communication and behavior if organizations are willing to invest considerable time and effort coaching and counseling. The cost may be high, but if the narcissistic bully is valuable, their "talents may be worth it" (p. 277] [442].

The third bully type is the *psychopathic bully*, a rare personality type (1% to 2% in general population, 15% - 25% in prisons) that is thought to be found in higher proportions in senior-level organizational positions (up to 3.5%) [445]. These aggressors are also called industrial psychopaths, organizational psychopaths, organizational sociopaths, and corporate psychopaths [438]. These non-criminal or successful psychopaths, deemed *successful* because unlike criminal psychopaths they have evaded legal authorities, are "not prone to outbursts of impulsive, violent, criminal behavior" (p. 301] [446]. Psychopathic (like narcissistic) bullies are grandiose, but they come across as friendly and charming at first. They are highly motivated to gain power and exceedingly talented at ingratiating themselves with powerful others. They often rise almost meteorically in organizations "because of their manipulative charisma and their sheer, single minded dedication to attain senior levels of management" (p. 124] [438]. These bullies can be authoritarian, aggressive, and domineering but in a way that imbues a sense of safety, particularly when organizations face an external threat.

Psychopathic bullies usually work to attract a follower base of patrons who can assist in their ascendancy. They also identify pawns to use or manipulate and potential opponents they attempt to undermine or disenfranchise (e.g., auditor, HR staff, safety and security personnel). Developing a cadre of followers is important to the psychopathic bully, and they are likely to react aggressively to those whom they perceive as disloyal or oppositional to their goals [443]. These bullies may perform feelings of remorse if the situation calls for it but these are not *felt* emotions; they are more likely to be displayed for manipulative effect [442]. Their personalities are marked by cold-heartedness, manipulativeness, ruthlessness, and lack of emotions including fear, empathy, guilt, and remorse when they harm others [438]. Psychologists believe that this personality type has no capacity for empathy or perspective taking [445].

A disturbing part of communicating with psychotic bullies is that they may distort what others say in self-serving ways. They typically blame others if their own actions bring about negative ramifications. If this bully type is challenged about his or her behavior their reaction is as volatile as the narcissist but often involve threats of litigation, claims of being a victim of bullying, threats of divulging information about others, and escalated bullying. Counseling or mentoring has little effect as the psychopathic bully is unlikely to change their communication or behavior [447].

General bully characteristics or traits for all types. Most bullies are unlikely to praise others [448] and are prone toward verbal aggressiveness. In fact, there is convincing medical-communication research arguing that high-aggressives are born with the trait [449]. Thus, bullies are likely to have the aggressiveness trait to a higher degree than those who do not bully others, regardless of the situation or pressure. Because high-verbal aggressives have lower scores on perspective taking and higher scores on social dominance orientation [450], they are unlikely to perceive aggressive messages as hurtful. Motivations do differ somewhat, however, based on unique profile markers.

Motivations. Accidental bullies are motivated predominantly by *economic resource goals*, the desire to gain or keep something of economic value. Their drive for achievement comes from this motivation. Typically the accidental bully wants to reach high standards and meet organizational goals (regardless of human costs). They respond readily to demands from higher-placed organizational members, especially as those demands deal with output or the organization's financial survival. Certain antecedents can drive the accidental bully by evoking additional stress around work production, which evokes aggression, venting negative emotions, and pushing subordinates and peers even harder. Quite likely, frustration exacerbates accidental bullies' aggression if they believe employees are stifling production goals [420].

Narcissistic bullies, on the other hand, are driven by *social identity goals* (e.g., face saving, identity-preservation, maintaining their self-perception of someone exceptional). They justify aggressive treatment as a means of bolstering their persona and maintaining their image- or identity-management work. Secondarily they may be motivated by economic goals of obtaining something of value but only if it serves the primary goal of bolstering grandiose self-identities. These bullies are want to protect others' perceptions of them as competent and excellent [367, 400]. Narcissistic and psychopathic bullies are often motivated to act aggressively because of a tendency to ascribe others' actions and words as having malevolent intent and see themselves as victims [451, 452]. As such, *justice goals* are activated for both types, as they believe they have been wronged and so seek retribution. Other indirect motivating factors are psychopathology (e.g., transference of negative emotions towards someone who represents unresolved conflict) and argumentative skill deficiency (e.g., lacking ability to communicate position effectively) that can trigger verbal aggression. Narcissistic bullies as high-verbal aggressives can be motivated by their own anger and bad mood—emotions they rarely control very well [428].

Psychopathic bullies are motivated predominantly by *power-hostility social goals*, the drive to establish dominance, gain power, and punish anyone who stands in the way of achieving these. As part of a drive for power and influence, psychopathic bullies are often motivated by *social identity goals* and will cover up errors and bad decisions or scapegoat and shift blame onto others [443]. As high-verbal aggressives, they can be driven by the desire "to appear 'tough,' ... to be mean..., and to express disdain for" the other person (p. 122] [428]. Self-defense, reprimanding someone, winning arguments, expressing anger, and manipulating the another person's behavior are also motivations for verbal aggression [453]. They may be motivated

288

by *social justice goals* because they often have a retribution bias (belief that retaliation is better than reconciliation); they might also be motivated by a potency bias (tendency to frame conflict as a contest in which to demonstrate dominance or submissiveness) [452], another form of a *power-hostility social goal.*

Tactics. Primarily, bullying involves a hostile, forcing-dominating conflict management style—bullies want their way and often shift conflicts over tasks (cognitive conflicts) to conflicts attacking targets' identity or values (affective conflict) [89]. Conflict management tactics are aggressive, and bullying conflicts, rather than being marked by a single form of negativity, involve numerous barbs, jabs, and machinations. Instead, exchanges are far more extreme and intense than everyday incivilities. Tactics vary by bully type, as might be expected, but all bullies use verbal aggressiveness (passive or active) to varying degrees. Most bullies derogate their targets, often to justify their own abuse of others in the conflict. Caustic humor is a common tactic bullies use against targets because it is ambiguous and provides plausible deniability. "High verbal aggressives [claim] that about 46% of their verbally aggressive messages ... [involve] trying to be humorous.... [As such,] "using humor may be a tactic for being mean, [in order] to a disdain another, or it may be an 'evasive' device which masks the use of personal attacks and avoids provoking physical violence" (p. 125) [428].

Depending on the bully type, tactics can include blaming targets for the bullies' errors (narcissistic, psychopathic), making unreasonable demands (accidental), criticizing targets' work ability (all types), yelling and screaming (accidental, narcissistic), inconsistently referring to made-up rules (narcissistic, psychopathic), threatening job loss (all types), discounting targets' accomplishments (all types), socially excluding targets (narcissistic, psychopathic), insults and put-downs (all types), taking credit for targets' work (narcissistic, psychopathic) [454], and scapegoating (narcissistic, psychopathic). Psychopathic bullies disparage, belittle, emasculate, and destroy anyone who appears to be blocking their aspirations. Tactics can include physical and psychological intimidation intended to cause fear, distress, or harm to the target [450]. This type of bully employs third-party tactics quite often; depending on the protection of patrons, the important or powerful others with whom the bully has developed power-based relationships. In fact, they are quite adept at *managing up*, so to speak.

This overview of the involved employee groups outlines many of the issues involved in bullying conflicts and illustrates why bullying can be so difficult to stop. Table 13.3 summarizes involved party profiles, motivations, and associated tactics. There are many drivers of bullying in organizations beyond the involved parties we have focused on in this paper. This look at the three central employee groups suggests areas of research necessary so that we might improve organizational efforts in resolving bullying conflicts. We now move to possibilities for change.

So What Can We Do?

We now bring some optimism to the chapter and talk about directions for transformation or change. We believe that bullying is an organization-wide issue, but individual employees are keen to improve these situations, so we touch on both. Fleshing out the different types of targets, bystanders, and bullies, as well as their motivations in these conflicts, underscores the complexity of bullying conflicts.

Clearly—no "one size fits all" solution will work. Rather, the dynamic nature of the resource and social goals in combination with the differing tactics to managing conflicts will result in negative spirals of retaliation and war zone like workplaces. Then where does this leave organizations? The experience suggests that organizations dealing with bullying conflicts should carefully consider this chapter's discussion to be forewarned of the involved bullies and how they are situated in workgroups. Organizations will necessarily have to conduct a careful analysis of the history (e.g., involved parties, motivations, tactics to date) surrounding the conflict to unravel the situational dynamics unique to the involved workgroup.

Bullying really is an organization-wide issue rather than something individuals alone can solve. Solving the problem is not only an organization-wide responsibility but successful efforts require the total commitment of top-level organizational leadership, involvement of middle-management, and engagement of employees. Short-term approaches such as identifying lone perpetrators while ignoring initiating and maintaining factors ultimately fails to produce meaningful, lasting change.

Some people believe that bullying results from management being inadequately prepared for the pressures of globalization. According to this viewpoint, organizations need "new rules" such as "clearly defined channels for support and advice in addition to clear reporting standards, times, and lines Not surprisingly, this merges with a higher concern for *communication*" (p. 47) [455].. Indeed, for there is a "need for new managerial skills such as strong interpersonal, communication, and listening skills and an ability to engage in reciprocal rather than manipulative behavior." We would add that *all* organizational members need these communication skills.

In fact, the most effective come about from changing the very nature of day-to-day conversations. Policy development, while important for victim redress, has little effect on reducing bullying if the organizational climate and culture does not change at a fundamental level. Similarly, training individuals about workplace bullying is important, labels the phenomenon, and should be part of an overall plan for staff training, but training alone rarely has a determinable effect on interpersonal aggression [456]. Rather, organizational members need to learn new ways of day-to-day interacting.

From interventions with the US Veterans Affairs, we summarize the following steps for an effective organization-wide approach [101]. This approach requires the involvement of four groups. First, top-level persons must be committed to organization-wide change regarding dignity for all workers. Second, middle-managers must be involved at each step. Third, members from support staff such as HR, Employee Assistance Program, ombudspersons, and unions should be involved. Finally, representatives chosen by direct-line staff in each program or division must be involved. Organizations may benefit from bringing someone in from outside to help facilitate analysis and planning, as an outsider may be more objective and less likely to have a vested interest in outcomes.

Teams comprised of persons from these groups carryout the following steps: (1) in each workgroup conduct a base-line evaluation of aggression using a validated measure (WAR-Q Workplace Aggression Revised Questionnaire is outstanding); (2) based on the types of aggression and the unique make up of each group, teams develop tailored interventions and implement them; (3) after three to six months, teams conduct a follow-up evaluation using the same measure as in step (1). If desired change has not occurred, teams assess the follow-up findings, design new approaches, implement, and measure again in a pre-determined time frame. We cannot stress the importance of this approach if true change is desired. However, if there is no support for this plan, we suggest the following individual-level actions for targets, bystanders, and bullies.

Individual responses to managing bullying conflicts constructively begin when involved parties are able to recognize when a simple conflict has become a bullying conflict. In particular for targets *and* by-

291

standers, is being able to name abusive conflicts "workplace bullying"; this is an important first step to understanding what's occurring and what to do about it. Information about bullying (e.g., research articles, books) coupled with being able to name bullying as a distinct phenomenon also bolsters employee claims to upper-management and HR. Targeted workers may also decide to file formal or informal complaints to unions, EEOC, the bully's boss, or attorneys, reports that typically require detailed documentation (e.g., dates, times, events). Targeted workers may also consider filing lawsuits against employers but should understand that such suits are rarely won and take enormous resources and personal energy.

Ensuring self-care and social support is especially important for effectively dealing with bullying conflicts. This may mean taking time off, trying not to take the experience personally, and spending time with trusted others. Gaining peer support is easier if other organizational members understand bullying and know it is occurring. Informally educating peers can be done by distributing articles and talking about bullying in a manner that protects vulnerable persons. If and when individual conflict management tactics fail, which is often the case, workers may choose to quit or transfer, and we argue, should frame their exits as a victory rather than defeat.

Bystanders are very important in bullying conflicts. Directly confronting bullies can be risky and make situations worse, but there are other actions available to bystanders. Scully and Rowe [457] suggest that bystanders can do two things that will reduce bullying, mobbing, verbal aggression, and so forth: "discouraging negative behaviors, and, ... encouraging *positive* behaviors" (p. 89). This means helping "people in all cohorts to note—and to commend—the achievements of their fellow workers. Such commendations often matter to the person concerned and are thought to be useful in encouraging future, socially desirable behavior" (pp. 89-90). Bystander action also means "helping people in all job categories to react, and then act appropriately, when they see unsafe, unprofessional, offensive, discriminatory, or illegal behavior in the workplace" (p. 90).

In addition, bystanders can be very helpful for supporting targets' stories and breaking the bullying cycle; concerted voice simply increases believability. Collective voice also reduces some of the risk of being labeled troublemakers, mentally ill, or problem-employees. Non-targeted workgroup members may not be as stigmatized, since they lack the victim-label. But even with collective resistance, there is the risk of being pejoratively branded when speaking out against abuse and oppression. William Ury's book *The Third Side: Why we fight and how we can stop* [458] outlines an instructive approach for building others' competence in workgroups, so that they can help prevent, handle, and in some cases stop aggressive communication behavior.

As for bullies, the organizational and communication literatures are sparse regarding what they could do to better manage conflicts and keep conflicts civil and constructive. Infante et al. [428] and Rancer and Avtgis' [459] work does provide constructive pointers, however, regarding persons with high trait verbal aggressiveness—likely present in some degree with all bully profiles. Their research suggests that one of the reasons people use verbal aggression is that they lack argumentation skills. Thus, if organizational members who bully others realize they tend to become aggressive in interactions that are conflictual, one remedy could be to learn how to constructively argue.

Infante [460] has developed a curriculum specifically for this purpose. Another useful skill is improving one's ability to read others' emotions. Laura Crawshaw, who coaches abrasive managers, argues that these individuals tend toward aggression because they have little ability to empathize with others so they do not fully see the effect their aggression has on others. Learning empathy is not a simple task, but persons in the medical profession often complete courses in this skill [461]. Indeed, the steps that high-verbal aggressive might take is an for future research.

Conclusion

Workplace bullying is a unique type of conflict because it involves power disparities, aggression, and persistence that affect a wide group of employees. An exploration of these parties' goals and tactics helps trace the likely motivations and how those differ for targets, bystanders, and bullies. Additionally, some motivations are at odds with others (e.g., targets and bullies want supporters, neutral bystanders want to stay neutral). If we say there are roughly three different types of target (provocative, rigidly conscientious, passive), three types of bystander (bully allies, target allies, neutral bystander), and three types of bully (accidental, narcissistic, psychopathic) and all nine of these general types have different motivations and tactics driven by those motivations, then we have some idea of how impossible it can feel to address bullying conflicts once they develop and how these conflicts can be a *nasty piece of work*.

CHAPTER 14

How Positive Experiences at Work Can Reduce Some of the Effects of Workplace Bullying[M]

Pamela Lutgen-Sandvik & Jacqueline Hood

Chapter Summary: Positive organizing is associated with a number of desirable outcomes for both organizations and their members. Focusing exclusively on positive phenomena and their relationships with desired outcomes, however, can lead to overlooking how destructive communication processes might cancel out these relationships. This chapter presents a study that examined the effects of interpersonal positivity and organizational virtuousness on three outcomes: intent to leave, perceived mental health, and workplace stress. The study also looked at these relationships when bullying was present to see if bullying negated or cancelled out these positive relationships. Results indicate that positive variables are associated with positive outcomes. When bullying was present, it negated one-third of the positive associations, suggesting that looking solely at creating workplace positivity without simultaneously looking at reducing aggression may doom efforts to fail.

Keywords: positive organizing, workplace bullying, stress, mental health, job satisfaction

----

Communication at work generally includes both positive-productive and destructive-counterproductive patterns, but research in these two areas typically doesn't cross-pollinate, so to speak. Because most organizing includes constructive and destructive dualisms [462], examining these in tandem makes sense in order to discern how they might interact. We analyze two forms of positive organizing and one form of destructive organizational communication and the relationships among these variables in terms of certain outcomes. Specifically, we study organizational virtuousness, interpersonal positivity, and workplace bullying for two purposes: (a) to determine the associations among these positive phenomena and three employee outcomes: intent to leave, perceptions of personal mental health, and workplace stress; and (b) to explore the extent to which positive phenomena moderate bullying communication's effects on these outcomes.

Interpersonal Positivity at Work

Interpersonal positivity is communication that emphasizes what's admirable, hopeful, constructive, and supportive and includes both relation- and task-related interactions. Relational interactions provide emotional support, consider others' feelings, and engender camaraderie and companionship [463]. Positive relational communication supports employee retention, reduces stress and burnout [439], contributes to preferred self-identities [464], and enhances health [465].

Task-related interpersonal positivity is affirmative, valuing communication about work assignment, planning, implementation, and evaluation. It includes receiving instrumental (e.g., time, resources, and help to complete tasks) and informational (e.g., how-to instructions, background about job/role) support. Task-related interpersonal positivity can reduce role ambiguity and conflict [466], buffer stress, enhance mental health, and reduce intentions to leave the organization [467]. As such, we hypothesize:

H1: Higher levels of interpersonal positivity will be associated with lower intentions to leave, lower stress levels, and enhanced perceptions of mental health.

Organizational Virtuousness

Organizational virtuousness involves systemic, organizational-culture processes that enable, foster, and perpetuate excellence, virtue, ethics, human dignity, and so forth [468]. Virtuousness is associated with meso-level discourse and meaning-centered features that systems, groups, or collectivities exhibit. Typically, moral goodness, positive effect on humans, and social betterment are evidence of organizational virtuousness [469]. Organizational virtuousness includes both internal (how members are treated) and external (effect on extended community) foci. Positivity at the organizational level is essential because some argue that the "organizational context in which people work is more important than the work itself in determining psychological outcomes" [470] (p. 150).

Organizational virtuousness can reduce employee turnover and increase social capital and social behavior among organizational members [471]. Social capital and affiliation, in turn, are thought to reduce stress and improve mental health [472]. Organizational virtuousness can also enhance flexibility and resilience, assist in building solidarity and commitment, and increase perceived efficacy or effectiveness [473]. Flexibility and resilience mediate the effects of stressors at work and can enhance mental health [474]. Solidarity, commitment, and perceived effectiveness are also associated with reduced turnover [475]. As such, we hypothesize:

H2: Higher levels of organizational virtuousness will be associated with lower intentions to leave, lower levels of stress, and enhanced perceptions of mental health.

Bullying Communication and Degree

There are a wide variety of destructive processes in organizations; we focus on workplace bullying because we see it as an issue of grave concern. Workplace bullying is *an extreme stressor* and is linked to serious health issues including symptoms of post-traumatic stress disorder, depression and anxiety, suicidal ideation (i.e., thinking about killing yourself), suicide, and physical illness. It increases intentions to leave and actual turnover, for targets and witnessing bystanders, and leads to higher stress for both groups. As such, we hypothesize:

H3: Higher degrees of adult bullying will be associated increased intentions to leave, higher stress levels, and perceptions of poorer mental health..

Does Bullying Moderate Positivity or Visa Versa?

Organizational cultures and climates typically are more complex than being either employee-abusive or virtuous. Rather, destructive and constructive communication processes coexist at work, processes that may be in tension and operate on separate but associated continua. As such, employees can experience (and organizations can be marked by) both affirmative and abusive interactions and processes. Positive peer relationships can stand in stark contrast to coexisting abusive supervision, or bullied employees can work in organizations with missions to which they strongly identify.

Past research offers contradictory arguments regarding the strength of positive and negative phenomena. Psychological research suggests that negative is stronger than positive [476], and some organizational studies report that negative phenomena explain more variance (particularly regarding stress) than do positive phenomena [477]. Other researchers argue that the positive effects gained from positive emotion and positive experiences are far more durable and long-lasting than the effects of negative phenomena [478, 479]. Given these different claims, currently we do not know if positivity might moderate the path between negative phenomena (like workplace bullying) and desired outcomes or if negativity might moderate the path between positive phenomena and desired outcomes. Because of the growing interest in both positive organizing and workplace bullying, we posed two RQs:

RQ1: Does interpersonal positivity moderate the relationship between bullying degree and intent to leave, stress levels, and perceptions of mental health?

RQ2: Does organizational virtuousness moderate the relationship between bullying degree and intent to leave, stress levels, and perceptions of mental health?

Method

Data Collection and Sample

This study was using Survey Monkey (www.surveymonkey.com) and a university-based sampling service (StudyResponse, see Glossary) coupled with on-line advertisements. (I have used StudyResponse data in many research studies.) In total, 2,846 US workers responded to the survey; 43.4% were male, and mean age was 42 (range 18-84, SD 10.6). A large portion of the sample included white-collar employees.

Instrumentation

Independent variables were interpersonal positivity, organizational virtuousness, and bullying degree. The dependent variables were intent to leave, stress level, and perceived mental health.

Interpersonal positivity. Interpersonal positivity was assessed using indexes adapted from past research [54, 480]. Respondents rated their level of agreement with statements regarding interpersonal treatment at work and working conditions over the past six months. Choices ranged from 5, strongly agree to 1, strongly disagree. The measure included two forms of interpersonal positivity: relational and task.

Organizational virtuousness. Organizational virtuousness was measured using an adapted form of Cameron and colleague's measure [469]. In the current study, respondents rated their level of agreement with statements regarding the organization where they worked over the last six months. Responses ranged from 5, strongly agree to 1, strongly disagree. The measure included two forms of virtuousness: organizational purpose (overarching mission-related features) and interpersonal principles (norms about how people were treated in organization).

Bullying degree. Bullying was measured with the Negative Acts Questionnaire, a widely used measure of workplace bullying assessing the intensity and frequency of 24 negative acts over the past six months. Responses were 0 never, 1 occasionally (less than monthly); 2 monthly; 3 weekly, and 4 daily. We derived bullying degree following past research as a continuous measure of abuse duration, intensity of abuse (number of negative acts experienced), and frequency (number of negative acts experienced daily or weekly) (See Chapter 2 for full discussion of measure development).

Intent to leave, stress, mental health. The study examined positive and negative independent variables' relationships with three dependent outcome variables: intent to leave, workplace stress, and perceptions of mental health. For intent to leave we used a cumulative measure of two items ("I often think of finding another job." "I am currently looking for another job." 5, strongly agree to 1, strongly disagree). Workplace stress and perceived mental health were assessed using single-item measures. (Stress: "How would your rate your stress level at work?"; 5, high stress to 1, little or no stress; Perceived mental health: "In general, would you say your general mental health is" 5, excellent to 1, poor). Single-item measures were used to assess stress and mental health.

Results

Main Effects

In total we measured four positive variables, two for organizational virtuousness (interpersonal principles, organizational purpose) and two for interpersonal positivity (relational positivity, task positivity). As such, main effects examined four positive variables' influence on three outcome variables (12 possible associations). Moderating effect analyses examined whether bullying interfered with (reduced, negated, canceled out, buffered) main effects. To review full statistical figures see citation [481].

H1proposed that interpersonal positivity would be inversely associated with intent to leave and workplace stress and directly associated with perceptions mental health quality. Similar H2 proposed that organizational virtuousness would have corresponding relationships to the outcome variables. We tested these hypotheses using hierarchical regression analysis. In the first step, the control variables of age and gender were entered into the regression equations. Older workers had lower intentions to leave than younger workers. Men had higher intentions to leave, lower workplace stress, and perceptions of better mental health than women. In the second step, we entered two interpersonal positivity factors and two organizational virtuousness factors into the regression.

The relational factor of interpersonal positivity was inversely related to intent to leave and workplace stress, and directly related to high quality perceptions of mental health. (*Inversely related* means as one variable increased, another variable decreased. *Directly related* means as one variable increased or decreased, another variable changed in the same direction.) The task-related factor was also inversely related to intent to leave and workplace stress. The task-factor was not linked to perceptions of mental health. Five of the six possible associations were significant, providing strong support for H1.

Regarding organizational virtuousness, the interpersonal principles factor was inversely related to intent to leave and workplace stress, and directly related to perceptions of mental health. The organizational purpose factor was non-significant regarding intent to leave and mental health, and directly related to workplace stress. As such, we found support for H2 only in terms of the interpersonal principles factor.

H3 proposed that bullying degree would be directly associated with intent to leave and workplace stress and inversely associated with perceptions of mental health. Bullying degree was directly related to both intent to leave and workplace stress and inversely related to perceptions of being mentally healthy. Thus, H3 was confirmed.

Moderating Variable Results

RQ1 asked if bullying degree would interrupt the relationships between interpersonal positivity and outcome variables. We found five main effects for the two factors, and bullying moderated one of these (relational interpersonal positivity and workplace stress). That means that even in the face of interpersonal positivity, which usually decreased stress, bullying created significant stress. On the other hand, bullying had no significant moderating effect on intent to leave or mental health in terms of relational interpersonal positivity. Bullying degree also had no significant moderating effect on workplace stress and intent to leave in terms of task interpersonal positivity. (Moderating effects means that one variable buffered or interrupted the path between two other variables. For example, workplace bullying increases stress when interpersonal positivity is absent. When interpersonal positivity is present, it interrupts (decreases) the impact of bullying on stress.)

Similarly, RQ2 asked if bullying degree would moderate the relationships between the organizational virtuousness and the three outcomes. (For RQ2 we looked only at the three relationships with the interpersonal principles aspect of organizational virtuousness, as the organizational purpose aspect lead to none of the hypothesized positive outcomes.) Bullying degree moderated two of the three relationship between interpersonal principles and key outcomes—intent to leave and mental health perceptions. Bullying had no significant moderating effect on stress.

Discussion and Implications

Overall, positive phenomena engender positive outcomes and bullying does not counteract all of these positive benefits. For both positive variables, the interpersonal/relational factors appear more resistant to the moderating effects of bullying.

Interpersonal Positivity: Relational, Task

Interpersonal positivity that is *relational in character* (praise, social
300

support, treated with dignity, etc.) seems most beneficial for workers and is associated with lower turnover and workplace stress and better perceptions of mental health. Bullying moderates only the link to reduced stress; it seems when bullying degree is high, even relational positivity cannot counteract the high stress that comes from being abused.

Task interpersonal positivity (access to resources and information, working on tasks that best use potential) also appears beneficial regarding turnover and stress but does not appear to improve employees' perceptions of their mental health. The beneficial relationships appear strong too; bullying degree does not moderate the affirmative effects. Thus it appears that when workers have positive task support, such support may keep them at their jobs and buffer stress even when bullying is a part of the organizational climate.

Organizational Virtuousness: Organizational Purpose, Interpersonal Principles

Organizational purpose does not seem to be associated with positive outcomes for employees (in terms of stress, mental health, turnover), and contrary to the expectations, it also increases employee stress. Organizational purpose means having a profound sense of purpose, being dedicated to doing good, and being optimistic about succeeding even when faced with challenges. Quite possibly, such intensity creates stress for employees. And organizational purpose, which is potentially good for organizations, does not seem as positive for employees and may even increase their stress levels.

Working in an organization supporting positive employee treatment (labeled *interpersonal principles*) does seem to have a positive effect on stress, intentions to leave, and mental health perceptions. However, bullying degree counteracts the positive effects on both turnover and mental health. Thus for this factor of organizational virtuousness that does provide positive benefits for employees, much of that is lost when bullying degree is high. Cameron and colleagues [482] argue that organizational virtuousness buffers against the negative outcomes associated with downsizing (e.g., increased voluntary turnover, stress, and negative attributions about the organization and decreased commitment, trust, innovation, and loyalty), but the findings in this study suggest that if workplace bullying is present organizations lose most of the positive benefits.

Bullying degree did not moderate the effect on stress, however, which seems a bit at odds with the relational interpersonal positivity factor finding (i.e., bullying moderates relationship with stress). The key difference between these two factors is that interpersonal principles represent how the organization treats people and relational positivity represents how the respondent is treated directly. So it seems that even in organizations where employees personally experience bullying, if the organization also features interpersonal principles of respect and dignity, these principles can buffer stress.

Workplace Bullying

Analysis confirms H3 and links workplace bullying to turnover, employee stress, and damaged perceptions of mental health. Regarding bullying degree's power to moderate the constructive outcomes associated with positive phenomena, the findings temper psychological and organizational literature, which argues that negative phenomena are stronger than positive.

If negative were always stronger, we would expected bullying to have stronger moderating effects. Bullying degree seems to negate the affirmative effects of relational positivity on stress and interpersonal virtuousness on intent to leave and mental health perceptions. Bullying did not, however, moderate positive effects of relational positivity on intent to leave and mental health, task positivity on stress and mental health, and interpersonal virtuousness on stress. Taken together, bullying reduced the effect of positive experiences on only 3 (37.5%) of the 8 desired outcomes; the other 5 remained relatively durable. In other words, we found that positive experiences buffered or reduced the negative effects of workplace bullying on 8 of 12 desired outcomes at work.

The findings may present conundrums for employees. Stress and intent to leave are good examples for the sake of discussion. If, as the findings suggest, relational positivity's effect on stress is nullified by bullying but bullying does not moderate the association with intent to leave, employees may be staying in high stress bullying workplaces. Anecdotal evidence does suggest that bullied workers stay long after they believe staying is still a good decision for them because of commitment to their peers.

Positive, Negative as Different Phenomena

Positive and negative communication in organizations appears to be independent continua rather than opposite ends of one continuum—

302

both can be present in varying degrees. As such, organizational inter-ventions should assess the presence and degree of both positivity and negativity when working toward the desired organizational cultures and climates. Without assessing both, negative dynamics can, at best, decrease the hoped-for positive outcomes or, at worst, nullify those positive outcomes.

Additionally, it is likely that negative and positive phenomena *do* different things in organizations. Emotions are a good example. Posi-tive emotions foster approach behavior, encourage engagement with the external environment (e.g., taking part in activities) and "*broaden* people's momentary thought-action and repertoires, widening the array of thoughts and actions that come to mind" [478](p. 122). Nega-tive emotion, on the other hand, restricts or narrows an individual's "momentary thought-action repertoire by calling to mind an urge to act in a particular way" (p. 122) (e.g., retaliate or seek escape when aggressed against). As such, measuring how negative and positive phenomena affect the same variables might be less useful than deter-mining which aspect of organization life are most strongly affected by each of these.

Conclusion

Positive organizational research and counterproductive workplace behavior research are somewhat insulated from one another. The current study underscores the importance of cross-pollination among these researchers studying and points to the importance for organiza-tional members or practitioners to examine both features in tandem, features that likely coexist in the complex world of work. We believe that interventions focusing solely on positive inquiry and neglecting the challenges posed by destructive communication will fail or at least fail to live up to their promise. Such approaches may even be coun-terproductive, engendering skepticism, disengagement, and aversion.

CHAPTER 15

Reversing the Effects of Bullying on Workers, Workgroups, Workforces, and Workplaces

Pamela Lutgen-Sandvik

Chapter Summary: When adult bullying goes on unaddressed, the persistent negativity creates toxic communication climates in which, employees suffer, workgroups polarize, workforce capital thins and declines, and organizations lose positive images and fail to reach their potential. Too often, organizational members can see only the individual-level effects of adult bullying and believe change should occur at the individual level. Such views fail to recognize adult bullying as the systemic phenomenon that it is—one that takes organizational efforts at multi levels to change. This essay explains the widespread damage that results from unaddressed adult bullying and outlines organizational changes at the individual- workgroup-, and organizational-levels to being reversing the negative effect.

Keywords: workplace bullying, workgroups, effects of bullying, ending bullying, respectful climates

---

Adult bullying/mobbing is a genuinely horrifying experience for those targeted, but it is also traumatizing to bystanders who witness and sympathize, toxic to workgroups and workforces, and damaging to organizational goals and reputations. Unaddressed workplace bullying can be a death knell for respectful communication climates and, by association, organizational goals. Problems go unsolved and can accumulate into crises, because bullying encourages "fixing the blame rather than fixing the problem" [124](p. 140). Terrorized workers hide mistakes rather than using them as improvement opportunities in an environment of "fear and mistrust, resentment, hostility, feelings

304

of humiliation, withdrawal, and play-it-safe strategies" (p. 141). This chapter fleshes out the extensive negative effects of unaddressed bullying and suggests approaches for multi-level organi-zational change to reduce and eliminate the problem.

In the following discussion, in addition to workplace bullying (defined in earlier chapters), I talk about communication climate, bullies, by-standers, targets, and upper-management. The communication climate is the social tone or psychological feel of working environments [483]. All types of organizational communication make up the com-munication climate in a workplace: face-to-face interactions, written or verbal messages from unseen upper-managers, beliefs about the motivations behind upper-management communiqués, gossip or buzzing among workgroup members about past interactions, formal policies and practices, and interactions employee have heard about but not directly witnessed, and so forth.

Bullies are the alleged perpetrators of persistent aggression and others who actively engage in aggression with the bullies. Bullies are also referred to as bullies, perpetrators, and aggressors. Bystanders are witnessing coworkers and can be bully-allies, target-allies, or silent onlookers. Targets are employees subjected to persistent emotional abuse. Upper-management are those whom others perceive to be key decision-makers in organizations: upper-managers, supervisors, board members, and so forth.

Why Bullying is Often Ignored or Inadequately Addressed

Because bullying occurs in communal settings—in front of or involving many people—researchers see it as a systemic, rather than individual psychological issue. Quite the opposite is the case in organizations, where members often blame victims or witch-hunt bullies—both responses rooted in the notion that bullying is a micro-level issue. With this mindset, the typical responses are ignoring aggression hoping it will go away or removing targets hoping their elimination ends abuse—neither typically works. In the United States, organizational responses to bullying are successful or partially successful in only a third of cases; in the other two-thirds, leadership does nothing, intervenes with little or no effect, or intervenes in ways that worsen targets' plights. When bullying is unaddressed or addressed ineffectively, workplace climates grow more toxic over time.

So why do organizational members fail to effectively address (or address at all) bullying? First, most members, including upper-management, have no effective strategies or tactics for dealing with aggression. Rather, people have the assumption that coworkers and bosses will interact politely and civilly; interactions only become problematic when members breach this assumption. When breaches occur, people simply do not know how to respond. Second, employees, including upper-managers, are put off, shocked, and even immobilized (i.e., they freeze) by aggression so are apprehensive about approaching aggressors. In many cases, even bullies' supervisors fear bullies and so are loathe to discipline or terminate employment. Additionally, they may have little idea how to coach or advise aggressive employees except to provide vague directives such as, "You need to improve your interpersonal skillls." Rarely can receipients of this advice do anything with the advice [484].

Third, as Ryan [197] notes, "the generic process of blaming the victim is applied to almost every American problem," (p. 8) and targets of workplace bullying are no exception. Organizational members typically believe the issue is a personality conflict, a personal rather than organizational problem. They see only the micro-, individual-level aspects of bullying and fail to acknowledge that bullying is a complex problem requiring complex interventions—requisite variety applies here (i.e., issue complexity/ambiguity requires intervention complexity) [335]. Finally, many managers may agree with aggressors and believe the best way to get results from people is to goad and terrorize them. When such people are decision-makers, the likelihood of addressing bullying is slim.

To strategize interventions that get to the root of the problem (v. its symptoms), organizations need requisite variety, that is, multi-pronged interventions. Changes focused solely at the micro-level are rarely effective, especially if organizational cultures reward aggression or upper-managers fear aggressors. And those who advise targets to go it alone—confront the bully—are giving dangerous advice. Research is quite clear that individual-level efforts have dismal outcomes and usually re-victimize targets [184, 431]. Complex interventions are required to ameliorate the effects of unaddressed bullying.

Effects of Unaddressed Bullying:
Workers, Workgroups, Workforces, and Workplaces

When bullying goes unaddressed and creates toxic communication

306

climates, employees suffer, workgroups polarize, workforce capital declines, and organizations fail to reach their potential. Aggression negatively affects workers, workgroups, workforces, and workplaces.

Workers (Targets, Witnesses)

Targets. Ostensibly, targets suffer the most direct harm from unaddressed bullying. Overwhelming evidence indicates that persistent harassment distresses all aspects of target lives. They suffer physical ailments including gastrointestinal programs (e.g., irritable bowel syndrome), insomnia, weight gain and loss, and musculoskeletal problems [485]. They also have increased risk of chronic stress, high blood pressure, and coronary heart disease [340].

Targets' emotional health also suffers; they experience depression, elevated anxiety, and anxiety attacks at much higher rates than non-bullied employees. Targets live with incredible levels of persistent fear. Bullying erodes target self-esteem and self-worth and contributes to symptoms of post-traumatic stress disorder (PTSD): hypervigilance, thought intrusions, and avoidance-disassociation. Abused employees have high rates of alcohol consumption and abuse and often think about suicide.

Work productivity can also flounder, cognitive functioning suffer and performance dwindle. Some targets are so damaged that they cannot reintegrate into the workforce, or can do so only after intensive remedial therapy. Their entire perspective is altered. "Exposure to bullying shatters employees' perceptions of a (reasonably) just world in which things happen as they should, thereby leading to perceived injustice" [486](p. 768).

Witnesses, bystanders. Employees who see coworkers abused but are not abused directly are considered witnesses or bystanders, organizational members whose "perceptions, fears, and expectations are changed as a result of being vicariously exposed to violence" [103](p. 35). The harm witnesses experience underscores the communal features of adult bullying. Witnesses experience "destabilizing forces at work, excessive workloads, role ambiguity and work relationship conflict" [104](p. 495). They have increased intentions to leave and exit rates compared to non-exposed workers and report higher rates of workplace negativity and stress and far less job satisfaction than non-exposed workers.

Bystanders feel daily dread and fear at work and practice

hypervigilance. When coworkers see and hear about others being bullied, they make the logical assumption that they could be next. Additionally, if witnessing coworkers pull back their support for targets, they can end up feeling quite guilty. "They may feel they stood by and did nothing, the organizational equivalent of watching a mugging on a daily basis" [18](p. 26). If bullying continues, negative emotions spread—fear, anger, emotional exhaustion, and guilt, plague bystanders and infect workgroups. Witnessing others' abuse leads to bystanders' reduced motivation, commitment, and efficiency in part due to "anticipating being targeted and being/feeling unable to help targets" [487](p. 270). The various ways bystanders involve themselves changes workgroups, typically by the materialization of insular factional cliques.

Workgroups

In workgroups affected by persistent abuse, goal displacement occurs, and the primary goal shifts from workgroup tasks to self-protection. The constant hypervigilance is corrosive to workgroups and typically pushes members into a number of relatively insular bystander factions. Three sub-groups are bullies and their allies, targets and their allies, and silent bystanders who try distancing themselves. Workplaces become marked by networks with warring sub-cultures and isolates who simply disconnect.

The bullies and their allies form a the first loosely structured sub-culture. Bully allies are "passive bullies, followers, ... henchmen," [39](p. 67), bully bystanders [488], patrons, or pawns [434]. Allies in this group can be passive followers who symbolically side with bullies but not be actively directly aggressive [39] or aggressive followers who collude with bullies to undermine, remove, and sometimes even destroy target reputations [383]. Patrons are persons who help bullies ascend to power and persons to whom bullies turn as third-party allies. Pawns are initially loyal to the bullies but later discover they are being manipulated and often emerge later as targets.

Targets and their allies comprise another sub-culture, typically including bystanders who believe abuse is wrong or are targets' friends [487]. Targets often gravitate to one another. In fact, targets are "nominated by other [targets] as preferred people to work with in the team" [102](p. 309). Over time, others may join the target's faction, especially if former followers, pawns, or silent onlookers become targets. Silent onlookers at times form a third pseudo-group but more commonly are an assortment of isolates. They strive to be uninvolved non-combatants.

Membership in all sub-groups is fluid; factions continuously shift and morph with the emotional tides. Subordinates, peers, managers, and upper-managers can fall into any of the three groups. In terms of upper-managers, some are also autocratic and aggressive and can view targets as weak links to be rooted out. The majority of managers, however, fall into the silent bystander group—passive, negligent, and inactive—a laissez faire approach that often encourages bullying. Rarely do managers side with targets, but at times this does occur, usually if managers have been plagued by bully aggression for extended periods of time [489]. In addition to these cliques and war-zone undercurrents, bullying seriously erodes workgroup effectiveness and cohesiveness. Workgroups become less satisfied with leadership and the social climate, and experience increased role conflict and decreased commitment and loyalty.

Workforces

Toxic workplaces can breed impoverished workforces as an indirect result of worker-exit waves [170]. During the crests of exit waves, talented employees leave without a fight or briefly fight, give up, and then exit. When bullying begins, employees often flee the environment. In these early exit waves, the brightest and most talented quit or transfer, taking their occupational capital (skills, technical knowledge, experience, etc.) with them. These first exit waves typically occur in two ways: first, if a new manager enters the workforce and employees see that bullying is part of the manager's approach, talented people assess the situation as undesirable and decide to exit rather than invest the energy to fight abuse. Quitting is their form of resistance—resignation communicates their unwillingness to be subjected to or witness abuse. This group includes workers who have occupational capital so can easily find other positions, those who have very little invested in the job, and people whose identity precludes being mistreated or devalued.

Others who have been at their jobs for a number of years, may feel they have a significant investment in the job, organization, or benefits (e.g., retirement). These employees may stay for a time and try to stop bullying. Many, however, become part of a second-exit wave as they see their efforts met with escalating abuse, upper-management ambivalence, or both. After fighting what feels like a losing battle the second wave of employees exit the organization [184]. In a third intermittent wave, new employees come in but go shortly after assessing the toxic climate [124], unless they lack occupational capital.

Unfortunately, waves of employee-exit leave behind a less talented cadre with fewer occupational skills, persons who are burned out and cynical, or high-aggressives who thrive in cut-throat environments. Reasonably, one might expect that those left behind will continue to experience or witness abuse and become increasingly frustrated, angry, and potentially even vengeful. The toxic climate, mounting frustration and anger, erosion of human resources, growing sense of impotence, and increased work loads can contribute to powder-keg climates likely to explode given the right spark [275, 490].

Organizations

Bullying costs organizations—they hemorrhage resources when aggression goes unchecked. Organizations in which people are bullied can pay higher premiums for workers' compensation and medical insurance [30, 124]. Law suits associated with bullying (e.g., wrongful or constructive discharge), are rare but when they occur can cost organizations dearly, both in legal fees and staff hours [491]. Quite commonly, organizations lose positive reputations and may find recruiting quality workers increasingly difficult.

Other losses are associated with reduced "opportunity costs ... such as lack of discretionary effort, commitments outside the job, time spent talking about the problem rather than working, and loss of creativity" [124](p. 137). Organizational citizenship behaviors, the discretionary acts that promote organizational effectiveness, wane in toxic climates, and presenteeism can also be a problem. Presenteeism means that employees are physically at work but not there mentally because they are ill or otherwise impaired [492]. In toxic climates presenteeism occurs because workers fear missing work—much might transpire in their absence (e.g., rumors, work destruction, key task removal).

Recommendations

Given the toxic effects of workplace bullying, this section suggests ideas for both prevention and intervention at the micro- and meso-levels. No solitary action will resolve adult bullying, especially if aggression has taken root and extensive damage occurred. The following suggests actions with the greatest potential for positive organizing.

Individual-Level Actions

Target actions. Given that target reactions seldom end bullying, the following are offered with caution and suggested more to assist suffering workers than to create substantive organizational change. First and foremost, targets need to take care of themselves and find social support. These ensue by taking time off and being around supportive friends and family members [147]. Coworkers play an incredibly important part in targets' experiences of abuse, as coworker social support can effectively protect targets from psychological harm [493]. Colleague support involves two processes: First, coworker support reinforces targets' feelings of sanity. Coworker agreement that mistreatment is occurring reassures targets that they really are experiencing something tangible; bullying is indeed happening [494]. Second, coworkers have been there, so to speak; they have witnessed bullying and its effects. As such, targets can talk to coworkers without the need to recount extensive contextualized histories of abuse.

Targets may want to inform colleagues unofficially about bullying—what is it, what it does, what to do—which can encourage coworker support. Targets can inform others at work by placing articles in break rooms or mail boxes or talking about the bullying phenomenon [495]. Such information leads to labeling the experiences *workplace bullying;* naming these experiences is incredibly powerful and shifts the experience from targets' subjective perspectives to an objective-feeling phenomenon external to the targets [104]. Labeling, reading published research, or both designates bullying as a substantive thing and not merely something imagined (as the term *sexual harassment* labeled experiences that had occurred for decades, but had been unspecified).

In addition to naming and self-care, friends, family members, coworkers, and external professionals consistently advise targets to confront bullies. Targets and others believe that if targets talk to the aggressors, the two will find common ground and understanding—a problem-solving approach. However, the problem-solving efforts that can be effective in conflicts over ideas are ineffective in bullying conflicts [89]. In fact, confrontation can be *extremely* risky. Rayner et al. claim [3] that *in some cases,* if done at the first indications of aggression, non-aggressive confrontation may slow or blunt hostility.

311

But the results are unpredictable—many, many targets say that abuse escalates after these talks.

Targets can also lodge formal or informal complaints to unions, EEOC, the aggressor's supervisor or governing body, or lawyers. Such reports typically require detailed documentation (e.g., dates, times, events), as decision-makers need "hard" evidence to take action. Targets sometimes take legal action and sometimes even win, which creates legal precedents (See http://www.workplacebullying.org/ category/workplace-bullying-laws/courts/). Others may have grounds for sexual harassment, racial discrimination, constructive discharge, or wrongful termination cases [99].

If and when individual tactics fail targets may consider building collective efforts; these demand a considerable investment of time and energy but are more likely to result in negative sanctioning of the aggressor than individual action. Targets may consider leaving the workplace to salvage their health, even though quitting can feel like defeat. Reframing exit as *resistance*—a take-this-job-and-shove-it perspective—can make exit feel better. In fact, when past targets are asked what advice they would give to others, their most frequent recommendation is "get out" before damage is irreversible [3, 184]. Many said they stayed too long fruitlessly trying to be vindicated, have aggressors sanctioned, or both.

Bystander, coworker actions. Bystanders are powerful agents who can use their influence to build respect or to embolden aggression. As Tremlow et al. [496] note, "bystanding may either facilitate or ameliorate victimization. The bystander is propelled into the role by dint of his or her interaction with the victim and victimizer, and the ongoing interaction can be activated in a helpful or harmful direction" (p. 271).

Bystanders can help in a number of ways. First, they can accompany targets at talks with upper-management or HR, even if their presence is silent and symbolic. Second, they can learn how to pivot aggressive conversations, that is, focus on a neutral or positive element of an aggressive statement and move the conversation in a different direction. For example, if Kelly says, "Leslie is such a bitch. What does she know about working with funders?," bystander Steve could *pivot* or turn the conversation by saying, "Speaking of funders, we should contact XYZ, Inc. I think they might contribute."

Third, bystanders can "discourage negative behaviors, and, ... encourage positive behaviors" [457] (p. 89). Encouraging the positive means commending and helping other to openly recognize colleagues' successes, which potentially encourages future, socially desirable behavior. Bystanders can discourage negativity by helping other to "react, and then act appropriately, when they see unsafe, unprofessional, offensive, discriminatory, or illegal behavior in the workplace" (p. 90). Fourth, bystanders can act as witnesses, referees, and peacekeepers to prevent, handle, and stop aggressive conflicts [458]. Because of their once-removed status, bystanders can be very influential in conflict resolution. Finally, bystanders can give weight to target accounts; bystander input intensifies target credibility. Non-bullied bystanders are less denigrated because no one has labeled them as *victims*. Bystander voice decreases some of the hazards of speaking out (e.g., being labeled pejoratively as rabble-rousers, insubordinate, or mentally deficient).

Manager actions. Because of the power and voice vested in hierarchical position, managers have incredible influence in changing abusive climates. First, managers who receive reports of bullying should take them seriously and take immediate action. Managers will want to avoid framing the issue as just-the-way-we-do-business-here or as a personality conflict [497], two responses that can encourage bullying. Bullying is not a personality conflict; it is a gross abuse of power. Effective managerial actions involved four inter-related actions: (a) accepting the reports as truth, (b) acknowledging that emotional abuse is inappropriate and harmful, (c) investigating complaints immediately, and (d) taking remedial action with bullies. These are challenging, time-consuming actions and typically raise the ire of high-aggressives. However, the way that managers respond to reported abuse is meta-communicative—responses communicate the value the organization places on its employees and their well-being.

Crawshaw suggests a straightforward, fair way to investigate allegations and remediate aggressors' behavior [484]. Three tactics are crucial: First, investigators (whomever they are) must avoid at all costs he-said-she-said exchanges with aggressors, as these are communicative vortexes that suck managers into drowning spirals. Second, investigators need to avoid discussions of aggressor intent, as intentions to harm are irrelevant. As with sexual harassment, the effect on others and the perceptions of others are the relevant concerns. Third, feedback about behavior change has to be very specific.

To reduce he-said-she-interactions, which nearly always come up during remediation, investigators can tell aggressors, "Exactly who said

313

what and what you intended do not matter as much as how others *perceive* your actions. What we want to do together is change the negative *perceptions* of your communication and behavior." This approach can reduce defensiveness because it externalizes the problem—it is not the bully him or herself who needs fixing but others' perceptions. Typically aggressive organizational members are quite insecure and fearful, so direct criticisms targeting their self or identity will likely back-fire. To avoid the intent issue, investigators simply need to speak with persons others peceive as aggressive and explain that intent is less important than are others' peceptions. Finally, to provide specific direction for behavior modification, investigators/coaches should speak with a variety of coworkers (chose both by the investigator and the alleged aggressor) to discover specific behavior that is in question. The investigator removes identifying information and clusters coworker feedback into themes and then works with the aggressive member on changing those particular behaviors [484].

Organizational-Level Actions

"Organizational culture arises spontaneously whenever groups of people come together for any length of time and focus on tasks long enough to create common traditions, rites, and histories" (p. 266)[153]. Taking action to change organizations means thinking of organizations as living organisms comprised of all members' individual identities, organisms that may not be able to be engineered but nonetheless can change, evolve, and grow. Certainly to reduce the toxic character of workplaces, an organizational-wide approach will be most effective and should involve explicitly talking about "basic beliefs, guiding principles,, and philisophical princples that ... guide decisions, decision-making processes, conflict reslution, and interpersonal" communication [758].

Organizational-level changes need to involve organizational systems, member beliefs, policies and practices, and various workgroups, specialties, and sectors. Efforts to address aggression speak volumes to organizational members. "When employees perceive that the organization is supportive and committed to them and helps employees to meet their socio-emotional and tangible needs, employees will reciprocate by helping the organization to achieve its goals" [486](p. 770). Effective meso-level efforts require engagement of top-level governance, middle-management, direct-line employees, HR, and union stewards from start to finish—from assessment, intervention development, and implementation to follow-up evaluation.

The commitment of upper-management is fundamental to change efforts; the communication and everything the communication implies of persons perceived to be organizational representatives sets the overall tone for change efforts. There is no question that "employees will quickly become cynical when ... exhort[ed] ... to behave in a way that bears little relationship to the action behaviors of the managers they observe in their daily life" [498](p. 136). Similarly, middle-management must be engaged; these managers serve as conduit between direct-line staff and upper-managers or governing bodies. As such, their actions can model the organization's commitment to respectful climates. If middle managers are tyrannical and think aggression is the source of their power, they can be quite guarded about changes that might remove that power. In such cases, upper-management provide reassurances, require education on positive managerial communication skills, and offer incentives and rewards for those who shift their aggressive communication in respectful, egalitarian directions. The core training should be interpersonal communication skills—skills that are the most trying during times of change.

In terms of organization-wide involvement cross-level, cross-functional teams, or a number of teams are needed and could be paired with external experts (e.g., academics, consultants). Cross-functional team approaches use high-involvement work practices (HIWP), which include "involvement, trust, goal alignment, empowerment, development, performance-enabling work structures, teamwork, and performance-based rewards" [499](p. B1). Team members collectively identify the issues unique to their workgroup and outline potential solutions tailored to those unique issues. Indeed, climates that "support the development of healthy relationships are rooted in communication patterns that are fact-based, open, and supportive of dialogue" [500](p. 90). The following reviews a facts-based, open approach that relies on cross-functional dialogue.

Organization-wide assessment. Organizational members are seldom entirely aware of the extent of workplace aggression because it is under-reported. To determine the extent of bullying and the extent of change effort success, organizations should assess the destructive

315

and constructive aspects of the communication in each workgroup. The constructive aspects are important because workgroups will later build on their strengths. Options for assessing workplace negativity include the Workplace Aggression Research Questionnaire—WAR-Q [501] and the Negative Acts Questionnaire Revised—NAQ-R. Measures of workplace interpersonal positivity should be coupled with WAR/NAQ. Communication audits assess both positive and negative communication [502]. Organizations may add items to the assessment tool such as intent to leave, days off work sick, self-report health inventories, and so forth, depending on unique goals. Assessment typically includes anonymous surveys followed by off-site interviews or focus groups. Outside professionals are helpful for developing measures, conducting interviews, and analyzing-reporting data.

The assessment is organization-wide and identifies each specific workgroups. This identification allows workgroups to see the degree to which negativity and positivity are present in their sector and which types are most common. Each workgroup will be distinctive. Baseline data should be widely distributed with some cautions: each workgroup receives its own positive and negative score averages and group-level scores for all survey items. Groups should also receive organization-level positivity and negativity average scores and organization-level scores for all survey items. A specific workgroup's scores *should not* be distributed to other workgroups. Rather, only organization-level averages are released, which serve as a baseline for follow up evaluation and provide a point of comparison (i.e., benchmark) for workgroups. Assessment data suggests areas workgroups may wish to change, as well as areas of strength so helps teams craft tailored action plans.

Intervention and follow-up. Teams develop action plans (i.e., interventions) to address the reduction of negativity and build on strengths. They also develop criteria (e.g., reduce negativity score by 20%, increase positivity score by 20%, reduce intentions to leave, etc.) against which the team or workgroup will later assess their intervention's effectiveness. Plans could include training to improve interpersonal communication skills, rewards for respectful communication, and ways to build on workgroup strengths. After plans have been implemented for 6 months or so, follow-up measures are collected to evaluate progress (e.g., reduced aggressive communication, increased respectful communication). Organizations

316

should use *the same measures* as in the initial assessment so easy comparisons can be made. Again, organization-level data is distributed to all workgroups, and group-level data given only to the group assessed (and upper-management). Groups compare the second measure to baselines to determine the effectiveness of their efforts and examine where the group stands in relation to organization-level averages. If plans fail to achieve their desired effect, teams will choose or craft other interventions, being sure they accurately identified causes of negativity.

Rewarding respectful communication. Visibly rewarding respectful interaction and relationships is an indispensable tactic for encouraging civil discourse. Incentive might begin by widely distributing the name of the workgroup with the highest positivity score (*never* distribute individual workgroups' scores publically, which can evoke humiliation, discouragement, etc.). Organizational members will, in most cases, do what's rewarded, especially if the incentive is meaningful. "Recognition is particularly important to achieve changes in culture .... [and] does not have to be financial to be effective" [498](p. 148). Changes in organizational cultures need to "ensure that high status is closely associated with conformity to prosocial norms" (p. 270) [758].

The persistent belief that negative feedback (i.e., punishment) causes discomfort and moves people to action leads some to focus solely on punishing alleged abusers; however, such an approach is far too one-sided to effectively change toxic climates [503]. Punishing undesirable behavior as a way to build respectful climates is counter-intuitive. As such, determining ways to *reward and celebrate respectful communication* is vital to success, and even small changes can result in large shifts over time in a butterfly effect [504]. Sadly, organizational members should celebrate the positive and reward the positive, but if bullying is present, some negative sanctions may be required to stop the aggression.

Negatively sanctioning destructive communication. An element of group action plans (or organization-level plans) is developing negative sanctions for those who persist in harassing, abusing, and disrespecting others. When aggression in any form occurs or continues, managers *must* take action. Failure to intervene marks managers as ineffective, cowards, bully-allies, or dull-witted [497] and destines efforts to fail. Beyond negative sanctions, organizations will also want to strategically analyze system forces to look for direct or indirect rewards that champion aggressive communication—even ignoring aggressive behavior in the hope that it will go away. When aggressive members refuse to stop abusing others, strong oversight and negative sanctions, up to and including employment termination, may be required to communicate that aggression is unacceptable. And dealing with aggression is quite difficult because it involves confrontation — interactions that are nearly always unpleasant.

Other prevention, intervention actions. Other meso-level changes support and maintain assessment and intervention. These include developing anti-bullying policies, enforcing of and training about policies, using external professionals, providing education about bullying and aggression, taking restorative action, and implementing multi-rater employee evaluation systems.

Anti-bullying policies. Policies alone will not end aggression and bullying, but policies do communicate organizational commitment to reducing the problem. Such policies can be stand-alone anti-bullying policies or adding anti-bullying provisions to supplement existing anti-harassment or violence prevention policies [505]. Policies need to declare precisely the unacceptability of passive or active aggression but avoid using zero tolerance terminology—when initially working toward more respectful communication, multiple offenses may need to be allowed (not ignored). Changing the climate takes time and could mean giving employees time to learn how to communicate more constructively.

Policies should define bullying because employees will be uncertain what "counts" as bullying and provide a list of bullying types with examples of each. Categories of bullying include *verbal abuse*; threatening, intimidating or humiliating communication and behavior; *social ostracism* and isolation; and *work obstruction*. Writing the policy should include various stakeholders—non-supervisory staff, union representatives, middle- and senior-managers, legal counsel, human resource staff, members of governing boards, and so forth. Organizational makeup will determine the stakeholder group's makeup.

Policy education, communication training. For anti-bullying policies to be effective and put aggressive employees on notice, employees at all levels need to be made aware of policy goals, provisions, enforcement procedures, especially what counts as

318

bullying and what happens to violators. Mandatory education, similar to what employers currently provide about sexual harassment, conveys the organization's intolerance for aggression. Ideally, handouts, brochures, flyers and posters mounted permanently in prominent places, accompany training. Training should also be repeated at designated intervals (e.g., annually).

Organizations may also want to provide mandatory training in argumentation. This represents an investment of resources, but aggression should decline as a result. There is convincing research suggesting that people who lack skills in argumentation (e.g., debate) easily become frustrated when conflicts arise and so become aggressive as a means to press their side of the issue [506]. Argumentation skills are particularly important for managers who, if they lack such skills, will fall back on aggressive position-based power (i.e., "I'm the boss so you'll do as I say.")

Another area for training is positive, constructive interpersonal communication skills. One of the simple practices used in an extensive US Veterans Affairs project was use of a *talking stick*—an item passed around to people in teams [101]. When any person has the talking stick, no one else speaks or interjects opinions; the speaker solely has the right to speak until the stick is passed on to another person, who is then the sole speaker. The practice trains people to listen and practice self-control in conversations. Another tactic was the Right-Hand/Left-Hand Column exercise [507]. Using this tool, communicators record in the right column the actual spoken interaction; in the left-hand column, communicators record what they are thinking but not saying (assumptions about others, what speaker is withholding, etc.). The left-hand column reflects what Argyris calls *undiscussables* to label this critical, though rarely shared information. The exercise helps communicators see how what they think but do not say affects interactions and helps speakers figure out ways of effectively expressing undiscussables.

Policy enforcement. When aggression and other forms of disrespectful communication occur, organizational administrators will be faced with enforcing policies and demonstrating to all members a true commitment to building a better climate. Sadly, if upper-managers are confirmed violators, enforcement can be dicey; however, enforcing expectations for respectful communication with upper-managers can be watershed events for shifting abusive communication to respectful communication. No stronger message

319

can be sent to organizational members than when employees discover that even the most powerful cannot get away with abusing others. (Commitment to create respectful climates might only occur when there is a shift in personnel at the organization's highest levels. Change may not be possible without a major shift in upper-management.) Conversely, unenforced policies will promote employee cynicism and disengagement from any further change processes because internal grapevines will swiftly spread news of hypocritical behavior or ersatz-investigations. Because of potentially conflicting (real or perceived) upper-management interests, trained neutral external investigators can be very effective at overcoming employee doubts [367, 508]. Policy enforcement practices must appear just and sincere to employees, especially to targets, but also to alleged aggressors.

Regarding reports of abuse, an effective first stage remedy is encouraging informal target complaints. When targets have the chance to talk confidentially to someone without fear of retaliation, many will not proceed to formal complaints. Targets are often disbelieved and discounted, so providing an opportunity simply to be heard and *believed* can be quite powerful. Informal complaints may lead to formal complaints, but only if the targeted workers chooses to move forward. Ombudspersons or practical listeners can provide the informal listening service.

When complaints are lodged, investigations and final decisions should progress as quickly as possible, and the involved parties (i.e., targets, bullies, witnesses—anyone called for statements) should be informed of the final decision (confirmation, non-confirmation of policy breach). Currently in HR or other investigations, complainants and affected co-workers never hear about the outcomes because upper-management believes it must protect offenders' confidentiality.

In the case of adult bullying, organizations need to waive privacy regarding the final decisions, which can be as simple as *confirmation, non-confirmation of policy breach,* because cynicism and distrust typically result if employees are left in the dark. Indeed, communicating the decision to involved parties should be written into the policy itself. For the new anti-bullying policy to transform the communication climate, all participants in the fact-finding process should be informed of results in a way that is respectful to all involved.

When organizational leadership makes it clear that aggression will be punished rather than rewarded, most employees will abandon aggressive ways of interacting. Organizational leadership *must be sure* that aggression is not indirectly rewarded. Sometimes managers transfer or promote bullies to get rid of them. Bullies are at times paid off to leave quietly because management fears that bullies will file lawsuits. These responses are rewards, regardless of the actual goal of the response. News of such actions roars through the grapevine and undermines efforts to build respectful climates. Punishing targets (in any way) also rewards aggression. Leadership must avoid negative judgments of targets and remember that social norms about victims being weak or "asking for it" operate in often unrecognized ways. Antivictim beliefs can color managers' responses, so being fully aware of these biases will help avoid punitive responses to target reports.

Behavior modification principles apply in making this change. When learning new ways to communicate, the offenders need to be encouraged to behave in a respectful ways through positive and negative reinforcement coupled with education. In time, high-aggressives will come to associate the pleasure or displeasure of the reinforcement with the behavior. As such, managers of aggressive employees will want to use negative consequences to reduce aggression and positive consequences for any signs of desired change.

If progressive discipline policies are in place they can be used, beginning with verbal warnings, moving to written warnings, suspension, and employment termination. With multiple confirmed violations, penalties should be increasingly severe. Constraint of unacceptable communication and behavior should be the organization's goal, with the idea that "the perpetrator *could* and *should* have acted differently" rather than focusing on any "intent to harm" [486](p. 771).

In some cases, management will have to terminate the employment of intractable, repeat offenders who are unwilling or unable to change. But negative penalties are insufficient for building respectful climates. Training in constructive interpersonal communication is vital; people need to learn replacement communication behaviors to fill the void when aggression is no longer tolerated as a means of managing or working with people. Training focuses on building respectful replacement communication.

External investigators, coaches. In some cases organizations may want to bring in external investigators to assist in investigation and policy implementation. External experts are warranted in cases where organizational members have little experience or expertise dealing with bullying, where alleged perpetrators hold senior management positions, and when the authority of an external person may be helpful during, or dealing with the aftermath of, the investigation. Investigations might be conducted by impartial, outside professionals specializing in adult bullying interventions. These experts can also coach upper-managers on how to deal more effectively with similar situations should they arise in the future and provide specific coaching for aggressive organizational members (see Crawshaw's work).

Training. In addition to policy training, organizations will want to provide ongoing, organization-wide training on both bullying and respectful communication. As an element of hands-on training, some organizations have "bullying drills... similar to fire drills" [495](p. 675) to prepare them with appropriate responses in the event that bullying occurs. Training must include human resources or employee assistance program professionals and focus on recognizing bullying and protecting reporting workers from harm. Managers, in particular, need to recognize the warning signs of bullying and respond swiftly to complaints, so they can intervene early when intervention is most effective. Furthermore, managers should be encouraged to develop a more compassionate, caring style that includes developing and using emotional intelligence skills.

Recuperative actions. Developing a means to provide emotional support to negatively affected employees is an appreciated response when dealing with bullying. Organizations can provide confidential support for targets by persons other than those whose first loyalty is to the employer (e.g., HR, EAPs). (Workers should understand that the primary loyalties of HR and EAPs are typically to the employing organization rather than the suffering employee.) An effective example is the "practical listeners" program implemented by the UK's postal service; trained peer volunteer staff members provide social support, validate targets' experiences, listen nonjudgmentally, suggest possible choices of action, help handling formal procedures, and maintain confidentiality [347]. (For a full discussion of a Practical Listener program in a public organization see citation # [165]) On a smaller scale, organizations can establish an ombudsperson with explicit training in bullying.

Multi-rater assessment techniques. Multi-rater systems, such as 360° evaluations, can provide a means of tracking and rewarding respectful or discouraging aggressive communication. (Without an overall commitment to respect, however, employees will fear honestly responding to these techniques.) They can also reduce the likelihood of high-aggressives receiving positive evaluations; remembering that managers who supervise bullies often fear them and so fail to honestly evaluate their performance. Multi-rater systems also include confidential staff evaluation of supervisors—a communicative channel that has the added benefit of identifying supervisory bullyings. Be informed, however, that multi-rater techniques will uncover general trends but rarely be specific enough information for coaching and changing aggressive members' behavior.

Conclusion

This chapter addresses the systemic outcomes associated with un-addressed bullying and suggests avenues for redress at the worker-, workgroup-, and workplace-levels. As these ideas suggest, addressing toxic communication climates and building respectful climates is not simple. Organizational and workgroups will use the applicable ideas and reject ideas that fail to fit their group's dynamics. The basic idea is that organizational members must change the very nature of every day conversations if they are to be successful. Policies alone, while important for target redress and stating an organization's position regarding adult bullying and incivility, will not stop disrespectful abusive communication or create respectful climates. Real change takes people at all levels, with managers leading the charge.

CHAPTER 16

What We Know about Workplace Bullying:
A Review of Organizational Communication
Research [N]

Pamela Lutgen-Sandvik & Sarah J Tracy

Chapter Summary: Organizational communication research is vital for understanding and addressing workplace bullying, a problem that affects nearly half of working adults and has devastating results on employee well-being and organizational productivity. A communication approach illustrates the toxic complexity of workplace bullying, as it is condoned through societal norms and cultural beliefs (macro-level forces), sustained by receptive workplace cultures (meso-level forces), and perpetuated through face-to-face individual interactions (micro-level forces). This chapter examines adult bullying in terms of these three levels, specifically addressing the following issues: (1) how abuse comes about, (2) how employees respond, (3) why it is so harmful, (4) why resolving it is so difficult, and (5) how it might be resolved. This chapter provides tips for addressing and transforming workplace bullying, which may be of particular interest to consultants and human resource professionals. The chapter also offeris a theoretical synthesis and launching pad for future academic research.

Keywords: workplace bullying, organizational communication, bullying-as-communicative, resistance, harm, solutions

----

The Just World Hypothesis: A societal-level assumption that the world is fair and orderly and that victims of misfortune deserve what happens to them.

Workplace Policies: Organizational-level structures that regularly address racial discrimination and sexual harassment but do not include information about how to deal with an "equal opportunity" office bully.

Giggles, eye rolls, threats, and silence: Some of the many individual-level interactions sustaining and perpetuating workplace bullying.

These are some of the perspectives of workplace bullying in action—from societal (macro) to individual (micro) respectively. Adult bullying is catastrophic for those targeted and devastating to organizations. Most of the typical ways of responding to bullying fail to change the situation and can even worsen the target's plight As such, exploring and addressing the issue from multiple perspectives is essential. Communication research provides a unique perspective, one with the potential to reinvigorate research by weaving together multi-disciplinary voices.

A communicative perspective provides valuable insights into how bullying is driven by macro-level Discourses (see Glossary; e.g., cultural, societal values and beliefs), propped up by meso-level policies and practices (e.g., organizational, educational, communal),and perpetrated or resisted through micro-level (person-to-person discourse) talk and interaction. This chapter explores how communication-based research provides key insights on the pressing questions about adult bullying, mobbing, and psychological abuse at work. These questions include

* What does bullying look like, and how does it manifest in organizations?

* How do employees and organizations make sense of and respond to bullying?

* Why is adult bullying at work so harmful?

* Why is workplace bullying so difficult to address and stop?

* How can workplace bullying be addressed or ameliorated?

To contextualize the communication field's responses to these questions, this chapter focuses on research conducted by communication scholars, both organizational and interpersonal.

Organizational Communication and
Research on Bullying and Aggression

Organizational communication researchers joined the academic conversation about workplace bullying in the early 2000s. This research provides a complex interdisciplinary hub, richly attending to the pressing questions about adult bullying. The communication field thinks and works in interdisciplinary spaces. Because of being interdisciplinary, communication research serves as a cross-pollinator for the varied perspectives and fields concerned with bullying (e.g., education, nursing, law, management, psychology, etc.). Communication research offers a unique perspective while also reinvigorating other research by weaving together diverse disciplinary voices.

Relatedly, organizational communication research argues that bullying is a complex multilevel issue and serves as a cross-pollinator for the varied perspectives and fields concerned with bullying (e.g., education, nursing, law, management, psychology, etc.). That is, communication research not only provides a unique perspective, but reinvigorates other research by weaving together diverse voices. As such, communication research shows that bullying is a complex multilevel issue occurring not only *inside* organizations but is inextricably interconnected with larger social/cultural values and beliefs (i.e., Discourses) and organizational polices.

Organizational Communication—
A Critical Voice and View

Organizational communication has a rich tradition of questioning hidden power relations at work [509]. Moving beyond the surface appearance of organizational communication means questioning our unquestioned beliefs and knee-jerk ways of interacting. As demonstrated in the review below, communication researchers ask, for example, "Why are target narratives so often disbelieved?" and "What beliefs lead to stigmatizing targeted workers?"

When pondering such questions, the issue of *voice* is crucial. Hierarchal position is often equated with voice in a way that designates highly placed bullies as truth-tellers and targeted workers as troublemakers or mentally ill. Communication researchers critique, for example, the nearly religious adherence to chain-of-command. We remind organizational members and practitioners that the chain-of-command is something organizational members have created, something that can be recreated or sidestepped simply by deciding and having the courage to do so [510].

A Multi-Level View of Workplace Bullying

Organizational communication research takes as a guiding premise that to understand workplace bullying, researchers and practitioners must move beyond examining abuse as a solely psychological, one-on-one issue manifesting "inside" organizations. Verbal aggressiveness has interconnections with biology and psychology [86, 449] and can look like only a bully and a target, but bullying occurs and continues only when organizational cultures condone, model, or reward it. A strengths of the communication perspective is recognizing that communication at many different levels work in such a way that they can create, sustain, or transform our social realities [511].

The importance of recognizing the forces at societal-, organizational- and individual-levels gets at the roots of bullying and its surface symptoms. Efforts focused solely on the individual-level are rarely effective, usually because organizational cultures reward aggression or upper-managers fear confronting bullies. Similarly, efforts focused on rebuilding organizational cultures falter if they don't consider overriding social and cultural beliefs that support aggression as a means of gaining success and power. The value of organizational communication research is its inclination to take all three levels into consideration when analyzing problems and suggesting interventions.

A richer understanding comes from examining how the three different levels of communication contribute to bullying and make it exceedingly difficult to address. Organizational members, for the most part, easily recognize the micro-level processes that comprise bullying—the everyday talk and interaction marked by interpersonal aggression. Members intimately *feel and experience* this communication in their daily work lives.

The meso-level (organizational-community-workgroup) of communication includes organizational culture and climate, organizational policies and procedures, community norms and organizational positioning within that community, and so forth. Targets typically point first to bullies' mental states, but they subsequently move on to ask, "Why doesn't upper-management do something?" This move from individual- to organizational- suggests that affected workers can see that bullying involves more than mental pathology. Abuse only continues if organizations ignore or reward it, even if only indirectly.

327

In the "big picture," societal/cultural-level communication processes are the beliefs, norms, and values that less obviously support and encourage aggression. These processes are the "relatively consistent ... emotionally-charged viewpoints, morals, and customs" that filter our perceptions of what is happening at work [151](p. 4). These macro forces are a bit more challenging to recognize because they are simply taken-for-granted. When recognized, these forces can evoke feeling overwhelmed and resigned, feelings represented by comments such as, "This is just the way things are here" and "You can't fight city hall." At times, organizational members glimpse macro forces, but they can seem so huge, so overwhelming, that for the exceptional few who take up social issues as moral causes, most turn away in defeat with slumped shoulders.

Taking to heart the importance of macro, meso and micro levels, this chapter reviews organizational communication research that has responded to key questions about bullying. Tables 17.1 through 17.5 summarize these contributions. In each table, we organize published research into three levels, provide brief descriptions of the studies' contents, and give citations [in brackets, see References at the end of the book]. Following the conventions I've used throughout the book, the word *discourse* indicates "every day talk and interaction" and *Discourses* indicate the "social forces such as norms, values, beliefs, ideologies, and so forth" that guide discourse [300] (p. 6) (see also Glossary).

Table 16.1: How does bullying come about?

Societal, Cultural	Organizational, Community, Workgroup	Individual
✳ A collection of beliefs support employee abuse & encourage employee abuse [2, 283] ✳ Gender, ethnicity make some people easier to target with abuse [74, 512]	✳ Cyclical, escalatory process silences onlookers, drives targets out & new targets emerge [7] ✳ Highly placed aggressors silence, encourage others to go along [7, 128] ✳ Communal activity involving many members, levels [128, 136]	✳ Essentially communicative [513] ✳ Bullying has specific features, forms [68, 170] ✳ Talk constitutes bullying [2, 151, 170]

How Does Workplace Bullying Come About?

Naysayers often ask, "Isn't bullying something that just happens to kids at school?" Communication research has shown that bullying is socially constructed via a complicated combination of communicative processes informed (usually in unrecognized ways) by macro-level beliefs, values, and norms.

Society/Cultural-Level Manifestation

Bullying involves individual psychology and aggressive one-on-one communication, but many Discourses encourage it. One of the ways organizational communication researchers have explored social/historical forces is a communication types theory that illustrates how five communication functions in organizations contribute to toxic organizations. This explanation is illustrated through a case study and shows that different message types combine to affect and change each other. That is, "messages in one type merge with, shape, and influence—usually in unseen, unintended ways—messages in other types" [283](p. 311). Considering this, it's clear to see that workplace bullying is more than just aggressive communication between two people.

Organizational communication researchers suggest that in asking "What does workplace bullying look like?" we need to incorporate the socially constructed categories of race, ethnicity, and gender. These classifications mute certain members of the workforce and make them easier targets [74, 512, 514]. Gender, ethnicity, and race are historically stigmatizing markers that contribute to bullying some people. Women and persons of color are often targeted by aggressive organizational members because they are easier targets of a variety of negative social interactions [515].

From the macro-level, adult bullying manifests in organizations because multiple beliefs, values, and meanings disregard or minimize (or both) worker mistreatment. Such Discourses condone the goading of people at work in the name of productivity, or objectifying them by treating people as if they are property or things. I argue that employee abuse emerges from the people's beliefs in contemporary workplaces. These beliefs come from an combination of economic theory, religious and secularized ideals of work, the merger of corporate interests and governing bodies, belief in rugged individualism, the dogma of meritocracy, the ideology of entrepreneurialism, and so forth. These Discourses, of course, also affect meso-level workplace bullying policies and practices.

Organizational/Community-Level Manifestation

At the organizational- or community-level, bullying is a cycle that generates when a target is singled out, bullied, and driven from the workplace and regenerates when another target is singled out, bullied, driven from the workplace, and so on. Because bullying has this cyclical quality, simplistic solutions (e.g., terminating employment of targets) give the short-lived impression of solving the problem without actually fixing anything. Especially in cases of bullying where targets are singled out, bullied, and then driven from the organization, firing target after target shifts focus from the communal character of the problem. Sadly, organizations are likely to see that bullying is a problem only after recognizing these cyclical communication patterns over time and many good people have fled.

At the organizational-level, bullying mutes some employees, especially when managers or other influential employees perpetuate abuse. Powerful persons' persistent hostility toward lower-ranking employees silences most onlookers, evokes fear, and discourages resistance. That said, communicative structures can also provide space for alternative expressions of workplace experience beyond those from managers, spaces that include the perspectives from subordinate staff.

Organizational communication research also debunks the popular misconception that a few lone aggressors are at fault for bullying. A nationally representative communication study of US workers suggests that in most bullying cases, many organizational members—perpetuators, henchmen and women, and silent witnesses—are involved.

Individual-Level Manifestation

At its heart, workplace bullying is communicative; it is talked into being. Indeed, all current measures of workplace bullying quantify bullying through the frequency and duration of negative acts, the majority of which are different types of communication. Bullying manifests by the use of particular communicative *forms*, such as public humiliation and spreading rumors [68]; rude, foul and abusive language [516]; persistent criticism; and explosive outbursts such yelling, screaming, swearing [517].

Bullying is not only about *forms* of communication but is characterized by specific communicative *features*—intensity, persistence, and power disparity between targets and perpetrators. Thus, if a certain form of communication (such as screaming or spreading a rumor) lacks these specific *features*, researchers wouldn't consider this bullying. The primary feature of bullying is persistence (frequency, repetition, duration), which essentially alters messages' meanings and effects. Screaming occasionally does not equate with bullying. Screaming over and over at the same person, day after day, week after week, and month after month—that is workplace bullying.

Communication is not only central in the perpetuation of bullying, but also key to the way targets make sense of it. Targets come to the awareness that they are being bullied through conversations or intersubjective sensemaking . By talking with friends, family, and co-workers, targets begin to label their treatment as *mistreatment*, and sensemaking generates and to some degree cements this meaning. In a very real sense then, involved parties *talk workplace bullying into being*. Perpetrators verbally abuse targets, targets feel and talk about feeling abused, witnesses talk about and concur that targets are being treated aggressively, and non-witnesses listen to and affirm target accounts. If someone in the chain of conversation reads published research or popular press articles about bullying, involved parties grow even more convinced that the experiences equate with *workplace bullying*. Once so convinced, they face the challenge of how to make sense and respond to the problem.

Table 16.2: How do employees and organizations respond to bullying?

Societal, Cultural	Organizational, Community, Workgroup	Individual
✳ Moral emotions [518], moral imperatives to resist [137] ✳ Beliefs drawn on in explanations [151]	✳ Organizational leadership knows bullying occurs [68] ✳ Organizational responses rarely effective, often blame targets [68] ✳ Responses to collective reports = disciplining bullies; individual reports = disciplining targets [137] ✳ Organizations take constructive action in 1/3 of cases [128]	✳ Most targets fight back [74, 137, 519] ✳ Resistance mixed in terms of effectiveness [137, 519] ✳ Targets not as powerless as past research suggests [74, 137, 519] ✳ Face-saving, recreating life stories [9] ✳ Targets tell stories, describing pain; stories may lead to fight, flight, flee [2, 74]

At the societal-level, organizational communication researchers are interested in how societal assumptions and Discourses inform employee responses to adult bullying.

Social/Cultural-Level Effects on Responding to Bullying

Vince Waldron, a professor at Arizona State University, [518] argues that emotions like outrage, anger, and indignation are indicators of what people believe is moral or immoral regarding human interactions at the global level. Employees who resist bullying often do so because they feel a *moral imperative* to act.

Moral Discourses that are embedded in religious doctrine and other ideologies inform individual-level responses to adult bullying at work. On one hand, the moral imperative that people should "fight the good fight" propels targets to battle injustice and bullying. On the other hand, targets typically make sense of their situations by drawing on beliefs about individualism (I can handle this myself), omnipotent leaders (the upper-managers are able to fix this), and unbeatable evil-demon bullies (the bully is unbeatable because he/she has supernatural power). These beliefs can intensify feelings of powerlessness and contribute to a sense of helplessness.

Organizational-Level Effects on Responding to Bullying

Organizational communication researchers see bullying as a *systemic problem* that develops from organizational beliefs, values, and policies/practices. Interestingly, upper-managers and HR rarely doubt or deny that bullies act the way targets describe [68]. Nonetheless, even when upper-managers accept the truth of target reports, their responses typically fail to end abuse. A recent study shows that in only one-third of cases, organizational responses improve situations for targets [128]. Most often targeted workers are unsatisfied with organizations' responses [68].

The organization's response largely depends on whether leaders believe the target is at fault. When managers blame the target they are more likely to minimize complaints, punish the target, or frame bullying as a personality conflict. If the organization blames the bully, upper-managers are more likely to take action. The organizational response also depends on the number of people complaining. When a contingency of workers report abuse, organizations are more likely to negatively sanction bullies.

Responses at the Individual-Level

Organizational communication research provides considerable insight to the ways individuals make sense of and resist workplace bullying through the field's focus on *voice*, particularly whose voice is privileged in organizations [511, 520]. Communication research extends ideas about target coping [184] with a critical conceptualization of power and resistance in unevenly matched workplace relationships.

333

Prior research typically characterizes targeted workers as powerless, as the term *target* might suggest. However, targets appear to resist abuse in many ingenious ways [74, 519]. These studies demonstrate the social processes involved in resistance and the forms of resistance most likely to result in providing relief from abuse. Taken together, communication researchers reconsider and critique the notion of the "powerless" target that has dominated workplace bullying research.

In addition to resistance, communication researchers have found that employees engage in a full range of face-saving when abused. This includes confirming self-image with others and re-storying one's life in order to "live with" or "live around" past abuse. Targets experience bullying as unexpected and undeserved and feel especially stigmatized because onlookers watch and hear them being mistreated in public settings Targets also ask themselves, "What kind of person am I, if this could happen to me?" They feel traumatized because bullying includes personal attacks, social ostracism, and a many other condemning messages.

Communication research also provides a distinctive contribution by exploring how narrative and metaphor teach us about the essence of bullying [74]. Targets can make sense of their abuse through rich metaphors. Bullies are "demons"; bullying feels like "water torture"; and targets feel like "chattel and slaves." Showcasing target narratives and metaphors is crucial for understanding the heart-breaking human pain from bullying, something unavailable in variable-analytic research. Narratives and metaphors underscore why bullying feels so horrible and why persistently abusive communication pushes targets toward fight, flight, or (most often) freeze/paralysis. Such responses can be extremely harmful—a topic the chapter turns to next.

Table 16.3: Why is bullying so harmful?

Societal, Cultural	Organizational, Community, Workgroup	Individual
✳ Anti-victim beliefs stigmatize target [283] ✳ Identity linked to paid work & consumer culture [9, 521, 522]	✳ Abuse silences, terrifies entire workgroups [7] ✳ Silent witnesses feel guilt [137] ✳ Abuse is social & lives on in hundreds of conversations [136] ✳ Poisons, makes workplaces toxic [283] ✳ Organization reputation damaged; workgroups become war zones [2, 283] ✳ Threatens deeply held beliefs about work, justice [9]	✳ Stigma, trauma & damaged self-image [9] ✳ Difficulty describing, explaining [225] ✳ Targets' explanations can be disempowering [151] ✳ Disorganized complaints reduce believability, increase harm[225] ✳ Metaphors increase sense of being trapped, hopeless [2]

Workplace bullying is linked to a wide range of negative physical, psychological, and organizational effects. These include psychosomatic illnesses, such as post-traumatic stress disorder (PTSD) and suicidal ideation, increased medical expenses, and reduced productivity. Organizational communication research offers a number of explanations for why bullying results in such harm.

Societal/Cultural-Level Forces Contributing to Harm

The importance of our identities is one of the reasons bullying is so harmful [521, 523]. Employees form their identity in relation to powerful and sometimes oppressive organizational experiences. What's more, workplace interactions significantly effect identity inside and outside of work [191, 523-525]. Adults typically look to their jobs to define who they are, whether that is being a good "X" (x = teacher, counselor, lawyer, etc.) or simply being a good/hard worker. This is especially true for persons who work in societies that emphasize paid employment, high salaries, and consumerism [232, 522]. Because work is such an important aspect of identity in such societies, bullying at work calls into question targets' very value as human beings.

Additionally, anti-victim beliefs, values, and norms increase the destructiveness of workplace bullying. Laypeople, journalists, peers, and targets themselves often stigmatize people who report abuse. Most of us stigmatize targets (in part) because of deep beliefs that people who are bullied are to blame, rather than the tormentors. Anti-victim beliefs and values such as the *Just World Hypothesis* associate being a victim with being weak, impotent, and child-like (See Glossary). If someone is being bullied, many believe that targets brought it upon themselves. We have this believe because of our overarching social and cultural beliefs about victimhood.

Organizational-Level Forces Contributing to Harm

The harms associated with bullying reach far beyond targets. Communication researchers recognize how abuse and aggression are profoundly social and, as such, exceedingly harmful to entire workgroups and organizations [136]. Bullying traumatizes and mutes bystanders or witnesses employees. In some cases, peers help fight back. At other times, witnesses are simply paralyzed; they are too terrified to sympathize with or support targets lest the bully turn attention to them. Regardless of the reasons for silence, failure to act can evoke extreme feelings of guilt for witnesses. Targets equate onlooker silence with consent, complicity, or support for bullies.

Communication researchers realize that abusive interactions "linger in a hundred conversations as members of the original audience re-encounter one another and negotiate the meaning of the original event" [136](p. 68). A single bullying incident can monopolize employee conversations for days and even weeks. Rehashing abuse re-victimizes targets, takes a severe emotional toll on other employees, and poisons organizational climates. Organizations lose valued reputations, and workgroups feel like war zones.

Bullying threatens people's deepest held beliefs about the world and their place in it. And bullying is conspicuously missing in society's grand narratives about work (we hear about "pulling yourself up by your boot straps," not "getting knocked down by your boss or coworkers"). Most people assume that if they work hard and are committed to their jobs, they will be rewarded or at the very least *not* punished. Abuse is not a requisite aspect of most work tasks and demands. Especially when targets lack social support or confirmation, bullying destabilizes their beliefs and threatens the bonds that anchor them to their social foundations. Once those bonds are destabilized or severed, targets are adrift, fending for themselves in a world that ostracizes the unemployed.

Individual-Level Forces Contributing to Harm

Past research points to many of the harms associated with bullying (PTSD, depression, suicidal thoughts), and organizational communication researchers have provided valuable insight into *why* harm is so extensive and enduring. Bullying stigmatizes through its content (e.g., accusations of poor work, personal shortcomings, mental illness) and traumatizes because it shakes deeply held beliefs about fairness and fair play. These two forces—stigma and trauma—make bullying an experience that severely disrupts lives and self-image.

Contributing to harm are targets' difficulties in describing and explaining the phenomenon. Bullying is difficult to explain and understand. Targets often talk about their plight as uncontrollable, unbearable, and impossible to stop. Targets tell stories and draw pictures that liken bullying to a battle, a nightmare, and a force-fed noxious substance. They view the bully as a narcissistic dictator (e.g., "a little Hitler") or a two-faced bully, and themselves as enslaved animals, prisoners, defenseless children, and heartbroken lovers. These interpretations graphically illustrate the level of pain and confusion targeted workers have when they try to name, describe, and manage their situations. These accounts point to why bullying is so emotionally devastating.

Bullying harms those targeted because, all too often, targets are stuck using stories and vocabularies that severely constrain action and exacerbate pain [151]. When targets compare abuse to torture, a likely response is completely zoning out, a response that further marginalizes target efforts and reduces coworker respect. When targets view themselves as children, they may cope by "hiding." If they take their role as slaves seriously, they may respond by becoming automatons that cannot differentiate the significant from the trivial. When bullying is likened to a nightmare and the bully to an evil demon, the target may believe the only path for survival is "waking up" or fleeing the

337

organization altogether [2].

A communication focus emphasizes how language informs and provides the material for making sense of abuse. For targets, these language choices combine with experiences to reinforce their feelings of "subordinate-ness." Some meanings also reinforce the reverence for hierarchy and the power-control tensions that favor dominant groups in organizations. Additionally, when targets attempt to explain their plight, their stories are often disorganized and confusing. Talking in a disorganized way can make them appear less credible, and targets can then feel re-victimized by others' disbelief [225].

In short, targets understand their experience through language. Language choices steer how people think about and experience what is happening to them [228]. Communication researchers study these choices and explain *why* an entrenched pattern of bullying is so devastatingly harmful, and, furthermore, why it is so difficult for targets alone to end abuse [3, 184]. Given the wide-ranging damage associated with workplace bullying, stopping it is crucial.

Table 16.4: Why is bullying unaddressed?

Societal, Cultural	Organizational-Community	Individual
✳ Certain stories become "truth"; oppressed voices often silenced [233]	✳ Many organizational members involved [128]	✳ Silence audience [7]
✳ Closed ways of talking about issues [191]	✳ Antagonistic, ambiguous policies [74, 140, 283]	✳ Silent assent, henchmen/ women [283]
✳ Difficulty naming experience due to confusing labels [6, 108]	✳ HR's perceived failures [2, 514, 526]	✳ Target reluctant to report abuse [68, 137]
	✳ Explanations limit empowerment [2, 151]	✳ Target defenses weakened by ongoing attack [9]
		✳ Embracing "problem-employee" label, desire for vengeance [137, 519]
		✳ Difficulty telling abuse story [225]

Workplace bullying affects upwards of half of all workers during their work histories, and once it becomes an entrenched pattern, targets, witnesses, and human resource managers alike face difficulties in effectively addressing or abating the issue. Organizational communication research provides a multifaceted lens for explaining why we so rarely do anything about bullying.

Societal/Cultural Forces Impeding Bullying Interventions

Victims of adult bullying face tremendous resistance in the public sphere when they try to solicit empathy or gain others' understanding. In large part this is due to beliefs and values that shape and inform the kinds of things that can be said at and about work [233]. These limiting beliefs include valorizing the economic, rational, and bottom-line aspects of organizations, and placing these above the emotional and relational features of organizing [522, 527, 528].

Social/cultural beliefs are powerful not because of their factuality, but because over time "they *become* 'truths' through their frequent repetition across a range" of settings and interactions [233](p. 254). They also become truths via associations with technical experts, such as psychologists, managers, and HR personnel who advocate these beliefs. Values championing strength and victory are believed and encouraged. In contrast, being a victim carries ideas of deservedness and weakness. Victims are subjected to questions about their behavior and what they did to protect themselves [213] or why they didn't protect themselves. Because other blame targets for their own abuse, targets keep abuse to themselves. Most people avoid talking about experiences that undermine their preferred self-image [529].

The concept called *discursive closure* [191] is particularly useful in explaining the difficulty of telling stories about bullying. Beliefs and values inform and shape meaning, which in turn enables powerful interests to retain and expand power and prevent alternate voices from being taken seriously. *Voice*, as opposed to expression, means having a say *and* having what is said taken into consideration in decision-making. Points of view that serve dominant organizational interests (e.g., bullying is a misperception of thin-skinned employees) become automatic and considered "common sense" [2].

There are five types of discursive closure: *disqualification, naturalization, neutralization, individualization of experience,* and *topical avoidance* [191]. First, *disqualification* excludes certain people from talking or at least disqualifies what they have to say if they do talk. For example, the comment, "She's just a disgruntled employee," negates what she has to say. Disqualification reinforces managerial and expert (consultant) accounts and disavows those of rank and file employees. "The presumption of credibility lays 'naturally' with the employer" [530](p. 97).

Second, *naturalization* strips away the social, historical, and cultural processes that have brought particular ways of seeing things to their current state. Naturalization treats certain ways of seeing things in organizational life as innate or natural in human beings. If employees see and hear enough about employee abuse, they come to believe that all managers are intrinsically abusive. When they encounter issues about bullying, they think, "That's just the way business works." Such a response naturalizes bullying and reduces chances of resistance and system change.

Third, *neutralization* masks the values and beliefs that support particular behavior and then treats particular behavior as if the behavior is value-free [531]. For example, rather than seriously standing up against bullying at work, organizational members take as a given that employee mistreatment is inevitable. Managers can and will treat subordinates anyway they desire; this is considered *managerial prerogative*. Neutral perceptions of some sort of inevitability close off discussions about the values or moral issues involved in allowing managers to do whatever they wish under the guise of getting work done (including psychological terrorizing).

Fourth, *individualizing* places the responsibility for social, systemic processes, outcomes, and conversations on individuals, usually those who have the most to lose. For instance, society and media valorize aggressive, win-at-all-costs business models, and upper-managers looks the other way when stronger organizational members bully those with less influence, but we often expect the target to resolve bullying independently of help. The questions "What did you do to make him/her (i.e., bully) mad?" or "What can you do to make him/her stop?" may seem innocent enough, yet such questions place responsibility solely on the target. Individualizing organizational processes like adult bullying removes organizational and social responsibility. Similarly, the assumption that bullying is causes by a few bad-apples bosses suggests that it is simply a personality issue and not the culmination of social norms condoning violence and aggression.

Finally, *topical avoidance* prohibits the discussion of certain subjects or issues at work, usually in indirect ways via rewards (e.g., offering friendship) and punishments (e.g., shunning). A few of the avoided topics at work are managerial shortcomings, personal life, and emotional reactions. Rewards and punishments make it unlikely that employees will publicly voice doubts about managerial actions, talk about the negative effects of work on home lives, or displays "inappropriate" emotion. Certainly, norms about appropriate workplace performance favor calm, rational displays over agitated, emotional displays [532]. When being angry, sad, or fearful are simply disallowed, then it is quite understandable why stories of bully victims remain silence or, when heard, difficult for others to accept.

These five language moves close off open, democratic communication and dialogue among involved organizational members. They point to the ways that social/cultural beliefs can severely curb telling and understanding bullying experiences. To some degree, discursive disclosure explains why the term *workplace bullying* is still in a state of denotative hesitancy (see Glossary) [214], which is a period of time in which we have yet to agree upon a vocabulary to name a social phenomenon. When a phenomenon is in a state of denotative hesitancy, people collectively question its existence (similar to the term *sexual harassment* prior to the 1970s). During this time, people will likely use a *dizzying array of terms* to refer to the same issue.

In addition to discursive closure, communication researchers see a language-related problem for targets that researchers have created. When researchers label workplace bullying using so many different terms (e.g., *generalized workplace abuse, work harassment, workplace mistreatment*), this mixed-up labeling causes confusion for people experiencing abuse at work. The unique, jargon-like terms may carve out a special niche for researchers and other authors but they are confusing and largely un-understandable for targets trying to identify, name, or fight against abuse [2]. Naming persistent abuse with the umbrella term *workplace bullying* helps targets to see that the problem is outside of them—not an internal mental deficiency or the beginning of losing their minds. Additionally, the term shines a light on the perpetrator's role.

Societal-Cultural Forces Impeding Bullying Interventions

Organizational communication researchers have suggested that there are a number of workgroup-level dynamics interfering with resistance to bullying that may even encourage its emergence and persistence. These include the collective nature of bullying, antagonistic or ambiguous policies, HR's perceived failures, and professional beliefs that inform how we make sense of bullying.

Communication researchers working with public advocates have found that workplace bullying involves many organizational members in addition to the targets and bullies. For example, my study with Gary Namie, cofounder of the Workplace Bullying Institute, looked at both targets' and non-bullied bystanders' perspectives. We found that nearly three-quarters of the cases, bullying included a host of co-conspirators and accomplices including bullies' peers, HR, and upper-managers. The complex cast of characters points to one of the reasons why creating effective organizational interventions is so difficulty. Bullying is not simply a personality conflict between two people. It is communal. (I hate to say *it takes a village,* but you get the idea).

In addition to all the people involved in bullying, policies and procedures can be reasons that bullying is unaddressed. The vague wording of "respect" policies can prevent abused workers from reporting [74] and make it nearly impossible for HR to respond effectively if they do report [514]. Other policies can also make things difficult. Communication research points to how the adversarial tendency of some personnel policies—progressive discipline [140], at-will employment, protracted probationary periods, one-way employment evaluations—can contribute to abusive organizational cultures. Such policies can be disguises that try to make bullying look like legitimate supervision.

They can mask power abuse in hostile supervisory employee evaluations, where employees can write a rebuttal to unfair damaging accusations, but no one ever reads the rebuttals. Drawn out probationary periods, for example, give bullies a slick means of getting rid new employees who dare to question abusive treatment. And as noted, employees are usually allowed to counter the disciplinary warnings and fabricated allegations placed in their personnel files, but communication researchers have found that the supervisor's version is counted as "reality," and the targets' version is rarely counted at all.

Indeed, targets have a tough time knowing to whom they should turn for help. Both targets and witnesses accuse HR personnel for making bullying situations worse—ostracizing abused employees, siding with bullies, and failing to protect workers [2, 128, 431]. Cowan's [514, 526] research, however, questions the blanket blaming of HR by showing the tensions, barriers, and struggles that staff in HR deal with when targets come to them. Despite these staff members' empathy and desire to help, the vagueness or lack of anti-bullying policies hinder their ability to take action or call abuse *bullying.* HR staff feels

342

challenged because they lack the power to take action. They do say they take bullying complaints seriously and act upon them when they can, but admit that they really have very little latitude for decision-making in bullying cases.

Professional-level (meso-level) framing vocabularies [335] or belief systems and values that inform sensemaking also discourage addressing adult bullying. Organizational members draw on these belief systems to decide what workplace experiences or cues mean, to pinpoint their meaning. In bullying situations, for example, when bullies persistently rage over targets' perceived shortcomings (cue), targets may weigh the outburst against a paradigm of professional decorum (framing vocabulary), connect the two and conclude that the bully is incompetent (derived meaning). Alternately, the target could connect raging (cue) to the ideology of individualism (framing vocabulary) and conclude that the bully has a personality disorder (derived meaning).

Once organizational members intersubjectively agree upon and thus settle on what a cue means by referring to the framing vocabularies, they then choose action that fits what they think the experience means. For example, targets often describe power as a zero-sum commodity, a commonplace vocabulary of power at work. Power norms necessarily vary, but targets talk about power as material, something that bullies lack or covet so seize from others via aggression.

Individual-Level Forces Impeding Bullying Interventions

Organizational communication researchers also point to a number of employee interactions that sustain rather than disrupt adult bullying. These include coworkers' silent assent or role as co-conspirators, ineffective target responses, and difficulty plotting bullying stories into believable narratives. Both silence and co-conspirators increase fear and reduce the odds of collective resistance that is needed to stop abuse. Onlookers often stay silent because they are afraid of being targeted, which is a very valid fear. Meanwhile, other coworkers might gravitate toward the bully, serving as henchmen/women. "Similar to schoolyard bullying, these [coworkers] ... participate indirectly in bullying but rarely take the initiative. They side with the aggressor most likely out of a desire for safety" [283](p. 316).

Absent or ineffective target responses can also contribute to ongoing bullying. Targets should *never be blamed* for being bullied at work. However, some responses do appear to encourage escalated abuse. Not only are some witnesses silent, targets also remain silent.

The trauma, terror, pain, and persistence of abuse weaken targets' personal defenses stunning them into a withdrawn *freeze* versus a *fight or flight* response. Some targets embrace negative labels, for example, by accepting the name "trouble-maker" as an sign of their workplace identity.

Targets also talk about the desire for vengeance but do so behind abusers' backs. They might debrief and depressurize during collective fantasies of revenge, such as one employee group that conjured ways to kill the bully by poisoning his tea, wiring a bomb to his car, and paying a professional hit man. One of the most common responses to bullying is *noisy* exit [533]—leaving their jobs (targets and witnesses) with a take-this-job-and-shove-it attitude. They leave like to send a message to upper-management. Revenge talk vents negative emotions and noisy exit removes people from harm, but it's unclear if they change the hostile environments. (There is reason to believe that worker exodus over long periods of time bring problems to the attention of upper-managers.) And directly speaking with the bully does not seem to help either, typically enflaming the bully and aggravating the problem.

The potential for targets telling their stories is that they can feel re-victimized by having others blame them for their own abuse [225]. Like other victims of severe trauma, betrayal, and pain, targets have trouble telling clear, consistent stories that persuasively and succinctly describe their situations. "Rather than [clear story line] plots, there are fragments of stories, bits and pieces told here and there, to varying audiences, so that no one knows a whole story; ... these are experiences that are just too shattering to put into words" [534](pp. 5,7). Even in the once-removed process of collecting stories from targets, researchers can become confused and anxious, sometimes trying to get research participants to the point more quickly. Despite the many challenges in halting workplace bullying, communication research provides promising solutions.

Table 16.5: How is bullying best addressed?

Societal, Cultural	Organizational, Community, Workgroup	Individual
✳ Increase public awareness [6, 128] ✳ Translational research, supporting academic reports with lay-friendly representations [225, 535, 536]	✳ Anti-bullying policies & culture changes [283, 537] ✳ Increased worker voice [7, 150, 517] ✳ Education, training on importance of language [517]	✳ Naming abuse *workplace bullying* and abuse victims *targets* [2, 9, 108] ✳ Learning how to tell credible stories when reporting [225]
✳ Academics partner with advocacy groups [128, 517, 538] ✳ Academic research in public-access outlets [128, 225] ✳ Campaigning for anti-bullying statutes [538]	✳ Teaching reframing tactics & communication skills [2, 101, 151, 283, 539] ✳ Training about what makes bullies bully [86, 459] ✳ Emphasizing collective resistance [137, 519] ✳ Bystander training [540, 541] ✳ Teaching argumentation; aggression prevention in schools [459, 460]	✳ Choosing empowering ways to talk about bullying (e.g., resistance = moral right action) [151, 519, 540] ✳ Encouraging collective voice, especially for witnesses [536] ✳ Securing social support; increasing support through educating peers, managers [2, 542, 543]

We now turn to how bullying might be best addressed from the social-, organizational- and individual-levels.

Social/Cultural Interventions

Public dialogue about bullying too often treats it as "an Emily Post problem" [544](p. 14), implying that it is merely a lack of politeness, rather than a *major cause of psychological terror and physical-mental damage*. One of the first steps to educating the public about the prevalence of bullying in US organizations. Organizational communication researchers have joined others to document its widespread occurrence.

Another way of educating the public is writing about the issue in formats and outlets that are accessible to people outside universities. Translating scientific research means writing in easily understood articles in popular outlets [535, 545]. Organizational communication researchers have traditionally focused on real-life communication [546]. Writing about the experience in a way that includes the shock and messiness is vital for meeting the realistic needs of contemporary organizations [547]. Practical impact also comes from academic-practitioner partnerships with professionals and community members outside of universities.

As my background is in managing nonprofit organizations, I realized the importance of building relationships with and learning from community activists early in researching this topic. Over the years I have spent time at the Workplace Bullying Trauma Institute (WBI), the leading target-activist center in the United States on the subject. During a 2003 internship, I learned about workplace bullying from targets' points of view, which has continued to inform later research. Throughout the years, I have become good friends and coauthored with the institute's cofounders Drs. Gary and Ruth Namie, two key public advocates on the topic. They regular appear as workplace bullying experts in the US media and lead the US movement to pass an anti-bullying law. Because of this relationship, the WBI website features many of the original studies revised or cited in this book. Online access to research increases the useful application of research.

Furthermore, organizational communication researchers have worked to improve the information about bullying available on public websites such as Wikipedia [546]. This work provides access to up-to-date information to anyone with a web connection. Several papers appear online and are free/downloadable to anyone (e.g., *How to Bust the Office Bully*; *Active and Passive Accomplices: The Communal Character of Workplace Bullying;* and *Compassion: Cure for an Ailing Workplace*). These papers are instantly available to targets, managers, journalists and anyone else interested and concerned with workplace bullying. (My own work with co-authors has generated hundreds of media stories. These, in turn, have triggered floods of calls and emails from targets seeking to understand and deal with abuse at work. Over the last 10 years, I've received hundreds and hundreds of personal emails and calls from targets or others seeking help and information.)

Finally, at the societal-level, communication research has helped, at least in a small way, to increase public awareness of the campaigns supporting anti-bullying laws [538]. Laws cannot singularly solve workplace bullying, but they are essential for moving topics into the public eye and building a critical mass of people who understand and can label the topic. Law has transformed sexual harassment from a hazy idea to an important issue to which organizations pay attention. Laws authoritatively stamp names on vaguely understood experiences. These societal-level processes contribute to *naming* and *understanding* bullying—both of which are necessary to stopping it.

Organizational-Community Interventions

Adult bullying can be addressed through organizational-level activities. Some of these are developing workplace policies and altering climate to reflect them, encouraging sidelined worker voice, and training people about workplace aggression and communication skills. Granted, workplace policies alone are insufficient for changing behavior. These must be coupled with changes in organizational members' attitudes, everyday talk, and behavior. Policies must also be matched to organizational rewards and punishments [537, 546, 548]. An important move for stopping bullying is incorporating *specific anti-bullying language* into organizational policies and coupling policies with culture change efforts. These may include creating public, sought-after rewards for treating others with respect and spreading efforts to improve climate into all levels of the organization [517].

Stopping abuse means creating opportunities for employees to be heard. Listening to non-supervisory employees and believing what they say could include hiring or electing an ombudsperson. It could mean providing direction for when employees should "go above supervisors' heads" when going to a direct supervisor is not safe [150]. Multi-rater 360° evaluations [517] provide some space for employee voice and reduce the odds of top managers glossing their middle-managers' abuse or fearing retribution [113]. These can be difficult,

347

however, if the climate is aggressive and people giving feedback can be identified (and retaliated against). These and other ways that employees can confidentially provide input can help organizations identify bullying.

Communication research also emphasizes the importance of education and training. Similar to learning about race and gender issues in terms of organizational policy [515, 549], simply understanding workplace bullying helps organizational members form new attitudes, respond more quickly to reported abuse, and counter bullying in constructive ways [517]. Areas of training that intersect with bullying include recognizing the roles of language use (framing vocabularies, narratives, metaphors) that are more or less empowering. Since the ways people *talk* about their experiences in part creates how they *feel* about those experiences, language shifts can be empowering [225]. For instance, rather than talking about bullying as a fight or the bullies as evil demons, employees may feel stronger when visualizing themselves as fighters in a moral crusade.

Knowing why bullies communicate aggressively is also crucial for intervention. More work is needed in this area, but communication research suggests that some people are born more verbally aggressive than others [86]. They can feel more justified using verbal aggression [550] and believe their aggression is less damaging to their targets than their aggression actually is [428]. Knowing this explains part of why abusers appear to lack empathy—to "not get it." Targets often believe that bullies are genetically aggressive and insensitive, which to some degree is true.

Despite research linking genetics with verbal aggressiveness, aggressive people control these tendencies depending on situation factors [459]. That is, aggressors will only behavior aggressively if they can get away with it. Targets and organizations can benefit from understanding the contextual factors that reduce bullying. For instance, some people resort to verbal aggressiveness when they are jealous in order to mask their own feelings of incompetence. When we recognize that bullies abuse others because of the bullies' fear and feelings of incompetence, it's easier to see other options for influencing the situation. Although a bitter pill, targets and witnesses might see that building up bullies' egos or lessening their fear might reduce the aggressors' abusive behavior.

Given that over half of targets blame themselves for being bullied, organizational training should also educate employees on the common patterns in bullying. Targets can feel better simply from learning that many different kinds of people are bullied, and there is not a single tried-and-true way to make it stop. Some targets think they are targeted for being too quiet and non-combative, and others believe they were bullied because they were too assertive. When targets stop blaming themselves, they can focus on taking care of themselves and getting the social support they deserves.

Employees would also profit from understanding the power of collective voice when resisting workplace abuse. Granted, organizations are unlikely to train employees in collective resistance, but peers can educate one another. Targets have described building coalitions of sorts, which include leaving articles about "busting bullies" in the break room or mailboxes.

Other ways to change things is to develop and use bystander training, an encouraging new organizational-level approach. In this training, workgroups learn how to provide immediate feedback in hostile workplace interactions [457, 541]. Bystander training can increase positive communication and pivot aggressive communication [540]. Pivoting means taking what someone else says and responding to a neutral or positive aspect of what otherwise might be a hostile statement. For example, if supervisor Bob says, "Ken is such an asshole. What does he know about working with community members?", Karen, a bystander, could pivot or turn the conversation by saying, "Speaking of community members, we really need to include that new client, and I have an idea."

Small changes like this in how people talk at work can lead to big changes over time. In an extensive intervention with the Veterans Administration, for example, teams learned and then used practices like passing a talking stick during meetings. When someone had the talking stick, no one else could interrupt him or her. The speaker then passed the stick to someone else when finished talking [101, 539]. The involved team members instituted the practice so firmly in how they talked with each other that even in restaurants they passed a salt shaker. The stick (or the salt shaker) reminded team members to listen and resist interrupting others. Small changes in communication resulted in enormous changes over time, reducing aggressive interactions among peers and aggressive supervisor-subordinate interactions. What was also very interesting and important was that veteran services improved when employee-to-employee aggression declined [539].

Moving out of the workplace and into educational institutions, to prevent verbal aggressiveness middle, high school and colleges might begin requiring courses in argumentation [459]. If people are verbally aggressive because they lack the skill to develop or generate responsible arguments, training can help to curb verbal aggressiveness. In terms of having this training, parents and students both report that their quality of life improved after completing argumentation training. To this end, Dominic Infante, Professor Emeritus at Kent State, developed a curriculum to help students develop strategies that control verbal aggressiveness [460].

Individual Interventions

The lion's share of bullying research suggests that targets should be the last ones to blame in these situations. Similar to advice about domestic violence, the most supportive thing someone can do is support targets' efforts or desires to *leave* the toxic workplace (if at all possible) [137]. Nonetheless, targets do have some options. Organizational communication research provides insight on individual-level interventions that might make them feel a bit better—naming abuse *bullying*, telling believable stories, building collective resistance, bolstering claims with published research, considering more empowering ways to make sense of abuse, and getting social support.

Research supports and confirms arguments made by the Workplace Bullying Institute (WBI) that simply *naming abuse workplace bullying and bullied persons as targets* are important steps move past knee-jerk target-blaming [147, 180]. Common terminology lets targets externalize the experience, recognize its identifiable patterns, feel better about themselves, and bolster their reports to peers, upper-managers, or HR staff.

Telling a believable story about abuse is crucial. Unfortunately, many people question targets' abilities, assume the abuse is petty, or believe targets brought it on themselves. To enlist others, targets must learn how to tell credible, relatively abbreviated stories. Such stories can eclipse a bit of the victim-stigma. Because targets usually have very little time to explain their claims to upper-managers, targets will benefit if they can frame their stories in relatively unemotional, brief ways that will be heard as professionally competent [225].

Tracy et al. [225] had independent raters evaluate anonymous target stories to see which were the most believable. The raters thought the stories that were least credible were those that were highly emotional, had inconsistencies, and featured unclear storyline lines. Raters thought the most credible were stories with the following characteristics: (1) clear beginning, middle, and end; (2) clearly identified bully; (3) focus on the bully's destructive behavior, not the target's; (4) specific details about bullying experiences, not other smaller complaints; (5) anticipation of potential objections and acknowledgement of others' perspectives; (6) vivid portrayal of the cost of the abuse, without being so emotional that the listener must console rather than work toward solving the problem; (7) consistency and the inclusion of detailed quotes, times, places, and people; (8) metaphors or examples that others may find familiar; (9) references to other people who have been bullied; (10) details about the negative effects of bullying on peers and workplace productivity; and (11) depiction of the target as a survivor not a victim.

Coworkers can also be very helpful supporters of target stories and breaking the bullying cycle. People in groups are more believable than people alone when group members agree on what's happening. If a target reports abuse and coworkers know about that report so also report that they've witnessed bullying, the coworker report makes the target report more credible. Quite simply, collective resistance is difficult to dismiss. Employers are more likely to intervene when affected targets have supportive (especially influential) allies; present their concerns through formal organizational procedures for grievance; and support their claims with research about adult bullying. Collective efforts also reduce the risk of being labeled as a troublemaking, mentally ill, problem-employee.

Targets feel stronger and better when they view their efforts as a moral imperative or honorable fight. Depending on how targets talk about bullying, they can frame themselves as survivors (versus victims) and thus transform the experiences in a way that affirms their positive self-image. As one woman told me, "Complaining and standing up and saying 'no' has given me opportunities to grow stronger, maybe more than I really wanted, but lots stronger. Today I can honestly say I am happy I stood up, because the greatest growth came with self respect." In many different ways, targets can resist the victim label, convince others of their value, impugn the bully, and move others to action.

As I have argued many times, the way we talk and label a situation shapes our perceptions of and responses to the situation [540]. When targets blame themselves or their bullies' eccentricities, they may feel paralyzed. When they view upper-managers as parental, all-knowing lords (of a sort), they feel frustrated and angry when these "parents" fail to stop the abuse. Targets can feel better if they talk about bullies and co-conspirators as people who are ignorant, fear-filled, and terrified of being unmasked and identified as bunglers [400]. When we recognize that upper-managers are uneducated about bullying rather than all-knowing scoundrels who simply ignore abuse, we might feel a bit better and make difference choices about how to react.

Finally, securing social support from friends, family, and coworkers is a powerful individual-level action that helps targets feel better [543]. Social support is helpful for a range of stressful, painful experiences on the job [542]. After conducting focus groups with targets, nearly every participant sent emails saying how much better they felt after sharing their experiences with others. In the group they found support and understanding and realized the problem was not isolated to themselves [2]. Targets say they feel better after talking with a variety of people, but conversations with supportive coworkers—even more so than family or friends—make the most positive difference in this regard [493]. Targets will want to keep from wearing people out, however, and thus losing others' support. When someone cares about the target, hearing over and over and over about abuse can drain the supporters' energy. Thus, finding a supportive counselor for ongoing conversations or speaking with a coach for targets of bullying can be incredibly helpful.

Table 16.6: Directions for Future Research

Societal/ Cultural	Organizational/ Communal	Individual
✳ Public health campaigns	✳ Wellness programs ✳ HR policies, practices ✳ Integrating superior-subordinate, communication competence, facework, & leadership research ✳ Research leaders tasked with addressing bullying ✳ Evaluate communication competence (argumentation) training ✳ Role of new communication technologies ✳ Effect of positive organizing & communication on bullying ✳ Exploring why organizations fail to intervene ✳ Examining how organizations successfully address bullying	✳ Bleed over of workplace bullying effects into family ✳ Exploring bullies' perspective ✳ Presence, absence of social support in bullying situations

Organizational communication research provides fertile ground for cultivating answers to future questions and concerns about workplace bullying. Given the important issues outlined in previous sections, what research is still needed for us to understand and better intervene in bullying situations?

Societal/Cultural-Level Directions

The intersections of health and organizational communication are vitally important for addressing workplace bullying at the societal-level. Partnering with those who have expertise in public health campaigns is sorely needed because workplace bullying *is* a public health issue. As such, development of and barriers to public health campaigns are important direction for raising awareness of adult bullying and its corrosive, toxic effects. Public health campaigns can discourage the popular belief that bullying is something that happens only at school or to a few thin-skinned weak people.

Target advocates and communication researchers have argued that strategic public health campaigns are needed to raise awareness and reduce general acceptance of adult bullying [155]. Knowledge gathered from successful past public health campaigns could provide some foundation for new efforts [551]. Once public health campaigns are developed and launched, the next step would be to examine and evaluate the effectiveness of campaigns at raising awareness and reducing acceptance.

Organizational/Community-Level Directions

Workplace wellness programs [552] could be part of organizational efforts to reduce workplace bullying. There is still have much to do, however, to build healthy workplace climates. Traditional workplace wellness programs have many advantages, but they also have the tendency to stigmatize those who suffer from various problems (overweight, substance abuse, social anxiety, etc.).

Workplaces would also benefit from improving and clarifying HR policies and practices [514] about workplace bullying. HR staff is relatively powerless to protect targets against abuse when policies are ambiguous or silent about bullying. Future research might investigate questions such as, What effect do anti-bullying policies have on abuse? or What problems exist in spite of clear policies? How do certain groups of people (status, tenure, age, etc.) interpret and respond to policies? Men and women typically interpret even seemingly clear policies about sexual harassment in very different ways [77, 553], so it would be interesting to see how people in different demographics (age, sex, position, etc.) interpret policies about workplace bullying.

Organizational communication has a long history of researching superior-subordinate communication, communication competence, facework, and leadership. Linking this work with bullying research might unearth ideas for bullying prevention or intervention. For example, in case of bullying, laissez-faire (i.e., hands-off) leadership is likely as ineffective at dealing with abuse as is aggressive authoritarian leadership. We currently know very little about the upper-managers tasked with addressing bullying. "Knowing why organizations fail to intervene is important.... Potentially, there are organizational or legal barriers to taking action in these situations. Surveying or interviewing upper-managers and HR professionals who deal with bullying could provide important insights" [128](p. 364).

Future research could also study if or how communication competence (or lack thereof) contributes to workplace bullying. People who lack competence in conflict management can become easily frustrated and aggressive in heated encounters. The "argumentative skill deficiency explanation for verbal aggressiveness" [459](p. 27) suggests that training people in competent argumentation might reduce verbal aggressiveness. This may or may not be true but finding out is important. Given that some people have doubts as to whether argumentation skill reduces aggressiveness [554], more research is needed. Similarly, research could evaluate the effectiveness of the curriculum teaching students communicative tactics for controlling verbal aggressiveness.

The role of new communication technologies suggests another fruitful direction for research. We know little about how technology is or could be used to make sense of, resist, or perpetuate bullying. Cowan [519] examined resistance to adult bullying through analyzing posts to the Yahoo group Bullyingonline, a support and information group developed by Tim Field, a target-turned-advocate in the UK [555]. Communication research has recently flourished in terms of cyberbullying and young adults [556] [557], but research about the workplace and cyberbullying is still somewhat rare. One study suggests the prevalence of organizational cyberbullying is lower than believed [558], but technological bullying is certainly an area for additional examination.

Focusing on workplace positivity, compassion, resilience, and wellness may also help solve bullying and other negative experiences like stress and burnout [549]. On one hand, bullying can neutralize some of the positive effects of constructive interactions. On the other hand, positive communication can buffer some of the negative effects of bullying on desired job outcomes. It's important to study the complex interactions of *negative* and *positive* organizational issues, not solely focus on the negative. Some argue that that negative events had stronger effect than positive events, but others propose that positive organizational events have longer lasting effects than negative . Future research could fruitfully examine which forms of positive organizing are most powerful at reducing the negative effects of bullying.

Indeed, this leads to the suggestion that future researchers not only explore why organizations fail to take action against bullying, but also seek out cases when organizational intervention was successful. About a third of working adults who saw or experienced bullying said that their organizations took action that improved situations for targets. And, collective resistance and targets' optimism about gaining justice are associated with bullying cessation. A variety of models show organizations how to craft respectful workplaces. These models could be improved with information about what reduces entrenched bullying.

Communication researchers concerned with organizational climate and culture [559] are well positioned to uncover the processes leading to positive culture shifts and bullying cessation. Along these same lines, we need to know the extent to which certain interventions (e.g., confronting bullies, mediation programs, conflict resolution approaches, etc.) improve or intensify bullying. Some bullying experts argue strongly against the use of mediation, saying it can place targets at enormous risk, a point with which I agree strongly.

Individual-Level Directions

The effects of workplace bullying on interpersonal relationships (e.g., marriage, domestic partnership) remain understudied and limited to target perspectives. Existing research suggests that bullying ripples into and harms family communication and relationships [37, 212]. Work-life balance researchers could usefully tap the perspectives of targets' partners and family members and ask them to describe how bullying "comes home" with targets. Because existing research is survey-based, new studies might examine how ideas like *family undermining* and *ripple effects* feel and show up in conversations.

Another direction for future study involves talking to perpetrators—from the horse's mouth, so to speak. Very few studies come from bullies' viewpoint. A communicative approach could valuably explore how perpetrators justify and narrate their behavior, characterize targets, naturalize aggression, or minimize others' pain. Interpersonal communication research on verbal aggressiveness has a rich history [428, 459, 550, 560], and collaborations between interpersonal and organizational researchers who study aggressive communication would be fruitful.

The role of social support is also a valuable avenue for communication research, one that has received little attention [543]. Past research has suggested that bullying silences onlookers and pushes them to avoid siding with targets. Meanwhile, some witnesses are so horrified by bullying that they are galvanized to fight against it. Communication researchers have explored social support in many contexts, but they have yet to look at social support in the face of workplace bullying or other forms of harassment [560]. Finally, the role of coworkers is still a bit vague. What is it that makes a coworker defend a target? Why would a coworker side with the bully? What have coworkers done that have improved situations? We have a bit of research in this area but need more so we can tap the power of bystanders in the social environment we call work.

Conclusion

Organizational communication research has enriched the understanding of workplace bullying in a number of ways. The field's attention to voice and its desire to uncover hidden systems of power, particularly those associated with oppression, have led the academic and professional conversation in new directions. Because of organizational communication's interdisciplinary roots, the work pulls together various threads of the conversation as researchers from communication, education, psychology, business, and health examine bullying and what to do about it.

This chapter illustrates the complexity of workplace bullying, as it is condoned through societal discourses, sustained by receptive workplace cultures, and perpetuated by interpersonal interactions. Examining these societal, organizational and individual aspects addresses the most pressing questions about adult bullying: (1) how abuse manifests, (2) employee/organizational responses, (3) why it's so harmful, (4) why resolution is so difficult, and (5) how it can be addressed. There is still much to do, particularly as research moves from identifying and understanding workplace abuse to addressing and combatting it. However, by approaching the adult bullying at various discursive levels, communication research has improved understanding, redressing, and ameliorating abuse at work.

Permissions

John Wiley and Sons

1. Licensed content title Burned by Bullying in the American Workplace: Prevalence, Perception, Degree and Impact*
License Number 3093201468015
License date Feb 20, 2013
Licensed content publisher John Wiley and Sons
Licensed content publication Journal of Management Studies
Licensed copyright line Copyright © 2007, John Wiley and Sons
Licensed content author Pamela Lutgen-Sandvik, Sarah J. Tracy, Jess
    K. Alberts
Requestor type Author of this Wiley article
Title of new book Workplace bullying-=A nasty piece of work: Research on adult bullying, non-sexual harassment, and psychological-emotional abuse on the job.

---

2. Licensed content title The Constitution of Employee-Abusive Organizations: A Communication Flows Theory
License Number 3093211477696
License date Feb 20, 2013
Licensed content publisher John Wiley and Sons
Licensed content publication Communication Theory
Licensed copyright line © 2008 International Communication Association
Licensed content author Pamela Lutgen-Sandvik, Virginia McDermott
Requestor type Author of this Wiley article
Title of new book Workplace bullying-=A nasty piece of work: Research on adult bullying, non-sexual harassment, and psychological-emotional abuse on the job

---

Taylor & Francis:

1. Licensed content "Take This Job and Shove It" (Communication Monographs)

2. Licensed content Making Sense of Supervisory Bullying (Southern Journal of Communication)
FOR FULL PERMISSIONS DETAIL SEE:
http://journalauthors.tandf.co.uk/permissions/reusingOwnWork.asp#top

Taylor & Francis: Copyright and reusing your own work
APPLICABLE SECTION:
3. Copyright
• **[PERTINENT TO THIS VOLUME]**: the right to use the article in its published form in whole or in part without revision or modification in personal compilations [in print or digital form] or other publications of your own articles, provided that acknowledgment to prior publication in the journal is made explicit;
• the right to expand an article into book-length form for publication provided that acknowledgment to prior publication in the journal is made explicit.
If you wish to use your article in a way which is not covered by the above license, please contact the Taylor & Francis Permissions Team: permissionrequest@tandf.co.uk

Sage:

1. Licensed content The cycle of employee emotional abuse: Generation and regeneration of workplace mistreatment. (Management Communication Quarterly)
2. Licensed content Nightmares, demons and slaves: Exploring the painful metaphors of workplace bullying. (Management Communication Quarterly)
3. Licensed content Intensive remedial identity work: Responses to workplace bullying as trauma and stigma. (Organization)
4. Licensed content. Answering five key questions about workplace bullying: How communication research provides thought leadership for transforming abuse at work. (Management Communication Quarterly)
FOR FULL AUTHOR PERMISSIONS DETAIL SEE:
http://www.sagepub.com/authors/journal/permissions.sp#7

APPLICABLE SECTION:
Journal Authors
Under the terms of your contributor agreement, without seeking per-

359

mission, you may:

- At any time, distribute on a not-for-profit basis photocopies of the published article for your own teaching needs or to supply on an individual basis to research colleagues.
- At any time, circulate or post on any repository or website the version of the article that you submitted to the journal (i.e. the version before peer-review) or an abstract of the article.
- At least 12 months after publication, post on any non-commercial repository or website the version of your article that was accepted for publication.
- [PERTINENT TO THIS VOLUME]: At least 12 months after publication, re-publish the whole or any part of the Contribution in a printed work written, edited or compiled by you provided reference is made to first publication by SAGE/SOCIETY.

Chapters without formal Permission entries are appearing in this book for the first time and have never been published in any other outlet, commercial or non-commercial.

All co-authors have given permission to include our work in this volume. For details contact author.

GLOSSARY

Vocabulary of terms (some in-text, others for your information)

Agency: the ability to take action, to mobilize resources and carve out spaces of control in their day-to-day lives and in respect of the activities of the more powerful; see also *Dialectic of Control*

Aggressive communication: tendency to attack others' self-concepts in order to deliver psychological pain or force others to believe something or behave in a particular way

Attribution: focus of causation that a person projects on someone in the process of judging why someone behaved as she or he did; in classical attribution theory, attributions are dispositional (focused on a characteristic of the person) or situational (focused on some feature of the physical or social environment)

Bounded emotionality: balancing individual needs for authentic and spontaneous emotional expression with relational requirements, rational decision-making, and organizational control

Burnout: a general "wearing out" from the pressures of work characterized by (1) emotional exhaustion; (2) depersonalization or a negative shift in responses to others, particularly clients; and (3) a decreased sense of personal accomplishment

Category deception: the intentional misrepresentation of an identifying demographic category such as one's sex, age, or status

Civility: the act of showing regard, respect, restraint, and responsibility for the social demands of the situation

Clique: narrow exclusive circle or group of persons held together by common interests, views, or purposes

Collective voice: when several employees talk amongst themselves about their experiences and what they could or should do; when several employees take action as a united group

Constructive discharge: when employees resign or quit because their employers' behavior or an implemented change makes the working climate so intolerable or makes worklife so difficult that the employees have no choice but to resign; because the resignation is not truly voluntary, it is in effect an employment termination

Contagious voice: when employees' decision to speak out incites others; when employee voice influences and spreads to others, encouraging them to speak out also

Cordial hypocrisy: the strong tendency of people in organizations, because of loyalty or fear, to pretend that there is trust when there is not; being polite in the name of harmony when cynicism and distrust are the norm

Counterproductive technology use: behaviors related to the use of communication technology that conflict with organizational goals and place employers at risk either legally or financially

Cyberbullying: actions that use information and communication technologies to support deliberate, repeated, and hostile behavior by an individual or group, that is intended to harm another or others

Dark side of teams: confluence of individual, dyadic, subgroup, group, organizational, and environmental forces that lead many teams to organize and communicate in ways destructive to individuals, subgroups, organizations, and the groups themselves

Dialectic: any systematic reasoning or argument that contrasts opposing or contradictory ideas and usually seeks to resolve the conflict; a tension or opposition between two interacting forces or elements

Dialectic of power and control: power and control is social process that exists as a push-and-pull dynamic between people with organizational position-power or influence and those without that power; employees in lower-level jobs are dependent on supervisors but supervisors are also dependent on subordinates; even the lowest-level employees have some agency and control over their superiors

Discourse, discourse: Big-D *Discourses* are the overarching social, historical, cultural meanings, values, beliefs, and norms that are, for the most part, taken for granted and unrecognized; little-d *discourse* is the numerous individual-level interactions and conversations, talk and text in micro=level social practices

Discursive formations: the total set of relations that unite, at a given period, the communicative and behavioral practices that give rise to what we know, how we know, and who has the expertise to be able to speak about "truth" or "reality"

Deceptive communication: communication that is dishonest, involves lying, or is unfair, or that entails messages and information knowingly transmitted to create a false conclusion, by virtue of evasive or deliberately misleading messages, as well as euphemisms designed to cover up defects, conceal embarrassment, or make things appear better than they are

Denotative conformity: when terms have an agreed-upon meaning or reference in system of language

Denotative hesitancy: when new terms are introduced in how we talk about experiences (e.g., workplace bullying) definitions are usually challenged or contested for a time before language-users come to agree on what the new terms mean; a situation in which there are no agreed-upon terms/meanings to describe a phenomenon; see also *denotative conformity*

Destructive communication: intentional or unintentional communication that attacks receivers' self-esteem or reputation, or reflects indifference towards others' basic values, and is harmful to organizational members, groups within organizations, or organizations as a whole

Discrimination: the discernment of qualities and recognition of the differences between things and the subsequent prejudicial treatment of those who are different based on certain characteristics

Discursive framework: understanding communication as shaping and framing social realities

Discursive knowledge: the ability to verbally express knowledge.

Distrust: cognitive and emotional process in which bullies are suspicious of motives, doubt the veracity, and have a lack of confidence in organizations or their members

Diversity: the ideology of including people with different backgrounds and beliefs

EEOC, Equal Employment Opportunity Commission: US government office responsible for enforcing federal laws making it illegal to discriminate against a job applicant or an employee because of the person's race, color, religion, sex (including pregnancy), national origin, age (40 or older), disability, or genetic information

Emotional contagion: transfer of moods among people, tendency to express and feel emotions that are similar to and influenced by those of others; can involve caregiver taking on client emotions or organizational members assuming other members' feeling states; when employees move to polar extremes of emotional contagion (complete emotional involvement), they are more likely to burn out

Emotional labor: a process whereby workers manage their emotions in response to organizational and occupational expectations and display rules

Emotional tyranny: use of emotion by powerful organization members in a manner that others perceive to be destructive, controlling, unjust, and even cruel

Empathic concern: an emotional stance in which the caregiver experiences concern about the welfare of the other without feeling parallel emotions of the other; correlated with employee satisfaction

Employee-abusive, toxic organizations: workplaces in which employees experience persistent emotional abuse and hostile communication that is unfair, unjust, and unwanted; in such workplaces ongoing hostility results in workers suffering heightened fear, dread, and job insecurity

Employee emotional abuse: repetitive, targeted, and destructive form of communication directed by more powerful members at work at those less powerful; see also workplace bullying, mobbing

Entrepreneurialism (or entrepreneurial culture): an economic and social shift that favors enterprise

Entrepreneurial self: an autonomous, reflexive being who steers his or her life, taking initiative and assuming responsibility for his or her own success

Ethnicity: an aspect of social identity based on cultural phenomena such as place of origin, language, rituals, and traditions

Exodus: quitting, intentions or threats to quit, transfers or requests for transfers, and aiding others' exit from the organization

Face-work, face-saving: a common conversational want and need that compels people to act in ways that preserve their own and others' public self-images

Fateful moments: points at which people feel compelled to make decisions that are particularly consequential for their ambitions, and more generally for their future lives

Flaming: hostile and aggressive interactions via text-based computer-mediated communication

Fundamental attribution error: a biased judgment about the cause of someone's behavior, in which an individual makes a dispositional attribution without considering likely situational factors; see *attribution*

Gender identity: a person's own sense of sex identification as male or female

Glass ceiling: a barrier so subtle that it is transparent, yet so strong that it prevents women and minorities from moving up in the management hierarchy

Grouphate: people's predisposition to detest, loathe, or abhor working in groups

Homophobia: hatred, hostility, disapproval, or prejudice toward homosexuals or homosexual behavior

Horizontal violence: hostile and aggressive behavior by individual or group members towards another member or groups of members of the larger group. This has been described as inter-group conflict

Hostile work environment: when an employee experiences workplace harassment and fears going to work because of the offensive, intimidating, or oppressive atmosphere generated by the harasser based on race, religion, sex, national origin, age, disability, veteran status, or, in some jurisdictions, sexual orientation, political affiliation, citizenship status, marital status, or personal appearance

Hypervigilance: enhanced state of sensory sensitivity accompanied by an exaggerated intensity of behaviors whose purpose is to detect threats; accompanied by a state of increased anxiety which can cause exhaustion resulting in a constant scanning of the environment for threats; a perpetual searching for sights, sounds, people, behaviors, smells, or anything reminiscent of threat or trauma; being on high alert in order to be certain danger is not near

Identity anchors: a relatively enduring set of identity discourses upon which individuals rely when explaining who they are and want to be to themselves and others

Identity work: continuous emotional and social effort people put in for the purposes of forming repairing, maintaining, strengthening or revising their preferred sense of personhood or self that produces a sense of coherence and distinctiveness

Impoverished workforce: a collection of employees that is left behind after multiple waves of employee exit due to hostile workplace dynamics (bullying, harassment, etc.); remaining employees

* lack sufficient career capital to exit and secure employment elsewhere, or

* are simply putting in their time until they can retire because they have too much invested in retirement or other benefit systems to quit their jobs, or

* are demoralized and hopeless about the organization's future, or

* some combination of these

Incivility: rude, offensive and demeaning behaviors that vary in intensity and intention to harm others; behaviors that demean, demoralize, and degrade others; can be a subtle or overt attempts to disarm, distance, disrespect or silence another in ways that privilege one's own views, position, and possibilities

Intrusive activities: communication events that interrupt work tasks or workers' cognitive concentration and are, consequently, burdensome or destructive

Isolate: individual separated or cut off from others by physical or social barriers

Just-World Hypothesis: tendency for people to want to believe that the world is fundamentally just; as result, when they witness an otherwise inexplicable injustice, they will rationalize it by searching for things that the victim might have done to deserve it; deflects their anxiety, and lets them continue to believe the world is a just place, but often at the expense of blaming victims for things that were not, objectively, their fault; also called just-world theory, just-world fallacy, just-world effect

Marginalization: being relegated to an unimportant or powerless position within a society or group by prejudice, bias, norms, rules, or belief systems

Marginalized: the exclusion of groups of people from meaningful participation in society generally because of a minority status

Micro-inequities: seemingly minor unpleasant experiences or small differences in how people are treated that can have negative effects on employees

Minority: a sociological group that does not constitute a political plurality of the total population

Moral emotions: affective reactions to violations or affirmations of moral obligations governing the conduct of individuals, relationship partners, or larger communities

Mutual advocacy: support and defense of one employee by another employee, "having each others' backs"

Negative face: desire for autonomy and freedom from imposition; acts or behaviors that compromise this desire

Negative anticipatory socialization: messages that repel people from organizations before people enter the organization through gossip, word-of-mouth, organizational reputations, and so forth; messages that repel potential recruits; unintended messages to external audiences unique to toxic organizations

Opportunity costs: what it takes to regain or produce anew something lost or valued; cost incurred (sacrifice) by choosing one option over the next best alternative (which may be equally desired)

Oppressed group: social group (e.g., women, African Americans, persons with disabilities) categorized by some imagined or actual differences that stigmatize group members; part of oppressed group behavior can include aggressive behavior by members toward others of the same group

Organizational discourse: refers broadly to the communication that takes place during the organizing process and the associated meanings that arise for organizational members

Organizational irrationalities: everyday practices that pull organizational members in different and sometimes competing directions (e.g., paradox, tension, contradiction, irony)

Organizational trust: members' faith in or reliance on the integrity, strength, ability, and surety of organizations and their leaders; confidence and belief in the uprightness of organizational actions and bullies

Ostracism, social: the act or process of shunning, banning, or excluding an individual from a larger group

Outcast: individual intentionally separated from or shunned by others

Positive face: desire or want for connection with others; acts or behaviors that threaten one's desire and need to be viewed positively by and connected to others

Power-distance: the extent to which the less powerful members of organizations and institutions (e.g., family) accept and expect that power is distributed unequally

Practical consciousness: the knowledge and skills that humans bring to the tasks required by everyday life, which is so integrated into how they live that it is hardly noticed

Presenteeism: slack productivity from ailing workers; workers in hostile environments may be at work, but they are not producing at their peak potential

Psychologically-safe communication climate: working environment that is characterized by support, openness, trust, mutual respect, and risk taking; one that facilitates innovation, constructive discussion, information provision, openness to new perspectives, and suspension of judgment

Quarantining bullies: taking aggressors out of a position of power over others in order to reduce their potential to harm individuals, workgroups, or organizations

Racial harassment: unwelcome conduct engendered by racism that unreasonably interferes with an individual's work performance or creates an intimidating, hostile, or offensive work environment

Racism: any theory or belief that a person's inherited physical characteristics associated with racial designations (e.g., skin color, hair texture or facial features) determine human intellectual capacity and personality traits

Racism, types:

* ✳ *Institutional (structural) racism*: systemic, collective patterns and practices that help to entrench racial inequality in organizations and institutions

* ✳ *Internalized racism*: a belief among persons of color that white persons are superior and persons of color are inferior

Reduplication: linguistic repeating of certain words or phrases (e.g., he attacked me, and attacked me, and attacked me)—in which more of the word or phrase (attacked me) stands for more of the content (more attacks)

Resilience: social processes of rebounding from or reintegrating after negative life experiences (e.g., disruptions, tragedies, crises, destructive organizational relationships and situations)

Resistance: (in workplace bullying cases) any active or passive, direct or indirect communicative or other behavior with the purpose of countering, disrupting, or defying the aggressor; any action or message that erodes the an aggressor's material or symbolic base of influence

Reverse discourse: turning repressive practices and messages to liberating advantages for those targeted; resisting abuse by engaging or co-opting the very managerial controls that provided alternative readings without directly confronting more powerful organizational members (e.g., taking pride in being a "troublemaker")

Scapegoating: assigning blame or failure to another to absolve one's wrongdoing or responsibility and deflect attention away from oneself; taking out frustrations out on a weaker, more vulnerable organizational or group member

Sexual harassment: unwelcome sexual advances, requests for sexual favors, and other verbal or physical conduct of a sexual nature constitute sexual harassment when this conduct explicitly or implicitly affects an individual's employment, unreasonably interferes with an individual's work performance, or creates an intimidating, hostile, or offensive work environment

Sexual harassment, types:

* *Hostile-environment sexual harassment:* situations where employees are subject to unwanted sexual behavior from persons other than a direct supervisor in which authorities fail to take steps to discourage or discontinue such behavior; unwanted sexual attention so prevalent or so severe that workplace becomes destructive or damaging

* *Quid pro quo sexual harassment*: situations where employees are subject to unwanted sexual behavior from a person in a hierarchically-superior position that makes employment, promotion, or raise contingent on the receipt of sexual favors

✳ *Third-person sexual harassment*: victim not directly harassed but negatively affected by witnessing or hearing about others' sexual harassment

Sexual orientation: broadly understood as enduring emotional, romantic, sexual, or emotional attraction towards others; distinguished from other components of sexuality including biological sex, gender identity (psychological sense of being male or female) and social gender role (adherence to cultural norms for feminine and masculine behavior)

Social stigma: severe social disapproval of personal characteristics or beliefs that are contrary to cultural norms

Social support: physical and emotional comfort given by family, friends, co-workers and others; helpful interactions that can ameliorate stress, burnout, and emotional pain

Social support, types:

✳ *Emotional support*: providing empathy, caring, acceptance and assurance

✳ *Instrumental support*: giving time, resources, or labor

✳ *Informational support*: helping others define their role, providing general facts about a job or issue, and offering skills training

Stress: a process of (1) alarm reaction, (2) resistance, and (3) exhaustion; difference between worker satisfaction (as represented by individual need fulfillment) and realities of the work situation as experienced by individuals

Study Response: The StudyResponse project is a paid sampling service of Syracuse University, facilitates sampling for many university studies and, as such, is not a collaborator or subcontractor in this study (StudyResponse disclaimer). The service sends an email with a link to the study's survey to respondents who have agreed to participate in social science research. As an incentive, respondents' names are placed in a drawing for gift certificates from Amazon and other online retailers. The service protects respondent identity; respondents are identified by a unique, anonymous ID, which they enter when beginning the survey. For an in-depth explanation of the sampling service, see studyresponse.com.

Subversive (dis)obedience: tactics in which workers alter work output or communication patterns in ways that disadvantage aggressors (e.g. labor withdrawal, working-to-rule, resistance through distance, and retaliation

Surveillance: watching over and monitoring employees, often using technology to do so

Synergy: the results of people working or talking in groups that is more than a simple sum of the whole—something entirely new comes from the group dynamic and produces an overall better result than if each person within the group were working toward the same goal individually

Toxin handlers: the managers, secretaries or intermediaries who address, eliminate, and assuage the conflicts, stressors, problems, abuse, and hurt feelings common in organizations

Toxic organizations: See employee-abusive organizations

Typology: a system used for putting things into groups according to how they are similar; the study of how things can be divided into different types

Verbal aggressives, high: people born with trait aggressiveness who are predisposed to attack others' self-concepts

Working-to-rule: doing no more than the minimum required by the rules of contracts or job requirements; following safety or other regulations precisely in order to cause a slowdown, rather than to serve organizational purposes

Workplace aggression: efforts by individuals to harm others with whom they work or the organizations in which they are employed

Workplace bullying: persistent verbal and nonverbal acts directed toward one or more workers that cause humiliation, offense, distress, or interference with work and create a hostile, counterproductive environment; typically involves power disparity between targets and bullies

Workplace bullying, types of

＊ *Authoritative bullying:* the persistent abuse of power granted through organizational position; most commonly reported type

* *Discriminatory bullying*: abusing someone out of prejudice, usually workers who differ from, or refuse to accept the norms of, the rest of the workgroup or "belong to a certain outsider group

* *Displaced bullying*: scapegoating or aggressing against someone other than the source of strong provocation because aggressing against the source of such provocation is too dangerous

* Dispute-related bullying: *bullying sparked by interpersonal disagreements that build into extremely escalated, entrenched conflicts*

* *Organizational bullying:* indicts organizational practices that are oppressive, exploitive, and over-controlling as seeding abuse (e.g., corporate downsizing, outsourcing jobs, forcing uncompensated overtime work, closing entire plants to relocate for low-cost labor).

* *Serial bullying*: many workers are bullied, usually one after the other by an authoritative bully

Zogby International: polling organization whose missing is "to offer the best polling, market research, information services, and business solutions worldwide based on accuracy and detailed strategic information" http://www.zogby.com/about/index.cfm

\

REFERENCES

Further Reading

1. Leymann, H, Gustafsson, A. Mobbing at work and the development of post-traumatic stress disorders. *European Journal of Work and Organizational Psychology.* 1996;5(3):251-275

2. Tracy, SJ, Lutgen-Sandvik, P, Alberts, JK. Nightmares, demons and slaves: Exploring the painful metaphors of workplace bullying. *Management Communication Quarterly.* 2006;20(2):148-185.10.1177/0893318906291980

3. Rayner, C, Hoel, H, Cooper, CL. *Workplace bullying: What we know, who is to blame, and what can we do?* London: Taylor & Francis; 2002.

4. Leymann, H. Mobbing and psychological terror at workplaces. *Violence and Victims.* 1990;5(1):119-126

5. Namie, G. The WBI 2003 report on abusive workplaces. *Workplace Bullying Institute.* Accessed 10/19/03, 2003.

6. Lutgen-Sandvik, P, Tracy, SJ, Alberts, JK. Burned by bullying in the American workplace: Prevalence, perception, degree, and impact. *Journal of Management Studies.* 2007;44(6):837-862

7. Lutgen-Sandvik, P. The communicative cycle of employee emotional abuse: Generation and regeneration of workplace mistreatment. *Management Communication Quarterly.* 2003;16(4):471-501.10.1177/0893318903251627:

8. Adams, A, Crawford, N. *Bullying at work: How to confront and overcome it.* London: Virago Press; 1992.

9. Lutgen-Sandvik, P. Intensive remedial identity work: Responses to workplace bullying trauma and stigma. *Organization.* 2008;15(1):97-119.10.1177/1350508407084487:

10. Einarsen, S, Hoel, H, Zapf, D, Cooper, CL. The concept of bullying at work. *Bullying and emotional abuse in the workplace: International perspectives in research and practice.* London: Taylor & Francis; 2003:3-30.

11. Vartia, M. Consequences of workplace bullying with respect to the well-being of its targets and the observers of bullying. *Scandinavian Journal of Work Environment and Health.*

2001;27:63-69

12. Namie, G, Namie, R. *The bully at work: What you can do to stop the hurt and reclaim your dignity on the job.* Naperville, IL: Sourcebooks; 2000.

13. Lutgen-Sandvik, P. Take this job and ... Quitting and other forms of resistance to workplace bullying. *Communication Monographs.* 2006;73(4):406-433

14. Liefooghe, APD, MacKenzie-Davey, K. Accounts of workplace bullying: The role of the organization. *European Journal of Work and Organizational Psychology.* 2001;10:375-392

15. Salin, D. Ways of explaining workplace bullying: A review of enabling, motivating and precipitating structures and processes in the work environment. *Human Relations.* 2003;56(10):1213-1232

16. Keashly, L, Nowell, BL. Conflict, conflict resolution and bullying. In: S Einarsen, H Hoel, D Zapf, CL Cooper, eds. *Bullying and emotional abuse in the workplace: International perspectives in research and practice.* London: Taylor & Francis; 2003:339-358.

17. Keashly, L. Emotional abuse in the workplace: Conceptual and empirical issues. *Journal of Emotional Abuse.* 1998;1(1):85 - 117

18. Crawford, N. Organisational responses to workplace bullying. In: N Tehrani, ed. *Building a culture of respect: Managing bullying at work.* London: Taylor & Francis; 2001:21-31.

19. Namie, G. Workplace bullying: Escalated incivility. *Ivey Business Journal.* 2003;68(2):1-6

20. Zapf, D, Einarsen, S. Individual antecedents of bullying. In: S Einarsen, H Hoel, D Zapf, CL Cooper, eds. *Bullying and emotional abuse in the workplace: International perspectives in research and practice.* London: Taylor & Francis; 2003:165-184.

21. Einarsen, S. The nature and causes of bullying at work. *International Journal of Manpower.* 1999;20(1/2):16-27

22. Lutgen-Sandvik, P. Water smoothing stones: Subordinate resistance to workplace bullying, Doctoral dissertation, Arizona State University. *Dissertation Abstracts International 66/04, 1214.* 2005

23. Hoel, H, Cooper, CL, Faragher, B. The experience of bullying in Great Britain: The impact of organizational status.

European Journal of Work and Organizational Psychology.
2001;10(4):443-465

24. Rayner, C. The incidence of workplace bullying. *Journal of Community and Applied Social Psychology.* 1997;7(1):199-208

25. Neuman, JH, Baron, RA. Social antecedents of bullying: A social interactionist perspective. In: S Einarsen, H Hoel, D Zapf, CL Cooper, eds. *Bullying and emotional abuse in the workplace: International perspectives in research and practice.* London: Francis & Taylor; 2003:185-202.

26. Randall, P. *Bullying in adulthood: Assessing the bullies and their victims.* New York: Brunner-Routledge; 2001.

27. Neuman, JH, Baron, RA. Aggression in the workplace: A social-psychological perspective. In: S Fox, P Spector, eds. *Counterproductive work behaviors.* Washington DC: American Psychological Association; 2005:13-40.

28. Andersson, LM, Pearson, C. Tit for tat? The spiraling effect of incivility in the workplace. *Academy of Management Review.* 1999;24(3):454-471

29. Adams, A, with Crawford, N. *Bullying at work: How to confront and overcome it.* London: Virago Press; 1992.

30. Brodsky, C. *The harassed worker.* Lexington, MA: D.C. Health and Company; 1976.

31. Einarsen, S, Mikkelsen, EG. Individual effects of exposure to bullying at work. In: S Einarsen, H Hoel, D Zapf, CL Cooper, eds. *Bullying and emotional abuse in the workplace: International perspectives in research and practice.* London: Taylor & Francis; 2003:127-144.

32. Keashly, L, Harvey, S. Emotional abuse in the workplace. In: S Fox, P Spector, eds. *Counterproductive work behaviors.* Washington DC: American Psychological Association; 2005:201-236.

33. Rospenda, KM. Workplace harassment, service utilization, and drinking outcomes. *Journal of Occupational Health Psychology.* 2002;7(2):141-155

34. Soares, A. When darkness comes: Workplace bullying and suicidal ideation. In: N Tehrani, ed. *Workplace bullying: Symptoms and Solutions.* London: Routledge; 2012:67-80.

35. Kivimäki, M, Ferrie, JE, Brunner, E, et al. Justice at work and reduced risk of coronary heart disease among employees. *Archives of Internal Medicine.* 2005;165:2245-2251

36.   Crawford, N. Conundrums and confusion in organisations:
        The etymology of the word "bully". *International Journal of
        Manpower.* 1999;20(1/2):86-93
37.   Hoobler, JH, Brass, DJ. Abusive supervision and family
        undermining as displaced aggression. *Journal of Applied
        Psychology.* 2006;91(5):1125-1133
38.   Sperry, L, Duffy, M. Workplace mobbing: Individual and
        family health consequences. *The Family Journal.*
        2007;15(4):398-404. 10.1177/1066480707305069:
39.   Olweus, D. Bully/victim problems in school: Basic facts and an
        effective intervention programme. In: S Einarsen, H Hoel, D
        Zapf, CL Cooper, eds. *Bullying and emotional abuse in the
        workplace: International perspectives in research and practice.*
        London: Francis & Taylor; 2003:62-78.
40.   Einarsen, S, Raknes, BI, Matthiesen, SB. Bullying and
        harassment at work and their relationships to work
        environment quality: An exploratory study. *European Work
        and Organizational Psychologist.* 1994;4(4):381-401
41.   Björkqvist, K, Österman, K, Hjelt-Bäck, M. Aggression among
        university employees. *Aggressive Behavior.* 1994;20(1):173-
        184.10.1002/1098-2337(1994)20:3<173::AID-
        AB2480200304>3.0.CO;2-D:
42.   Rayner, C. The incidence of workplace bullying. *Journal of
        Community and Applied Social Psychology.* 1997;7(2):199-
        208
43.   Sheehan, MJ, Jordan, PJ. Bullying, emotions and the learning
        organisation. In: S Einarsen, H Hoel, D Zapf, CL Cooper,
        eds. *Bullying and emotional abuse in the workplace:
        International perspectives in research and practice.* London:
        Taylor & Francis; 2003:359-369.
44.   Marais-Steinman, S, Herman, M. *Corporate hyenas at work:
        How to spot and outwit them by being hyenawise.* Pretoria,
        South Africa: Kagiso Publishers; 1997.
45.   Niedl, K. Mobbing and wellbeing: Economic and personal
        development implications. *European Journal of Work and
        Organizational Psychology.* 1996;5:239-249
46.   Hubert, AB, van Veldhoven, M. Risk factors for undesired
        behavior and mobbing. *European Journal of Work and
        Organizational Psychology.* 2001;10:415-424
47.   Zapf, D. Organisational, work group related and personal
        causes of mobbing/bullying at work. *International Journal of*

Manpower. 1999;20(1/2):70-85

48. Ahmed, E, Braithwaite, J. Shame, pride, and workplace bullying. In: S Karstedt, I Loader, H Strang, eds. *Emotions, Crime and Justice.* Oxford: Hart Publishing; 2009:55-80.

49. Zapf, D, Escartin, J, Einarsen, S, Hoel, H, Vartia, M. Empirical findings on prevalence and risk groups of bullying in the workplace. In: S Einarsen, H Hoel, D Zapf, CL Cooper, eds. *Bullying and emotional abuse in the workplace: International perspectives in research and practice.* London: Taylor Francis; 2011:107-128.

50. Cox, H. Verbal abuse nationwide, Part II: Impact and modifications. *Nursing Management.* 1991;22:66-67

51. Sheehan, KH, Sheehan, DV, White, K, Leibowitz, A, Baldwin, DC. A pilot study of medical student abuse. *Journal of the American Medical Association.* 1990;263:533-537

52. Keashly, L, Jagatic, K. North American perspectives on hostile behaviors and bullying at work. In: S Einarsen, H Hoel, D Zapf, CL Cooper, eds. *Bullying and harassment in the workplace: Developments in theory, research and practice.* 2nd edition. Boca Rotan, FL: CRC Press/Taylor & Francis Group; 2011:41-71.

53. Baron, RA, Neuman, JH. Workplace violence and workplace aggression: Evidence on their relative frequency and potential causes. *Aggressive behavior.* 1996;22:161-173

54. Keashly, L, Trott, LM, MacLean, LM. Abusive behavior in the workplace: A preliminary investigation. *Violence and Victims.* 1994;9(4):341-357

55. Rospenda, KM, Richman, JA, Wislar, JS, Flaherty, JA. Chronicity of sexual harassment and generalized workplace abuse: Effects on drinking outcomes. *Addiction.* 2000;95:1805-1820

56. Aquino, K. Structural and individual determinants of workplace victimization: The effects of hierarchical status and conflict management style. *Journal of Management.* 2000;26:171-193.10.1177/014920630002600201

57. Fox, S, Spector, PE, Miles, D. Counterproductive work behavior (CWB) in response to job stressors and organizational justice: Some mediator and moderator tests for autonomy and emotions. *Journal of Vocational Behavior.* 2001;59(3):291-309

58. O'Leary-Kelly, AM, Duffy, MK, Griffin, RW. Construct

confusion in the study of antisocial work behavior. *Research in Personnel and Human Resources Management.* 2000;18:275-303

59.   Lee, D. Gendered workplace bullying in the restructured U.K. Civil Service. *Personnel Review.* 2002;31(2):205-222

60.   Fox, S, Spector, PE, eds. *Counterproductive work behavior.* Washington DC: American Psychological Association; 2005.

61.   Cropanzano, R, Randall, ML. Injustice and work behavior: a historical review. In: R Cropanzano, ed. *Justice in the Workplace: Approaching Fairness in Human Resource Management.* Hillsdale, NJ: Lawrence Erlbaum Associates; 1993:3-20.

62.   Harlos, KP, Pinder, C. Patterns of organizational injustice: A taxonomy of what employees regard as unjust. In: J.Wagner, ed. *Advances in Qualitative Organizational research.* 2nd edition. Stamford, CT: JAI Press; 1999:97-125.

63.   Vardi, Y, Weitz, E. *Misbehavior in organizations: Theory, research, and management.* New York: Psychology Press; 2003.

64.   Baron, RA, Neuman, JH. Workplace aggression--the iceberg beneath the tip of workplace violence: Evidence on its forms, frequency, and targets. *Public Administration Quarterly.* 1998:446-464

65.   Schat, ACH, Frone, M, R., Kelloway, EK. Prevalence of workplace aggression in the U.S. workforce: Findings from a national study. In: EK Kelloway, J Barling, JJ Hurrell, eds. *Handbook of workplace violence.* Thousand Oaks, CA: Sage; 2006:47-89.

66.   Bennett, RJ, Robinson, SL. Development of a measure of workplace deviance. *Journal of Applied Psychology.* 2000;85(3):349-360.10.1037/0021-9010.85.3.349:

67.   Kelloway, EK, Barling, J, Hurrell, JJ. *Handbook of workplace violence.* Thousand Oaks, CA: Sage; 2006.

68.   Keashly, L. Interpersonal and systemic aspects of emotional abuse at work: The target's perspective. *Violence and Victims.* 2001;16(3):233 - 268

69.   Leymann, H. The content and development of mobbing at work. *European Journal of Work and Organizational Psychology.* 1996;5(2):165-184

70.   Zapf, D, Einarsen, S. Mobbing at work: Escalated conflicts. In: S Fox, P Spector, eds. *Counterproductive work behaviors.*

Washington DC: American Psychological Association; 2005:237-270.

71. Duffy, MK, Ganster, DC, Shaw, JD, Johnson, JL, Pagon, M. The social context of undermining behavior at work. *Organizational Behavior and Human Decision Processes* 2004;101(1):105-126

72. Einarsen, S, Hoel, H, Zapf, D, Cooper, CL, eds. *Workplace bullying: Developments in theory, research and practice.* London: Taylor & Francis; 2011.

73. Richman, JA, Rospenda, KM, Flaherty, JA, Freels, S. Workplace harassment, active coping, and alcohol-related outcomes. *Journal of Substance Abuse.* 2001;13:347-366

74. Meares, MM, Oetzel, JG, Torres, A, Derkacs, D, Ginossar, T. Employee mistreatment and muted voices in the culturally diverse workplace. *Journal of Applied Communication Research.* 2004;32(1):4-27.10.1080/0090988042000178121:

75. Aquino, K, Bradfield, M. Perceived victimization in the workplace: The role of situational factors and victim characteristics. *Organization Science.* 2000;11:525-537.10.1287/orsc.11.5.525.15205

76. Schneider, KT, Hitlan, RT, Radhakrishnan, P. An examination of the nature and correlates of ethnic harassment experiences in multiple contexts. *Journal of Applied Psychology.* 2000;85(1):3-12

77. Dougherty, D, Smythe, MJ. Sensemaking, organizational culture, and sexual harassment. *Journal of Applied Communication Research.* 2004;32(4):293-317.10.1080/0090988042000275998:

78. Pryor, JB, Fitzgerald, LF. Sexual harassment research in the U.S. In: S Einarsen, H Hoel, D Zapf, CL Cooper, eds. *Bullying and emotional abuse in the workplace.* London: Taylor & Francis; 2003:79-100.

79. Tepper, BJ. Consequences of abusive supervision. *Academy of Management Journal.* 2000;43(2):178-190

80. Pearson, CM, Andersson, LM, Porath, Cl. Workplace incivility. In: PE Spector, S Fox, eds. *Counterproductive Workplace Behavior: Investigations of Actors and Targets.* Washington, D.C: American Psychological Association; 2004:177-200.

81. Sypher, BD. Reclaiming civil discourse in the workplace. *Southern Communication Journal.* 2004;69:257-269

82. Ashforth, BE. Petty tyranny in organizations. *Human Relations.* 1994;47:755-778. 10.1177/001872679404700701

83. Williams, KD, Sommer, KL. Social ostracism by co-workers: Does rejection lead to loafing or compensation? *Personality and Social Psychology Bulletin.* 1997;23(7):693-706

84. Braun, K, Christle, D, Walker, D, Tiwanak, G. Verbal Abuse of Nurses and Non-Nurses. *Nursing Management.* 1991;22(3):72-76

85. Infante, DA, Rancer, AS. Argumentativeness and verbal aggressiveness: A review of recent theory and research. *Communication Yearbook.* 1996;19:319-351

86. Beatty, MJ, McCroskey, JC. It's in our nature: Verbal aggressiveness as temperamental expression. *Communication Quarterly.* 1997;45(4):446-460.10.1080/01463379709370076:

87. Mikkelsen, EG, Einarsen, S. Bullying in Danish work-life: Prevalence and health correlates. *European Journal of Work and Organizational Psychology.* 2001;10(4):393-413

88. Einarsen, S, Hoel, H. The Negative Acts Questionnaire: Development, validation and revision of a measure of bullying at work. Paper presented at: 10th European Congress on Work and Organisational Psychology; May, 2001; Prague.

89. Keashly, L, Nowell, BL. Conflict, conflict resolution, and bullying. In: S Einarsen, H Hoel, D Zapf, C Cooper, eds. *Bullying and harassment in the workplace: Developments in theory, research, and practice.* 2nd edition. Boca Rotan, FL: CRC Press/Taylor & Francis Group; 2011:423-445.

90. Cowie, H, Naylor, P, Rivers, I, Smith, PK, Pereira, B. Measuring workplace bullying. *Aggression and Violent Behavior: A Review Journal.* 2002;7:33-51

91. Salin, D. Prevalence and forms of bullying among business professionals: A comparison of two different strategies for measuring bullying. *European Journal of Work and Organizational Psychology.* 2001;10(4):425-441

92. Rayner, C. A comparison of two methods for identifying targets of workplace bullying. *Ninth European Congress on Work and Organizational Psychology Conference.* Helsinki: Finnish Institute of Occupational Health; 1999.

93. Magley, VJ, Hulin, CL, Fitzgerald, LF, DeNardo, M. Outcomes of self-labeling sexual harassment. *Journal of Applied Psychology.* 1999;84(3):390-402.10.1037/0021-9010.84.3.390:

94. Hoel, H, Cooper, CL. *Destructive conflict and bullying at work* Manchester: University of Manchester Institute of Science and Technology (UMIST); 2000.

95. Alberts, JK, Lutgen-Sandvik, P, Tracy, SJ. Workplace bullying: A case of escalated incivility. Paper presented at: International Communication Association; May, 2005; New York.

96. Hofstede, G. *Culture's consequences: International differences in work-related values.* Vol 5. Beverly Hills: Sage; 1980.

97. Newman, KL, Nollen, SD. Culture and congruence: The fit between management practices and national culture. *Journal of International Business Studies.* 1996;27(4):753-779

98. Hofstede, G. Cultural constraints in management theories. *The Academy of Management Executive.* 1993;7(1):81-94.10.5465/AME.1993.9409142061:

99. Davenport, N, Schwartz, RD, Elliott, GP. *Mobbing: Emotional abuse in the American workplace.* 2nd edition. Ames, IA: Civil Society Publishing; 2002.

100. Einarsen, S, Skogstad, A. Bullying at work: Epidemiological findings in public and private organizations. *European Journal of Work and Organizational Psychology.* 1996;5(2):185-201.10.1080/13594329608414854:

101. Keashly, L, Neuman, JH. Bullying in the workplace: Its impact and management. *Employee Rights and Employment Policy Journal.* 2005;8(3):335-373

102. Coyne, I, Craig, J, Chong, PS-L. Workplace bullying in a group context. *British Journal of Guidance and Counseling.* 2004;32(3):301-317

103. Barling, J. The prediction, experience and consequences of workplace violence. In: GR VanderBos, EQ Bulatoao, eds. *Violence on the job.* Washington, DC: American Psychological Association; 1996:29-50.

104. Jennifer, D, Cowie, H, Anaiadou, K. Perceptions and experience of workplace bullying in five different working populations. *Aggressive Behavior.* 2003;29(4):489-496

105. Vartia, M. *Workplace bullying: A study on the work environment, well-being and health*: Finnish Institute of Occupational Health, People and Work Research Reports; 2003. 56.

106. USDOL. Industry at a glance. In: UDo Labor, ed; 2007.

107. Keashly, L, Neuman, JH. Exploring Persistent Patterns of Workplace Aggression. In: A Workplace Abuse, Bullying, and

Incivility: Conceptual and Empirical Insights' symposium, ed. *Meeting of the Academy of Management.* Denver; 2002.

108. Keashly, L, Jagatic, K. By any other name: American perspectives on workplace bullying. In: S Einarsen, H Hoel, D Zapf, CL Cooper, eds. *Bullying and emotional abuse in the workplace: International perspectives in research and practice.* London: Taylor Francis; 2003:31-91.

109. Burnazi, L, Keashly, L, Neuman, JH. Aggression revisited: Prevalence, outcomes and antecedents. Paper presented at: Annual meeting of the Academy of Management; August 5-10, 2005; Honolulu.

110. Neuman, JH. Injustice, stress, and aggression in organizations. In: RW Griffin, AM O'Leary-Kelly, eds. *The dark side of organizational behavior.* San Francisco: Jossey-Bass; 2004:62-102.

111. Hornstein, HA. *Brutal bosses and their prey: How to identify and overcome abuse in the workplace.* New York: Riverhead Books; 1996.

112. Yamada, D. The phenomenon of "workplace bullying" and the need for status-blind hostile work environment protection. *Georgetown Law Journal.* 2000;88(3):475-536

113. Pearson, CM. Organizations as targets and triggers of aggression and violence: Framing rational explanations for dramatic organizational deviance. In: PA Bamberger, WJ Sonnenstuhl, eds. *Research in the Sociology of Organizations.* Vol 15; 1998:197-223.

114. Skarlicki, DP, Folger, R. Retaliation in the workplace: The roles of distributive, procedural, and interactional justice. *Journal of applied psychology.* 1997;82(3):434

115. BNA. Work and stress: The work/family connection. Special report # 32. In: BoN Affairs, ed. Washington, DC: Author; 1990.

116. Tehrani, N. Introduction to workplace bullying. In: N Tehrani, ed. *Workplace bullying: Symptoms and Solutions.* London: Routledge; 2012:1-18.

117. Ellis, A. Workplace bullying in the retail industry. Oxford, UK: Ruskin College Oxford; 2000.

118. Price Spratlen, L. Interpersonal conflict which includes mistreatment in a university workplace. *Violence and Victims.* 1995;10:285-297

119. Hirigoyen, M-F. *Stalking the soul: Emotion abuse and the*

erosion of identity. New York: Helen Marx Books; 2000.

120. Wyatt, J, Hare, C. *Work abuse: How to recognize it and survive it.* Rochester, VT: Schenkman Books; 1997.

121. Infante, DA, Gorden, WI. How employees see the boss: Test of an argumentative and affirming model of supervisors' communicative behavior. *Western Journal of Communication (includes Communication Reports).* 1991;55(3):294-304

122. Rayner, C, Hoel, H. A summary review of literature relating to workplace bullying. *Journal of Community & Applied Social Psychology.* 1998;7(3):181-191

123. Thomas - Peter, BA. Personal standards in professional relationships: Limiting interpersonal harassment. *Journal of Community & Applied Social Psychology.* 1998;7(3):233-239

124. Bassman, ES. *Abuse in the workplace: Management remedies and bottom line impact.* Westport, CT: Quorum Books; 1992.

125. Kontorovich, E. The Mitigation of Emotional Distress Damages. *The University of Chicago Law Review.* 2001:491-520

126. Lockhart, K. Experience from staff support service. *Journal of Community and Applied Social Psychology.* 1997;7(1):193-198

127. Gorden, WI, Infante, DA. Employee rights: Context, argumentativeness, verbal aggressiveness, and career satisfaction. In: CAB Osigweh, ed. *Communicating employee responsibilities and rights.* Westport, CT: Quorum; 1987:149-163.

128. Namie, G, Lutgen-Sandvik, P. Active and passive accomplices: The communal character of workplace bullying. *International Journal of Communication.* 2010;4:343-373

129. Kramarae, C. *Women and men speaking.* Rowley, MS: Newbury House; 1981.

130. Orbe, MP. *Constructing co-cultural theory: An explication of culture, power, and communication:* Sage Publications, Incorporated; 1997.

131. Ardener, S. Introduction: The nature of women in society. In: S Ardener, ed. *Defining females: The nature of women in society.* 2nd edition. New York: John Wiley & Sons; 1993:1-33.

132. Spender, D. Defining reality: A powerful tool. In: C Kramarae, M Schult, W O'Barr, eds. *Language and power.* Beverly Hills, CA: Sage; 1984.

133.   Beasley, J, Rayner, C. Bullying at work (after Andrea Adams). *Journal of Community & Applied Social Psychology.* 1998;7(3):177-180.10.1002/(SICI)1099-1298(199706)7:3<177::AID-CASP415>3.0.CO;2-Y:

134.   Bies, RJ, Tripp, TM. Two faces of the powerless: Coping with tyranny in organizations. In: RM Kramer, MA Neale, eds. *Power and influence in organizations.* Thousand Oaks, CA: Sage; 1998:203-219.

135.   Harlos, KP, Pinder, C. Emotion and injustice in the workplace. In: S Fineman, ed. *Emotions in organizations.* Thousand Oaks, CA: Sage; 2000:255-276.

136.   Waldron, VR. Relational experiences and emotions at work. In: S Fineman, ed. *Emotion in organizations.* Thousand Oaks, CA: Sage; 2000:64 - 82.

137.   Lutgen-Sandvik, P. Take this job and ... : Quitting and other forms of resistance to workplace bullying. *Communication Monographs.* 2006;73(4):406-433

138.   Matusewitch, E. Constructive discharge: When a resignation is really a termination. *Employment Discrimination Report.* 1996;6(7):1-5

139.   Heller, M. A return to at-will employment. *Workforce.* 2001;80(5):42-46

140.   Fairhurst, GT, Green, SG, Snavely, BK. Managerial control and discipline: Whips and chains. *Communication yearbook.* 1984;9:558-593

141.   Lesly, E. Good-bye Mr. Dithers. *Business Week;* 1992:41, 52.

142.   Tracy, K, Dusen, D, Robinson, S. "Good" and "bad" criticism: A descriptive analysis. *Journal of communication.* 2006;37(2):46-60

143.   Namie, G, Namie, R. Workplace bullying: The silent epidemic. *Employee Rights Quarterly.* 2000;1(2):1-12

144.   Ray, EB, Miller, KI. The influence of communication structure and social support on job stress and burnout. *Management Communication Quarterly.* 1991;4(4):506-527

145.   Andersen, PA, Guerrero, LK. Principles of communication and emotion: Basic concepts and approaches. In: PA Andersen, LK Guerrero, eds. *Handbook of communication and emotion: Research, theory, applications, and contexts.* San Diego, CA: Academic Press; 1998:3-27.

146.   Gaines, J, Jermier, JM. Emotional exhaustion in a high stress organization. *Academy of Management Journal.* 1983:567-586

147. Namie, G, Namie, R. *The bully at work: What you can do to stop the hurt and reclaim your dignity on the job.* 2nd edition. Naperville, IL: Sourcebooks; 2009.

148. Corman, SR. "That works fine in theory, but . . ." In: SR Corman, SP Banks, CR Bantz, ME Mayer, eds. *Foundations of organizational communication: A reader.* White Plains, NY: Longman; 1995:3-10.

149. Tracy, SJ. Becoming a character of commerce: Emotion labor, self subordination and discursive construction of identity in a total institution. *Management Communication Quarterly.* 2000;14:90-128

150. Kassing, JW. Breaking the chain of command: Making sense of employee circumvention. *Journal of Business Communication.* 2009;46(3):311-334

151. Lutgen-Sandvik, P, McDermott, V. Making sense of supervisory bullying: Perceived powerlessness, empowered possibilities. *Southern Communication Journal.* 2011;76(4):342–368

152. Ryan, KD, Oestreich, DK. *Driving fear out of the workplace: Creating the high-trust, high-performance organization:* Jossey-Bass; 1998.

153. Bloom, SL. Building resilient workers and organisations: The Sanctuary® Model of organisational change. In: N Tehrani, ed. *Workplace bullying: Symptoms and Solutions.* London: Routledge; 2012:260-276.

154. Stohl, C, Schell, SE. A communication-based model of a small-group dysfunction. *Management Communication Quarterly.* 1991;5(1):90-110

155. Namie, G, Namie, R, Lutgen-Sandvik, P. Challenging workplace bullying in the USA: An activist and public communication. In: S Einarsen, H Hoel, D Zapf, CL Cooper, eds. *Workplace bullying: Developments in theory, research and practice.* 2nd edition. London: Taylor & Francis; 2010:in press.

156. Hogh, A, Mikkelsen, EG, Hansen, A, Marie. Individual consequences of workplace bullying/mobbing. In: S Einarsen, H Hoel, D Zapf, CL Cooper, eds. *Bullying and harassment in the workplace: Developments in theory, research, and practice.* 2nd edition. Boca Rattan, FL: CRC Press/Taylor & Francis Group; 2011:129-148.

157. Tepper, BJ, Duffy, MK, Shaw, JD. Personality moderators of

the relationship between abusive supervision and subordinates' resistance. *Journal of Applied Psychology.* 2001;86:974-983

158. Ezzamel, H, Willmott, H, Worthington, F. Power, control, and resistance in "the factory that time forgot.". *Journal of Management Studies.* 2001;38:1053-1079

159. Humphreys, M, Brown, AD. Narratives of organizational identity and identification: A case study of hegemony and resistance. *Organization Studies.* 2002;23:421-447

160. Mulholland, K. Workplace resistance in an Irish call centre: Slammin', scammin', smokin' and leavin'. *Work, Employment and Society.* 2004;18:709-724

161. Burawoy, M. *Manufacturing consent: Changes in the labor process under monopoly capitalism.* Chicago: University of Chicago Press; 1979.

162. Collinson, DL. Strategies of resistance: Power, knowledge and subjectivity in the workplace. In: JM Jermier, D Knights, WR Nord, eds. *Resistance and power in organizations.* London: Routledge; 1994:25-68.

163. Witten, M. Narrative and the culture of obedience at the workplace. In: D Mumby, ed. *Narrative and social control: Critical perspectives.* Newbury Park, CA: Sage; 1993:97-118.

164. Hodson, R. Worker resistance: An underdeveloped concept in the sociology of work. *Economic and Industrial Democracy.* 1995;16:79-110

165. May, T. From banana time to just-in-time: Power and resistance at work. *Sociology.* 1999;33:767-783

166. Tucker, J. Everyday forms of employee resistance. *Sociological Forum.* 1993;8:25-45

167. Kondo, DK. *Power, gender, and discourses of identity in a Japanese workplace.* Chicago: University of Chicago Press; 1990.

168. Trethewey, A. Resistance, identity, and empowerment: A postmodern feminist analysis of clients in a human service organization. *Communication Monographs.* 1997;64:281-301

169. Mumby, DK. Theorizing resistance in organization studies. *Management Communication Quarterly.* 2005;19:19-44

170. Lutgen-Sandvik, P. Water smoothing stones: Subordinate resistance to workplace bullying (Doctoral dissertation, Arizona State University, 2005). *Dissertation Abstracts International.* 2005;66(04):1214

171. Clegg, S. Power relations and the constitution of the resistant

subject. In: JM Jermier, D Knights, WR Nord, eds. *Resistance and power in organizations.* London: Routledge; 1994:274-325.

172. Foucault, M. The subject and power. *Critical Inquiry.* 1982;8:777-795

173. Giddens, A. Power and the dialectic of control and class structuration. In: A Giddens, G MacKenzie, eds. *Social class and the division of labour* Cambridge: Cambridge University Press; 1982:29-45.

174. Giddens, A. *The constitution of society.* Berkeley, CA: University of California Press; 1984.

175. Foucault, M. *The archeology of knowledge.* New York: Pantheon; 1972.

176. Glaser, BG, Strauss, AL. *The discovery of grounded theory.* New York: Aldine de Gruyter; 1967.

177. Carey, B. Fear in the workplace: The bullying boss. Accessed 8/12/05.

178. Childers, L. Bullybusting: Nurses in hostile work environments must take action against abusive colleagues. Accessed 4/26.

179. Guynn, J. Mean business: Benecia couple lead fight against workplace bullying. *Contra Costa Times.* 10/7, 1998; Business: B2.

180. Namie, G. The challenge of workplace bullying. *Employment Relations Today.* 2007;34(2):43-51

181. Ashforth, BE, Mael, FA. The power of resistance: Sustaining valued identities. In: RM Kramer, ME Neale, eds. *Power and influence in organizations.* Thousand Oaks, CA: Sage.; 1998:89-120.

182. Martin, J, Meyerson, D. Women and power: Conformity, resistance, and disorganized coaction. In: RM Kramer, MA Neale, eds. *Power and influence in organizations.* Thousand Oaks, CA: Sage; 1998:311-348.

183. Rothschild, J, Miethe, TD. Whistle-blower disclosures and management retaliation. *Work and Occupations.* 1999;26:107-128

184. Zapf, D, Gross, C. Conflict escalation and coping with workplace bullying: A replication and extension. *European Journal of Work and Organizational Psychology.* 2001;10(4):497-522

185. Sass, JS, Mattson, M. When social support is uncomfortable: The communicative accomplishment of support as a cultural

term in a youth intervention program. *Management Communication Quarterly.* 1999;12:511-543

186.   Barsade, SG. The ripple effect: Emotional contagion and its influence on group behavior. *Administrative Science Quarterly.* 2002;47:644-675.10.2307/3094912

187.   Schoenewolf, G. Emotion contagion: Behavioral induction in individuals and groups. *Modern Psychoanalysis.* 1990;15:49-61

188.   Fiori, J. American Airlines pilots stage militant job action. *Socialist Action.* 3/01. Accessed 5/02, 2005.

189.   Jones, J. Northwest pilots' victory encourages other unions [The Militant]. 9/28. Accessed 5/2/05, 2005.

190.   Jordan, JW. Sabotage or performed compliance: Rhetorics of resistance in temp worker discourse. *Quarterly Journal of Speech.* 2003;89:19-40

191.   Deetz, SA. *Democracy in an age of corporate colonization.* Albany, NY: SUNY; 1992.

192.   Hafen, S. Organizational gossip: A revolving door of regulation and resistance. *Southern Journal of Communication.* 2004;69:223-240

193.   Martin, D. Humor in middle management: Women negotiating the paradoxes of organizational life. *Journal of Applied Communication Research.* 2004;32:147-170

194.   Varallo, SM, Ray, EB, Ellis, BH. Speaking of incest: The research interview as social justice. *Journal of Applied Communication.* 1998:254-271

195.   Collinson, DL. *Managing the shopfloor: Subjectivity, masculinity and workplace culture.* Berlin: DeGruyter; 1992.

196.   Fleming, P, Spicer, A. Working at a cynical distance: Implications for power, subjectivity and resistance. *Organization.* 2003;10:157-179

197.   Ryan, W. *Blaming the victim.* New York: Vantage Books; 1976.

198.   Namie, G. The WBTI 2007 U.S. Workplace Bullying Survey. *Workplace Bullying and Trauma Institute.*

199.   Farrell, A, Geist-Martin, P. Communicating health: Perceptions of wellness at work. *Management Communication Quarterly.* 2005;18:543-592

200.   O'Driscoll, MP, Cooper, CL, Dewe, PJ. *Organizational stress: A review and critique of theory, research, and applications:* Sage Publications, Incorporated; 2001.

201.   Tattersall, AJ, Farmer, EW. The regulation of work demands

and strain. 1995

202. Lakoff, G, Johnson, M. *Metaphors to live by.* Chicago: University of Chicago Press; 1980.

203. Morgan, JM. Moldy bagels and new toasters: Images of emotion in workplace relationships. *Iowa Journal of Communication.* 2003;35:207-232

204. Aristotle. *Rhetoric:* Lee Honeycutt. Accessed May 12, 2005, http://www.public.iastate.edu/~honeyl/Rhetoric/; 1954.

205. Cialdini, RB. *How and why people agree to things.* New York: Morrow; 1984.

206. Planalp, S. Communication, cognition, and emotion. *Communication Monographs.* 1993;60(1):3-9

207. Weiss, HM, Cropanzano, R. Affective events theory: A theoretical discussion of the structure, causes and consequences of affective experiences at work. *Research in Organizational Behavior.* 1996;17:1-74

208. Freud, S. Inhibitions, symptoms, and anxiety. In: J Strachey, ed. *Standard Edition.* Vol 20. London: Hogarth Press; 1926:70-176.

209. Hochschild, AR. *The managed heart: Commercialization of human feeling.* Berkeley: University of California Press; 1983.

210. Fineman, S. *Understanding emotion at work.* London: Sage; 2003.

211. Tracy, SJ. The construction of correctional officers: Layers of emotionality behind bars. *Qualitative Inquiry.* 2004;10:509-533

212. Lewis, SE, Orford, J. Women's experiences of workplace bullying: Changes in social relations. *Journal of Community and Applied Social Psychology.* 2005;15(1):29-47

213. Ferraro, KJ. The dance of dependency: A geneology of domestic violence discourse. *Hypatia.* 1996;11:77-91

214. Clair, RP. The use of framing devices to sequester organizational narratives: Hegemony and harassment. *Communication Monographs.* 1993;60:113-136

215. Lewis, D. Workplace bullying -- interim findings of a study in further and higher education in Wales. *International Journal of Manpower.* 1999;20(1/2):106-118

216. Einarsen, S, Raknes, BI. Harassment at work and the victimization of men. *Violence and Victims.* 1997;12:247-263

217. Zapf, D, Knorz, C, Kulla, M. On the relationship between mobbing factors, and job content, social work environment, and health outcomes. *European Journal of Work and*

Organizational Psychology. 1996;5(2):215-237.10.1080/13594329608414856:

218. Scott, MJ, Stradling, SG. Trauma, duress and stress. In: N Tehrani, ed. *Building a culture of respect: Managing bullying at work*. London: Taylor & Francis; 2001:33-42.

219. Lindlof, TR, Taylor, BC. *Qualitative Communication Research Methods*. 3rd edition. Thousand Oaks, CA: Sage; 2011.

220. Vince, R, Broussine, M. Paradox, defense and attachment: Accessing and working with emotions and relations underlying organizational change. *Organization Studies*. 1996;17(1):1-21

221. Zuboff, S. *The age of the smart machine. The future of work and power*. New York: Basic Books; 1988.

222. Liebermann, M. *Art therapy for groups: A handbook of themes, games and exercises*. London: Routledge; 1991.

223. Meyer, A. Visual data in organizational research. *Organization Science*. 1991;2(2):218-236

224. Mischler, E. *Research interviewing: Context and narrative*. Cambridge, MA: Harvard University Press; 1986.

225. Tracy, SJ, Alberts, JK, Rivera, KD. How to bust the office bully: Eight tactics for explaining workplace abuse to decision-makers; 2007.

226. Marshak, RJ. Metaphors, metaphoric fields and organizational change. In: D Grant, C Oswick, eds. *Metaphor and organizations*. London: Sage; 1996:147-165.

227. Morgan, G. *Images of organizations*. Thousand Oaks, CA: Sage; 1997.

228. Kirby, EL, Harter, LM. Speaking the language of the bottom-line: The metaphor of "managing diversity". *Journal of Business Communication*. 2003;40:28-54

229. Deetz, SA. Metaphor analysis. *International and Intercultural Annual*. 1984;8:215-228

230. Miles, MB, Huberman, AM. *Qualitative data analysis*. Thousand Oaks, CA: Sage; 1994.

231. Innes, B. *The history of torture*. New York: St. Martin's Press; 1998.

232. Buzzanell, PM, Turner, LH. Emotion work revealed by job loss discourse: Backgrounding-foregrounding of feelings, construction of normalcy, and (re)instituting of traditional male masculinities. *Journal Applied Communication Research*. 2003;31:27-57.10.1080/00909880305375:

233. Lawler, S. Narrative in social research. In: T May, ed. *Qualitative research in action.* London: Sage; 2002:242-258.

234. Djurkovic, N, McCormack, D, Casimir, G. The physical and psychological effects of workplace bullying and their relationship to intention to leave: A test of the psychosomatic and disability hypothesis. *International Journal of Organizational Theory and Behavior.* 2004;7:469-497

235. Mikkelsen, EG, Einarsen, S. Basic assumptions and post-traumatic stress among victims of bullying at work. *European Journal of Work and Organizational Psychology.* 2002;11(1):87-111

236. Fraser, B. The interpretation of novel metaphors. In: A Ortony, ed. *Metaphor and thought.* 2nd edition. Chicago: University of Chicago Press; 1993:329-341.

237. Hart, J. Organizational orienteering: Charting the terrain. *American Communication Journal.* 2003;6(2):1-9

238. Hershcovis, MS. "Incivility, social undermining, bullying... oh my!": A call to reconcile constructs within workplace aggression research. *Journal of Organizational Behavior.* 2011;32(3):499-519.10.1002/job.689:

239. Grant, D, Oswick, C. The organization of metaphors and the metaphors of organization: Where are we and where do we go from here? In: D Grant, C Oswick, eds. *Metaphor and organizations.* London: Sage; 1996:213-226.

240. Koch, S, Deetz, SA. Metaphor analysis of social reality in organizations. *Journal of Applied Communication Research.* 1981;9:1-15

241. Smith, RC, Turner, P, K. A social constructionist reconfiguration of metaphor analysis: An application of "SCMA" to organizational socialization theory. *Communication Monographs.* 1995;62:152-181

242. Sheenan, KH, Barker, M, McCarthy, P. Analysing metaphors used by victims of workplace bullying. *International Journal of Management and Decision Making.* 2004;5(1):21-31

243. Schön, DA. Generative metaphor: A perspective on problem-solving in social policy. In: A Ortony, ed. *Metaphor and thought.* New York: Cambridge University Press.; 1993:254-283.

244. Scott, JC. *Domination and the arts of resistance.* New Haven, CT: Yale University Press; 1990.

245. Kay, P, Kempton, W. What is the Sapir-Whorf hypothesis?

American Anthropologist. 1984;86:65-79

246.   Richardson, L. Narrative and sociology. In: JV Maanen, ed. *Representation in ethnograp.* Thousand Oaks, CA: Sage.; 1995:198-221.

247.   Ólafsson, RF, Jóhannsdóttir, HL. Coping with bullying in the workplace: The effect of gender, age and type of bullying. *British Journal of Guidance and Counselling.* 2004;32(3):319-333

248.   Bolger, N, DeLongis, A, Kessler, RC, Wethington, E. The contagion of stress across multiple roles. *Journal of Marriage and The Family.* 1989;51:175-183

249.   Giddens, A. *Modernity and self-identity.* Stanford, CA: Stanford University Press; 1991.

250.   Richman, JA, Rospenda, KM, Nawyn, SJ, et al. Sexual harassment and generalized workplace abuse among university employees: Prevalence and mental health correlates. *American Journal of Public Health.* 1999;89(3):358-363

251.   Zapf, D, Einarsen, S, Hoel, H, Vartia, M. Empirical findings on bullying in the workplace. In: S Einarsen, H Hoel, D Zapf, CL Cooper, eds. *Bullying and emotional abuse in the workplace: International perspectives in research and practice.* London: Taylor Francis; 2003:103-126.

252.   Glomb, TM. Workplace anger and aggression: Informing conceptual models with data from specific encounters. *Journal of Occupational Health Psychology.* 2002;7:20-36

253.   Keashly, L, Neuman, JH, Burnazi, L. Persistent hostility at work: What really hurts. Paper presented at: Society for Industrial and Organizational Psychology Annual Meeting; April 1-4, 2004; Chicago.

254.   Geddes, D, Baron, RA. Workplace aggression as a consequence of negative performance feedback. *Management Communication Quarterly.* 1997;10:433-454

255.   Kruml, SM, Geddes, D. Catching fire without burning out: Is there an ideal way to perform emotion labor? In: NM Ashkanasy, CEJ Hartel, WJ Zerbe, eds. *Emotions in the workplace.* Westport, CT: Quorum Books.; 2000:177-188.

256.   Conrad, C. Stemming the tide: Corporate discourse and agenda denial in the 2002 'corporate meltdown'. *Organization.* 2003;10:549-560

257.   The downsizing of America. *New York Times.* , 1996: 55.

258.   Salin, D. Bullying and organisational politics in competitive

and rapidly changing work environments. *International Journal of Management and Decision Making.* 2003;4(1):35-46

259. Fairhurst, GT, Cooren, F, Cahill, DJ. Discursiveness, contradiction, and unintended consequences in successive downsizings. *Management Communication Quarterly.* 2002;15:501-541

260. Tourish, D, Paulsen, N, Hobman, E, Bordia, P. The downsides of downsizing: Communication processes and information needs in the aftermath of a workforce reduction strategy. *Management Communication Quarterly.* 2004;17:485-516

261. Mishra, AK, Spreitzer, GM. Explaining how survivors respond to downsizing: The roles of trust, empowerment, justice, and work redesign. *Academy of Management Review.* 1998;23:567-588

262. Taylor, E. Workplace bullying: ASU team studies intimidation on the job. *Arizona Republic.* 3/8, 2004; Business: 1-2.

263. Deetz, SA. Discursive formations, strategized subordination and self-surveillance. In: A McKinley, K Starkey, eds. *Foucault, management and organizational theory.* London: Sage; 1998:151-172.

264. Mercer, K. Welcome to the jungle. In: J Rutherford, ed. *Identity: Community, culture, difference.* London: Lawrence & Wishart; 1990:43-71.

265. Alvesson, M, Willmott, H. Identity regulation as organizational control: Producing the appropriate individual. *Journal of Management Studies.* 2002;39(5):619-644.10.1111/1467-6486.00305:

266. Kerby, AP. The language of the self. In: LP Hinchman, SK Hinchman, eds. *Memory, identity, community: The idea of narrative in the human services.* Albany, NY: State University of New York Press; 1997:125-142.

267. Du Gay, P. *Consumption and identity at work.* London: Sage; 1996.

268. Howard, JA. Social psychology of identities. *Annual Review of Sociology.* 2000;26(3):367-393

269. Linstead, A, Thomas, R. "What do you want from me?" A poststructuralist feminist reading of middle managers' identities. *Culture and Organization.* 2002;8(1):1-20

270. Ainsworth, S, Hardy, C. Discourse and identities. In: D Grant, C Hardy, C Oswick, LL Putnam, eds. *The Sage handbook of*

organizational discourse. Thousand Oaks, CA: Sage; 2004:153-174.

271. Gergen, KJ, Gergen, MM. Narratives of the self. In: LP Hinchman, SK Hinchman, eds. *Memory, identity, community: The idea of narrative in the human sciences.* Albany, NY: State University of New York Press; 1997:161-184.

272. Ibarra, H. Provisional selves: Experimenting with image and identity in professional adaptation. *Administrative Science Quarterly.* 1999;44(5):764-791

273. Layton, L. Trauma, gender identity and sexuality: Discourses of fragmentation. *American Imago.* 1995;52(1):107-125

274. Breslau, N, Kessler, RC, Chilcoat, HD, Schultz, LR, Davis, GC, Andreski, P. Trauma and Posttraumatic Stress Disorder in the Community. *Archives of General Psychiatry.* 1998;55(7):626-632.10.1001/archpsyc.55.7.626.:

275. Allen, RE, Lucerno, MA. Beyond resentment: Exploring organizationally targeted insider murder. *Journal of Management Inquiry.* 1996;5(2):86-103.10.1177/105649269652002

276. Kaufman, JM, Johnson, C. Stigmatized individuals and the process of identity. *The Sociological Quarterly.* 2004;45(4):807-833

277. Roschelle, AR, Kaufman, P. Fitting in and fighting back: Stigma management strategies among homeless kids. *Symbolic Interaction.* 2004;27(1):23-46

278. Deitch, EA, Butz, RM, Brief, AP. Out of the closet and out of a job? The nature, import, and causes of sexual orientation discrimination in the workplace. In: RW Griffin, AM O'Leary-Kelly, eds. *The dark side of organizational behavior.* San Francisco: Jossey-Bass; 2004:187-234.

279. Gerschick, TJ. Sisyphus in a Wheelchair: Men with physical disabilities confront gender domination. In: J O'Brien, JA Howard, eds. *Everyday inequalities: Critical inquiries.* Malden, MA: Blackwell Publishers; 1998.

280. Goffman, E. *Stigma: Notes on the management of spoiled identity.* Englewood Cliffs, NJ: Prentice-Hall; 1963.

281. Charmaz, K. Grounded theory. In: RM Emerson, ed. *Contemporary field research.* Prospect Heights, IL: Waveland Press; 2001:335-352.

282. Ashforth, BE, Humphrey, RH. Emotional labor in service roles: The influence of identity. *Academy of Management*

Review. 1993;18(1):88-115.10.5465/AMR.1993.3997508

283. Lutgen-Sandvik, P, McDermott, V. The constitution of employee-abusive organizations: A communication flows theory. *Communication Theory.* 2008;18(2):304-333

284. Perrone, J, Vickers, MH. Emotions as strategic game in a hostile workplace: An exemplar case. *Employee Responsibilities and Rights Journal.* 2004;16(3):167-178

285. Crossley, ML. Narrative psychology, trauma and the study of self/identity. *Theory & Psychology.* 2000;10(4):527-546

286. DeGarmo, DS, Kitson, GC. Identity relevance and disruption as predictors of psychological distress for widowed and divorced women. *Journal of Marriage and the Family.* 1996;58(4):983-997

287. Kubler-Ross, E. *On death and dying.* New York: Scribner; 1997.

288. Sonnenfeld, JA, Ward, AJ. Firing back: How great leaders rebound after career disasters. *Harvard Business Review.* 2007;January:1-9

289. Gilmore, L. Limit-cases: Trauma, self-representation, and the jurisdictions of identity. *Biography.* 2001;24(1):128-139

290. Ashcraft, C. Naming knowledge: A language for reconstructing domestic violence and systemic gender inequity. *Women and Language.* 2000;23(1):3-10

291. Collinson, DL. Identities and insecurities: Selves at work. *Organization.* 2003;10:527-547

292. Balthazard, PA, Cooke, RA, Potter, RE. Dysfunctional culture, dysfunctional organization: Capturing the behavioral norms that form organizational culture and drive performance. *Journal of Managerial Psychology.* 2006;21(8):709-732.10.1108/02683940610713253:

293. Lee, D. An analysis of workplace bullying in the UK. *Personnel Review.* 2000;29(5):593-612

294. Craig, RT. Communication theory as a field. *Communication Theory.* 1999;9:119-161

295. Cooren, F, Taylor, JR. Organization as an effect of mediation: Redefining the link between organization and communication. *Communication Theory.* 1997;7:219-259

296. McPhee, RD, Zaug, P. Organizational theory, organizational communication, organizational knowledge, and problematic integration. *Journal of Communication.* 2001;51:574-591

297. McPhee, RD, Zaug, P. The communicative constitution of

organizations. *Electronic Journal of Communication.* 2000;10(1&2):1-17

298.   McPhee, RD. Formal structure and organizational communication. In: RD McPhee, PK Tomkins, eds. *Organizational communication: Traditional themes and new directions.* Beverly Hills, CA: Sage; 1985.

299.   Fineman, S. Emotion and organizing. In: SK Clegg, C Hardy, WK Nord, eds. *Handbook of Organization Studies.* 2nd edition. London: Sage; 2006:675-700.

300.   Fairhurst, GT, Putnam, LI. Organizations as discursive constructions. *Communication Theory.* 2004;14:5-26

301.   Lammers, JC, Barbour, JB. An institutional theory of organizational communication. *Communication Theory.* 2006;16:356-377

302.   Falcone, P. The fundamentals of progressive discipline. *HR Magazine.* 1997;42(2):90-94

303.   Falcone, P. Adopt a formal approach to progressive discipline. *HR Magazine.* 1998;43(12):55-59

304.   Barth, S. Pros and cons of progressive discipline. *Lodging Hospitality.* 2002;58(4):10

305.   Dulebohn, JH, Ferris, GR. The role of influence tactics in perceptions of performance evaluations' fairness. *Academy of Management Journal.* 1999;42(3):288-303

306.   Thomas, SL, Bretz, RDJ. Research and practice in performance appraisal: Evaluating employee performance in America's largest companies. *SAM Advanced Management Journal.* 1994;59(2):28-35

307.   Di Martino, V, Hoel, H, Cooper, CL. *Preventing violence and harassment in the workplace*: European Foundation for the Improvement of Living and Working Conditions; 2003.

308.   Folger, R. Reactions to mistreatment at work. In: JK Murningham, ed. *Social psychology of organizations.* Englewood Cliffs, NJ: Prentice-Hall; 1993:161-183.

309.   Hamilton, C. *Communicating for results: A guide for business and the professions.* 6th edition. Belmont, CA: Wadsworth; 2001.

310.   Marcus, JH. *The complete job interview handbook.* New York: Harper Collins; 1994.

311.   Feldman, DC. A contingency theory of socialization. *Administrative Science Quarterly.* 1976;21(3): 433-452

312.   Gibson, MK, Papa, MJ. The mud, the blood, and the beer

guys: Organizational osmosis in blue-collar work groups. *Journal of Applied Communication Research.* 2000;28(1):68-88

313. Johns, N, Menzel, PJ. "If you can't stand the heat!"... Kitchen violence and culinary art. *Hospitality Management.* 1999;18(1):99-109

314. Hoel, H, Salin, D. Organisational antecedents of workplace bullying. In: S Einarsen, H Hoel, D Zapf, CL Cooper, eds. *Bullying and emotional abuse in the workplace: International perspectives in research and practice.* London: Taylor & Francis; 2003:203-218.

315. Lyon, A. The forms of capital and systematically distorted communication in organizations: A rereading of Enron's collapse. Paper presented at: Western States Communication Association; February, 2006; Palm Springs, CA.

316. Hoel, H, Rayner, C, Cooper, CL. Workplace bullying. In: CL Cooper, IT Robertson, eds. *International review of industrial and organizational psychology.* Vol 14. Oxford: Wiley; 1999:195-230.

317. Hatfield, E, Cacioppo, JT, Rapson, RL. Emotional contagion. *Current Directions in Psychological Science.* 1993;2:96-99

318. Crawford, N. Bullying at work: A psychoanalytic perspective. *Journal of Community & Applied Social Psychology.* 1997;7(3):219-225.10.1002/(SICI)1099-1298(199706)7:3<219::AID-CASP420>3.0.CO;2-Q:

319. Lynch, J. Institution and imprimatur: Institutional rhetoric and the failure of the Catholic church's pastoral letter on homosexuality. *Rhetoric & Public Affairs.* 2005;8(3):383-403

320. Lutgen-Sandvik, P, Fletcher, CV. Conflict motivations and tactics of targets, bystanders, and bullies: A thrice-told tale of workplace bullying In: JG Oetzel, S Ting-Toomey, eds. *Sage Handbook of Conflict Communication.* 2nd edition. Thousand Oaks, CA: Sage; 2014:349-376.

321. Lawrence, C. Social psychology of bullying in the workplace. In: N Tehrani, ed. *Building a culture of respect: Managing bullying at work.* London: Taylor & Francis; 2001:61-76.

322. DiMaggio, PJ, Powell, WW. The iron cage revisited: Institutional isomorphism and collective rationality in organization fields. *American Sociological Review.* 1983;48:147-160

323. Abrahamson, E. Management fashion. *Academy of*

Management Review. 1996;21:254-285

324. Pfeffer, J. Working alone: What ever happened to idea of organizations as communities? *Destructive Organizational Communication: Processes, Consequences, and Constructive Ways of Organizing.* New York: Routledge; 2009:363-388.

325. Nicotera, AM, Cushman, DP. Organizational ethics: A within-organization view. *Journal of Applied Communication Research.* 1992;20:437-462

326. Kalwies, HH. Ethical leadership: The foundation for organizational growth. *Howard Journal of Communication.* 1988;1(3):113-130

327. Silliance, JAA. Organizational context and the discursive construction of organizing. *Management Communication Quarterly.* 2007;20(4):363-394

328. Young, M. *The rise of the meritocracy, 1870–2033: An essay on education and equality.* Baltimore, MD: Penguin Books.; 1961.

329. Johnson, LM, Mullick, R, Mulford, CL. General versus specific victim blaming. *The Journal of Social Psychology.* 2002;142(2):249-263.10.1080/00224540209603898:

330. Dumaine, B. America's toughest bosses. *Fortune.* Vol 18 October; 1993:39-49.

331. Drucker, P. The new society of organizations. *Harvard Business Review.* Vol 70; 1992:95-104.

332. Friedman, M. The social responsibility of business is to increase its profits. *The New York Times Magazine.* Vol 9; 1970:2-14.

333. Deetz, SA. *Transforming communication, transforming business: Building responsive and responsible workplaces.* Cresskill, NJ: Hampton Press; 1995.

334. McGregor, D. *The human side of enterprise.* New York: McGraw-Hill; 1960.

335. Weick, KE. *Sensemaking in organizations.* Thousand Oaks, CA: Sage; 1995.

336. Abrams, D, Marques, JM, Bown, NJ, Henson, M. Pro-norm and anti-norm deviance within in-groups and out-groups. *Journal of Personality and Social Psychology.* 2000;78(5):906-912

337. Cialdini, RB, Reno, RR, Kallgren, CA. A focus theory of normative conduct: Recycling the concept of norms to reduce littering in public places. *Journal of Personality and Social*

Psychology. 1990;58(6):105-1026

338. Sutton, RI. *The no asshole rule.* New York: Warner Business Book; 2007.

339. Schultz, V, Fricdman, BS, Saguy, AC, Hernandez, TK, Yamada, D. Global perspectives on workplace harassment law. *Employee Rights and Employment Policy Journal.* 2004;8(2):151-193

340. De Vogli, R, Ferrie, JE, Chandola, T, Kivimäki, M, Marmot, MG. Unfairness and health: evidence from the Whitehall II Study. *Journal of Epidemiology and Community Health.* 2007;61(3):513-518

341. Nelson, CG, Halpert, JA, Cellar, DF. Organizational responses for preventing and stopping sexual harassment: Effective deterrents or continued endurance. *Sex Roles.* 2007;56:811-822

342. Baron, RA, Neuman, JH. Social antecedents to bullying: A social interactionist perspective. In: S Einarsen, H Hoel, D Zapf, C Cooper, eds. *Bullying and harassment in the workplace: Developments in theory, research, and practice.* 2nd edition. Boca Rotan, FL: CRC Press/Taylor & Francis Group; 2011:201-226.

343. Domagalski, TA, Steelman, LA. The impact of gender and organizational status on workplace anger expression. *Management Communication Quarterly.* 2007;20(3):297-315

344. Zak, MW. "It's like a prison in there": Organizational fragmentation in a demographically diversified workplace. *Journal of Business and Technical Communication.* 1994;8(3):281-298

345. UNISON. *UNISON members' experience of bullying at work.* London: UNISON; 1997.

346. Graham, JW, Keeley, M. Hirchman's loyalty construct: Employee voice to supervisors. *Employee Responsibility and Rights Journal.* 1992;5(3):191-200

347. Rains, S. Don't suffer in silence: Building an effective response to bullying at work. In: N Tehrani, ed. *Building a culture of respect: Managing bullying at work.* London: Taylor & Francis; 2001:155-164.

348. Wild, A, Brady, J. Women bullies often target other women [Television broadcast]. ABC News. February 24, 2009.

349. Meese, M. Backlash: Women bullying women at work. *The New York Times.* May 9, 2009;

http://www.nytimes.com/2009/05/10/business/10women.html.

350.   Simpson, R, Cohen, C. Dangerous work: The gendered nature
        of bullying in the context of higher education. *Gender, Work
        & Organization.* 2004;11(2):163-186.10.1111/j.1468-
        0432.2004.00227.x:

351.   Salin, D, Hoel, H. Workplace bullying as a gendered
        phenomenon. *Journal of Managerial Psychology.*
        2012;28(3):235-251.10.1108/02683941311321187:

352.   Lee, D. *A feminist study of men's and women's experiences of
        workplace bullying and sexual harassment* [PhD Thesis].
        Coventry, U.K.: Center for the Study of Women and Gender,
        University of Warwick; 1998.

353.   Buzzanell, PM. Reframing the glass ceiling as a socially
        constructed process: Implications for understanding and
        change. *Communication Monographs.* 1995;62(327-
        354).10.1080/03637759509376366:

354.   Schieman, S, McMullen, T. Relational demography in the
        workplace and health: An analysis of gender and the
        subordinate-superordinate role-set. *Journal of Health and
        Social Behavior.* 2008;49(3):286-300

355.   Rayner, C, Cooper, CL. The black hole in "bullying at work"
        research. *International Journal of Decision Making.*
        2003;4(1):47-64

356.   Hutchinson, M, Vickers, MH, Jackson, D, Wilkes, L.
        Workplace bullying in nursing: Towards a more critical
        organisational perspective. *Nursing Inquiry.* 2006;15(2):118-
        126

357.   Hatcher, C. Becoming a successful corporate character and the
        role of emotional management. In: S Fineman, ed. *The
        emotional organization: Passions and power.* Carlton, Victoria,
        Australia: Blackwell Publishing Ltd; 2008:153-166.

358.   Neilson, A. Is Chest Beating as Good for People as It Is for
        Primates? *Stanford GBS News.* Accessed June 6, 2009.

359.   Britton, DM. Cat fights and gang fights: Preference for work in
        a male-dominated organization *Sociological Quarterly.*
        1999;40(3):455-474.10.1111/j.1533-8525.1999.tb01729.x:

360.   Freire, P. *Pedagogy of the oppressed.* New York: Continuum;
        1970.

361.   Wall, CJ, Gannon-Leary, P. A sentence made by men: Muted
        group theory revisited *European Journal of Women's Studies.*
        1999;6(1):21-29

362. Lerner, JS, Tiedens, LZ. Portrait of the angry decision maker: How appraisal tendencies shape anger's influence on cognition. *Journal of Behavioral Decision Making.* 2006;19:115-137

363. Kanter, RM. *Men and women of the corporation.* 2nd edition. New York: Basic Books; 1993.

364. Mooney, N. *I can't believe she did that!: Why women betray other women at work.* New York: Saint Martin's Press; 2005.

365. Baumeister, RF, Leary, MR. The need to belong: Desire for interpersonal attachments as a fundamental human motivation. *Psychological Bulletin.* 1995;117(3):497.10.1037/0033-2909.117.3.497:

366. Sachs, J, Blackmore, J. You never show you can't cope: Women in school leadership roles managing their emotions. *Gender and Education.* 1998;10(3):265-279

367. Crawshaw, L. *Taming the abrasive manager: How to end unnecessary roughness in the workplace.* San Francisco, CA: John Wiley & Sons; 2007.

368. Norander, S. Surveillance/discipline/resistance: Carly Fiorina under the gaze of *The Wall Street Journal. Communication Studies.* 2008;59(2):99-113

369. Tannen, D. *Talking from 9 to 5: Women and men in the workplace: Language, sex, and power.* New York: Harper Collins; 1994.

370. Ely, R. Unshackling the 'double bind' of the female leader. August 21. Accessed July 16, 2009.

371. Barrett, LF, Bliss-Moreau, E. She's emotional. He's having a bad day: Attributional explanations for emotion stereotypes. *Emotion.* 2009;9(5):649-658.0.1037/a0016821:

372. Brescoll, VL, Uhlmann, EL. Can an angry woman get ahead? Status conferral, gender, and expression of emotion in the workplace. *Psychological Science.* 2008;19(3):268-275.10.1111/j.1467-9280.2008.02079.x

373. Mavin, S. Queen bees, wannabees and afraid to bees: No more 'best enemies' for women in management? *British Journal of Management.* 2008;19:S75–S84.10.1111/j.1467-8551.2008.00573.x:

374. Tracy, K, Eisenberg, E. Giving criticism: A multiple goals case study. *Research on Language & Social Interaction.* 1990;24(1):37-70

375. Oakley, JG. Gender-based barriers to senior management

positions: Understanding the scarcity of female CEOs *Journal of Business Ethics.* 2000;27(4):321-334

376. hooks, b. *The will to change: Men, masculinity, and love.* New York: Washington Square Press; 2004.

377. Hodson, R, Roscigno, VJ, Lopez, SH. Chaos and the abuse of power: Workplace bullying in organizational and interactional context. *Work and Occupations.* 2006;33(4):382-416

378. Lutgen-Sandvik, P, Tracy, SJ. Answering five key questions about workplace bullying: How communication scholarship provides thought leadership for transforming abuse at work. *Management Communication Quarterly.* 2012;26(1):3-47.10.1177/0893318911414400:

379. Ashcraft, KL. Gender, discourse and organization: Framing a shifting relationship. In: D Grant, C Hardy, C Oswick, L Putnam, eds. *The Sage handbook of organizational discourse.* London: Sage; 2004:275-298.

380. Hall, E. Interview with George Miller. *Psychology Today.* 1980;58(6):38-50, 97-88

381. Rowe, AC. *Power lines: On the subject of feminist alliances.* Durham, NC: Duke University Press; 2008.

382. McIntyre, MG. Don't be a victim of co-worker. *Albuquerque Journal.* November 30, 2008: H2.

383. Westhues, K. *Workplace mobbing in academe: Reports from twenty universities.* Lewiston, NY: Edwin Mellen Press; 2005.

384. Tehrani, N. *Building a culture of respect: Managing bullying at work.* London: Taylor & Francis; 2001.

385. Notelaers, G, Einarsen, S, Hans, D, Vermunt, JK. Measuring exposure to bullying at work: The validity and advantages of the latent class cluster approach. *Work & Stress.* 2006;20(4):289-302

386. Coyne, I, Chong, PS-L, Seigne, E, Randall, P. Self and peer nominations of bullying: An analysis of incident rates, individual differences, and perceptions of working environment. *European Journal of Work and Organizational Psychology.* 2003;12:209-228

387. Lewis, SE. Recognition of workplace bullying: A qualitative study of women targets in the public sector. *Journal of Community and Applied Social Psychology.* 2006;16:119-135

388. Lewis, D. Voices in the social construction of bullying at work: Exploring multiple realities in further and higher education. *International Journal of Management and Decision Making.*

2003;4(1):65-81

389.   !!! INVALID CITATION !!!

390.   Westhues, K. *The envy of excellence: Administrative mobbing of high-achieving professors.* Lewiston, NY: Edwin Mellen Press; 2006.

391.   Hershcovis, MS. "Incivility, social undermining, bullying...oh my!": A call to reconcile constructs within workplace aggression research. *Journal of Organizational Behavior.* 2010:in press

392.   Hershcovis, MS, Barling, J. Towards a multi-foci approach to workplace aggression: A meta-analytic review of outcomes from different perpetrators. *Journal of Organizational Behavior.* 2009;31:24-44

393.   Hoel, H, Beale, D. Workplace bullying, psychological perspectives and industrial relations: Towards a contextualized and interdisciplinary approach. *British Journal of Industrial Relations.* 2006;4(2):239-262.10.1111/j.1467-8543.2006.00496.x:

394.   Keashly, L, Jagatic, K. The nature, extent and impact of emotional abuse in the workplace: Results of a statewide survey. Paper presented at: Academy of Management Conference, 2000; Toronto, Canada.

395.   Westhues, K. *Winning, losing, moving on: How professionals deal with workplace harassment and mobbing.* Lewiston, NY: Edwin Mellen Press; 2006.

396.   Harvey, MG, Buckely, MR, Heames, JT, Zinko, R, Brouer, RL, Ferris, GR. A bully as an archetypal destructive leader. *Journal of Leadership & Organizational Studies.* 2007;14(2):117-129

397.   Strandmark, M, Hallberg, L-M. Being rejected and expelled from the workplace: Experiences of bullying in the public service sector. *Qualitative Research in Psychology.* 2007;4(1):1-14

398.   Hauge, LJ, Skogstad, A, Einarsen, S. Relationships between stressful work environments and bullying: Results of a large representative study. *Stress & Work.* 2007;21(3):220-242

399.   Schaller, M. Unintended influence: Social-evolutionary processes in the construction and change of culturally-shared beliefs. In: J Forgas, K Williams, eds. *Social influence: Direct and indirect processes* Philadelphia: Psychology Press; 2001:77-93.

400. Fast, NJ, Chen, S. When the boss feels inadequate: Power, incompetence, and aggression. *Psychological Science.* 2009;20(11):1406-1413

401. Weick, KE. *Making sense of the organization.* Malden, MA: Blackwell Publishing Professional; 2001.

402. Weiner, B. *Achievement motivation and attribution theory.* Morristown, NJ: General Learning Press; 1974.

403. Berger, PL, Luckmann, T. *The social construction of reality: A treatise in the sociology of knowledge.* 2nd edition. New York: Open Road; 2011.

404. Canary, HE, Canary, DJ. Making sense of one's career: An analysis and typology of supervisor career stories. *Communication Quarterly.* 2007;55(2):225-246

405. Raes, AML, Glunk, U, Heijltes, MG, Roe, RA. Top management team and middle managers: Making sense of leadership. *Small Group Research.* 2007;38(3):360-386

406. Tracy, SJ, Myers, KK, Scott, CW. Cracking jokes and crafting selves: Sensemaking and identity management among human service workers. *Communication Monographs.* 2006;73(3):283-308

407. Wallace, DM, Hinsz, VB. Group members as actors and observers in attributions of responsibility for group performance. *Small Group Research.* 2009;40(1):52-71

408. Saxena, S, Shah, H. Effect of organizational culture on creating learned helplessness Attributions in R&D professionals: A canonical correlation analysis. *Vikalpa: The Journal for Decision Makers.* 2008;33(2):25-45

409. Weiner, B. An attributional theory of achievement motivation and emotion. *Psychological Review.* 1985;92(4):548-573

410. Trice, HM, Beyer, JM. *The culture of work organizations.* Englewood Cliffs, NJ: Prentice Hall; 1993.

411. Barker, JR. Tightening the Iron Cage: Concertive control in self-managing teams. *Administrative Science Quarterly.* 1993;38(3):408-437

412. Tompkins, PK, Cheney, G. Communication and unobtrusive control in contemporary organizations. In: RD McPhee, PK Tompkins, eds. *Organizational communication: Traditional themes and new directions.* Newbury Park, CA: Sage; 1985:179-210.

413. Kimmell, SB. *The gendered society* Oxford: Oxford University Press; 2000.

414. Lerner, MJ, Miller, DT. Just world research and the attribution process: Looking back and ahead. *Psychological Bulletin.* 1978;85(5):1030-1051

415. Bird, FB. *The muted conscience: Moral silence and the practice of ethics in business.* 2nd edition. Westport, CT: Quorum Books; 2002.

416. Monroe, C, Borzi, MG, DiSalvo, VS. Managerial strategies for dealing with difficult subordinates. *Southern Journal of Communication.* 1993;58:247-254

417. Fukushima, O, Ohbuchi, K-i. Antecedents and effects of multiple goals in conflict resolution. *International Journal of Conflict Management.* 1996;7(3):191-208

418. Ohbuchi, K-i, Tedeschi, JT. Multiple goals and tactical behaviors in social conflicts. *Journal of Applied Social Psychology.* 1997;27(24):2177-2199

419. Putnam, LL, Poole, MS. Conflict and negotiation. In: FM Jablin, LL Putnam, KH Roberts, LW Porter, eds. *Handbook of organizational communication.* Beverly Hills: Sage; 1987:549-599.

420. Infante, DA, Trebling, JD, Shepherd, PE, Seeds, DE. The relationship of argumentativeness to verbal aggression *Southern Communication Journal.* 1984;50(1):67-77

421. Lewin, K, Llippit, R, White, RK. Patterns of aggressive behavior in experimentally created social climates. *Journal of Social Psychology.* 1939;110:271-301

422. Knapp, ML, Putnam, LL, Davis, LJ. Measuring interpersonal conflict in organizations: Where do we go from here? *Management Communication Quarterly.* 1988;1:414-429

423. Rahim, MA. Toward a theory of managing organizational conflict. *The International Journal of Conflict Management.* 2002;13(3):206-235

424. Aquino, K, Lamertz, K. A relational model of workplace victimization: Social roles and patterns of victimization in dyadic relationships. *Journal of Applied Psychology.* 2004;89:1023-1034

425. Olweus, D. *Aggression in schools: Bullies and whipping boys.* Washington DC: Hemisphere; 1978.

426. Infante, DA, Wigley, CJI. Verbal aggressiveness: An interpersonal model and measure. *Communication Monographs.* 1986;53:61-69

427. Coyne, I, Seigne, E, Randall, P. Predicting workplace victim

status from personality. *European Journal of Work and Organizational Psychology.* 2000;9:335-349

428. Infante, DA, Riddle, B, Horvarth, C, Tumlin, S. Verbal aggressiveness: Messages and reasons. *Communication Quarterly.* 1992;40(2):116-126

429. Lind, K, Glasø, L, Pallesen, S, Einarsen, S. Personality profiles among targets and nontargets of workplace bullying. *European Psychologist.* 2009;14(3):231-237

430. Schuster, B. Rejection, exclusion, and harassment at work and in schools. *European Psychologist.* 1996;1:293-317

431. D'Cruz, P, Noronha, E. Protecting my interests: HRM and targets' coping with workplace bullying. *The Qualitative Report.* 2010;15(3):507-534

432. DeDreu, CKW. Productive conflict: The importance of conflict manaement and conflict issue. In: CKW DeDreu, E Van De Vliert, eds. *Using conflict in organizations.* Thousand Oaks, Ca: Sage; 1997:9-22.

433. Ayoko, OB, Callan, VJ, Härtel, CE. Workplace conflict, bullying, and counterproductive behaviors. *International Journal of Organizational Analysis.* 2003;11(4):283-302.10.1108/eb028976

434. Boddy, CRP, Ladyshewsky, RK, Galvin, P. The influence of corporate psychopaths on corporate social responsibility and organizational commitment to employees. *Journal of Business Ethics.* 2010;97(1):1-19.10.1007/s10551-010-0492-3:

435. Vickers, MH. Toward employee wellness: Rethinking bullying paradoxes and masks. *Employee Responsibilities and Rights Journal.* 2006;18:267-281

436. Ferguson, M, Barry, B. I know what you did: The effects of interpersonal deviance on bystanders. *Journal of Occupational Health Psychology.* 2011;16(1):80-94.10.1037/a0021708:

437. McCroskey, JC, Richmonda, VP. Applying reciprocity and accommodation theories to supervisor/subordinate communication. *Journal of Applied Communication Research* 2000;28(3):278-289

438. Boddy, CRP, Ladyshewsky, R, Galvin, P. Leaders without ethics in global business: Corporate psychopaths. *Journal of Public Affairs.* 2010;10(3):121-138.10.1002/pa.352:

439. Tracy, SJ. Managing burnout and moving toward employee engagement: Reinvigorating the study of stress at work. In: P Lutgen-Sandvik, BD Sypher, eds. *Destructive organizational*

communication: *Processes, consequences, and constructive ways of organizing.* New York: Routledge/Taylor & Francis; 2009:77-98.

440. Bowes-Sperry, L, O'Leary-Kelly, AM. To act or not to act: The dilemma faced by sexual harassment observers. *Academy of Management Review.* 2005;30(2):288-306.10.5465/AMR.2005.16387886

441. Hoel, H, Einarsen, S, Cooper, CL. Organisational effects of bullying. In: S Einarsen, H Hoel, D Zapf, CL Cooper, eds. *Bullying and emotional abuse in the workplace.* London: Taylor & Francis; 2003:145-162.

442. Kelly, DJ. Workplace bullying -- a complex issue needing IR/HRM research? In: B Pocock, C Provis, E Willis, eds. *21st Century Work: Proceedings of the 20th Conference of the Association of Industrial Relations Academics of Australia and New Zealand.* Adelaide: University of South Australia; 2006:274-284.

443. Egan, K. People risks, motivation and culture: Human factors and compliance motivations. Paper presented at: 6th Annual Financial Services and Compliance Conference; February 9-11, 2009; Sydney.

444. Kernis, MH, Grannemann, BD, Barclay, LC. Stability and level of self-esteem as predictors of anger arousal and hostility. *Journal of Personality and Social Psychology.* 1989;56:1013-1022

445. Babiak, P, Hare, RD. *Snakes in suits: When psychopaths go to work.* New York: Harper Collins; 2006.

446. Boddy, CRP. Corporate psychopaths and organizational type. *Journal of Public Affairs.* 2010;10(4):300-312.10.1002/pa.365:

447. Clark, J. *Working with monsters: How to identify and protect yourself from the workplace psychopath.* Sydney: Random House; 2005.

448. Wigley, CJ, Pohl, GH, Watt, MGS. Conversational sensitivity as a correlate of trait verbal aggressiveness and the predisposition to verbally praise others. *Communication Studies.* 1989;2(2):92-95

449. Shaw, AZ, Kotowski, MR, Boster, FJ, Levine, TR. The effect of prenatal sex hormones on the development of verbal aggression. *Journal of Communication.* 2012;62(5):778-793.10.1111/j.1460-2466.2012.01665.x:

450. Parkins, IS, Fishbein, HD, Ritchey, PN. The influence of

personality on workplace bullying and discrimination. *Journal of Applied Social Psychology.* 2006;36(10):2554-2577

451.   Bing, MN, Stewart, SMH, Davison, K, Green, PD, McIntyre, MD, James, LR. An integrative typology of personality assessment for aggression: Implications for predicting counterproductive workplace behavior. *Journal of Applied Psychology.* 2007;92(3):722-744.10.1177/1094428107301148

452.   Burroughs, SM, James, LR. Advancing the assessment of dispositional aggressivenes through conditional reasoning. In: S Fox, P Spector, eds. *Counterproductive work behavior: Investigations of actors and targets.* Washington, DC: American Psychological Association; 2005:127-150.

453.   Infante, DA, Bruning, SD, Martin, MM. The verbally aggressive individual: Experiences with verbal aggression and reasons for use. Paper presented at: Speech Communication Association Annual Convention; November 18-21, 1994; New Orleans.

454.   Smith, PK, Cowie, H, Olafsson, RF, Liefooghe, APD. Definitions of bullying: A comparison of terms used, and age and sex differences, in a 14-country international comparison. *Child Development.* 2002;73(4):1119–1133

455.   Vandekerckhove, W, Commers, MSR. Downward workplace mobbing: A sign of the Times? *Journal of Business Ethics.* 2003;45:41-50

456.   Vartia, M, Leka, S. Interventions for the prevention and management of bullying at work. In: S Einarsen, H Hoel, D Zapf, CL Cooper, eds. *Bullying and harassment in the workplace: Developments in theory, research and practice.* 2nd edition. Boca Rotan, FL: CRC Press/Taylor & Francis Group; 2011:359-379.

457.   Scully, M, Rowe, M. Bystander training within organizations. *Journal of the International Ombudsman Association.* 2009;2(1):89-95

458.   Ury, WL. *The third side: Why we fight and how we can stop.* New York: Penguin Books; 2000.

459.   Rancer, AS, Avtgis, TA. *Argumentative and aggressive communication.* Thousand Oaks, CA: Sage; 2006.

460.   Infante, DA. Teaching students to understand and control verbal aggression. *Communication Education.* 1995;44:51-63

461.   La Monica, E. Empathy can be learned. *Nurse Educator.* 1983;8(2):19-23

462. Putnam, LL. Dialectical tensions and rhetorical tropes in negotiations. *Organization Studies.* 2004;25(1):35-53.10.1177/0170840604038179

463. Keyton, J. Relational communication in groups. In: L Frey, DS Gouran, MS Poole, eds. *The handbook of group communication theory and research.* Thousand Oaks, CA: Sage; 1999:192-222.

464. Roberts, LM. From proving to becoming: How positive relationships create a context for self-discovery and self-actualization. In: J Dutton, BR Ragins, eds. *Exploring positive relationships at work: Building a theoretical and research foundation.* Mahwah, NJ: Psychology Press; 2007:29-46.

465. Heaphy, ED. Bodily insights: Three lenses on positive organizational relationships. In: J Dutton, BR Ragins, eds. *Exploring positive relationships at work: Building a theoretical and research foundation.* Mahwah, NH: Psychology Press; 2007:47-72.

466. Fried, Y, Shirom, A, Gilboa, S, Cooper, CL. The mediating effects of job satisfaction and propensity to leave on role stress-job performance relationships: Combining meta-analysis and structural equation modeling. *International Journal of Stress Management.* 2008;15(4):305-328

467. Spreitzer, G, Sutcliffe, K, Dutton, JE, Sonenshein, S, Grant, AM. A socially embedded model of thriving at work. *Organization Science.* 2005;16(5):537-549

468. Cameron, KS. Organizational virtuousness and performance. In: KS Cameron, JE Dutton, RE Quinn, eds. *Positive organizational scholarship.* San Francisco: Berrett-Koehler; 2003:48-65.

469. Bright, DS, Cameron, KS, Caza, A. The amplifying and buffering effects of virtuousness in downsized organizations. *Journal of Business Ethics.* 2006;64(3):249-269. http://dx.doi.org/10.1007/s10551-005-5904-4

470. Hart, PM, Wearing, AJ, Headey, B. Police stress and well-being: Integrating personality, coping and daily work experiences *Journal of Occupational and Organizational Psychology.* 1995;68(2):133-156

471. Straw, BM, Sutton, RI, Pellod, LH. Employee positive emotions and favorable outcomes at the workplace. *Organizational Science.* 1994;5(1):51-71

472. Baum, F. Social capital: is it good for your health? Issues for a

public health agenda. *Journal of Epidemiology and Community Health.* 1999;53:195-196

473. Cameron, KS, Dutton, JE, Quinn, RE. An introduction to positive organizational scholarship. *Positive organizational scholarship.* San Francisco: Berrett-Koehler; 2003:3-13.

474. Davydov, DM, Stewart, R, Ritchie, K, Chaudieu, I. Resilience and mental health. *Clinical Psychology Review.* 2010;30(5):479-495

475. Mitchell, TR, Holtom, BC, Lee, TW, Sablynski, CJ, Erez, M. Why people stay: Using job embeddedness to predict voluntary turnover. *Academy of Management Journal.* 2001;44:1102-1121

476. Baumeister, RF, Bratslavsky, E, Finkenauer, C, Vohs, KD. Bad is stronger than good. *Review of General Psychology.* 2001;5(4):323-370.10.1037//1089-2680.5.4.323:

477. McDermott, V, Lutgen-Sandvik, P. Communicating subtle messages: Creating hostile and supportive environments. In: B Brushan, ed. *Communication in perspectives.* Kiel, Germany: Amani International Publishers; 2009:31-57.

478. Fredrickson, BL. Positive affect and the complex dynamics of human flourishing. *American Psychologist.* 2005;60:678-686

479. Herzberg, F, Mausner, B, Snyder, BB. *The motivation to work.* New York: Wiley; 1959.

480. Lutgen-Sandvik, P. An exploratory study of U.S. workplace bullying. Paper presented at: National Communication Association Annual Conference; November, 2003; Miami Beach, FL.

481. Lutgen-Sandvik, P, Hood, J. Positive Organizing and Bullying Communication: Do Positive Phenomena Moderate the Effects of Workplace Bullying on Desired Outcomes? *Western States Communication Association.* Reno, NV; 2013.

482. Cameron, KS, Bright, D, Caza, A. Exploring the relationships between organizational virtuousness and performance. *American Behavioral Scientist.* 2004;47(6):766-790.10.1177/0002764203260209

483. Albrecht, TL. The role of communication in perceptions of organizational climate. In: D Nimmo, ed. *Communication Yearbook 3.* New Brunswick, NJ: Transaction Books; 1979:343-357.

484. Crawshaw, L. Caoching abrasive leaders: Contradictory tales of the Big Bad Wolf. In: N Tehrani, ed. *Workplace bullying:*

Symptoms and Solutions. London: Routledge; 2012:132-148.

485. Vranceanu, A-M, Barsky, A, Ring, D. Psychosocial aspects of disabling musculoskeletal pain. *Journal of Bone & Joint Surgery.* 2009;91:2014-2018

486. Parzefall, M-R, Salin, DM. Perceptions of and reactions to workplace bullying: A social exchange perspective. *Human Relations.* 2010;63(6):761-780.10.1177/0018726709345043:

487. D'Cruz, P, Noronha, E. The limits to workplace friendship: Managerialist HRM and bystander behaviour in the context of workplace bullying. *Employee Relations.* 2011;33(3):269 - 288

488. Twemlow, SW, Fonagy, P, Sacco, FC. The role of the bystander in the social architecture of bullying and violence in schools and communities. *Annals of the New York Academy of Science.* 2004;1036(1):215-232

489. Roundy, C. The impact of leadership on workplace bullying. *In The Refractive Thinker, Volume One: An Anthology of Higher Learning.* Vol 1; 2009:23-40.

490. Folger, R, Baron, RA. Violence and hostility at work: A model of reactions to perceived injustice. In: GR VanderBos, EQ Bulatoao, eds. *Violence on the job.* Washington, DC: American Psychological Association; 1996.

491. Hananel, S. Workplace Bullying Emerging As Major Employment Liability Battleground. *Insurance Journal.* March edition; 2013.

492. Cascio, W, Boudreau, JW. *Investing in People: Financial Impact of Human Resource Initiatives.* 2nd edition. Upper Saddle River, NJ: FT Press, Pearson Education; 2011.

493. Soares, A. Bullying, post-traumatic stress disorders, and social support. Paper presented at: 4th International Conference on Bullying and Harassment in the Workplace, 2004; Bergen, Norway.

494. Farmer, D. Workplace Bullying: An increasing epidemic creating traumatic experiences for targets of workplace bullying. *International Journal of Humanities and Social Science.* 2011;1(7):1-8

495. Macintosh, J. Tackling workplace bullying. *Issues in Mental Health Nursing.* 2006;27(6):665-679

496. Twemlow, SW, Sacco, FC, Williams, P. A clinical and interactionist perspective on the bully-victim-bystander relationship. *Bulletin of the Menninger Clinic.* 1996;60(3):296-313

497. Ferris, P. A preliminary typology of organisational response to allegations of workplace bullying: See no evil, hear no evil, speak no evil. *British Journal Of Guidance & Counselling.* 2004;32(3):389-395

498. Tehrani, N. A total quality approach to building a culture of respect. In: N Tehrani, ed. *Building a culture of respect: Managing bullying at work.* London: Taylor & Francis; 2001:135-154.

499. Harmon, J, Scotti, DJ, Behson, SH, et al. Tthe impact of high-involvement work systems on staff satisfction and service costs in veterans health care. *Academy Of Management Proceedings.* 2003:B1-B6

500. Sloan, LM, Matyok, T, Schmitz, CL, Short, GFL, Sloan, LM. A story to tell: bullying and mobbing in the workplace. *International Journal of Business and Social Science.* 2010;1(3):87-97

501. Neuman, JH, Keashly, L. Development of the Workplace Aggression Research Questionnaire (WAR-Q): Preliminary data from the Workplace Stress and Aggression Project. *Society for Industrial and Organizational Psychology.* Chicago; 2004.

502. DeWine, S, James, AC. Examining the communication audit: Assessment and modification *Management Communication Quarterly.* 1988;2(3):144-169

503. Froman, L. Positive psychology in the workplace. *Journal Of Adult Development.* 2010;17(2):59-69.10.1007/s10804-009-9080-0:

504. Senge, PM. *The fifth discipline: The art and practice of the learning organization.* New York: Crown Business; 2006.

505. Richards, J, Daley, H. Bullying policy: Development, implementation and monitoring. In: S Einarsen, H Hoel, D Zapf, CL Cooper, eds. *Bullying and emotional abuse in the workplace: International perspectives in research and practice.* London: Taylor & Francis; 2003:247-269.

506. Infante, DA, Chandler, TA, Rudd, JE. Test of an argumentative skill deficiency model of interspousal violence. *Communication Monographs.* 1989;56(2):163-177

507. Argyris, C. *Knowledge for action: A guide to overcoming barriers to organizational change.* San Francisco: Jossey-Bass; 1993.

508. Merchant, V, Hoel, H. Investigating complaints of bullying. In:

S Einarsen, H Hoel, D Zapf, CL Cooper, eds. *Bullying and emotional abuse in the workplace: International perspectives in research and practice.* London: Taylor & Francis; 2003:259-269.

509. Mumby, DK, Ashcraft, KL. Organizational communication studies and gendered organization: A response to Martin and Collinson. *Gender, Work and Organization.* 2006;13(1):68-90

510. Kassing, JW. *Dissent in organizations.* Vol 4. Malden, MA: Polity; 2011.

511. Mumby, DK, Stohl, C. Disciplining organizational communication studies. *Management Communication Quarterly.* 1996;10:50-72

512. Lutgen-Sandvik, P, Dickinson, E, Foss, KA. Painting, priming, peeling, and polishing: Constructing and deconstructing the woman-bullying-woman identity at work. In: S Fox, TR Lituchy, eds. *Gender and the dysfunctional workplace.* Northampton, MA: Edward Elgar Publishing.; 2012:61-77.

513. Lutgen-Sandvik, P, Alberts, JK, Tracy, SJ. The communicative character of workplace bullying and responses to bullying. Paper presented at: Western States Communication Association Annual Convention; February 15-19, 2008; Denver/Boulder, CO.

514. Cowan, RL. It's complicated: Defining workplace bullying from the human resource professional's perspective. *Management Communication Quarterly.* 2012;26(3)

515. Allen, BJ. Racial harassment in the workplace. In: P Lutgen-Sandvik, BD Sypher, eds. *Destructive organizational communication: Processes, consequences, and constructive ways of organizing.* New York: Routledge/Taylor & Francis; 2009:164-183.

516. Vega, G, Comer, DR. Sticks and stones may break your bones, but words can break your spirit: Bullying in the workplace. *Journal of Business Ethics.* 2005;58(1):101-109

517. Lutgen-Sandvik, P, Namie, G. Workplace bullying from start to finish: Bullies' position and supporters, organizational responses, and abuse cessation. Paper presented at: Western States Communication Association Annual Conference; February 13-17, 2009; Mesa, AZ.

518. Waldron, VR. Emotional tyranny at work: Suppressing the moral emotions. In: P Lutgen-Sandvik, BD Sypher, eds. *Destructive organizational communication: Processes,*

consequences, and constructive ways of organizing. New York: Routledge/Taylor & Francis; 2009:9-26.

519.   Cowan, RL. "Rocking the boat" and "Continuing to fight": Un/productive justice episodes and the problem of workplace bullying. *Human Communication.* 2009;12(3):283-301

520.   Mumby, DK. Power and politics. In: FM Jablin, LL Putnam, eds. *The new handbook of organizational communication.* Thousand Oaks, CA: Sage; 2001:585-624.

521.   Tracy, SJ, Trethewey, A. Fracturing the real-self--fake self dichotomy: Moving toward "crystallized" organizational discourses and identities. *Management Communication Quarterly.* 2005;15(2):168-195

522.   Wieland, SMB, Bauer, JC, Deetz, SA. Excessive careerism and destructive life stresses: The role of entrepreneurialism in colonizing identities. In: P Lutgen-Sandvik, BD Sypher, eds. *Destructive organizational communication: Processes, consequences, and constructive ways of organizing.* New York: Routledge/Taylor & Francis; 2009:99-120.

523.   Scott, CW. Communication and Social Identity Theory: Existing and potential connections in organizational identification. *Communication Studies.* 2007;58(2):123-138

524.   Ashcraft, KL, Mumby, DK. *Reworking gender: A feminist communicology of organization.* Sage: Thousand Oaks, CA; 2004.

525.   Trethewey, A. Reproducing and resisting the master narrative of decline: Midlife professional women's experiences of aging. *Management Communication Quarterly.* 2001;15:183–226

526.   Cowan, RL. *Walking the tightrope: Workplace bullying and the human resource professional* [Doctoral Dissertation]: Communication Studies, Texas A&M; 2009.

527.   Mumby, DK. Discourse, power and ideology: Unpacking the critical perspective. In: D Grant, C Hardy, C Oswick, LL Putnam, eds. *The Sage handbook of organizational discourse.* London: Sage; 2004:237-258.

528.   Mumby, DK, Putnam, LL. The politics of emotion: A feminist reading of bounded rationality. *Academy of Management Review.* 1992;17(3):465-486

529.   Riessman, CK. *Narrative analysis.* Newbury Park, CA: Sage; 1993.

530.   Eisenhart, M, Lawrence, N. Anita Hill, Clarence Thomas and the culture of romance. *Genders.* 1994;19:94-121

531. Leonardi, PM, Jackson, MH. Technological determinism and discursive closure in organizational mergers. *Journal of Organizational Change Management.* 2004;17:615-663

532. Tracy, SJ. Locking up emotion: Moving beyond dissonance for understanding emotional labor discomfort. *Communication Theory.* 2005;15:in-press

533. Gossett, LM, Kilker, J. My job sucks: Examining counterinstitutional web sites as locations for organizational member voice, dissent, and resistance *Management Communication Quarterly.* 2006;20(1):63-90

534. Boje, DM. *Narrative methods for organizational and communication research.* London: Sage; 2001.

535. Frey, LR. What a difference more difference-making communication scholarship might make: Making a difference from and through communication research. *Journal of Applied Communication.* 2009;37(2):205-214

536. Lutgen-Sandvik, P. *Adult bullying—A nasty piece of work: A decade of research on non-sexual harassment, psychological terror, and emotional abuse on the job.* St Louis, MO: ORCM Press; 2013.

537. Deetz, SA, Tracy, SJ, Simpson, JL. *Leading organizations through transition: Communication and cultural change.* Thousand Oaks, CA: Sage.; 2000.

538. Namie, G, Namie, R, Lutgen-Sandvik, P. Challenging workplace bullying in the United States: An activist and public communication approach. In: S Einarsen, H Hoel, D Zapf, C Cooper, eds. *Bullying and Harassment in the Workplace: Developments in Theory, Research, and Practice.* 2nd edition. Boca Rotan, FL: CRC Press, Taylor & Francis Group; 2011:477-468.

539. Keashly, L, Neuman, JH. Building a constructive communication climate: The Workplace Stress and Aggression Project. In: P Lutgen-Sandvik, B Davenport Sypher, eds. *Destructive organizational communication: Processes, consequences, and constructive ways of organizing.* New York: Routledge/Taylor & Francis; 2009:339-362.

540. Foss, SK, Foss, KA. *Inviting transformation: Presentational skills for a changing world.* Long Grove, IL: Waveland Press; 2003.

541. Keashly, L. From observation to engagement: Building coworker efficacy to address bullying. Paper presented at:

National Communication Association 96th Annual
Convention; November 14-17, 2010; Chicago.

542. Miller, KI, Stiff, JB, Ellis, BH. Communication and empathy as precursors to burnout among human service workers. *Communication Monographs.* 1988;55:250-265

543. Pörhölä, M, Karhunen, S, Rainivaara, S. Bullying at school and in the workplace: A challenge for communication research. In: CS Beck, ed. *Communication Yearbook* Vol 30. Mahwah, NJ: Lawrence Erlbaum; 2006:249-301.

544. Kinosian, J. Workplace bullying, Do we need a law? *Parade.* July 18, 2010: 14.

545. Giles, H. Accommodating translational research. *Journal of Applied Communication Research.* 2008;36(2):121-127

546. Rush, EK, Tracy, SJ. Wikipedia as public scholarship: Communicating our impact online. *Journal of Applied Communication Research.* 2010;38(3):312-318

547. Tracy, SJ. Taking the plunge: A contextual approach to problem-based research. *Communication Monographs.* 2007;74(1):106-111

548. Kirby, EL, Krone, KJ. "The policy exists but you can't really use it": Communication and the structuration of work-family policies. *Journal of Applied Communication Research.* 2002;30:50-77

549. Tracy, SJ. Compassion: Cure for an ailing workplace? *Communication Currents.* 2010;5(6)

550. Martin, M, Anderson, C, Horvath, C. Feelings about verbal aggression: Justifications for sending and hurt from receiving verbally aggressive messages *Communication Research Reports.* 1996;13(1):19-26

551. Dunlop, SM, Wakefield, M, Kashima, Y. Pathways to persuasion: Cognitive and experiential responses to health-promoting mass media messages. *Communication Research.* 2010;37(1):133-164

552. Zoller, HM. Health on the line: Identity and disciplinary control in employee occupational health and safety discourse. *Journal of Applied Communication Research.* 2003;31(2):118-139

553. Scarduzio, JA, Geist-Martin, P. Making sense of fractured identities: Male professors' narratives of sexual harassment. *Communication Monographs.* 2008;75(4):369-395.10.1080/03637750802512363:

554. Hamilton, MA, Minero, PJ. Argumentativeness and its effect on verbal aggressiveness: A meta-analytic review. In: M Allen, RW Preiss, BM Gayle, N Burrell, eds. *Interpersonal communication research: Advances through meta-analysis.* Mahwah, NJ: Lawrence Erlbaum; 2002:281-314.

555. Field, T. *Bully in sight: How to predict, resist, challenge and combat workplace bullying.* Oxfordshire, UK: Success Unlimited; 1996.

556. Roberto, AJ, Eden, J. Cyberbullying: Aggressive communication in the digital age. In: TA Avtgis, AS Rancer, eds. *Arguments, aggression, and conflict: New directions in theory and research.* New York: Routledge; 2010:198-216.

557. Vandebosch, H, Van Cleemput, K. Cyberbullying among youngsters: Profiles of bullies and victims. *New Media & Society.* 2009;11(8):1349-1371.10.1177/1461444809341263:

558. Lea, M, O'Shea, T, Fung, P, Spears, R. Flaming in computer-mediated communication: Observations, explanations, implications. In: M Lea, ed. *Contexts of computer-mediated communication.* New York: Harvester Wheatsheaf; 1992:89-122.

559. Sopow, E. The impact of culture and climate on change programs. *Strategic Communication Management.* 2006;10(6):14-17

560. Palazzoloa, KF, Robertoa, AJ, Babin, EA. The relationship between parents' verbal aggression and young adult children's intimate partner violence victimization and perpetration. *Health Communication.* 2010;25(4):357-364

ABOUT THE AUTHOR

Brief Bio

Pam Lutgen-Sandvik was born and raised in Anchorage, Alaska and moved to Arizona in 2000 where she earned her Ph.D. in organizational communication at Arizona State University. Prior to her tenure as a university professor, she worked as a social service organization administrator, first in the field of women's advocacy and then in outpatient substance abuse treatment. She accepted her first professor's position in 2005 at the University of New Mexico and subsequently moved to North Dakota State (NDSU) in 2013 to join the Department of Communication in Fargo. She continues to research, publish, and teach in the area of organizational communication at NDSU and serves as the Director of the Center for Applied Communication Research. Dr. Lutgen-Sandvik is married, has two children, and lives in Moorhead, MN.

Co-Authors (in alphabetical order)

Jess K. Alberts. Professor, Hugh Downs School of Human Communication, Arizona State University

Elizabeth Dickinson. Assistant Professor of Communication, Kenan-Flagler Business School, University of North Carolina

Lisa Farwell. Department Chair, Department of Psychology, Santa Monica College

Courtney Vail Fletcher. Assistant Professor, Department of Communication Studies, University of Portland

Karen A. Foss. Professor, Department of Communication & Journalism, University of New Mexico

Jacqueline Hood. Professor, Anderson School of Management, University of New Mexico

Virginia McDermott. Associate Professor, Nido R. Qubein School of Communication, High Point University.

Gary Namie. Director, Workplace Bullying Institute

Sarah J. Tracy. Associate Professor, Hugh Downs School of Human Communication, Arizona State University

FIRST PUBLICATION CITATIONS

Original Articles/Papers

[A] Lutgen-Sandvik, Pamela, Tracy, Sarah J., & Alberts, Jess K. (2007). Burnedby bullying in the American workplace: Prevalence, perception, degree, and impact. *Journal of Management Studies, 44* (6), 837-862. doi: 10.1111/j.1467-6486.2007.00715.x

[B] Lutgen-Sandvik, Pamela. (2003). The Communicative Cycle Of Employee

[C] Lutgen-Sandvik, Pamela. (2006). "Take this job and ...": Quitting and other forms of resistance to workplace bullying. *Communication Monographs, 73*(4), 406-433. doi: 10.1080/ 03637750601024156

[D] Tracy, Sarah J., Lutgen-Sandvik, Pamela, & Alberts, Jess K. (2006). Nightmares, demons and slaves: Exploring the painful metaphors of workplace bullying. *Management Communication Quarterly,* 20(2), 148-185. doi: 10.1177/0893318906291980.

[E] Lutgen-Sandvik, Pamela. (2007). "But words will never hurt me": Abuse and bullying at work, a comparison between two worker samples. *Ohio Communication Journal, 45,* 81-105. http://www. ohiocomm.org/journal .html

[F] Lutgen-Sandvik, Pamela. (2008). Intensive remedial identity work: Responses to workplace bullying trauma and stigma. *Organization, 15*(1), 97-119. doi: 10.1177/1350508407084487

[G] Lutgen-Sandvik, Pamela, & McDermott, Virginia. (2008). The constitution of employee-abusive organizations: A communication flows theory. *Communication Theory, 18*(2), 304-333. doi: 10.1111/j.1468-2885.2008.00324.x

[H] Lutgen-Sandvik, P., J.K. Alberts, and S.J. Tracy. *The communicative character of workplace bullying and responses to bullying.* Paper presented at Western States Communication Association Annual Convention. 2008. Denver/Boulder, CO.

[I] Lutgen-Sandvik, Pamela, Dickinson, Elizabeth, & Foss, Karen A. (2009, February 15-19). *Cat Fights, Bitches, and Alpha-Females?: Exploring and Critiquing the Women-Bullying-Women Pattern in Bullying Survey Research.* Paper presented at the Western States Communication Association, Mesa, AZ

[J] Namie, G., & Lutgen-Sandvik, P. (2010). Active and passive accomplices: The communal character of workplace bullying. *International Journal of Communication, 4,* 343-373. Available at http://ijoc.org

[K] Lutgen-Sandvik, P., & McDermott, V. (2011). Making sense of supervisory

420

bullying: Perceived powerlessness, empowered possibilities. *Southern Communication Journal, 76*(4), 342–368.

L Lutgen-Sandvik, P., & Fletcher, C.V. (2013, February 15-20). *A Nasty Piece of Work: Goals and Communicative Actions of Parties in Workplace Bullying Conflicts.* Paper presented at the Western States Communication Association, Reno, NV.

M Lutgen-Sandvik, P., & Hood, J. (2013, February 15-20, 2013). *Positive Organizing and Bullying Communication: Do Positive Phenomena Moderate the Effects of Workplace Bullying on Desired Outcomes?* Paper presented at the Western States Communication Association, Reno, NV.

N Lutgen-Sandvik, P., & Tracy, S.J. (2012). Answering five key questions about workplace bullying: How communication research provides thought leadership for transforming abuse at work. *Management Communication Quarterly, 26*(1), 3-47. **DOI** 10.1177/08933 18911414400

CPSIA information can be obtained
at www.ICGtesting.com
Printed in the USA
LVOW04s0546251116
514391LV00008B/52/P